THE LONG RUN.
(a rather pragmatic romance)

by

Zig

Cover image, cover & book design by Zig using KDP templates

Copyright © assigned to Zig.
First Published, 2020.
Published: Independently.
ISBN (paperback) 9798673575956.

No part of this publication may be reproduced, stored in an electronic retrieval system, or transmitted in any form or by any means, electronic, mechanical, photocopying, recording, scanning or otherwise without the prior permission of Zig (merziggerman@gmail.com)

Limit of Liability/Disclaimer of Warranty: While the publisher and author have used their best efforts in preparing this book, they make no representations or warranties with respect to the accuracy or completeness of the contents of this book and specifically disclaim any implied warranties of merchantability or fitness for a particular purpose. No warranty may be created or extended by sales representatives or written sales materials. The advice and strategies contained herein may not be suitable for your situation. You should consult with the appropriate professional where necessary. Efforts have been made to conceal identities within this text. Should any party identify themselves or others, intentionally or otherwise, they will carry their own liability for so doing including onward liability for any consequences of their actions. Neither the publisher nor the author shall be liable for damages arising therefrom.

Author's note (1).

This story is a true romantic travelogue/autobiography where an 18,000 mile round trip between the U.K. and The Philippines was needed for the couple to meet face-to-face.

The currency exchange rates provided are the live rate offered at www.xe.com at 2pm 23rd July, 2020, (B.S.T.). These were: £1 = 62.71 Philippine Pesos; £1 = €uros 1.097; and, £1 = $(U.S.) 1.268.

The original text was written as a guide for genuine men considering a relationship with a woman from a different culture. It was released in 2017 under the questionable title of 'Hello Daddy!' which may go some way to explaining why sales struggled to reach double figures. The original text has been substantially revised and updated, a further chapter being added to cover changes and the events which have occurred subsequent to the original publication.

This text has been spellchecked and proof-read several times but there is always the one that got away. I hope this can be forgiven.

CHAPTERS:

Author's Note (1).	4
Why this book, and why now?	7
The prologue.	9
In the beginning.	11
Why am I even looking for a relationship?	17
So, what path to take?	25
Three sorry stories, and a fourth!	33
Progress.	42
Do dating websites have any genuine users?	44
A complete change of focus.	58
Preparing a visit/money!	70
Note on the Empire Windrush.	87
Website shenanigans.	89
Planning the first trip.	107
Prelude to the first visit.	117
April.	125
"Water, water, everywhere, nor not a drop to drink."	138
From April to May.	151
May.	164
From May to June, (and five highly forgettable ladies).	190
July, (well, Julia actually)!	207
Post Julia.	223
The realities and stupidities of bureaucracies.	234
Yolanda.	247
Visas and Jo(e).	258
Ongoing negotiations.	283
One step forward, one step sideways!	324
Success at last.	381
Together forever.	402
Author's Note (2).	414
Appendix 1.	415
Appendix 2.	416
Appendix 3.	424

Why this book, and why now?

At any one time there are around a quarter of a million people online actively grooming children for sex. Almost all male and overwhelmingly from the 'developed' world, Europe, North America and Australasia. With some it will have gone far beyond grooming to active engagement. Cyber paedophilia has proliferated over recent years. This was a conclusion of research published by the Swiss headquartered charity Terre des Hommes in 2013. The charity has bases in several European cities and this research emanated from their Dutch offices. I first became aware of these numbers when watching a Stacey Dooley documentary on TV (BBC - British Broadcasting Corporation) and Phil Ambrose on 101 East (al-Jazeera). Some of their work in this area is readily available for viewing on YouTube.

Many youngsters in the developed world are the target of these perverts. However in poor countries there are fewer resources to tackle similar issues. I'm no expert in Filipino affairs but have a Philippine wife and family in the Philippines, a country I have visited on many occasions. I'm essentially a private man but there are occasions when we must stick our heads above the parapet. This is one such occasion. The Philippines is a country where there are serious extremes of poverty. People routinely move around over significant distances in the search for work. At any one time around 10% of the population of the country will live and work overseas. Broadband, a laptop and web cam are ever more accessible and money exchange, to support OFWS, (overseas foreign workers), is well-developed, simple, straightforward and everywhere, a combination which has led to online sex tourism and a proliferation of child sexual exploitation, cyber-paedophilia, sometimes with the active encouragement of their own parents. Whilst the Philippine authorities are doing their best to tackle these crimes, demand is huge and comes from the West.

This book is about a journey looking for love across international boundaries; a genuine search for a healthy adult relationship. I have first-hand experience over several years of the environments Stacey Dooley and Phil Ambrose reported on. With the best will in the world local law enforcement is fighting a serious uphill battle. Any profits made from the sale of this book will be used to employ an educator in the part of the Philippines in which our family live. Their role will be to work with teachers and schools to flag up online dangers and how to manage them. My wife is undertaking a sponsored 15,000 foot tandem parachute jump in support of the same cause. Should there be insufficient funds to do this then profits will be donated to Terre des Hommes in support of their ongoing efforts to catch the perpetrators of these awful crimes.

The prologue.

"I want a baby!"

That call is rarely heard from a man who is drawing his state pension, but that is the position I find myself in. As you will discover my lack of family does not reflect a lack of effort! Maybe I was a late starter but, over the last quarter of a century, I've made up for a lot of lost time whilst being thwarted to some extent by circumstance.

Whilst events in my earlier life are alluded to, this part of my story begins around 2008 and publication will be in 2020. So the story begins with its author, me, as a divorcee in his mid-fifties. He is based in the United Kingdom, was in full-time employment and on the Boards of two international charities, but has now retired.

The story is based on experiences of online dating across continents, travel, passports and visas; lying, cheating, loving and marrying. It is not a story I ever expected to write, and has only been written as a consequence of the various events which occurred between deciding to look abroad for a long term partner, finding her, finding a woman who felt equally strongly towards me and subsequent events.

It has been written because my change of circumstances has opened my eyes to the huge differences we experience as a consequence of where we happen to be born, our genders and the generation we are born into.

It has also been written as the story developed during a period where wide access to online services became available to impoverished people. Whilst there have been many positive consequences of developing technologies there is also an unpleasant underbelly. Cyber paedophilia is part of this and I have family members whose circumstances could lead to them being targeted so, if I can raise awareness and maybe a bit of income to help prevent that, I would very much like to do so. If we could put some of these perverts behind bars that would be an added bonus.

You will be on the top side of a quarter of the way through the book before we first set foot in the Philippines. The opening section gives you background on the person doing the travelling and, hopefully, a bit of an insight into his mind-set. It also sets out the reasons for me looking to distant shores for a relationship and how I went about doing that.

It is also very obvious when dating websites are being discussed that the story is being told by a man looking for a woman. That is my reality but I am sure the issues I describe will be have resonance for women looking for a man online and for those seeking same sex relationships.

So, here we go …

In the beginning.

I am in my mid-sixties with a something of a chequered past in the leg-over stakes, or maybe I should say in terms of successful personal relationships. A poorly conceived five year marriage was preceded and succeeded by a variety of wholly inappropriate relationships, or attempts at relationships. I am no misogynist; the fault has mostly been mine. When I look back at what lies behind this litany of errors the reasons for these outcomes have been fairly predictable.

However I am a hopeless optimist and, when the opportunity arose, I was happy to once again launch myself into the seemingly lush pastures of romance. I did not take much encouragement to embark upon the search for that special lady; perhaps by unusual means for someone of my vintage. Having failed to meet the right woman by what would be viewed as the conventional route for someone of my generation, I have been through the process of setting up a relationship using twenty-first century methods, or trying to! A process which, from the outset, has had disaster written all over it. That's right; I've been trying online dating.

Was I destined for failure? We will see but, currently, the portents are good. That said there can't be many men my age looking at the possibility of starting a family! Looking for sex, yes, but babies?! I must be crackers. The prospect of beginning to draw state pension and child allowance simultaneously is one entertained by a tiny minority. The unconventional searching out the unlikely; perhaps impossible!

This part of my life's story began around twelve years ago and will run right up to the date of publication; warts and all.

The good news is that, after several years of online dates, having met a couple of dozen of the women concerned in person, I am now regularly interacting with officialdom and the reams of paperwork necessary to secure the right for my new foreign, non-European wife to continue living with me in the U.K and hoping the day will soon arrive when she is granted the permanent right to remain and raise our family here. Oops, have I given away the happy ending?! No. This is the story of the ongoing journey one has to make through lies, deceit, chicanery and bureaucracy, to find happiness when using international online dating websites.

(My activities began two or three years before the arrival of today's technology allowed a swipe right or left; but the principles are very similar. Clickbait and swipe bite are much the same!)

Before getting into the nuts and bolts of online dating and its consequences I will introduce the 'me' of the late-noughties to you. At that time I was working as a project manager in the health sector having previously had a police career following which I set up my own research and training company. I am very tall, overweight, grey haired and starting to bald. I am also a recovering alcoholic. I have now been dry for approaching six years and am writing in mid-2020 but, for most of the time I was dating online, in fact for most of my adolescent and adult life, I have been a heavy drinker. From adolescence to my forties I was, by and large, in control of the drink. However for the last ten years of my drinking career there were times when the booze controlled me. Realising this and to ensure I kept my job and driving licence I had several years where I would completely abstain from alcohol consumption from Sunday to Friday. But I was routinely paralytic on Friday and Saturday nights. I was never a violent or nasty drunk. Mostly I would collapse and sleep. But I have been lifted off an urban dual carriageway on which I decided to nap; have discovered the morning after that I have lost a shoe of shoes and, on one occasion, a temporary denture. I have found myself waking up in a bush! Granted these were rarities but they do describe my problem with booze and I am glad to now have it under control. But there would undoubtedly have been times when I was online and inebriated. Does online dating whilst drunk have disaster written all over it? Damned right it does. However how relevant that is to my story is for you, the reader, to judge. When I began the online dating game I had realised I had a problem and was working round to doing something about it. I can say that I first met the woman who is now my wife online as a drinker. However when we first met face to face, three or four months later, I had been completely dry for a few weeks and have remained so.

The woman I have married we will call Rosa Beth, or RB for short. We have celebrated our leather wedding anniversary, (that's the third), and she seems to be settling well into life in the U.K.. But, when we first met, she was just over a third of my age, under a third of my weight and reached my chest when standing on tip-toes. Academically we both left school with nothing much in the way of qualification, me at the age of sixteen, she at fourteen. I left school in 1971, she left school in 2007. Subsequently I have gone on to gain two degrees, study at Doctorate level and publish a couple of books (aside from this one) and a few academic papers. She has had neither the opportunity nor the time to do this. I own a decent sized house, have no debt and reasonable index-linked pensions which supplement the state pension. Thanks to my late father's will there is also a modest investment income. In terms of economic assets she had nothing. To my eye she has beauty in abundance, a mischievous sense of humour, plenty of common sense and plenty of enthusiasm. Prior to our getting together she had worked full-time for several years looking after a quadriplegic child with cerebral palsy; she has no children of her own. When she first arrived in the U.K. she had no savings or resources and, once she arrived here, had a visa condition stipulating no work, unless and until she married me. For around twenty months prior to her arrival I had to financially support her whilst the necessary paperwork and associated bureaucratic processes were negotiated. Now we are married she has, rightly, most of the same rights as other married people here. However she does not have rights to access public funds; i.e. social benefits. Following the current rules it will take seven to twelve years from her arrival in the U.K. before she can be granted a right of permanent residence and access to the same range of benefits available to those born here. That is despite paying income tax and national insurance from the moment she began paid employment. This, of course, assumes the Immigration Rules do not change. Over the past few years these Rules have been tightened frequently and the seven to twelve years could increase. Once the right to remain has been established she can then consider an application for

British citizenship. Should that be granted she will then be able to apply for a British passport; with citizenship will come the right to vote. The idea of 'no taxation without representation', (enshrined in the US constitution), is still completely meaningless insofar as British law and the U.K. Home Office, (Ministry of Internal Affairs), are concerned.

Keeping all this in mind as I began my journey I spent some time considering my mental health. Was I was cracking up; going through a mid-life crisis? I was aware of my drinking problems but was not properly dealing with them. This led to the real question which is still unanswered. Is the relationship I am in, and heavily committed to, going to work? Much of my situation defies common or any other kind of sense. Am I risking the assets built up over a working lifetime for the hope of a regular roll with a young woman who, at any time, could sue for divorce, claim half the assets, and then return to her home country a very wealthy woman by local standards? Is this madness on my part?! I ask again – does this have disaster written all over it? Is it right we consider starting a family when, statistically, I will be dead in a round fourteen years? What sort of father knowing lays that burden on the presently unborn child?

In putting my thoughts and experiences into writing I guess I am trying to justify to myself the hopes and dreams I hold. But, when embarking upon this journey, I was seriously considering my sanity, or lack of, whilst endeavouring to provide an explanation for those who, with my best intentions at heart, made it clear they considered my actions to be folly.

I also know that when it comes to choosing women I have a long history of either reckless optimism or complete abstention. Always one extreme or the other; never a happy medium. This attitude has its positives but contains one very big negative. I can be a very easy target.

Whilst this story is aimed at those readers who enjoy romance, travel and autobiography, the original audience for whom I was writing, were men looking for a serious long term relationship with a woman from a different culture, possibly where there would be a significant age gap. In the developed world the difference in ages between a couple beyond five years begins to stretch traditional concepts of normality. Ten years or more might raise an eyebrow or two. In some parts of the world there are much larger differences in age between couples. Whilst it is often the man who is older than the woman that is not always the case. To my mind such issues should only be the concern of the two people involved so long as each is of sufficient age and maturity. So, whilst tongues might wag, it is no one else's business. However, now I have remarried my in-laws are around fifteen years younger than me and I have a brother-in-law who is my junior by fifty-seven years. I can feel the chattering classes warming up already!

This book should also still be a useful reference for those men who are genuinely looking for love and trying to find that special someone. If you might travel into the developing world then my comments could well be of interest as I lay out some of the pitfalls and the sorts of issue you are likely to come across. The main one of these is to ask you to take a good look at what is really motivating you before setting out to develop a relationship with a partner living in the developing world; often a much younger person. Have good look in the mirror before embarking on this type of journey. I am writing about the search for a genuine, serious, long-term adult relationship. For me it is not about playing games. So my thoughts, experiences and recollections will be of little or no relevance to the man who wants to visit a developing country for casual sex. In any case that is something which can be found with relative ease across the western world.

If you are an adult and using someone online or travelling thousands of miles for sex, whether you admit it to yourself or not, the likelihood is that you are seeking a particular kind of sex or relationship which cannot easily be fulfilled in your own country. Whilst your intentions may be legal, where do they stand in terms of general morality? If your aims are not legal, i.e. sex with children or young people or maybe involving some kind of violence then be warned. This book is not for you. I have no time for such behaviour or that type of person. As was highlighted in

'Why this book, and why now?' above, the driver for this book is to help prevent children and young people getting caught up with anyone seeking to engage them in abuse, sexual or otherwise.

Why am I even looking for a relationship?

Well, despite my age and having lived much of my adult life alone, that has not been through choice; not entirely anyway. When I embarked upon my current search for romance I had 40-45 years of adulthood behind me depending upon the age when the counting begins; old enough to legally have sex, old enough to vote or old enough to be voted for. For around the first quarter of a century of working life I was a police officer. Whilst much of my work was routine one never knew from one moment to the next what might happen. Elements of the work were very risky and the working environment was a health and safety nightmare. The role of a street cop means having the constant risk of being engaged in or recovering from dangerous work at all hours of the day and night, at weekends and public holidays. Whilst actual danger is not there 24/7 the risk is.

By the time I reached my mid-twenties I had had dealings with a couple of murderers. Dealt with men twice my age who had had sex with children. Met a mother who was twelve years old and a thirteen year girl who was offering sex for cigarettes. I had collected up the body of a person who had committed suicide by putting their head on a railway line and witnessed a couple of dozen post mortems, including those of a baby and young children. This was in amongst the routine road traffic accidents, burglaries and thefts and the pub fights which were guaranteed on Friday and Saturday nights when it wasn't raining. A wet night did have significant benefits. These are just a few incidents off the top of my head and this was the first few years; there were many more before I finished.

Whilst being contracted to work a forty hour week on a twenty-four hour shift system my reality was probably a further ten to twenty hours worked off the record weekly, an employment situation which would have put serious pressure on any relationship, and did on several occasions until I learned better. That may be just an excuse. However it was a very macho environment devoid of any subtlety or small talk. My armoury consisted mostly of an anti-intellectual blend of sarcasm, cynicism, arrogance and stupidity; attributes I learned from colleagues who knew no better and a management system which encouraged sameness. There were one or two exceptions to this but they were very much the exception rather than the case. On a daily basis I looked up into the arse hole of society and saw just how human beings can treat each other. Houses were often smelly, behaviour aggressive, language course, whether dealing with punters or colleagues, and it was rare to find anyone in possession of a brain. My colleagues and I had fairly high opinions of ourselves. Until I returned to education I did not understand how dim, as a group, we really were. Overall it was not a pretty sight. Working in such an environment changes people, and not for the better. Add to this that for much of that time I was a heavy smoker and drank like a fish and you will see that, from the perspective of any potential partner, from youth to early middle age I was seriously high risk. With any new girlfriend discontent would became apparent on both sides; fairly quickly. The women I did get involved with rarely went beyond a few weeks before we both, very happily, went our separate ways.

Another factor which came into play was that as a teenager I suffered a serious accident. I fell down a steep rocky hillside and my progress was halted after a couple of hundred feet by a boulder. Various cuts, bumps, bruises and minor fractures accompanied a multiple compound skull fracture and three weeks of unconsciousness. When my parents attended the hospital they were initially told there was a greater likelihood of my dying than surviving and there was no way of knowing if any long term damage had occurred. I gradually recovered without being aware of any permanent disability but was absent from school for the best part of a year which had to be repeated, the first year of G.C.S.E.s, the equivalent of year ten in the current education system. Dropping back a year also meant the peer group relationships I had been forming continued their development in my absence. It dropped me into an environment in which friendships amongst others had been flourishing for several years. Whilst my presence was not a problem I was regarded by my new peer group as something of an interloper; this had significant implications for the development of normal adolescent relationships.

Whilst I did not realise it at the time, the accident must have also had a major impact of my memory. I cannot recall anything from my childhood with confidence. There are snippets here and there but, when I hear others talk about childhood memories, whether fondly or otherwise, I reflect that I have none in which I have any confidence before the age of around fourteen; when I regained consciousness.

Whilst I left school with nothing much by way of qualification as I reached the end of my teens and during my early twenties I developed a keen interest in learning but had very little by way of formal education. I dipped into adult self-learning materials and night school classes from time to time studying, briefly, subjects as diverse as music and organic chemistry. At one point I sent off for information on higher education from the Open University, but was put off by my mother telling me that, as I had failed to get any meaningful qualification at school, I would be wasting my time studying at that level. I always felt more comfortable with people who had had an education rather than those I found myself working alongside. A knock-on effect of this was having a peer group of people, most of whom had left school at the earliest possible opportunity. None had any experience of higher education; in fact many would have struggled to spell 'university'! The women I met saw me as being something a bit weird; I routinely used words with more than four letters and my interests from the outset went well beyond simply negotiating the horizontal jog. Conversely educated women quickly found my lack of formal education a turn off; unless they fancied a bit of rough – perhaps not a nice way of describing myself but, from their perspective, at that time that's what I was.

So, whilst my contemporaries were playing the field, marrying, settling down, having their families, etc. I continued on the razzle. It was a razzle that contained a lot of booze and tobacco and little by way of long term company. This continued for many years. I am not complaining. By and large I had a lot of fun and generally had a good time. I thoroughly enjoyed having complete freedom and a lack of responsibility for anyone or anything beyond myself. But it did create a situation in which good opportunities for serious romance were progressively eroded. The single women with whom I shared social similarities became engaged, married, married with children, divorced with children, etc. and the pool of possible dates diminished. Whilst I might have been embroiled in a crazy work situation and used both tobacco and alcohol to manage this, (without really realising so at the time), the only times when I used controlled drugs were in my final year at school and then perhaps on half a dozen occasions; just sharing a wrap as it was passed around a group of friends and chipping in a bit of cash for the privilege. I've always assumed it was a bit of hash we smoked but I never really knew. The only impact it had on me was to make me feel a bit tipsy and seriously randy. And that would likely be a fairly normal state of affairs for a young man at that age around 1970! I did retain a fairly high level of morality. To this day I have never knowingly had an intimate relationship with anyone who is married or still in a relationship; nor have I sought to split anyone up or allowed myself to be used for that purpose. I am a firm believer in monogamy; serial monogamy for the unmarried and believe in fidelity within relationships. A bit of a bore I guess.

By the time I reached my forties I had been able to make several changes to my life. These occurred gradually and were completely unsupported by family, friends or employer. In fairness to them I should say that I dealt with these issues quietly not seeking support so they were largely unaware of developments. The main change was around education. I could not fully understand why things happened in my bit of the world in the way they did. So I set out to discover the answer. A year or two into this project I realised that I did not have the intellectual framework and tools to go very far. So I returned to education. I took the plunge with the Open University, and, studying on a part-time basis gained a B.A. Honours. I then registered with the University of Bristol where, after two years of part-time study I was awarded a Master's degree; much to the surprise of immediate family and colleagues. I began working on my Doctorate but, during a divorce, all my research materials were destroyed, so that project fell by the wayside. I still do not fully understand why things happen in my bit of the world in the way they do - but I am now comfortable in the knowledge that no one else does either. The big danger is that many of us think we do! Throughout this time I had continued with the police but ultimately, reached a point where we parted company. The easiest explanation would be to say I burned out. A financial settlement was agreed and my employer and I parted company; it has to be said not on the best of terms. I was obliged to sign a 'confidentiality' agreement on the advice of their solicitor before pension arrangements would be agreed. I knew a bit too much about them and could have opened up various cans of worms. They considered themselves safer if I was outside the organisation where I would be less able to let loose the worms; and they would not have the hassle of finding a bigger can to put them in.

So I had reached a position where I had some financial independence. I could get by without working but, were I to take that path, would have very little free cash. But now I did have good qualifications. So I set up my own business and got on with life. By this time I had also stopped smoking but was still the consummate drinker; however much of that was now done behind closed doors; not a healthy situation.

My lifestyle changed dramatically. I became my own boss, ran my own show and, once the business was up and running, quickly reached a similar level of disposable income to that which I had pre-burnout. I don't know if it is lack of ambition but I have never really been motivated to try and make a fortune; it is just not in my make-up. I am happy just jogging along and doing my own thing. Perhaps the near death experience in my youth created a frame of mind where I know I am lucky to be alive; or maybe I am just using that as an excuse for idleness and underachievement! However, within a few months I met the woman who was to become my first wife and, within two years, we married. I met her whilst working abroad and she was around fifteen years younger than me.

We were together for around seven years and married for five but, for me, the marriage effectively ended within the first six months. The reason was quite simple. Prior to marrying, in fact prior to proposing, we had talked about having a family and agreed this was the path we wanted to travel on; parenthood. I would have been happy with one or two children, she had suggested four, (and I thought about the snip). However my belief was that she wanted children. Within six months of the wedding, whilst on holiday in the home town of her family on the opposite side of the world, she dropped on me that she had no intention of ever of having children but that she did intend having a good career and the lifestyle to go with it. I immediately took the view that I had been tricked. Had she expressed her true feelings toward parenthood before marriage I would have never popped the question. She had probably intuited this. What she was saying was about as opposite to my ambitions as it was possible to get. I was angry and felt I had been tricked into marriage. We had a comfortable lifestyle which I wanted interrupting whilst I was still of an age where I could be a fully effective parent. I know as a man I do not have the biological clock to worry about, but I do want to properly support any children I father. As time progresses I may become debilitated in some way and would not want to put the burden of having to look after me on any offspring.

What to do? In retrospect what I should have done was immediately walk out of the relationship and institute divorce proceedings. Hindsight may be a wonderful thing, and the only exact science we have, but it cannot change the path I chose. I was in love, married and wanted a family, so I endeavoured to persuade her to change her mind. This went on for three or four years during which time I was told she would consider children once she had completed her higher education; she would consider children once she had her career on track. Over time it became blindingly obvious that what she had told me during the holiday six months into our marriage was true; she had no intention of ever having a child. The implication of these events for me was that, if I wanted a family, I needed to divorce and to find another woman. As I write we have been divorced for the best part of twenty years and I know she was good to her word and has never had a child and is now of an age where she probably never can. Lovers, I hope so, but no family of her own.

It took a few years for me to get over the divorce. That surprised me. It was something I had initiated and wanted but, psychologically, it affected me far more deeply than I had ever thought it would. It knocked the stuffing out of me and left me carrying a lot of anger which needed dealing with before considering another relationship. By the time the decree nisi was issued I was around fifty years old. I was now a well-educated man; several years removed from the work which funded my early retirement; and gradually coming to terms with a failed marriage. I had learned a fair bit about myself and had generally developed a much more positive self-image. I had also developed some very definite ideas of what I was looking for from the rest of my life; more importantly what I was not prepared to put up with. Perhaps this goes some way to answering the question – "Why am I even looking for a marriage or relationship?"

I knew I had my faults, don't we all, but I was what most would consider a decent person. I had no criminal record, my most serious formal indiscretions have been twice getting three points on my driving licence on occasions separated by sixteen years. The next time I get into a fight with anyone will be the first time. I will certainly fight in terms of debate and defending my position, (although tend to engage only where I think the subject is worthwhile and where I do not expect to lose). I don't sleep around or have unhealthy sexual interests; I no longer smoke. I am not taking any medication or drugs, prescribed or otherwise. I am well read, articulate, financially independent, and enjoy a comfortable lifestyle. However I do not have my own family. There was a big gap in my life where I wanted a wife; and, despite my age, I was open to the possibility of a child or two. I also have to add that, on the horizon, I can see old age beginning to stalk me and have no desire to spend any of the time I have left bed blocking in a hospital or vegetating in a nursing home.

Given my situation I considered that looking for a relationship and marriage was a fairly healthy and relatively normal position to be in.

It also needs to be said that whilst my drinking was very moderate whilst married, once divorced I hit the bottle with a vengeance. I am not blaming my ex for this. I suppose she was involved in the circumstances leading up to it, but it was me who bought the booze and did the drinking. All that said the five years following the divorce probably saw the peak of my drinking activities. The only good news about that was that I retained enough common sense to understand that, as I was driving 30,000 to 40,000 work related miles each year, I needed to keep my weekday drinking in check. The last thing I needed was to get a conviction for driving under the influence by being caught the morning after. So I separated alcohol consumption from work. However, when I was not working the following day, or on holiday, I drank very heavily. But I was beginning to understand (grudgingly) that booze and I were not a positive mix. By the time I started online dating I was beginning to settle down and get my consumption under control before eventually stopping altogether.

So, what path to take?

The problem I faced was that, whilst it is normal and healthy for an adult to be in a relationship, my circumstances were anything but normal. My wish was to move from single status to a healthy adult relationship with a woman where we worked out our issues as and when they arose and shared a mutual respect and happiness. Of itself this should not have presented a problem. However the type of relationship I was looking for, with a childless woman who would be interested in starting a family if she met the right man, was most unusual for a man my age. In consequence, in the society in which I live, my options were seriously limited.

To keep open the opportunity for a family I needed to find a women who was a good few years pre-menopause. Whilst I am not at all averse to children, in a career which has routinely engaged me hands on in the social sector, I have come across many broken homes, single parent families and relationships where each partner brought children into the relationship. Many of these worked well but the percentage which did not work well seemed to me to be far higher than that which occurred when both parents stayed together and reared the children. Solely because of this I convinced myself of the need to find a woman who was currently childless but open to starting a family with the right man. I acknowledge that was perhaps not the best of decisions but it was the decision I took,

I am now in my mid-sixties. This search began over a decade ago. So I am describing a woman likely to be ten to twenty years younger than me, potentially more than that. Age of itself is not a problem but finding a woman in her late thirties or early forties who is childless but wants to breed with a man likely to be old enough to be her father was a major challenge. The pool of women fitting this description is tiny. The few I have met have been very career oriented and seem to measure success largely in terms of income and assets. They were looking for a man who shared that outlook and the accompanying lifestyle. I wish them well in finding their partner but it is certainly not me. I am way beyond that debate. I know I have the resources (as a single person) to be comfortable for the rest of my days. The last thing I need is some high flyer who considers position, job title and money to be a vital, or even an important, goal. Life has far more to offer than constantly nosing that grindstone up the hill to a perceived success. I was looking for someone who was bright and chatty, someone who could and would use her brain, someone who shared my enjoyment of music and the arts, life in general; someone who was open-minded. Someone who worked to live rather than lived to work.

I mentioned earlier that I have my faults. In terms of developing a relationship my biggest handicap was likely to be where I stood on beliefs. This is something most of us don't think about very much. They may have been given to us by our parents or they may have developed as we grew up. But few of us give them much thought. When starting out in life and looking for someone with whom to share it these are issues which don't get much of an airing. One normally meets someone within ones circle of friends or colleagues at college or work and, because of that, similar belief systems are already in place. At the stage of life when this usually occurs we are in a position where, as a couple, there is every likelihood of growing together and developing shared belief systems going forward. That was not my position.

My studies as an adult learner and subsequent research, teaching and publications related in part to the human condition and its development and about the ways in which societies/workplaces are organised and operate. This work has involved discussing belief systems and how they develop and can be changed in organisations, communities and at the nation-state level. To do this meant knowing where I stood. Whilst I do not discuss what I believe very often, it does have a bearing on who I will feel comfortable with. More importantly, when seeking a partner for life, who will feel comfortable with me. For example, whilst I am happy to engage in debate and prepared to change my mind and alter my beliefs if I feel it to be necessary, I can be a stubborn old bugger. I have been around long enough to feel justified in holding the belief that our parliament consists of six hundred and fifty pigs with their noses, to a greater or lesser extent, in the trough, whichever party holds a majority in parliament. I think the Scottish comedian Billy Connolly had it right about politics. I paraphrase: "Politicians take my money to pay for their projects! Nice work if you can get it. Anyone who says they want to be involved in politics should be banned from politics for life!" I think the House of Lords is a joke; a particularly bad joke given that the twenty-six bishops of the church of England are automatically given seats. Their beliefs reflect a view of the world which places belief above scientific rigour. At best this is a belief in the supernatural; at worst it is a belief system based upon the visions, views and opinions of people in the poorest parts of the Middle East one to five thousand years ago. People who could not read and write, who looked for mystical explanations of things like eclipses and comets, etc. People who, if you read the old testament of the bible, supported the most vicious forms of ethnic cleansing and discrimination imaginable. Their way of life was written up a few generations later to codify the reality existing in those ancient times. We now have a lot more evidence and understanding of our world. The content portrayed in the old books gives believers what is known as 'received' knowledge; the knowledge received from these books. Those wishing to run their lives based on these outdated texts need to constantly reinterpret the rules of the world today as new evidence and information arises. So, for me, the concept bishops in government; theocracy, is not only discrimination against all other religious beliefs and non-beliefs, it also encourages an acceptance of unevidenced 'faith based' ideas. At best I am sceptical about all religion and everything which develops from that. However, in terms of relationship building, the bottom line is that anyone for whom religion is of any consequence should avoid me. Whilst I would count people holding religious beliefs to be amongst my closest friends that is because we share similar moral and ethical values. They may attribute this to their religion; I don't. From a scientific perspective religion cannot be completely and totally disproved, but nor can U.F.O.s, ghosts, witches or fairies at the bottom of the garden. In any case it is for those claiming religious beliefs to prove their case rather than those who do not believe to prove they are in the right.

I think the monarchy are the biggest shower of freeloaders we have in the U.K. As a society we encourage them to continue a benefit fraud which surpasses any other in the country, and probably across the world. This follows from a belief that hereditary revenue from national assets and the Civil List equate to state sanctioned benefits. In the highly unlikely event I were offered some award in the birthday or New Year's honours list my response would be to suggest those doing the offering stick it where the sun don't shine. A consequence of this is that I think our national anthem is an awful thing. Slight variance around 'god save our gracious queen' does not go down well with someone who does not believe in the existence of a god and does believe that monarchies should be abolished. I think the national anthem should be replaced. In deference to some of our sporting personalities who demonstrate a marked inability to remember the words we should replace it with an instrumental. I would suggest Henry Mancini's Pink Panther theme!

Enough of this tirade. As you can see I am not an easy person to please when it comes to issues of this nature. So I needed to be clear with any prospective partner that, if they supported 'the establishment' or the status quo, we would probably be best going our respective ways.

In terms of finding someone with whom I could comfortably spend the rest of my life it would need to be either someone who does not concern themselves much with these issues, or someone who shares some of my beliefs and is up for some pretty invigorating debate. I guess the point I am making is that someone who has found success by supporting the traditional norms and values of our society is not likely to find much comfort around me; nor me with her. If you consider me to be an assertive man you would be right; I am quite happy to relate with equally assertive women; but finding such a person has proved impossible. In fairness to myself I should say that, on a day to day basis, I hardly ever gave these issues a thought. That might be a consequence of living alone; but, in the safety of home, I have thrown many an obscene line at the TV when issues of religion, politics and monarchy are being aired. And with our current government the mute button gets a hammering!

When I returned to dating, a few years after my divorce, the type of women I met had very mainstream values and opinions. Good for them, I wish them well and have no wish to change them, but we were terrible potential matches for each other and that usually became apparent within a few minutes. The type of woman I was meeting had chosen to put having a family to one side whilst she built her career and was now considering the pitter patter of tiny feet to the backdrop of an approaching menopause. Aside from the issue of breeding these ladies all had similar aims and targets to the woman I had divorced. They offered a bland and cosy future that I had no intention whatever of revisiting! I also gained the impression that around half of those I met were looking for a house-husband with elements of a father figure. Knowing my sirloin from my silverside scored points; dropping a donner kebab on top of a meat feast pizza didn't! Distinguishing Canaletto from Caravaggio and Shostakovich from Stravinsky was relevant; differentiating Whitesnake from Judas Priest and Pink Floyd from Genesis not so. My enjoyment and knowledge across these areas was challenging. Throw in an appreciation of the art of Banksy, David Hockney and Grayson Perry with a love of the music of Santana, Frank Zappa, Leonard Cohen and top it all off with a love of all things jazz and the confusion was complete.

The bottom line was that I was presented with a problem. I could probably meet someone of a similar age to myself, adult children so no issues there, perhaps divorced or widowed, and develop a relationship. That could work but denied the possibility of family together and I would probably be finding friendship over a full blooded relationship. I have female friends so that is not what I was seeking. Perhaps I could find someone around twenty years younger than myself; but the few possibilities I had met seemed to have very different lifestyles and aspirations. Could I consider someone over twenty years my junior? Maybe, but more to the point, what is the likelihood of a woman that much younger than me having any romantic inclinations towards a man my age. Furthermore I would suggest that a man, at that time in his early to mid-fifties, trawling bars and cafes looking for single women so much younger than himself, at best might generate amusement, but the stronger likelihood is that he would quickly pick up the wrong type of reputation altogether. I looked around some of the more popular dating websites and found that assumption to be fully validated. Unsurprisingly western women in their twenties and thirties showed no romantic interest whatever in a man my age. So where was I to turn to next?

Whilst I know many people meet their lifetime partners as a consequence of their work, perhaps as a consequence of the type of work I was engaged in during the early part of my life, I always tried to separate work and pleasure. Work can be a pleasure; non-working time should also be a pleasure as much as possible. However, until I was in my forties, an overlap between the two domains was asking for serious trouble, so I avoided it. As an aside I would add that I have had some recent work experience in environments populated by young adults. There do appear to be some major differences between the ways in which people now in their twenties and thirties behave compared to the recollections I have of the way the world worked when I was that age. Maybe this is no more than a reflection of the generation gap. The biggest shift, between the workplace I entered almost fifty years ago and the workplace today, appears to me to be along lines espoused by the late Malcolm McLaren, former manager of the Sex Pistols and sometime cultural guru. He commented that it is often better to be a flamboyant failure than a benign success. Whilst I cannot, hand on heart, completely agree with this I do think it goes some way to describing my feelings towards the current crop of developing career professionals. Age precludes me from being a viable part of their groups and cliques but, generalising, they do seem to be a brittle and fickle bunch. So McLaren's benign success would be an excellent description for the ones advancing furthest up the greasy pole. That said I would prefer the company of a flamboyant failure every time. Scientist and astronomer Sir Fred Hoyle made a similar point when he commented: "It is better to be interesting and wrong than boring and right." What I am probably describing is a situation in which the environments we populate have gradually been changing and the differences in our situations make comparison and comprehension something of a challenge, both ways. Given my current situation this could be a challenge to which I will have to rise!

To conclude this part of my story, a few years after my divorce I began to look seriously for a relationship which could lead to marriage. I had taken the time to get a failed marriage out of my system first otherwise I would have been behaving unfairly towards both myself and any potential future partner. I had occasional dates with people who I met through friends, colleagues or on dating websites. I met some good people, some nice people, but none of them pressed the right buttons. The women I met tended to reflect the traditional values of British society. I see myself as a citizen of the world first and cannot really be described as traditional in any real sense of that word.

During this time I was operating in a middle management position for public and private sector organisations; occasionally I would represent them at regional and national level. I have had involvement with three of the Directorates of the European Union; DG XIII B Telecomms, information and research (people and peace; international dialogue and aid effectiveness); DG XV Internal market and financial services (copyright and data protection); and, DG XXII Education, training and youth (around vocational training and distance learning). I have also held senior positions on the boards of two charities, one position elected, the other nominated; one U.K. based the other located in Europe. The former related to the literary arts, the latter involved secondary and university level education. Both had international mandates and I have spent some of my working life in continental Europe, Asia and North and South America, and have undertaken Middle East and Africa based projects. As a consequence I have met many women of all ages and from a variety of very diverse cultural backgrounds. Most seemed to be happily married or settled in their relationships. The relationships we had were what I would describe as normal, functional working relationships. Outside of the workplace we rarely, if ever, socialised.

As a consequence of my work with one of these organisations I was invited to undertake a piece of original research around personal risk management to present at an A.G.M. The remit was to fill a one hour spot reporting a piece of original research and to be topical, quirky and relevant to youth in 21st century society.

Three sorry stories, and a fourth!

Whilst I was looking around for ideas I saw a satellite TV programme about the perils of online dating across cultures. It featured negative outcomes for two women and one man.

The first woman came to the U.K. from the Ukraine as the wife of a British man. She had married in her home country and been granted a visa to return to the U.K. with him. What she did not know was that the man was an alcoholic who could be violent. He had previous convictions in the U.K. for committing offences of violence against women. When she arrived at his house she became a virtual slave. Her English language knowledge was minimal, she had no access to any finance, was only allowed to leave the house with her husband, and was expected to perform in the kitchen and bedroom on demand. Whilst with her family in the Ukraine she had seen photographs and video of the house they would be living in. However the husband had only portrayed those aspects which looked acceptable. What they did not show was that part of one of the external walls was in the process of collapsing. Nor did they show the room which was full of empty bottles together with various items of clothing and paper which were rotting in the damp. She eventually managed to communicate with a local woman who, in turn, contacted a support group. They helped to get her out of this appalling situation and back home to her family.

The second woman had arrived in the U.K. on a visitor visa; as I recollect she was Vietnamese. She had been working in one of the Gulf States and became friendly with a U.K. based Arabian man who had been visiting his extended family. They continued their friendship online and she obtained a visa to come to the U.K. as a visitor for up to six months. As soon as she arrived it became obvious she had been tricked. She was met at the airport by her sponsor and taken to his home. She discovered he was married with children. Her passport was taken from her and she was immediately put to work as a child-minder and housekeeper. Her day began before six in the morning and finished once the children were sleeping and she had cleaned their clothes and prepared whatever was needed for them the following day. There were no days off, no holidays, various aspects of her life with this family belied bad treatment and cruelty and she had no opportunity to leave the house without being accompanied. She finally escaped after three years.

The man had been using a Russian dating website which claimed to find young attractive wives for the 'older western man'. He met his 'hearts' desire' online and then visited her in her own city. He was met at the local office of the dating agency by two men to whom he paid his fee; they then took him to the home of his 'girlfriend'. After the initial introduction, for the week or so he was in town, the couple set their own itinerary, rarely outside the company of her family and friends. Everything went well and they agreed they would marry in her city a few months later. As a married couple they would then apply for a visa so she could return to the U.K. with him. He sent money across to support her and to progress these arrangements. They maintained regular e-mail contact and exchanged photographs and video clips. He returned to her city the week before the scheduled wedding with the intention of getting the paperwork sorted out. Close to the company offices was a park in which they had arranged to meet. The lady did not appear. He waited but eventually, after finding the company offices were also closed, went to an internet café and sent her a message. By return he received an apology from her saying she had needed to have some emergency dental work attended to but was now on her way. She asked him to return to the park. He did this and the two men he recognised from his previous visit to the company office appeared with a rather agitated woman he had never seen previously. One of the men asked for the money he had agreed to pay for the wedding. When he baulked a gun was pulled on him and his wallet and papers stolen. The men then pushed the woman towards him and told him that this was person they were working for and that if he wished to marry her she was willing. This was not the woman he had met previously and was nothing like her. Nor was she anything like the woman he had been hoping to meet and marry when he joined the website. He reported the matter to the local police who, with some amusement, returned with him to the company offices only to find the rooms had been stripped of any identifiable material. Other users of these buildings had, of course, never heard of the company or family and did not recollect any callers.

So we have three stories of how two gullible woman and one rather silly man were preyed upon by unscrupulous people. Two of these utilised dating websites and all three had operated online. From a risk management perspective I considered that this might be the topical, quirky and relevant issue I could focus my presentation on for the A.G.M. So I did some preliminary scoping. What I was looking for was a means of discovering how these websites were abused and the risks faced by users.

I should be clear about my own position. It was thirteen years ago now. At the time I launched the project I was dipping my toe back into the matters romantic and trying to get a bit of love back into my life. However I had realised it was very unlikely I would be able to find anyone within my own culture where there was a likelihood of romance which could lead to family life. So it is legitimate to ask if I was using this 'research' as a means of testing the market for myself. At this stage I would say no; however I would agree that I was vulnerable to approaches generated through websites. I knew this from the get go but set out with the view that I would not take advantage of the situation; I would not 'go native' for want of a better phrase. However, as we will see, my position on this did change. But that occurred a couple of years later.

I did an online search for international dating websites. As the TV programme had mentioned Ukraine and Russia I decided to look in that area and joined a website. To do this I had to post my profile. Whilst not using my own name on the public profile I did otherwise try to keep reasonably close to a description of myself. A good liar needs a good memory and that is something I don't possess. I also needed to post a photograph. Then the website prompted me to describe the person I was searching for. So I posted that I was seeking a female, wanting a long term relationship where family was a possibility, she must not yet have children, and be prepared to marry and live in my country. Once the formalities had been completed I clicked the button to post my profile and sat back to wait for the results. Within an hour I had received ten messages; within a week I had received over five hundred. The response was incredible and overwhelming. Each message carried a photograph of the woman sending it, a link to her profile and further information. Most were very attractive and all were making the right kind of noise in my direction.

Shakespeare is often misquoted via 'Hamlet' to have written: "Vanity, thy name is woman." The actual line is: "Frailty, thy name is woman;" a line spoken by Hamlet as a response to his mother re-marrying, in his opinion, 'too soon' after his father's death. However, in retrospect, having been inundated with replies from stunning, nubile young women, I have to admit the phrase: "Vanity, thy name is man," would have been a very appropriate response to my initial reaction. However it did not take long for the penny to drop! I was not the attraction, the potential of my wallet very likely was.

And so it turned out. The only way to reply to any of these messages was by paying a fee to the website for their services which included translation costs. The fee paid bought me credits with the site. So, in the name of research, I made a payment of U.S. $ 50 which bought me 100 credits. Each woman had her own website credit rating between 0.5 and 10 and, to reply to her, cost a specified number of credits. I am not party to how an individual's credit score was calculated. However you will not find it surprising that the beautiful, single, childless woman in her late teens or early twenties looking for a western husband and prepared to relocate to his country carried the maximum tariff; 10 credits. A lady with a couple of children in her thirties or forties would range from 0.5 to 5.0 credits. Again unsurprisingly, almost all of my replies were from 10 credit ladies. The website claimed that the credit level of their client was based on the number of messages she received; the more messages, the more need to provide translation services for her, therefore the higher their charges. Maybe. If so my experience suggests a direct correlation between traditional good looks and messages received which would make some sort of sense. But, even if that were the case, the cost of translation has nothing to do with a person's visual appearance. It will reflect the number, length and complexity of the messages received. As the service is offered on behalf of 'all' women regardless of appearance, the cost of translation services should have had no bearing whatever on the appearance of the person to whom a message was sent. One would anticipate a set rate for translation based on the number of words or sentences or paragraphs. Whilst a provocatively dressed, single, 21 year old blonde may get more attention than a woman in her late thirties with young children, the status of the woman does not have any impact on the cost of translating a message. But there are major implications if translating ten words, a hundred words or a thousand words, etc.

The website had automatically set up an account for me where my credits were stored and which I could check at any point. When my number of credits dropped below ten I automatically received a reminder. A second reminder came when only one or two credits remained in the account. If an attempt was made to reply to a message when there were insufficient credits in the account a default message advising of this was received and a link to their payment page provided. A rule of the website was an absolute ban on harvesting information from members which could lead to contact being made 'off site'. Specifically this included e-mail addresses, telephone numbers, names and addresses. The site was monitored rigorously for this. On two occasions I tried to slip an e-mail address into the message; it was bounced back to me each time. On the first occasion I was told gently that I must have made a mistake; the second time I was told they operated a three strikes and you are out system and that I had just transgressed for the second time.

Going into the terms and conditions of the website I discovered that if two people met through the website and decided they wished to meet in person, this could only be arranged through the website where various criteria, all with a price tag, had to be met. The meeting would be at a location, convenient to the woman, which the dating website would nominate on her behalf. This brought back memories of the man in the TV programme who had been mugged at gun point.

Before any introduction could be considered the man had to produce proof that he had no criminal record. The reason given for this was that the website claimed it had to comply with the International Marriage Broker Regulation Act, (I.M.B.R.A.). This is a piece of U.S. legislation which seeks to protect foreign nationals who enter the U.S.A. to be with a partner or a person they intend to marry. It was enacted following an incident where a woman was murdered by the man she visited. The murder enquiry revealed the U.S. authorities knew this man to be a violent, predatory sexual offender who had convictions for committing serious sexual offences and violence against women with whom he had a relationship. This is a good piece of legislation provided the woman is involved with a U.S. citizen and is visiting that country. The website I was using, whilst ostensibly introducing Ukrainian and Russian women to western men, billed in U.S. dollars but was registered in Canada. I am a citizen of the U.K. In an e-mail exchange I pointed this out to the site managers who told me it was my problem but, for their standard fee of $150, they would ensure I had the I.M.B.R.A. paperwork in place. I pointed out to them that this would be meaningless. All it would do is tell the woman I was planning to meet that a person who was a U.K. national and resident had no convictions in the U.S.A. It would not, and could not, provide any meaningful information on any convictions I might have against me in the U.K. In fact what the website owners were offering was dangerous for any women concerned as they were proposing to present documentation advising her that I had no convictions when they were fully aware it was quite impossible for them to make a meaningful check.

This might be thought of as a relatively minor issue but think about the potential damage which could occur. Many women using this website had children; many posted photographs of themselves with their children. The service offered by this website was global. It is quite feasible that a paedophile who is not a U.S. citizen could use the website to target a female member as a means of getting access to her children. The website managers making it clear that, for a fee, they would tell their client a man has a clean bill of health in circumstances where it was impossible for them to properly check him out. All they could truthfully say would be that the man had no previous convictions in the U.S.A. So what they proposed to tell their female client was a completely meaningless piece of information. What is the likelihood of a man, who is not a U.S. citizen and has never lived in the U.S.A., having any criminal conviction recorded against him within the U.S. judicial system? Rather than protecting their client the website was proposing to jeopardise the woman and her children whilst taking a payment from the man. She would believe she had evidence from the website owners which demonstrated she was dealing with a genuine bona fide and trustworthy suitor with no criminal record. She would be making her decisions on that basis. So far as I am aware the website did not check addresses or attempt to verify the identity of any of their members. That suitor could easily be a non-U.S. citizen. When a website member was not a citizen of the U.S.A. the introduction agency was unable to make any check of his criminal record; it was impossible. Even if the man was a U.S. citizen, any meaningful check is contingent upon him providing full and accurate details of himself. Whatever his nationality is a predator using a website to find a victim likely to do this? Yet the site managers were happy enough, provided he paid his $150, to tell the woman he proposed to meet that he had a clean record. In doing so they would increase the likelihood of that man getting access to their female member and her child or children; an awful situation in which to put the woman and her family. I flagged this to the website managers. I also pointed out that as an organisation registered for business in Canada they were not legally bound by U.S. legislation. The I.M.B.R.A. clearance they were requiring was, therefore, not a legal obligation for them but a self-generated administrative issue. My implication was that they were deliberately creating an issue where it did not exist and then offering to provide a fake solution; for a fee. Their reply to both issues was in essence: "These are the rules, take it or leave it."

Going back to using this website, I responded to a few messages and several online conversations began. However it very quickly became obvious that either my messages were not being read or, if they were, the person responding did not understand them. I would send a message along the lines of: "I enjoy watching comedy and sports programmes on TV, what kind of things to you enjoy watching?" I would then get a reply which might answer the question but, just as easily, might not. I would respond. The reply to my second message would then ask: "What sort of things do you enjoy watching on TV?" All this website was effectively providing was employment for a pool of translators who may or may not have been interested in matching people up. They would answer messages for all clients, probably working from a crib sheet to ask questions, and not realise they were asking a question which had, very recently, been answered. Not only was I unlikely ever to meet anyone through this website, all I was doing was providing a bit of work for a not very proficient interpretation service.

To further test this proposition I split the people with whom I was chatting into two small groups. To one group I sent very long, complicated messages, and anticipated quickly being told to reign myself in. For the second group I used a computer based translation service and sent the following message in Ukrainian:

> Я насолоджуюся чаті з вами і думаю, що це було б набагато простіше для нас обох, якщо ви написали на своїй рідній мові. Я можу перевести без будь-яких витрат. Я можу також відправляти повідомлення на вашій мові так що це буде також означати, що ви не повинні платити.

The above is what I was provided with when I entered the following message in English:

I am enjoying chatting with you and think it would be much easier for us both if you wrote in your own language. I am able to translate at no cost. I can also send messages in your language so it will also mean you do not have to pay.

Whilst all the replies ostensibly came from the woman to whom they had been sent, the outcomes were all as predicted. The women who received my message in Ukrainian told me they had received warning messages from the website as they were expected to pay for translation services. They asked me to send no more messages in Ukrainian. They also told me that my membership and payment for credits included the costs of translation of their messages and that was the method the website owners expected their clients to use.

I also got the replies anticipated to the lengthy messages. It was along the lines of: "We are members of a small intimate organisation which cannot provide the resources to deal with the length of message you are sending; please will you just sent one or two paragraphs otherwise I will not be able to pay the translation costs."

Either way developing any kind of relationship was scuppered.

(Of course if we used an electronic translation service we would be far more likely to be able to make our own arrangements. And that would never do as we would be subverting their business model.)

Progress.

The experiment with the Russia/Ukraine website lasted a few months. I realised that the only way forward would be to use online dating sites which did not provide interpretation services. So I looked around for a website where the members routinely conversed using the English language. I also wanted a website which did not forbid its members from opening up full communications with each other.

When I looked at the geographic areas in which international dating websites operated I found they were global. However, when searching out what appeared to be professional sites in regions outside the west, these tended to be based in in a particular country or region, i.e. Far East, China, India, Japan, South-East Asia, Central America, Latin America, and the former Soviet Union states. Alternatively there were sites which specialised across religious groups or by sexuality. They offered their services with payments for different elements. There was typically an entry level where one could view the site but not interact with it. The next level would involve a level of payment just to be able to see and reply to e-mails sent through the website; further tiers of membership might offer a video conferencing facility and/or allow members to exchange personal details, etc.

Where a website introduces people to each other from different parts of the world this structure encourages citizens in a developing or underdeveloped country to open an entry level account. The only cost to them is that of being able to be online. There was no cost involved in setting up one's own profile with photographs. This would make that person visible to paying members in the developed areas of the world. So, whilst there were very few paying members of these websites based in the developing world, it is overwhelmingly the person based in the developed country who was paying the membership fee and therefore that was the person in control of all interactions. It is they who make the choices around levels of membership based on a version of the criteria outlined above. This could and did lead to a lot of abusive behaviour on these websites. Services unrelated to the website would be offered by some women; such services were requested by many men. The websites owners claimed to regulate their sites for misuse and asked all users to report improper behaviour. Some sites were better at this than others.

As I progressed my research I confirmed it would suit my purposes far better if I used a service which operated in the English language. I also decided to only use sites which were properly regulated whilst allowing participants to develop and manage their communications as they wished. I also did not want to be hampered with issues around proving a clean bill of health so far as a criminal record was concerned. I live in a country where proving this has costs attached and usually only makes the information available when applying for work in a sensitive area. I agree with this. In any case the clean bill of health from a criminal record check is only relevant on the day it is issued and assumes the person requesting the check has provided correct details. In the U.K. anyone with a criminal conviction trying to get around this would need to supply false details. That would be unlawful when applying for a job but, when supplying information to an offshore dating website, would that remain the case?

We can also be certain that, whilst I am sure there will be dating website users who have criminal records and use sites malevolently, that can happen both ways. That does not make it right. But we have to remember that, like it or not, a dating website is a market place. The product you offer is yourself and you are looking to invest in another person's self! The Latin phrase 'caveat emptor' (let the buyer beware) applies with full force. It is risky enough using a dating website in which the members share a common language and culture. When this is not the case opportunities for abuse rise. Many of these websites are scams through and through. The one I described based in Canada and supposedly seeking to provide western men with introductions to Russian and Ukrainian women was one such. I don't think I met a single genuine person on that website. It was all about providing money for sham translation services. Even with the best sites the risks are high.

Do dating websites have any genuine users?

At this stage of the process I was in my mid-fifties; the women with whom I was in contact, if the profiles on the websites were to be believed, were all under the age of forty and most claimed to be mid-twenties, single, not in a relationship and without children. A genuine person in this environment is asking for trouble, whichever side of the relationship/world they are on. Sorting the wheat from the chaff was a never ending process; it was not always straightforward and could be quite a challenge.

I did some digging around online and discovered there were many dating websites all over the world. There were also a wide variety of websites set up to warn of scammers and how to spot them. The reality is that in poor countries many will use such websites to try to get money from a would-be partner. Whilst this routinely happens on a one to one basis, it is also a small industry.

I spent around six months on and off trying to find the right website. Outside of the western world the only country I found where English was used extensively and on a daily basis was the Philippines. There may be others, my search does not claim to be exhaustive. I did not know at the time but English is the language of education from secondary school upwards in the Philippines. This means that most adults have some knowledge of it and can get by to a greater or lesser extent. Even so one should not hold any great expectations around language skill. Many Filipinas will be withdrawn from education early and encouraged to undertake some income generating activity. So a genuine woman in her twenties may have had three years of English at school and not have used it for over a decade.

I also chose the Philippines because I had heard, anecdotally, that Philippine women did not see an age gap with potential partners as being a barrier. I had heard the same of Thai women but did not venture there for two reasons. Firstly there was the issue of language. Secondly was the reputation for sex particularly involving underage girls. I wanted no part of that so had no contact with websites purporting to operate for a Thai audience. However subsequent experience has shown that the offering of sex with underage girls (or boys) is also rife in the Philippines.

Before going forward just a brief note here on word endings. A FilipinA is a female from the Philippines. A FilipinO is a male from the Philippines. However the word FilipinO, particularly in the plural, FilipinOS, can refer to a group of people or the population in general, not just the male part. The word FilipinAS, can only mean Philippine females.

I digress.

There are many dating websites which cover the Philippines. Some of them are explicitly sexual, some graphically so. However that was not what I was looking for. I was trying to establish what risks existed for users who were genuine whether they were Philippine or western based. I searched for websites which offered introduction services; a means for two people to get to know each other. I experimented with four of five sites which claimed to provide such services. For a few weeks I played around as a non-paying member of these sites. I finally settled on a website managed by an organisation registered for business in Australia which operated a variety of dating websites covering most geographic areas of the world and a variety of tastes; a significant player in the international dating websites field. I made this choice for a variety of reasons but principally because their systems were easy to use and well maintained; had a payment system in which I was confident; and, when I reported misuse to the website managers, they immediately removed that member profile or gave me a good reason for not doing. Others either didn't respond or required more 'evidence' than it was possible to provide; two or three provided nonsensical reasons for not taking action. There were also several websites where, after doing a bit of digging, I concluded they were more interested in collecting bank details than providing a useful website. The website I chose seemed to offer the highest likelihood of genuine users. That still wasn't very high. When I joined the website I thought the split was about 50% genuine, 50% scam of one sort or another. In light of five years membership and several visits to the Philippines I would revise that to about 30% genuine, 70% scam. However that was still considerably better than the other sites I tried where the scam rate was often close to 100%.

Learning to use the website was an interesting experience. Let's start with the profile. To post a profile on a dating website at that time all you need is a fairly modern mobile device or access to a computer. So, if you were based in a poor country, you could post a profile on a dating website free of charge and see what you attracted. If you are lucky you might find a meal ticket out of poverty and be able to support your family. When I first went into this project I thought that would be the only reason a young woman would consider a relationship with a man my age. For some it is, but not all are playing that game.

Having a photograph of yourself is very helpful but not essential. There are profiles on websites without a photograph. However I would never respond to a profile which did not have some images of the person behind it. There is a reason for the owner of a profile choosing to remain invisible and often that will be because they are a scammer, a fraudster. The one exception would be a new member to the site. For the first few hours, whilst completing their profile, it will appear on the site without a photograph. Adding images tends to be the final thing one is asked to do before your profile is fully completed. The managers of the website then need time to look at the photos submitted to ensure they are appropriate. As the new members are completing their profiles they can be viewed by paying members. So in these very limited circumstances you may find a genuine profile under development which has yet to have its photos approved and available. On a genuine website profiles will have a unique membership number. If a profile without a photograph interests you then check the member number. Compare it with your own membership number. A higher number indicates the profile has been set up after you joined and the higher the membership number the more recently the member joined the website. Conversely lower numbers mean the profile has been in use longer than yours and the lower the number is, the longer the profile has been in active use. If you are looking at a profile with a new number you may be okay. Make a note of the membership number and look again in a day or so. Otherwise, if there are no images, I would avoid it like the plague.

Each website will prescribe the maximum number of photographs a member is allowed to post. The site I used set that at five. It also asked the member to specify their 'main' image. This accompanies your profile whenever it is viewed. So it is logical to make it the one you consider shows you in your best light. To complete your profile you will also need to complete quite a lengthy pro forma. You need to describe yourself and what you are looking for and then repeat the process for the type of person you are seeking. A genuine person will take time doing this as it is effectively your advertising platform. When you search the website an incomplete profile tells you that its owner, for whatever reason, is not taking the process seriously. This is a warning sign which should be noted. By incomplete I am meaning that they do not specify their hobbies or their educational background, likes and dislikes, that sort of information. Nor will they specify the characteristics they are looking for in a partner. Insofar as the Philippines are concerned the absence of this level of information more often than not indicates the user is not very confident in using the English language. However it may also be a warning that, behind the profile, someone is lurking who will not provide that information as they do not want other members interrogating what the profile claims. It could be one of several fake profiles posted by a scammer. Be wary also where the profile owner posts a single image. They may only have one, but, given modern technology, is that likely? It is more likely that a scammer has got hold of one image of a person and is using that to front a fake profile. Photographs are an important element of the profile. As mentioned before this is a market place. Presentation matters. It tells you important things about the person behind the profile. The best way to sell your goods is to make sure they are visible, looking their best and are clearly labelled. In the case of this type of website, provided you are using it genuinely, you need to be honest and realistic. There is no point in a man describing himself as a slim, six foot tall male weighing in at 90 kilos if he is short in stature with a sixty inch waist and buttocks sagging down below the knees. If you are genuine at some point you will have to completely reveal yourself! Just as you expect the person you meet to come pretty close to their profile description and photographs, so your prospective partner deserves to have that expectation met. Ultimately, if you post a false profile, the only person you are fooling is yourself.

I soon learned that using this type of website has its learning curve. The good news is that, once you understand the way people are using the site, you can quickly weed out most of the opportunistic scammers. There are a lot of them so it is important to learn how to do this quickly. Just as occurred with the Russia/Ukraine website as soon as my profile went live on the website I began attracting interest but with two major differences. Firstly the number of contacts I had were fewer. After an initial flurry this settled at around the mid-thirties during an average week; five or six a day. More importantly the language used on these profiles and in messages was obviously written by someone using a second language without the support of an interpretation service. This made communication much more real. It became a genuine conversation or chat with a person doing their best in a second language. Having plenty of experience of working in far flung places I understood this well. It was a far superior experience to the Russian/Ukrainian website to which I had initially subscribed.

Staying with the profile let's take a look at how you might spot the scammer. It may be stating the obvious but when one uses a dating website it must be understood from the outset that the person behind a profile may not be the person shown on the profile. The profile might describe a slim attractive woman in her early twenties who claims to be seeking a man whose age and appearance is not important to her. Her photograph will confirm the written description. But that does not mean the profile is genuine. It may be. She may be genuine, she may be sharing a profile with a friend or relative, or she may be a scammer herself. But the profile may have been posted, with or without her knowledge, by anyone. The family unit is very important in the Philippines and some family members take advantage of this. So the profile you are looking at may have been posted by her brother, sister, father, mother, grand-parent, friend, etc. who is looking to hide behind a profile whilst trying to raise funds by whatever means possible. It may be a professional scammer who has found the photograph in a magazine, a newspaper, lifted it from another website or simply been taking photographs in the street. They have then built a profile around the image(s) they have. The only way you have to confirm that you are exchanging messages with the person whose image accompanies a profile is to see them. One of the attractions of the website I signed up with was that it provided a secure video link which was controlled by the paying member of the website. This worked in much the same way as Skype or Facebook video. If you are using an international dating website genuinely you need a site which offers this facility. Having exchanged a few messages you might suggest a video chat. Resistance to this is a big sign that all is not well; as is the suggestion by the other party that they prefer to use a video link not supported by the website. Why would they want to do this? Whichever system you use it is, technically, almost identical; the same equipment can be used at the same cost. Wanting to move off a managed and monitored dating website to a platform which is not managed and monitored is an indication that the person with whom you are chatting does not want to risk evidence of a scam being generated on the genuine website. That would make it very easy for the site managers to throw the profile they have spent time building off the site. For a live chat all a profile holder needs to be able to do is use a computer or mobile device which has a camera; even in a developing country as most of the Philippines is, almost all have some access to this technology. As the paying member you have complete control over who your video chat is with. Whilst all members of the website can send an 'invitation to chat' to any other member, only the paying member can open the link and set up a conversation; and that can only be done from your own profile page. The website I was using offered the paying member the opportunity to not see 'invitations to chat'. This was a useful facility as I was hit on by all and sundry in my first few weeks of use.

Many Filipinas live in poverty. Many will not have access to a computer but most have some access to a mobile phone. Provided the phone has a front facing camera this will support a video chat using the website. There are also thousands of internet cafes across the country in city, town and village. Whilst someone living in a rural area may genuinely have a difficulty in arranging a video chat, most will be able to provided they are given time to arrange it. One also needs to be cognisant that young Filipinas living with their families are kept on a fairly tight leash by their parents. They will have a curfew, even in their twenties, and the parents are likely to hold the purse strings. So be patient with any women when arranging a chat. She will be working with a completely different set of norms and values to yours. She may still be a scammer but taking time to set up a chat is not indicative of this. For the genuine user of the website they will also want to use the video link for the same reason that you do. They are also familiar with being scammed, albeit for different reasons, and want to see you. To want to use any system other than that provided through the dating website does not make sense for the genuine user until a good level of trust has been developed. Those who push for this to happen are likely to be doing so because they want to discuss things that are too risky to chat about on a properly managed website. A small percentage will be worried by having to use a system of which they have no previous experience; they will need to be talked through the process in very simple phrases.

As an aside, whilst there have been major improvements in broadband access and general IT infrastructure over the last few years in metropolitan areas of the Philippines, the telecommunications systems in the rest of the country are generally very poor in comparison with surrounding countries and the west. The basic infrastructure just isn't there. Breaks in power supply are a regular occurrence across much of the country and are referred to locally as brownouts or power outages. They may not last long but they can disturb all forms of communication. If you are chatting to someone you believe to be genuine and experience some kind of technical glitch, it is very likely this will be genuine and has happened at the Philippines end of the conversation. You need to be patient and remember it is just as frustrating at the other end of the chat.

However system break down is something which can be exploited by scammers. If you ask an awkward question they may just disappear and then try again a few days later in the hope you will not ask that question again. When you next meet them they will claim a failure with the connection.

Confusingly such a disappearance from the website can also indicate a cultural issue which most of us in the west will not be aware of. The question of 'amor-propio'. To understand this we need to take a look back at the history of the Philippines. The islands were originally influenced by Malaysia and Indonesia. However, from 1521-1898 the country was colonised by the Spanish. The main first languages are Tagalog, Cebuano and Bisaya; there are several local variants and dialects. All have influences from the Spanish language. For example the Cebuano numbers are the same as the Spanish. Spoken English is also heavily influenced by U.S. colonisation from 1898-1946.

Back to amor-propio. It is a Spanish phrase which literally translates as self-esteem. A very different aspect of culture from the west is a fear of publicly losing face. Coupled with this, and unlike in the west, Filipinos place a very high value of their kin group. Many live in extended family groups. As a race they go out of their way not to cause offence because this might bring into question the self-esteem of another. That would be a very serious social gaffe, particularly where it could impact on another family member. From birth it is imprinted on the child to respect all others and to not create a situation in which the self-esteem of another may become threatened. This means that most Filipinos do not challenge others and do not like being challenged. This also plays into notions we may have in the west of Filipinos being subservient. These are well documented aspects of Philippine culture and, when you are in their country, with them, they expect the same consideration from you. This is particularly important when dealing with those members of the community who have limited experience beyond their own family group. Outside the metropolitan areas this is just about everyone. However this drive not to cause offence to anyone in a face-to-face situation has led to a trait which can become unpleasant. As I don't speak the local language I make this observation based on what several Filipinos I know have told me. In Philippine communities there is a lot of talking about people going on behind their backs and much of this can be highly judgemental. In the U.K. we would probably refer to this a malicious gossip.

If two westerners have a serious disagreement they will deal with it themselves. If two Filipinos have a serious disagreement it is dealt with at the family level and family extends to second cousins three times removed. It will involve people you have never known and who may not be known to your partner. If you fall foul of one member of a family, you are likely to fall foul of all of them. You will not be taking on one person, you will be taking on dozens, many of whom you will have never previously met. Conversely when you marry a Filipina you become part of that extended family; whether you want to or not. The up side of 'amor-propio' is that Filipinos will go out of their way to avoid arguments and problems and this will help smooth a relationship through some stormy waters. This is a contributory factor to the belief, in some circles, that a Filipina wife will be a compliant wife! She will operate in a way which you are not familiar with and avoid dispute where possible, but that does not mean she will do your will; nor should you expect that. Just as you enjoy the freedom to operate in your way, so she has the right to be free to operate in her way. The downside of 'amor-propio' is that there can be more and deeper sulks than a westerner would ever imagine; these locally are known as 'tampo', which is discussed in greater depth later. Also issues which need to be resolved can go on and on and on as a way is sought to deal with them without having crossed words or causing offence. I mention this as a cessation of communication following an awkward question when using a dating website might be more a matter of 'amor-propio' than a technical problem. To check if the person you are chatting with feels your question challenges their self-esteem or pride, change the phrasing of it. Asking if there was a problem is much more likely to elicit a positive response than an accusation and request for explanation.

Dating websites attract thousands of scammers. They can be broken down into three main categories. The first is the professional scam where a group of people will create a number of profiles and manage them, each profile being a front behind which they will try to develop a 'profitable' relationship with as many gullible people as they can. The second is the individual who puts up a fake profile in the hope of 'profiting' by attracting as many donors as possible. The third is the opportunist site user who has posted a genuine profile and will try to draw you, and many others, in. Once connected they will take their time and peruse their options. They may take this as far encouraging you to visit and spend time with them. Once they have you in the flesh so to speak, then the scam hits. Before that they will give every sign of being genuine. As you will see as this story progresses I was caught out that way on a couple of occasions.

It matters not which type of scammer you come across, what the genuine user has to keep at the front of their mind is that the only reason for the scammer chatting with you is because they want something; from a western perspective this is usually money, from the Philippine perspective it is usually sex in one form or another. As a western man I acknowledge the latter and have had to knock back occasional approaches; I only really have direct experience of the former.

For the scammers I have come across, time is money, particularly for the professionals, and they will not waste their time making conversation unless they have to *and* think their efforts will be rewarded. They are looking for either a quick kill after which they will move on; or to develop a relationship where you will be continuing to pay them over a period of weeks, months, even years if they can get away with it. This can occur if you believe you are building a genuine relationship and dealing with a genuine website user. The scammer knows that the image you believe you are developing a relationship with does not exist. That image might be a set of photos on their profile or the image conveyed by the person in front of the camera when you have video chats. They know they are just stringing you, and probably a few others, along. This type of scam will continue for as long as you allow it. When money raises its head, however it happens, make it clear from the outset that you will not be sending money to anyone, for any reason, until you have met them in person and are confident you have a good working relationship which has a chance of staying the course. This might sound tough, particularly when the person sat in front of the camera is telling you some heart-breaking story of their own or their family's misfortunes, maybe decorated with the occasional sob or tear. But you have to assume that none of this is real until you can literally see it for yourself, in person. When a scammer understands they will not be getting your money (or whatever else might be under negotiation) they will quickly vote with their feet. You may wonder where this lovely person has disappeared to. The answer is that (s) he was not a lovely person; just another con artist after your hard earned assets.

The scammers only linger when they believe the rewards are there. To be able to use the website they have taken the time to create a profile. They do not want that profile to be compromised so the professional scammer will try to get you to operate off the website as soon as they can. If they try to scam you whilst using the dating site you have subscribed to then you, as the bona fide user, can and should report them to the site managers. More importantly, both you and the site managers will have evidence of what they have been up to. That information will be contained within the messages you have exchanged. The end result is that the profile behind which they are operating is likely to be struck off the website. For the scammer that is a headache. They have to create a new profile which means a new identity and a new set of photographs.

If you are encouraged to operate away from the dating website you can allow this to happen as a means of screening out the crooked. To do this you should set up a new e-mail address and/or new accounts for Facebook, Viber, or Skype as appropriate for this specific purpose as you do not want to compromise your day-to-day arrangements. If they do not try to cheat you then your confidence in them can grow.

The scammer will not linger. They will disappear, often without giving any reason. An easy way of flushing them out is to maintain a lengthy and time consuming dialogue. The scammer will make a move. They do not want to waste time chatting; they want to find out whether or not they have discovered an income. If not they will move on. This is also a way of testing how genuine someone is. The genuine site user will stick with you. However you are not out of the woods yet. That will not happen until you meet in person. A genuine Filipina tends to be a pleasant, quite shy woman by western standards. It is highly unlikely that she will ask for money until it is necessary and, by that time, you will have a greater understanding of her circumstances and finances. I discuss this later but it must be borne in mind just how poor many Filipinos are. What may happen is that a genuine user will find and chat with you, but, once their family realise she has hooked someone, they may put pressure on her to ask for money. But that is something the Filipina has to manage. From your perspective you need to keep yourself safe so, once a financial request is made, report it and, as the website allows you to place a block on members you wish to have no further contact with, block their profile.

Once you have established a rapport and think you can trust the person with whom you are chatting you should work towards a video chat using the dating website's facilities. If that works you might consider meeting off the website. If things progress really well you may arrange to visit her. Do not think she will visit you. Even if you are prepared to finance such a trip the likelihood of her obtaining a U.K. visa for a visit is virtually nil; something else to which I will return later.

Now let's return to basics. My reason for joining this website was to discover the risks to genuine users. Once I had paid my membership and set up a profile and photographs I went to work. I would estimate that around seven out of ten of the contacts I made were at best people playing silly games and at worst scams. But that does mean that around 30% of contacts seemed genuine. That came as something of a surprise. With the Russia/Ukraine website I was quickly sure that virtually every approach I received was from someone wanting to generate an income through translation. With the Philippine site I met a lot of cranks but I did begin to get into dialogue with some very pleasant and decent women who were interested in developing a long term relationship if they found the right man. For many, age difference was just not an issue. They would mention in conversation that their parents had an age gap of twenty or thirty years. I didn't know if this was true so I took to reading up on the Philippines. Whilst I found a lot of cautionary tales there was also confirmation that age did not seem to be much of an issue for the Filipina. One explanation which I came across several times advised that, in her own country, the Filipina gets a seriously raw deal. Men routinely play the field. This can begin during puberty and then continue into adulthood and marriage and having children together makes little difference. Provided the man has the income to support two families he will be quite content to operate that way and, so long as he is discreet and discrete, society generally keeps quiet about this. Obviously this practice is not appreciated by the women scorned. However the man can only behave this way if he finds another willing woman, so men, and some women accept this practice. When it emerges that a husband has a second family, the reaction will often be to question why his first wife allowed this happen. Why wasn't she a good enough wife? Why didn't she put right what she was doing wrong? In 21st century U.K. this is an antediluvian attitude. But, for the young Filipina, it is a reality she has grown up with and will probably have experienced somewhere within her own extended family or that of one of her friends. It also plays into the facet of character discussed earlier, being judgemental. What many Filipinas are looking for is a relationship where they feel safe and secure and reduce the risk of losing their man to a minimum. So they look for someone more mature and also look to other cultures.

In the first three months of using this website I had received a few dozen requests for money. Most said it was needed to fund health care or education. A few explicitly offered sexual services. I reported all of these to the website managers who took appropriate action. The worst example I came across was a profile that claimed to be of a woman in her mid-twenties. After exchanging a couple of messages I received one which commented that I was interested in women much younger than myself and asked if she was young enough. Whoever I was exchanging messages with went on to offer access to much younger women. I declined, reported the matter, and the profile disappeared from the site within a few minutes.

I have to say that the scams I came across on this website were not sophisticated. I would be surprised if many of them netted an income. However in a country where half the people are living on a dollar a day or less, where children as young as four and five are sent onto the streets to beg, then using a website to ask for support should be expected. For Filipinos this does not seem to be an area where large scale or complicated fraud will be practised. Although that does occur in the wider society as it occurs across the world.

Having chatted with many website members and seen their profiles it was also obvious to me that, whilst many scams were being attempted against western men, there were also many western men behaving very abusively towards Filipinas. Many of the profiles of female members stated quite clearly they were not interested in being contacted by men simply looking for sex. They would often couch this in terms which were not quite so blunt but their meaning was quite clear. That told me that many men using the website were explicitly requesting sexual favours. I did not make a habit of exploring male profiles on the site but did note that abuse was not a one way street. There is more on this to come.

A complete change of focus.

Within three months of using the new website I came to two conclusions which re-focussed my research. Having convinced myself the scams being attempted by Filipinas were generally fairly easy to spot I realised I knew I did not have an original piece of research to present to the conference. So, for that particular project, I completely changed focus. The research element of using the dating websites was over; finished.

Much more importantly I also realised that some of the women I was chatting with seemed to be very genuine in their search for a husband, that age and looks did not matter very much to them, and they were prepared to relocate to my country. I was a man well into middle age, certainly no Adonis, and seeking a relationship where a family was a potential outcome. Could I find a match here? It deserved some consideration. I also needed to shift from considering the women I was chatting with online as being an element in a research project. I had to get real and treat myself and the women I met with respect in a relationship sense.

I extended my membership, gave my profile and photographs some serious attention, and started searching the site with a view to finding a genuine user with whom I shared mutual interests. My images were genuine and recent, the description I provided of myself was accurate as was the description of the woman I was trying to find. It stated I would like to meet a single woman under the age of forty who was looking for a long term relationship. I was clear that I was not looking for a weekend or holiday shack-up. Educationally she should have completed secondary education and be able to communicate in English. If a relationship did develop she should be prepared to relocate to my country and marry. In terms of interests I was not particularly specific, however I did mention that if religion was important to her then I was the wrong man. I was also clear I was looking for someone who did not have children but would be interested in considering family if she met the right man. I mentioned earlier my reason for this. However Philippine law makes divorce almost impossible so the genuine online dater needs to be careful when developing a relationship with a single parent. There is more detail on this later.

Whilst the scams continued they were all of the type mentioned before, nothing which wasn't obvious fairly quickly. However my change of focus also meant that I needed to be ready to develop an online romantic relationship. This was something I had never done before; something I had never really thought much about. I was no longer searching for cheats and their explanations; I was now offering myself to the market and seriously looking around to see if I might find love. My responsibilities towards the women with whom I chatted changed. I had a responsibility to nurture. This opened up a variety of other issues, so it seemed prudent that I take a look at the country in which I was searching. I did some reading.

For many years it was believed that the Philippine Islands consisted of 7,107 islands. However, in February 2016, the National Mapping and Resource Information Authority in the Philippines announced that, using new technology, they were now able to put the total at 7,641. Most of these are uninhabited small outcrops of rock, but many are of significant size. The Philippines is after all the twelfth largest country in the world when measured by population; a population likely to reach 110 million during 2020. Births exceed deaths by just under 4,000 per day which means the population increases by around 1.4 million every year; 7 million every 5 years.

The Philippine Islands run north to south in the Pacific Ocean. In the big picture they lie between the northern coast of Australia, (close to the area where the provinces of Northern Territory and Western Australia meet), and China; north of the Equator but south of the Tropic of Cancer. The islands running off the south west of the Philippine archipelago border with Indonesia. The north coast of the northern islands are the closest to Taiwan and the Chinese mainland; to the west is Viet-Nam. They share latitude with Sri Lanka, Ethiopia, Nigeria and Venezuela. Perhaps a better way to get a feel for location is by typical flight times. The capital of the Philippines is Manila. A flight into

Manila from Hong Kong takes 2 hours 10 minutes; from Ho Chi Minh City, Vietnam, it is 2 hours 30 minutes and from Singapore 3 hours 40 minutes. Further afield but within package tour distance are Seoul, the capital of South Korea, just over 4 hours away and Tokyo, 4 hours 40 minutes. Manila may also be a stopover location for antipodean travellers en route to Europe and the U.S.A. as Perth is 6 hours 20 minutes away and Sydney, 7 hours 40 minutes. To the east, apart from a few scattered islands, i.e. Palau and Guam, the next mainland is thousands of miles away; the west coast of South America. To give an idea of the immensity of the Pacific, and allowing for changing time zones, a direct flight into Manila from Los Angeles is scheduled to take 14 hours 15 minutes; the 15 minutes is about all you have over land, the remainder is the Pacific Ocean. By contrast a direct flight from Los Angeles into London Heathrow is scheduled to take 10 hours 40 minutes.

Appreciating the size of the Pacific Ocean is an important feature of the geography of these islands because it is in this vast expanse of ocean that weather systems develop, build up momentum and deliver fifteen to twenty typhoons a year into the country. The energy builds up in the Pacific Ocean and moves west with prevailing winds and currents. Often the first land a typhoon will reach will be the east coast of the Philippines. Coupled with this the islands are located across what is called 'the Pacific Ring of Fire', an area in which volcanic eruptions are prevalent. This is a horseshoe shaped ring formed well beneath the surface of the planet where three of the Earth's major tectonic plates meet. These are effectively masses of rock which rub against each other. Such movements take place miles underground and are expressed at the surface as earthquakes. Because of this the Philippines is a country which has far more than its share of earthquakes. A visit to the website www.earthquaketrack.com will inform you of the number of earthquakes a country has. On the day I checked out the Philippines it advised me: none today, three in the past week, forty one in the past month and 329 in the past year. So, there is an earthquake more frequently than every other day somewhere in the Philippines. At 329 during a year that is approaching an earthquake every day! Most are small vibrations but there is the occasional big one. The Mariana Trench, the deepest part of the ocean, intersects with the Pacific Ring of Fire.

Ninety per cent of the world's active volcanos are found along the Pacific Ring of Fire, hence the name; again the Philippine Islands have more than their fair share. Whilst the economy will encourage a young person to seek a better quality of life away from the Philippines, so will risks attributable to the climate/weather.

Geographically the country splits into three areas. There is Luzon. This is the major northern island and its surrounds where over 50% of the population live, mostly in or within fifty miles of the capital, Manila. The actual city of Manila has a population recorded at just under two million. However this is part of a huge urban sprawl, generally referred to as Metro Manila, which includes a further fifteen cities. The largest, Quezon City, has well over two million inhabitants, and the third largest, Caloocan City, has a population close to that of the city of Manila. Overall Metro Manila has a measured population close to thirteen million. However there is a huge transient population living in unofficial settlements and the total urban area has an estimated head count over 21 million. Just providing these numbers only tells a part of the story. These people are all crammed into a relatively small area. This makes Manila the most densely populated area in the world. It clocks in at just under 43,000 residents per square kilometre; which is just over 111,000 people per square mile. For the purpose of comparison London and Chicago check in at close to 4,500 per square kilometre.

There are several islands in the south but far and away the largest and most significant is Mindanao. The central area between Luzon and Mindanao is a maze of islands under the banner of the Visayas. Tacloban, where the dreadful Typhoon Haiyan, struck in November, 2013 killing between 5,000 and 10,000 people is on Leyte Island, the eastern Pacific Ocean facing side of the Visayas. This was also the island to which U.S. General MacArthur promised to return to liberate the Philippines from Japanese occupation during World War Two. The country's second largest city, Metro Cebu, is on Cebu Island, also part of the Visayas.

There are many cultural differences between the Philippines and the west. Quite a few will get an airing here. Let us start with religion. The Philippines is a roman catholic country. Religion tries to worm its way into all aspects of Philippine life. And, in a country where there are very few effective social supports, it tries to bridge the gap, with some success. The island of Mindanao historically was entirely muslim. The western part still is but the remainder has been converted to catholicism. However there is still significant friction in this neck of the woods. For the purposes of dating it is a place I would avoid, but each to their own. Political organisation at the national level consists of the representatives of the Provinces and cities which make up the country. Within these are autonomous regions. Each are subdivided into what are called barangays (similar to local council areas), they are small sub-divisions of a city or province. The barangay can be further sub-divided into Sitios or Puroks. Barangay politics is an important aspect of Philippine daily life as the public services available to people are generally negotiated at barangay level building into provision by the city or province. Overseeing it all is the central government, elected across the country and based in Manila. I mention religion and politics because they are important elements of society to understand if you get involved with the Philippines. There are still religious and political assassinations in parts of the country. The Moro Liberation Front occasionally makes the international press as it pursues its claims for a muslim autonomous area. The U.K. government advises its citizens not to visit Mindanao unless there is good reason, even then they advise to avoid the muslim areas completely. Prior to the Coronavirus-19 pandemic this advice had been extended to the southern part of Cebu Island and the areas of Negros Island around Dumaguete City. This advice has a knock-on effect when buying travel insurance so, if you travel to the Philippines, be sure your travel insurance covers the areas you are visiting and travelling through.

(At the time of writing, during the pandemic, the U.K. government intervened to prevent international travel but is currently talking about travel bubbles and generally lifting restrictions with the aim of life assuming some sort of normality by Christmas, 2020.)

In some areas you will find that local militias still exist based around political support. It is still relatively common for there to be political assassinations as local factions vie with each other, particularly on the approach to elections. There are also revenge attacks. The reason for extending 'no travel' advice to include southern Cebu Island and Dumaguete City relates to an incident in mid-2017 when a rebel group, believed to be communist, travelled into Negros Island via southern Cebu following a bomb attack on Bohol Island. The advice from the U.K. Foreign Office is odd as the really risky part of Negros Island is around the town of Guihulngan. The hills in this area are where the communist 'rebels' live and where there have been the top side of sixty street murders in the last 2-3 years; a high ratio for an area with a population of around 30,000. Neither Dumaguete City nor southern Cebu Island have seen terrorism/criminality on this scale. It is also the area in which my in-laws and extended family live along with many friends of my wife.

I do not profess to be an expert on Philippine affairs however I have yet to meet a Filipino who does not have a story about political corruption. It would seem to be absolutely endemic; it is also routinely family based. It is a different world to the one we experience in the west. There are many areas of outstanding beauty and the islands are home to many endangered species and some fantastic coral beds. But it is also a country with densely packed areas of population and some of the most appalling living standards anywhere in the world. As a taxi driver who took me from my hotel to a family home in a very poor Sitio pointed out – the biggest export to the world from the Philippines is Filipinos. When you see the living conditions of the many it is little wonder.

Any westerner considering a relationship with the Philippines for whatever reason would do well to assume they are entering a modern day equivalent of the Wild West and prepare accordingly. It should also be kept in mind that this is a state of affairs which Filipinos grow up with. For the local people this is normal. It is their world and totally different to that which they see on imported TV programmes and films. These fire the imagination. It is a country where there are very, very few wealthy and powerful people; there is a modest sized middle class; and there is political patronage and acute poverty everywhere. A visitor to the Philippines is unlikely to run into religious or political problems if they stay on the beaten track. However there are plenty of other potential pitfalls.

Philippine women tend to start having their children earlier than generally occurs in the west and have larger families. A couple with 4-6 children is normal. In the Philippines a woman who is 25 and not in a relationship is more the exception than the rule. A single woman of thirty is likely to be either the youngest amongst siblings, and therefore expected to stay at home and support parents through their old age, or very worried about being left on the shelf, and probably both. A career woman is likely to have married. In consequence, by the time the typical Filipina reaches the age of thirty, she will have been married/in a relationship for several years and have a few children. From the perspective of the man looking for a woman who does not have children this presented me with much the same difficulty to that which I had faced in the U.K. However the women I found myself chatting with were usually in their early twenties. This threw up another risk which I thought I was well beyond; that of the age of consent for sex. Whilst the age of consent for sex in the U.K. is irrelevant to me, my understanding is that it is sixteen unless a duty of care is involved in which case it is eighteen. This is different to the Philippines. My understanding is that a woman cannot legally consent to sex as an adult until she is eighteen years old. Between 18-21 years she can marry but must have the written consent of her parents. However, where the husband is within ten years of the age of his wife, a marriage with a girl aged twelve and upwards is permissible; with parental consent. These are very different laws to those which exist in the U.K. and contribute to different understandings and practices of safe sex and what we in the west would consider to be unlawful, underage sex. A western paedophile adult cannot ride into town and marry a twelve year old girl then claim to be having consensual sex as a married person. However it does mean there can be a very different attitude to sexual activity involving young people. Whilst a girl cannot legally consent to sexual activity outside marriage until she reaches the age of eighteen that does not mean it doesn't happen. Of course it does. But this situation does provide a potential issue. If a seventeen year old girl has consensual sex with a western adult male, can that be considered as rape due to her being legally under the age when she can give consent? I ask this question rhetorically; I do not know the answer. That said, there are plenty of teenagers around with children. I also recall in one of the TV programmes fronted by Stacey Dooley she was chatting about the financial aspects of parental involvement in the sex lives of their teenage daughters with a Philippine colleague. The colleague expressed the opinion that the parents suspected their daughters were sexually active so took the view they might as well get paid for it!

A further important issue the online dater must be aware of are the Philippine laws around divorce. A marriage in the Philippines is for life. Divorce is not allowed.

Marriages can be ended in three ways. Firstly the couple can agree a legal separation. In this case the assets of the marriage are split 50:50 and the couple separate. If they wish they can get a legal document which will specify that, so far as they are concerned, they live separate lives and are completely independent of each other. However they are then faced with an anomaly. They may become legally separated but, legally, their marriage still exists. Legally the marriage is still recognised and they cannot re-marry. The only difference separation makes is that they are legally living apart. Many couples will separate and not bother with any paperwork because it does not come cheap!

So a westerner going to the Philippines looking for a partner with a view to marriage has to be very careful. Married people who have separated from their spouse are usually still legally married, even where they have a legal document proving they are legally separated. Despite being legally separated as a couple, in the eyes of the law they remain married and cannot re-marry. This is a concept I have not come across elsewhere. They are just able to legally live separately. No more than that. Confusing? You ain't seen nothing yet! The second way to end a marriage is to get a Declaration of Nullity issued. For an existing marriage to be annulled the couple must prove that, at the time they married, the marriage was illegal, i.e. incest or bigamy was occurring. If that happens then any children from that union are declared illegitimate which opens up a whole new ball game around the legal status, etc. of the child and parental rights. Thirdly there is Article 36 of the Philippine Legal Code. This allows for divorce if one or other party to a marriage is prepared to legally declare themselves to be psychologically impaired. However, especially where a divorce is contested, this can take decades rather than years to achieve. It can also be extremely expensive. Evidence must be presented to a Court which proves the declaration of psychological impairment to be accurate and genuine. The Court is, of course, at liberty to refuse it. In a country where divorce is so difficult to achieve there are likely to be thousands of attempts each year to use this potential loophole. Often the Court will not be convinced of the genuineness of the claim and refuse the divorce. In practice there are hundreds of thousands of Filipinos who live with a second partner, and have children, because they are unable to legally separate themselves from their first spouse in a way which leaves them free to re-marry. Provided they live in their native country this is a manageable situation; very unfair perhaps, but manageable. However when a westerner flies in with a view to offering a life of marriage in their home country you can see that problems may well arise. If a Filipino tells you they are divorced my advice would be to seek the advice of a Philippine lawyer and get the claim thoroughly checked out before going forward with any marriage plans of your own.

There is much ore that we could discuss here. However all I am wanting to demonstrate is that if you marry a Filipina in the Philippines, you will stay married. Grounds for divorce are so tight they may as well not exist.

This has a further very serious implication for the online dater. If your online relationship flourishes and you decide to marry then you must be certain your Philippine partner has not previously been married. If they have it is very likely that, whilst separated, they are still considered to be legally married under Philippine law. If you do marry such a person then you will become a bigamist. The situation will also have lifetime implications should a visa be issued for your partner to come to your country and marry. If at some point after your marriage it transpires your partner is still legally married in the Philippines and this has not been declared, there will be big problems around legality of all visas and a likelihood of a swift forced deportation to the home country, with all problems of custody, etc. of children to be dealt with.

A further relevant snippet of information comes from the 2019 World Development Indicators published by the World Bank. It tells us that 16.5% of Philippine women aged between 20 and 24 years report that they were married by the time they were 18 years old. That is one of every six women in the age group. The same number for the U.K. is too small to measure. So, when online dating, if you meet a single person looking for love, remember there may well be a partner somewhere and, if she is amongst the 16.5% who is married, you could be building up big problems for the future.

Compared to westerners Filipinos are generally a small, skinny race. A person in their mid-twenties, in general, will have a physique similar to a westerner in their mid-teens. This raises another issue. If Filipinas are small and skinny and western men are large and flabby, where does this leave us in terms of the practicalities of sex? Is it reasonable to assume that the smaller the woman the shorter the distance between the entrance to the vagina and the cervix? Does a larger man have a larger erection? Unless the answers to these questions are 'no', these could become issues which demand serious consideration. More on this later.

All of the dating websites I have seen will only allow membership of people aged eighteen years and upwards. However people posting profiles on websites are not always honest. A person claiming to the eighteen or older may be underage but post a profile saying she is old enough to be a member. It is also common practice amongst young women to share a profile. I know that the woman who is now my wife shared her profile with a sister four years younger than her. When we met online her sister was sixteen years old. This poses a risk for any man travelling across to meet a young woman so it makes sense to ask for proof of age before travelling. From a personal perspective what makes more sense for a mature man is to have nothing to do with members who are so young. They are barely adult in many respects and should have the freedom to grow up. However when living in poverty unpleasant choices will be considered. It is also obvious when using these websites that many very young women have been sexually active whilst underage as they have the child or children to prove it.

There is a potentially expensive scam which uses the underage scenario. It may be played out in a short period of time or over a few days. It works like this. The young woman meets the man in a café or a bar, in a shopping centre, if pre-arranged through a dating website it may even be at the place where he is staying. She tells him she is over the age of eighteen and is happy to share a bed with him. They go to the hotel room. As she begins to undress associates appear, one with a camera. (This scam can also be practiced by the woman acting alone where her room is used and a video camera is concealed). If operating in a team the two associates will claim to be law officers of some description. They will tell the man that the girl is under age. She will then admit this. They have film or video evidence of some level of sexual activity, maybe the beginning of removal of clothing. The man will be offered a hefty financial settlement to avoid arrest and prison, confiscation of passport, media attention, etc. If the woman is operating alone the hit will arrive later in the form of an associate(s) who have the video and/or photographic evidence.

There have been occasions when, after exchanging a few messages on the website, women have told me they have posted incorrect information. This occasionally involved age but, more usually, they wanted to tell me that they already had a child or children. Another thing that has occurred a couple of times is that a woman has tried to pass me on to a friend. I have also received a couple of blistering messages condemning my lack of religion and seeking to convert me to catholicism.

When I have received requests for money on the dating website I copied them to the site managers and the profile was removed. Occasionally an implicit request will be made. The message will claim something along the lines of a family member having an illness and being unable to buy medication or see a doctor. There have also been a few offers to get involved in paying college fees in return for a relationship. These have gone the same way. The site managers will either remove the profile or send a warning message. Either way my communication ended and another profile would hit the blocked list!

The genuine Filipina using the website will not ask for money. If she is genuinely wanting a relationship with a foreign national and is prepared to relocate to make that happen, what she will want is proof that you are genuine. She will be keen to see you in person but understands that this is something which cannot happen easily. The compromise is the video chat. I have only once had a problem with identity during video chats. I chatted a few times with a woman. She appeared a little agitated on one occasion and I did not know why. She told me it was because she was using a friend's laptop and that she was under pressure to return it. I thought no more of it until she missed an agreed chat time. A couple of days later we met again but I knew immediately that, although the image I was seeing was poor, the woman had been switched. It was definitely someone else. Another profile that went onto my blocked list.

If you are both happy with video chats over a period of a few weeks then the time might have arrived for the man to plan a trip to The Philippines. This is where the fun and games really start.

Preparing a visit/ Money!

If a Filipina has the resources to visit the west it is unlikely she will be using a dating website to find a western boyfriend; so maybe we need a reality check.

Your trip to the Philippines is essential if you are from the west and hoping to develop a long-term relationship with a Philippine citizen. At some point a visa will be needed. These are issued by U.K.V.I. (United Kingdom Visas and Immigration, until 2013 called the U.K. Border Agency. They will only give consideration to issuing a visa allowing a girlfriend or fiancée to visit the U.K. once they have evidence that a genuine relationship exists. They too are on the lookout for scammers. They have years of experience which is part of what we pay them for and, generally, they do a good job. As you will discover later they can be a seriously frustrating bunch of bureaucrats, but they do have an important job to do. You will have to provide evidence that you and your girlfriend know each other; part of this means proving that you have actually met, face to face, in the flesh, preferably more than once. So she cannot come to you! You have to go to her. In any case before your online girlfriend can apply for a visa to visit the U.K. she will need a passport. The likelihood is that she will not have one. Until she has she is unable to apply for a visa because the visa will be stamped into her passport. When she has a passport and evidence that you have met and know each other, then you can consider applying for a visa. However you should not think its issue will be a matter of course, a mere formality. U.K.V.I. take their work very seriously.

At the time of writing protection of our borders, (in the U.K.), is very high on the political agenda and, in consequence, a major issue for the media. The process of getting a legitimate non-European national into the U.K. has never been more difficult. Even if you marry in their country there are no guarantees that they will get a visa to live with you in your country. And, as we have seen recently with the Windrush Generation, the right to stay in the U.K. remains contestable for life, so there will be no guarantees your partner will be able to stay. (There is an explanatory note on the implications of 'Windrush' at the end of this chapter.)

I will discuss the issue of visas more fully later; for now we need to understand the reality of what we are trying to do and to get a handle on the issue of finance. Are Filipinas only interested in your money? The scammers are; that is all they are interested in. However the person looking for a genuine relationship wants what any person anywhere in the world wants. Money, or an ability to generate money, is an element of this. However it is more likely to be expressed in terms of seeking security, comfort and opportunity and this may be concealed somewhat behind what we culturally learn 'love' to be. In the west this is overtly-romanticised; Filipinos place a greater emphasis on pragmatism, (blended with a bewildering leaning to serendipity, or, 'que sera, sera! Whatever will be will be', taken to the extreme.) Perhaps a reflection on knowing what an empty belly feels like and having little opportunity to do much about it. The bottom line is that the genuine Philippine woman wants the same as any genuine woman anywhere else in the world. She wants to be loved and she wants to love and she is searching for the right partner for her; someone genuine.

It is particularly important when dealing with the Philippines to work alongside their cultural norms. Remember amor-propio, self-esteem? When you visit your girlfriend's country you will be placing your relationship at serious risk should you choose not to follow the local cultural norms. Most Filipinos, like most people in the rest of the world, are reasonable people. They will not expect you to understand everything and they will make allowances for your lack of understanding. But you will not get away with serious excesses and you will be expected to gain more understanding as time progresses. Open and frank discussion of their personal finance will not be expected; this is something foreigners in their country do not do, but, should you ask, the matter is likely to be dealt with openly and with candour. However your personal financial position will likely be brought up for discussion very early in proceedings. When this occurs you need to tread very carefully, particularly if your sub-text suggests the Filipino is seeking to financially exploit the westerner. How would you react if the Filipinos you met openly discussed the possibility that your interest was to sexually exploit their daughter or sister, etc.? As a mature western man seeking a young bride; you are on a potentially slippery slope. An implicit suggestion could be made that what you are really after is sex with a woman who, physically, in *your* mind's eye, might be under the age of sexual consent. Think about that. Other people certainly will, particularly if you intend to set up home in the west. If you think there may be some truth in this then you need to stop visiting these websites and seek help.

Let's think this through a bit further. Keep in mind the reference I made on the previous page to the media. We have a relatively free press and should do all we can to keep it that way. However it does mean that some reportage can be partisan and somewhat extreme. They have an interest in reporting on border control issues. It is right that they do. However border controls are not the only issue to provide a focus for the media. Anything to do with young people and sex, particularly potentially illicit sex, attracts their interest; it is journalistic clickbait and sells newspapers.

As an adult male seeking to bring a much younger, but adult, Filipina into the U.K., you may attract unexpected attention. Your actions directly involve a border control issue. You may be seen as an old(er) man seeking to bring a young girl into the country for the purpose of sex.

Your girlfriend has to apply for and be granted her visa before she can leave the Philippines for the U.K. An airline which brings someone to the U.K. with incorrect paperwork is liable to stand the cost of returning that person to their country of origin. Both the airline and Border Control, Philippines, will check this out before she is allowed to board a flight out of her country. So, without the right visa, she will not be allowed onto the plane. When she arrives in the U.K. the visa is already stamped into her passport. U.K.V.I. staff at the airport will check her visa is correct, that the photograph and thumb print match with the person presenting the document, then date stamp her passport to indicate she has legally entered into the country. At this point, should U.K.V.I. question the legality of her application, despite her having obtained a legitimate visa whilst in her own country, she can still be turned around and sent back. When she presents at the border check-in desk, although she may be in her mid-twenties or older, to the person checking her documents she is likely to look considerably younger, maybe mid-teens. (Today my wife bought some new clothes off the rack in our local supermarket. She shopped in the children's clothing section and her items were labelled as suitable for 11 year olds in the U.K.). So, visually she is likely to be small and slight by western standards. She may well be nervous as she is unlikely to have never gone through this process before. It is a long flight, and usually an overnight flight, so she is also likely to be tired. At home she will have heard of good outcomes but also some horror stories about entering a foreign country even with the correct paperwork. For a mixture of all these reasons she may come across to U.K.V.I. as being edgy, nervous, vulnerable, or a mix of these. Consider what you would do if the roles were reversed and you were the U.K.V.I. officer. You are at your desk when a girl who looks to be in her early teens presents herself. If you have been fortunate she will have a visitor visa, but this is very unlikely. Far more likely she will have a family of a settled person visa which, unless there is evidence of existing family already in the U.K., will tell the Border Control Officer they are looking at a person who has arrived in this country intending to be married within six months to the person named on the visa. She has documents saying she is in her twenties and identifying you as the husband to be. You may have flown in with her or you may be waiting on the arrivals concourse to collect her. But 'you', stereotypically, will be a middle aged male, past your peak in most departments and without the traditional family ties associated with a man of your age. U.K.V.I. has a duty of care to anyone arriving in the U.K. Their job is to spot people arriving in our country for reasons which are not genuine. They have been trained to look out for people who are vulnerable or may be being exploited. They will have heard of how documents might be applied for by a sister or cousin who looks similar to the family member who is travelling, or by using their documents. Their job is to be suspicious. They check to make sure a person is genuine and not trying to enter the country illegally, but they also check to protect people coming into our country who may be exploited. Iris and fingerprint recognition systems are now improving identification documents but that does not prevent a vigilant Border Control Officer from taking the view that your girlfriend or fiancée is much younger than it states on her passport. People have been known to make false statements around age. You could hit a big problem. When U.K.V.I. check her out and you show up they are being presented with a man in his 30's, 40's, 50's or older trying to bring a young female into the U.K. who claims to be mid-20's but looks pubescent. They may suspect she is being trafficked, they may be thinking about false documents. Whilst her passport carries a fiancée visa they will ask themselves if this man is offering marriage as a front when he has a different agenda. Maybe he is just after sex, or maybe he intends to traffic her for sex or for some other illegitimate form of work; i.e. modern slavery. What are they going to do? It's fairly obvious. They will refuse her entry and take her to a place of safety, at least initially, whilst a rigorous check of her bona fides is undertaken. As for you, they will certainly take steps to have you detained whilst they satisfy themselves that all the paperwork is correct. So you could end up being arrested on suspicion of attempting to commit a serious sexual offence or such like.

After this digression let's get back to the issue of money. It is a subject usually discussed around other issues. My experience in these matters is limited. In my own culture all the relationships I have been involved in have had a financial element. However, it has rarely been explicit; in fact, from my perspective, it is something rarely if ever discussed. Perhaps this is because I have been fortunate enough to have lived much of my adult life with stability, employment, financial security and, during courtship and marriage, money was never a major issue. The only time my ex-wife and I discussed money in detail was through our solicitors during divorce proceedings. Unsurprisingly we expressed radically different opinions! But it needs to be acknowledged that finance generally and hard cash in particular will be an issue when developing a serious relationship with in The Philippines. We all know that if you have no money your personal security is at greater risk, you are less comfortable, maybe homeless, and your opportunities are likely to be seriously restricted. When seriously looking for a husband or wife money might not be an explicit element of the courtship, but would you consider a relationship with someone who is penniless? Maybe. Would you have the opportunity to seriously consider a relationship with someone who was at the opposite extreme and considered you to be penniless? Probably not. These are the sub-plots of the modern day Cinderella stories. Remember Richard Gere and Julia Roberts in Pretty Woman? Dudley Moore and Liza Minelli in Arthur? Julia Roberts and Hugh Grant in Notting Hill. Great films maybe, but how much do they reflect real life? At one level they are modern fairy stories. The position of Julia Roberts' character 'Vivienne' in Pretty Woman keeping the clothes bought for her on Rodeo Drive is radically different to that the 'Anna Scott' character in Notting Hill presenting Chagall's 'The Bride' to her bookseller boyfriend 'William Thacker'. These portrayals are entertaining comment on the juxtaposition of money and power in the west. However I was moving into a position where east and west would meet. There are parallels but the positions are very different.

A chasm exists between the middle income man in the west and a poor woman in the developing world, particularly their financial circumstances. There is a topical example of earning capacity currently available to us. In connection with managing Coronavirus, track and trace staff are currently being recruited in both countries. The salary offered in the U.K. is around £20,000 per annum, £1,667; (€1829; $2114) per month. In The Philippines P. 12,000 per month about £191; (€210; $242) is being offered for the same position.

There may also be a temptation to assume that whoever holds the purse strings also holds the power in these relationships. Whilst I would argue that this would not be a healthy line to take, and could be a much bigger debate, it is something each party needs to think about. I have met men considering marriage with a Filipina and occasionally come across the view that she can be moulded into developing into the wife he is looking for. Any man thinking that way is implicitly making it clear he wants to rule the roost, keep his wife under the thumb, etc. Any man visiting The Philippines and thinking this way is not only ethically and morally out of order, but asking for serious relationship problems in the medium and long term. Another example from film/literature comes to mind, Pygmalion/My Fair Lady!

For now I just want to make the point that a man travelling out to meet a potential Philippine girlfriend must understand he will be in foreign climes and a different culture. Like it or not he controls the finances at this point. Money will play an explicit role in the relationship he is considering. Whether or not he likes that idea is irrelevant; that is the reality. In consequence he needs to have his financial plan explicit. It needs to be clearly thought through before physically meeting anyone from the website in person.

As soon as you arrive in the Philippines there will be people begging from you, and they are very explicit. If you can afford to fly you are rich, therefore, in their eyes, you are a legitimate target irrespective of your nationality, gender, etc. If you are a westerner to boot then you are rich beyond the wildest fantasies of many Filipinos. A return flight from the U.K. to Manila or Cebu booked well in advance will cost around £550, tourist class. (P34,490, €603, $695) For the average young adult Filipino this is getting towards their annual salary. For those forced to make a living from the streets it is a sum they would struggle to imagine. To them you are a legitimate target and they will hit on you at every opportunity and, in busy areas, many will pursue you doggedly not taking 'no' for an answer. Almost all these people are beggars; however, there are a handful who work in teams to commit distraction thefts, so you have to keep your wits about you and a very close eye on your baggage and pockets; whilst ensuring you have a good insurance policy!

One hour worked on minimum wage in the U.K. equates to around an average weekly wage for many Filipinos. Think about that. It sounds insane but here we have resources we cannot imagine living without, like three meals a day, a TV, wifi, and a roof over our heads. That is your reality, not theirs. You are entering an environment where you can attend a hospital for emergency medical care but, if you cannot produce cash or insurance, be left outside to die. It happens. Every Filipino has baseline access to a government based insurance company called PhilHealth. This guarantees health care providers in the country a standard fee for various services. I have a business contact who needed an appendectomy. He had standard PhilHealth insurance but there was no one available to do the operation so it was not done. Within a few days his appendicitis escalated to peritonitis. If his appendix was not removed quickly he would die. This young man became an emergency case and had to sign up to pay double the PhilHealth baseline payment because of a delay caused by a system which did not have the capacity to provide his operation when it was necessary. The additional amount he had to find equated to just over 20% of his anticipated annual salary. So, beware. You are likely to be entering a totally different world from anything you have ever been prepared for. There is also a likelihood you will be staying in a part of the country which draws you away from seeing poverty. Just because you cannot see something does not mean it ceases to exist! For millions of Filipinos a dollar a day is the norm; for the woman you are meeting it is likely to be close to the norm. So be prepared for this. You are entering a country where there are levels of poverty which you probably cannot imagine. In the U.K. I have worked in places where there are serious levels of poverty, where the employment rate, not unemployment rate, is less than 10% and benefits are a way of life, for life. These places are luxury compared to the poverty you will find in the Philippines if you look for it; you will not need to look very far and there is no benefit system whatsoever. So do not try to convince yourself that money is not an issue. It is a big issue and, if you are seeking a relationship with a Filipina, you must be clear in your own mind on how you are going to deal with it.

However, providing you are meeting someone who is genuine, and have taken your time and chosen well, you will not be meeting someone of low moral standards. You may well be meeting someone who had to leave secondary education at the earliest opportunity as their family needed them to generate an income, probably by offering domestic or child care services, maybe working on a market stall or at a supermarket or store. If they are city based then maybe at a factory. You will be dealing with someone who has a very limited experience of life, no experience of life as you know it and needs to have their hand held through what we in the west would consider to be simple and straightforward transactions. The work they do will deliver a financial contribution to the family. Their wages will automatically go into the family pot. They are unlikely to see any of it beyond their share in the context of overall family finance, i.e. food is provided with a roof over their head. They are also unlikely to play any part in the planning of the family budget.

If they have work then getting time out to meet you will be a challenge. Unemployment and underemployment rates are high, employers can hire and fire on a whim, there is no employment protection and no effective support for the workforce, financial or otherwise. If you look in the 'situations vacant' section of an online Philippine newspaper, like GMA or the SunStar, you will see that employers specify age limits, gender and, sometimes, marital status. Getting a job will have been tough enough for them and they need to keep it. When you arrive they will want to see you and spend time with you, but you will be secondary to their work until they are confident they can rely on you financially during their transition from worker in a developing country to spouse in a developed country. This might sound dramatic or harsh but look at their reality. They are part of an extended family and working. They have a job; this may well not be the norm in her family.

People in developing countries who use dating websites reflect the social structure of their communities. Many will be without parent(s) or the product of broken homes; being a child in a single parent family is common-place. Their relationship(s) will have a significant impact on the rest of the family. They are a wage earner. If they leave there will be one mouth less to feed but their financial input will disappear as well. Where they have both parents, given the parlous state of medical treatment, disability is common. They may have siblings who are also working, but they may also have siblings who are still in education. If they do not live in the family home it is likely they will be sending income back to it. When you arrive on the scene you are offering something very different. If, from their point of view, you are offering a better alternative, better opportunities, they will want to take you up on your offer. However, having had little experience of life and decision-making making for themselves, they are not likely to be able to take this decision easily, if at all. In the west we are educated to grow up, go out into the world, build our own relationships and become independent of the family whilst being a part of it. That relationship may become distant. In the Philippines you are educated to support your immediate family and be part of an extended family group for life. You are expected to help them and they are expected to help you. You are expected to stay close. It is a totally different situation to anything we would expect in the west. If you are genuine you will have to work with people who think very, very differently to the way you do. If you reach a position where you may be thinking of marriage there will be a need to provide your partner to be with support at a very basic level and this will involve money. They, and their family, will expect you to smooth the process. If you give the impression you are not prepared to offer that support then they will not be confident to move forward.

During the transition you are proposing there will be pressure from family to at least maintain the inputs your prospective partner provides; the family ties will be incredibly strong by any western standards. Unless you are explicit about the situation you want to develop and back that up financially your partner will not be socially and financially able to take the next step. Furthermore, if you are not prepared to take this step, you need to ask yourself how serious you really are in your search for a genuine long term relationship. If you are then you will put your hand in your pocket; if you are not you need to stop using the websites in this way because, in this environment, you are unfairly raising expectations and that is a form of cruelty. Yes, you will find people try to abuse you when operating on the dating website, but you choose to be there and it does not make it right for you to do likewise. To get an idea of the costs involved look at the websites through which visas and air tickets are issued and add up the price. It is not cheap; far from it.

If you believe many Filipinas are simply looking for a foreign partner as a means of escape you are wrong. That may be a starting point for some but, for the genuine website user, just like you and I, they are trying to find someone with whom they can develop trust, understanding and love. They are looking for a decent, honest and honourable person. Until you have visited their country and seen the type of western man who relocates there, and the typical unattached male tourist, you cannot appreciate how important this is. I am sure there any many genuine and decent western men in the Philippines; when there I would count myself amongst them, however there are many who leave an awful lot to be desired. My experiences are limited to the Central Visayas generally and Cebu City specifically. I have met and seen decent westerners but there are many who disgust me. My first visit to the Philippines took me in on a Cathay Pacific flight from Hong Kong to Cebu. I was travelling alone and sat at the rear of the plane. Several rows in front of me but on the opposite side were a group of 10-15 men. It seemed to me that they comprised two or three groups of travellers who met either at Hong Kong Airport or on the flight; they were aged 35-55 or thereabouts. They spoke loudly in English with the drawl I associate with North America. The topic of discussion was the sexual exploits they hoped to engage in and they were exchanging notes on which bars in the city's red light area had the youngest, cheapest and dirtiest girls. I was appalled. Aside from the objectification of these young women; either these men did not care about offending all the other passengers within earshot or assumed we did not understand English. This was not a brief exchange of opinions. It was a detailed examination of the subject which went on for the best part of three quarters of an hour. Unfortunately this type of vulgarity and loudness is a regular feature of the western ex-pat life I have witnessed in the Philippines. It is particularly prevalent in the tourist areas. It is not at all unusual to hear a western voice, usually speaking in English, which is loud, brash, arrogant and vulgar. Some of these people are British but I can tell by the accents that many are not. I'm not trying to excuse British men here; I have met several British people who treat the local people just as badly as the other ex-pats. Whilst I avoid them like the plague, local people can't. They need an income and working for and with the ex-pat is one way of achieving it. So, when you make your trip to the Philippines, do not assume that decent Filipinos will accept you without question. They won't; nor should they. You may not realise this because they will operate within their cultural norms which means them being circumspect. They will not be rude or bad mannered towards you. But there have been many English speakers before your arrival and a significant percentage of them represent the dregs of their home societies. Even in the four and five star hotels in which I have stayed this is the case. Many westerners treat Filipinos like dirt.

You also need to consider that, to the untrained Philippine ear, English is assumed to be spoken by people from the U.S.A., Australia, the U.K. and New Zealand. English is a second language not only for Filipinos but also many Europeans. In consequence Filipinos may not realise an English speaker is using English as a second language. In consequence native English speakers may carry the sins of all English speakers; and there are plenty of them.

The Filipino mind is no different to that of other nations; it is programmed by the culture in which it develops, and this culture will encourage them to avoid conflict and be polite, to make sure no one will lose face. Western cultures do not work that way. We will be familiar with having to justify our actions, to compete and to be challenged. Amongst decent Philippine society, and most of it is decent, such behaviour is not really understood. Just because someone comes from a poor background does not mean they have poor moral values. Most Filipinos have a high standard of moral behaviour. But most middle aged male tourists are not visiting the Philippines to engage with mainstream society. They are there to exploit one of the consequences of poverty, the trade in flesh. Wherever you go in the world you can find this. Whilst there is no correlation between poverty and poor moral standards; there is a correlation between poverty and the activities someone will engage in when they have no money and need to feed their baby or buy medicine for a sick parent.

Before planning a visit it would be beneficial to acquaint yourself as best you can with the local culture. There is plenty of material available online but you need to keep a keen eye on quality control. Some of it is worth a read but there is also a lot of garbage. As a western man considering a relationship with a Filipina you are right to be aware of the fact that you may be setting yourself up to be taken advantage of. Unless you are very lucky this will happen and you will need to deal with it. My experiences in the Philippines suggest that these attempts at extortion are generally very simple and can be headed off without much difficulty. But you do have to deal with them. So do the genuine Filipinas who use these websites. She may be on home territory, she may have family and friends close by, but she is unlikely to have had much experience of dealing with the day to day issues that crop up for us all and will have little or no experience of dealing with people from a different culture. However she will certainly know of people who have; and she will have heard the stories that circulate. The man using the dating website is visiting her country because, whatever it is he is looking for, he cannot find it on home territory. She will need to deal with this matter with her family and friends. They will pass judgement on you as much as she does and she will listen to them. This is the Philippines and this is family. For the Filipino you are engaging in one of the most important aspects of life, family. You are seeking to become part of their family in a way which may further extend it.

The western man looking to date a Philippine woman is unlikely to give much thought about the end game at this initial stage. For the Filipinos almost the opposite prevails. She lives in a society where leaving her home country, family and friends, routinely happens. Official Philippine sources inform us that, at any one time, 9% - 10% of the population of the country is either working or living out of the country. That's ten and half million people, give or take half a million. However, whilst five thousand Filipinos a day, on average, leave the country; many return. She, her family and friends, will be looking at outcomes from your visit at an early stage. At the second or third meeting with her family, the man may very well be asked what his plans are for the future with their daughter. They will want an assurance that he is not playing the field, that he intends to marry and that he is financially sound. This would never happen in the west, but this is not the west. He is at the beginning of a journey which may end in him joining her culture and, presumably, he will want to operate successfully. With the genuine Filipina her family are only asking about finance to assure themselves their daughter will be living properly; they are not after his money.

So these are matters the westerner will need to keep at the forefront of their mind throughout a visit. If the woman he has found is genuine she will listen to and deal with her family as best she can. He will have to acknowledge this, be supportive, and be prepared for the unexpected. He will need to keep in mind that, if there is a significant age gap, he will probably be the same age as her parents, maybe older. Whilst the age gap is not much of an issue in the Philippines it is still there. His partner to be, if all works out well, will need to prepare her family for this. Encouraging her to do this also has its rewards because he will be demonstrating to her and to her family that he is caring and supportive of the family relationship.

So we move on to the mechanics of meeting for the first time. Common sense needs to prevail; neither party has met face to face before so there is a need to find a place where both parties feel comfortable and safe; a public place with plenty of other people around. This offers both parties some protection. It is very likely that the genuine Filipina will be accompanied when you meet for the first time; it is a warning sign if she isn't. Chaperoning for the first few dates is normal in her culture although the practice is now diminishing a little in bigger cities and towns. This is likely to be her preferred position until she and her family can trust him. The man will be expected to cover any costs that come with this. Should this practice persist after the first few dates either he is not trusted or they are taking advantage. I am using the plural because, whether you like it or not, you are dealing with a family at this stage, not an individual. If you meet at a restaurant or café do not be surprised if a large amount of food is ordered. They have the doggy bag in mind because there will be many more mouths to feed back at home.

There are a couple of other issues which the dating traveller needs to be aware of. I am very much a one woman man. I do not play around and don't like the idea of doing. However when you have a return trip on the top side of 17,000 miles (27,000 km.) for a date a back-up plan makes sense. You will realise within a few minutes of meeting if the woman from the website is genuine. My trips to the Philippines number into double figures now. I will take you through most of these visits in more detail later. Before booking a trip I chatted online with my prospective dates. When I was confident there was enough of a chance of a good long term relationship developing which we both wanted I would arrange a trip. However the first woman I met was not genuine and the fourth was soon honest enough to acknowledge she had an ulterior motive once we met. The second and third I think were genuine but we met unanticipated interference from their respective families. The fifth visit was to meet again a woman I met towards the end of my fourth trip but things didn't work out. The following visits have been to the woman who is now my wife; a relationship we are still very happily working on together.

I learned from the first visit of the need for a fall-back position. If the woman you meet decides you are not the man for her or if she does not hit the right buttons for you, what do you do? My shortest trip has been for eight nights, my longest for twenty-six nights. If you discover on day one that you have met someone incompatible you need to deal with that. You will need to refocus the rest of your trip. This may be a nuisance but it is also an opportunity. It provides plenty of time to arrange other meetings. However putting in the ground work for this in advance is beneficial. Knowing in advance which other members of the website are both genuine and live in the area you are visiting is a very good start. Hopefully you will not need to go down this path, but it is the old boy scout adage of 'be prepared'.

On my first trip I went to see one specific woman. I had nothing else planned. Within the first couple of hours I knew that we might have been able to make things work but we were not really cut out for each other. As that section of the story is told, you will realise that this became something of a relief rather than a problem. For all the trips thereafter I had used the dating website to arrange what might crudely be referred to as a reserve list of other website users who lived within striking distance. The woman who I travelled out to meet would be the only one who knew I was in country; and she would only find out two or three days prior to my departure from the U.K. But, if my date did not work out for any reason, I would hit the reserve list to see if I could make arrangements to maximise my opportunities of meeting someone else.

The other issue occurs when the woman you propose to meet does not have work. You are likely to book your visit in advance. Travel over these distances at short notice can happen but tends to be more expensive. If you tell her well in advance of your plans, you will also be providing her with the opportunity to plan. If either the woman or her family, or both, are not genuine this also gives them time to plan how to maximise on the benefits your visit could bring. In these circumstances you may well find the woman looking to stay with you throughout the visit. That is fine if you are both happy to share a bed from the outset allowing the direction of the relationship to be dealt with separately. However if you are genuine and looking for a lifetime partner and discover she is not that woman, then you have an issue to manage. I mentioned earlier that if the woman has a job that meeting up can be difficult. It is just the opposite if she does not have a job. She will want to enjoy a few days of luxury living. She will also know that hotels in the Philippines charge a daily tariff for the room. This assumes two occupants and it usually makes sense to book the bed and breakfast option rather than room only. (A decent hotel may be some distance from a place where you can buy breakfast; shopping malls often don't open until ten in the morning so if you want to eat earlier than that you may have to wait or go native [which has its own problems, discussed later].)

From the woman's perspective and that of her family, if she stays with you that is one less mouth to feed at home for the duration of your visit and an opportunity for them to also benefit from your largesse. You will also probably have to buy her some clothing as her own wardrobe will be completely inappropriate for the new surroundings. If she is the wrong woman for you then you may have a problem in persuading her of the need to leave. Most Filipinas are fairly quiet and shy; they don't like friction and try hard to avoid trouble. When rejected this might raise their dander a little, but only a little. If heels are dug in a departure is refused, hotel security will help should it become necessary.

This leads to another anecdote. On my first three trips I stayed at the same four star beachfront resort. On each of my trips I saw the same Philippine women staying as guests at the hotel with a series of different western men. These women were obviously providing a full range of services. The hotels have very tight security. Hotel management must have been colluding with these arrangements; it was obvious to me what was happening the first time I visited. Whilst I would call this prostitution, possibly in U.K. law brothel keeping, I'm sure a high quality hotel chain would provide a far more subtle marketing term.

NOTE ON THE EMPIRE WINDRUSH.

The ship H.M.S. Windrush arrived in the U.K. on 22nd June 1948 from Jamaica carrying 492 West Indians (plus a handful of stowaways) who came to seek their fortune, take a chance of a new life and to help the U.K. to rebuild after World War II. Most intended to leave after a few years. Mostly young men, many settled, married, had families and happily lived out their lives in the U.K..

The seventieth anniversary of that landing was marked politically by the government, through U.K.V.I., with the news that the children and families of those who originally arrived on the Empire Windrush, who had been born and raised in the U.K., were routinely having their right of abode in their native country challenged. Families were being split apart with some members returned to the West Indies by U.K.V.I., on behalf of the government. These U.K. citizens were unable to prove their right of abode in the U.K.. Despite being born in the U.K. a right to continue residence was challenged as their parents, the original travellers on the Empire Windrush, and the other vessels which followed it, were unable to prove they had been legally allowed into the country. This was because the U.K. Border Agency had destroyed the paperwork (original landing cards) which proved that right of abode. Some had been forcibly removed from the U.K.

Windrush is a by-word for citizens of the British Commonwealth exerting their rights under the British Nationality Act of 1948 to live and remain in the mother country, i.e. the U.K..

The concept of 'Colonisation in Reverse' (thank you Miss Lou [Louise Bennett] for such a wonderful poem) has proved hard to swallow for many white people in that Mother

Country. As the Windrush sailed out of the West Indies in 1948, Clement Attlee, the Labour Prime Minister, made efforts to have it diverted to East Africa. Once it had landed his Colonial Secretary, Arthur Creech Jones, whilst acknowledging the arrivals were British passport holders, claimed they would not last beyond the first winter as the climate would be too harsh. Conservative politician Enoch Powell, in the 1960's, referred to the British Nationality Act as being the most evil piece of legislation ever enacted. We should not be surprised to find his colleague, former Home Secretary and later Prime Minister, Theresa May actively, and openly, created a hostile environment for non-Brits wanting to stay in the U.K.. What we should be ashamed of is the support she and her successor BJ receive from the electorate for pursuing this policy; the 'I am not racist, but ...' brigade. At its simplest, racism is dealing with someone differently because of their race. And that is precisely what their policies are designed to do.

Website shenanigans.

Having got to grips with the basics of dating websites, and being confident of identifying and getting rid of the more obvious scammers who came my way, I began to understand that the Philippines might be home to a woman who would be pre-menopause, childless, want children, be happy to get involved with a man my age and be prepared to relocate. Perhaps I could realise my ambition for a loving wife who would consider having children with me after all.

So my journey to find her online, chat for a while so we could both understand we were genuine, or as genuine as this medium allows, and then to meet face to face, began.

My intentions had changed totally from the initial research project eighteen months or so earlier. The A.G.M. had been and gone and I had delivered a lecture and workshop on a completely different topic. I set out my stall to find a woman who was keen on me and for whom I had the hots!

Given the title of this section refers to shenanigans, let me start by reinforcing the reasons behind this with some statistics. The underlying reason for the website scams are a mixture of greed and poverty; in the case of the Philippines it will almost always be the latter. I would not want to give the impression that these claims are simply my opinion. The poverty and lack of investment is obscene in parts of the Philippines and these claims can be supported with some real hard evidence, so let's take a look.

Please stay with me on this; don't be frightened off by numbers and tables. We'll keep things fairly basic. These figures simply provide the context to help the westerner visiting the Philippines understand the differences in day to day living; and vice-versa.

I have put the information into three small tables. It is taken from the annual World Development Reports, published by the World Bank. For simplicity the World Bank can be seen as the financial arm of the United Nations. It isn't quite that straightforward but, for our purposes here, it gives the right idea. Each of their reports follows a theme but each also contains a chunk of statistics which allow countries to be compared in detail with each other. The World Bank specifies where all its information comes from so we are able to check to make sure we are not being fed garbage.

The material presented here is all originated by the World Bank itself except for that relating to natural disasters which has been provided to the World Bank by the International Disasters Database. Whilst these sound like information sources which we should automatically trust I would suggest a caveat. If a government department provides information to an international organisation its civil service staff will ensure accuracy as best they can. However, before officers of a national government submit it, assurance as to its accuracy and appropriateness will need to be underwritten by their political masters. Now far be it from me to suggest that every politician is corrupt, however I would suggest it would be a very unusual politician who agreed to provide data showing *them* in a bad light. What I am getting at is that the accuracy of information provided by governments to the World Bank cannot be guaranteed. That said it is probably the best we can get given the nature of the system it needs to go through to be collected. When dealing with information provided by government departments, we can expect to get the information that the government wants us to have. It will probably have some semblance of reality but will be portraying an official perspective; which makes me think of lies, damn lies and statistics!

Tables 1, 2 and 3 provide information from the World Development Reports of 2014, 2016 and 2019 respectively. They compare things like income, child mortality, internet usage, etc. Each report uses historical information. The 2014 report cannot give income for that year as the information cannot be collected until after the end of the year. Usually the information relates to the previous year. Following the issue of the 2014 report the structure of the reporting lines were significantly changed. I have no information as to why this happened. However the reporting methods now seem to be aimed at the professional development economist; in consequence they are less accessible to the lay reader, a category in which I would place myself. Few of the reporting lines from the reports post-2014 are directly comparable with those of 2014 and earlier. Tables 2 and 3 provide direct comparisons of five measures. The first three of these lines also appear in Table 1.

All I am trying to do here is to put some real numbers to things that exist in both the Philippines and the U.K. so we can compare life in the two countries, and to do so using a source of information which is as close to unbiased as we are likely to get. The end result allows us to get a feel for how very different the countries and cultures are.

I have used £s sterling as the currency and provided the currency in P. or php which is the Philippine Peso; € which is the Euro and $ for the U.S.A dollar. As the World Development Reports use the U.S. dollar I have used the conversion rate shown on page 6. The number of natural disasters is a measure of droughts, earthquakes, floods and storms. The Philippines have plenty of these. What is not included are problems with active volcanos. As we noted earlier the Philippines stand on the Pacific Ring of Fire which hosts 90% of the active volcanos on the planet.

Table 1: Data comparing the Philippines and the U.K. taken from the indicators provided in the World Development Report, 2014.

Measure	Philippines	U.K.
Life expectancy at birth, female/male	72/66	83/79
% of population aged under 15 years	35%	18%
Average income per annum	£ 1,872 P 117,393 € 2,054 $ 2,374	£ 29,054 P 1,821,976 € 31,872 $ 36,840
% of people living on less than £7.88 ($10) per day	97.4%	Too small to measure
% of people living on less than £0.79 ($1) per day	53.3%	Too small to measure
Homicide rate per 100,000 people	5.4	1.2
Deaths of under 5's per 1,000 live births	25	5
Maternal deaths per 100,000 births	99	12
Number of natural disasters (2003-2012)	163	19
Deaths in natural disasters (2003-2012)	10,834*	58
% of people aged 15+ with health insurance	5.5%	100%
Number of electronic payments (in millions)	Too small to measure	13,468

* - These figures were collected before Typhoon Haiyan hit the Philippines. The death rate from that event alone comes close to doubling the natural disaster death rate figure given here for the Philippines as a whole.

So imagine yourself as a young adult woman living in a country where you cannot transact payment for anything electronically. A place where there are around twice as many children and young people than in a typical western country and where death comes 11 years earlier, (13 years earlier for men). The homicide rate is 4½ times higher, the chances of your baby dying before reaching school age are five times higher and the likelihood of you dying during childbirth is over eight times higher. It is a place where natural disasters are over eight times more frequent, and where, if you are caught up in such a disaster, lives are lost at a rate of 187:1 compared to what we would anticipate in the west. These figures will become more extreme if you allow for Typhoon Haiyan or are living within range of an active volcano. This is a country where almost everyone is living on less than £7.88 a day and over half the population have to get by on 79 pence per day or less, and, for good measure, whilst the National Health Service assures our health in the U.K., just over one in twenty people aged over fourteen have access to an equivalent level of health care. Within her own country, given her age and status, this young woman is likely to have below average earnings or be unemployed.

It is in these circumstances she finds there is a man on a dating website who lives in a country where the average income is over fifteen times higher than that in her own country. He is showing an interest in her; he has sent her an encouraging e-mail. How does she respond? As a scammer she will dive into the opportunity with a view to extracting the maximum possible from anyone daft enough to part with it. There will not be much evidence of guile or subtlety. However, if she is genuinely wanting to find love with a foreigner, her approach will be very different. There are likely to be elements of temerity, shyness and a bit of surprise that someone who might be genuine is showing an interest in her.

Given her situation she is likely to be very interested, however her interest is, at least in the first instance, is much more likely to be driven by things other than love. Or perhaps, more to the point, we in the west need to refine our understanding of what 'love' may be to her as her circumstances are so different to those of the westerner.

Culturally she lives in a country where age difference between potential life partners has little relevance. She lives in a country where emigration is common. She lives in a country where there is a great deal more poverty; where living on the edge is far more common than it is to most of us in the west. A major driver for her will be to secure a better opportunity for her future to that which faces her daily; the practical aspects of being able to stay alive. Before she sits at a computer or uses a mobile device the genuine Philippine web site user, will have made some serious decisions about where she wants her life to go. She is online to progress those plans. She is likely to be juggling feelings of affection and the tingling feeling of excitement one gets when a new romance is in the air with issues of safety and security; having some guarantees of a roof over her head, food and clean water. She will be considering what might happen if she leaves the relative safety and security of her family and friends.

To summarise; as we approach this situation we should understand there will be some genuine people among the scammers; on a well-managed website probably around three out of ten. Whilst many of the Filipinas using dating websites will be living on the edge, only a tiny percentage will turn to the sex trade. On the ground these activities occur far more obviously than the corresponding areas in the west. From media reports and online info it is also clear that those in the west searching for illegal or questionable sex will be catered for. However for those seeking these activities most cities have established centres. Away from these fairly well defined and tiny areas, the Philippines as a whole is much more conservative in its sexual expression than any other country I have ever visited.

Amongst women seeking romance with a foreigner their specific reasons will differ, everyone has their own influences and priorities. But, generally the view is that relocation to the west will provide a much higher quality of life. We have to acknowledge that, provided she has made a decent choice, having relocated, she will find this is reinforced. She will be secure in a far more affluent environment with good support systems. What word would we use to describe her feelings towards the person who helps her to achieve this? Love might not be the first word to come to the western mind, however from her perspective that could be just the word to use.

Once in the U.K. she will physically feel cold throughout the year. For me that means the domestic heating bill has shot up and, around the house, I am in shorts and sandals for much more of the year. Before arriving in the U.K. my wife had never experienced temperatures below 22°C. There is another important aspect to keep in mind here. Whilst in the Philippines, her diet may well have been be questionable, she will have been exposed to plenty of sunlight. Sunlight is a great way of getting vitamin E and vitamin E is important to the functioning of the thyroid gland. When vitamin E levels drop so does thyroid functionality. One of the main symptoms of this is constantly feeling cold. So, whilst she will feel the coldness simply because the U.K. climate is colder than anything she has previously experienced, this may well be exacerbated by a malfunctioning thyroid. This is something one is well advised to keep an eye on. It is a condition which is fairly easily diagnosed and treated. Furthermore because thyroid treatment is for life it entitles the sufferer to free prescriptions for life; for everything, not just thyroid treatment. In a perverse way one can view thyroid problems as being beneficial!

Being so far from her own family is likely to be stressful but, in the west, she will have a roof over her head and an improved diet. She will also, as time progresses, have the opportunity to generate an income. On the down side she will also find she is in a society which deals with issues and does not tiptoe around problems for fear of upsetting anyone. Until she becomes familiar with this her self-esteem (amor propio) is likely to regularly take a knock. This will be very challenging for her. She is also likely to feel some guilt as her parents and siblings are left in the Philippines and she will regularly be put under pressure to repatriate income to help them out.

Having relocated there will be further reinforcement to stay particularly because the woman knows only too well the environment and conditions she will be returning to if things don't work out. A further factor from my perspective was that she would check out my age from my profile. Her understanding of male life expectancy will be reflected in the position as it exists in her country. On that basis she would be likely to think that I would soon be shuttling off this mortal coil. So this was something I needed to be aware of; would she be tolerating what she anticipated would be a short term pain in the hope of a long term gain? What she couldn't know is that I had a grandfather who died at 96 which is also the age at which my father died. My personal expectations are to be around for a good while yet. I would love to meet my grandchildren, but who knows ... ?

The first three lines of Tables 2 and 3 below can be compared directly with the information provided in Table 1.

Table 2: Data comparing the Philippines and the U.K. taken from indicators provided in the World Development Report, 2016.

Measure	Philippines	U.K.
Average income per annum	£ 2,652 P 166,307 € 2,909 $3,363	£ 32,882 P 2,062,030 € 36,072 $41,694
Deaths of under 5's per 1,000 live births	28	4
Maternal deaths per 100,000 births	114	9
% of individuals using the internet	40	92
Days required to start a business	29	5

Table 3: Data comparing the Philippines and the U.K. taken from indicators provided in the World Development Report, 2019.

Measure	Philippines	U.K.
Average income per annum	£ 4,947 P31,226 € 5,427 $6,278	£ 31,318 P 1,963,952 € 34,356 $39.711
Deaths of under 5's per 1,000 live births	28	4
Maternal deaths per 100,000 births	121	7
% of individuals using the internet	60.1	98.5
Days required to start a business	33	4.5

Before comparing these numbers we need to acknowledge that the information in Table 3 reflects a position in the U.K. Our currency plummeted following the outcome of the Brexit referendum. The British currency dropped close to 20% of its value against the Philippine Peso before recovering a bit. Drops against the Euro and U.S. dollar are also significant but somewhat less. This will have a bearing on comparing incomes from the 2019 report in Table 3. Whilst U.K. wages have remained fairly static when viewed in country, when measured in U.S. dollars by the World Bank the drop in the value of the £ results in a drop in average income.

The main feature to draw out from these is around income. Whilst there has been an overall rise of 8% over the last five years, the Philippine average has risen 264%, i.e. the average wage is over 2½ times higher! By any standards this is a dramatic rise. However the average salary in the U.K. in 2019 is still over six times higher than that earned by the average Filipino. But that is a big drop from the 15 times higher which was the case on the early 2010's. Some of this will be explained by the fall in the value of the £ Sterling. Whilst this does represent a major change for the better, over the same period of time the number of Filipinos living in absolute poverty has also risen, albeit slightly. Those in waged income are earning more but those with nothing still have nothing and there are more of them. To make any real sense of these income figures we need to know what you can buy with the income generated in each of the countries and that is not provided by this dataset or by the World Development Reports.

The next two lines tell us that, whilst mortality rates for the under-fives and maternal mortality rates in the U.K. have reduced, i.e. improved as there are fewer deaths; in the Philippines the opposite applies, i.e. there are more deaths.

The remaining lines are new to the World Development Report and give an indication of two significant differences between our two countries. Whilst there is still much less internet use across the Philippines this is increasing rapidly; and, at the same time bureaucracy appears to be on the increase whilst it is slowly reducing in the U.K.

The New Scientist magazine (22nd October, 2016, p.30) provides an alternative and very interesting comparison across countries. It tells us that the value of a human kidney in the U.S.A. is $334,000 (£263,407, P16,518,253, €298,957); in China $62,000 (£48,896, P3,066,268, €53,639) and, in the Philippines $6,310 (£4,976, €5,459, P 312,045). The value of a Filipino kidney is 53 times cheaper if it is harvested in the country of birth rather than the United States – same person, same kidney!

Back to the dating website. As mentioned earlier, when joining the website you submit your profile and photographs to the site for posting. All site users go through this initial set up process. The site allocates a unique membership number to each member/user and, for the purposes of making changes, one can only access one's own profile. However you can see everyone else's. There are certain brief characteristics about you which will appear on the website continuously. They are the photograph you specify, your age, a short headline of up to six words, the town and region you are from, the gender and age group of people in whom you are interested and when you last used the website. You are also able to search across the website using these parameters. This is very important because there are thousands of profiles hosted on this one website alone.

Just as the City of London is a part of Greater London, so Manila is part of the area called Metro Manila. There are other huge population centres within Metro Manila and the population of Manila, as a part of Metro Manila, is a fraction of the twenty million or so total for Metro Manila as a whole. Whilst there are some lovely areas in the metropolis, much of it is racked with poverty. The view as one lands at the city's airport represents the area as a whole accurately. To give you an idea of the number of profiles held on the website I recall doing a search for women based in Manila (not Metro Manila) aged between 18 and 35. The website came up with one thousand profiles to scroll through at sixteen per page and provided me with a default message saying there were more and I needed to narrow my search criteria if I wished to see them all. So I tried the ages 27-35 and got the same result. The only way to ensure I saw all profiles for females aged thirty-five and under for

Manila was to search a single age band, i.e. 26 year olds or 32 year olds. Then I got a list of under a thousand profiles, but in some cases only just and never less than six hundred and fifty. On one evening I did this for all ages from 18-35 and the total number of profiles exceeded 15,000. That is an awful lot of women. Now most of these would be scammers; my estimate is 70% but, for the sake of argument, let us say 80%. That means over 3,000 profiles, the remaining 20%, will be genuine. And this search was simply for a small part of a massive metropolitan area. If we extend this across the archipelago of the Philippines we can see that, despite websites being overrun by scammers, there will still be huge numbers of genuine site users. However, discovering which of the profiles are authentic and which are fake is a continuous and time consuming job.

Fortunately it is possible to narrow the numbers down significantly. I was not looking for a teenager; the lowest age I was comfortable with contacting was early to mid-twenties. The website asks members how many children they have. This was the issue which reduced the numbers most for me. As I mentioned earlier Filipinas tend to start their families at a younger age than women in the west. Whilst this is probably a consequence of catholicism rather than choice (no teaching around issues of birth control and contraception) it is unusual to find a woman aged thirty or over who does not have children. Most women aged twenty five and over had at least one child. It was only when the age parameter was around 21 or 22 years that there was approximate parity between the profiles showing women who had children and those who didn't. As age reduced the number of members without children increased. Even so, amongst eighteen year olds, the figure for Mums was approaching 30% of profiles shown. This also assumes that the profile is posted by a woman who is real, genuinely looking for a relationship and contains information which is 100% accurate. That is not always the case and, as mentioned earlier, I would get into a conversation with some women who, after an exchange of messages for a few weeks, would disclose they had a family.

Another means of reducing the number of profiles to view was to see when the member had last been active on the website. When logging onto the website it was possible to do a search of those currently online. So you knew these members were active users of the site. But when doing a search, for example, for women from Manila aged 28, the website might flag up the top side of nine hundred profiles, these could be requested in the order of when they last logged onto the website. The profile headline would state either that the user was actually online or specify when that member had last logged onto the site. So the search would return a list of members showing those who were currently using the site first. The others would be listed in time order from when they had last logged off the site, i.e. two minutes, fifty-five minutes, ten hours, five days, three weeks, two months, etc. A genuine and unattached current user of the website will be online fairly frequently. Perhaps not every day but two or three times a week just to check if they have attracted any attention. Someone living in a rural area may check their profile less frequently as they may not have easy access to a computer or mobile; (more likely they will not have easy access to any network services). Anecdotally it would seem the female profile holders in the Philippines do not get a lot of attention and, when they do, it is routinely explicitly sexual. It was common to find a line in a profile making it abundantly clear the woman was not using the site to show off parts of her body at the request of male users; that she did not want any contact with men wanting sexual favours or otherwise playing games. When I looked at the profiles of western men, my competition, some were highly suggestive, (anything explicitly sexual would have led to the profile being removed by the site managers). A genuine Filipina using this website had the same problem I had. They had to wade through loads of garbage to have a chance of finding someone who was real. Someone sending a normal message was likely to get a reply and the first two or three exchanges of information often entailed tippy-toeing around each other.

Some profiles contained the absolute basic minimum of information. This was an indicator that a scammer could be behind that profile. Either that or someone with poor English or whose heart wasn't really in it. I guess there could be other reasons for this happening; perhaps concern about being recognised, however I tended to avoid such profiles unless there was a very good reason not to. I would also avoid profiles which had not been opened for longer than a couple of weeks. Also, when frequently searching the website, you begin to notice that some profiles are open at all times of the day and night. These profiles are probably the front for a scam so are to be avoided. Similarly if a profile has been open for an hour or more it suggests someone who is scamming. Many Filipinas will use a mobile phone or internet café to check their accounts and online time is bought on a pay as you go basis. The genuine site user is unlikely to have either the time, money or incentive to stay online so long. Someone there for an hour or more is probably 'doing business' in one way or another. Another way of identifying scammers is by exploiting the seven or eight hour time difference between our two countries. Seven in the evening in the U.K. will be two or three in the morning in the Philippines depending whether we are on Greenwich Mean Time or British Summer Time. Who will be using a dating website at that time? There will be those involved in the entertainment sector and other shift workers, someone who has been woken up by a baby or child, or it will be scammers working at an off peak time in their country but targeting the west at times of peak usage. For the European surfing during the early evening the chances of finding a genuine person actually online are probably reduced a bit. However Filipinas do have a fairly early start to the day so by the time we got to nine or ten the evening in the U.K. the number of genuine users would begin to gradually increase. Members able to check their accounts from home would often do this before going to work or college.

The website I was using had four ways of telling other members that you were out there and curious. For paying members, if you were using the site and another member was checking your profile, an automatic message would be sent to you. The other three ways were open to all members. You could click a button on the profile of another member which sent them a message that you were of 'interest' to them. Similarly there was a button to identify someone as a 'favourite', so a bit more than just interested. Finally you could an e-mail through the website.

Any member could use these means of communication but, to take things any further, one of them had to be a paying member. Now that my membership has lapsed I can see I have received 'interests', 'favourites' and e-mails, but I cannot read beyond the first line of text and cannot reply.

Most Filipinas post a profile and hope to attract some attention; a tiny number are paying members. In the seven or so years I used this website I can count the number of fully subscribed Filipinas I came across on the fingers of one hand. This puts the westerner, as the person who has paid to join the website, in control of any dialogue. Almost all of the women using the site would only be able to chat when they got a response from a paying member. In consequence one occasionally received suggestive messages trying to tempt a reply. I will re-iterate that this is what many male users of the site were looking for.

I decided that I would send a standard message to anyone who caught my eye. I would also click the 'interest' button. I did this because an odd anomaly of the membership I purchased was that, when I looked at the profile of another member, it told me if I had previously clicked their 'interest' button. However, I did not have an easily accessible record of members to whom I had sent an e-mail without going through a long trawl going back months. So, if I sent a message but got no reply, I could forget. In consequence I found it beneficial to click the 'interest' button whenever I first sent a message to a member. I received replies to around 40% of my messages.

Until I firmed up a visit and a meeting with a specific site member I followed the following procedure when I logged onto the website. Firstly I would look at my messages. The website automatically filtered these into two categories. There were those received from persons who fitted the description I had provided of the woman I was looking for; that was my 'new messages' folder; and there was a second batch of messages where the woman did not fully fit that criteria but had still sent me a message. These appeared in the 'new filtered messages' folder. I made a point of always responding to the former and checking through the latter perchance there was someone I might be interested in; perhaps someone a couple of years outside the age parameters I had set. There were three other folders which I would glance through now and again:

- 'new interests' - woman who had clicked the 'interest' button on my profile.;
- 'new profile views', women who had checked my profile but not made contact; and,
- 'new favourites', where the woman had clicked that button on my profile.

As an aside my membership of this website expired getting on for five years ago as I write; to get accurate information I returned to the site twice today as a non-paying member. The first visit triggered the settings of the website to shift my profile from being one which was last online five years ago to one who had been active very recently. When I returned the second time I found I had four new messages, twelve new filtered messages, and a number of new interests, profile views and favourites. There were three hours between the two visits I made to the web site. In that time I had received sixteen messages and eight interests from woman aged 23-57. In the following twenty-four hours I received two new filtered messages. In the following two weeks I received a further seventeen messages. I know this as I received an automatic e-mail from the website whenever a message was sent to me, even though my membership has expired. Probably the site owners are hoping I will pay to re-register and answer those contacts. However, I have not subsequently returned to the website because, if I do, my profile will automatically update again to indicate I am an active member. That tells women using the site they are looking at the profile of someone current. I do not want to give that impression, so I keep away.

I would spend time trawling through the website, sending messages and 'interests' to women whose profiles appealed to me and getting some replies. Many women stated on their profiles that they were only interested in men up to a particular age. Whilst the upper age specified was much older than I had found on the U.K. dating websites I had visited, often it was still well below my age. Looking at the life expectancy rates for the Philippine man, 66 years, could explain this. The same rate in the U.K. is 79 years. Most Filipinas under the age of thirty would set their upper age limit as somewhere between forty and fifty years. Some just entered eighteen to eighty years, but, even for the Philippines, that smacked of desperation or scamming rather than a genuine search for affection and love.

I thought there was a possibility some Filipinas were specifying forty to fifty years as they were looking for a man who still had the potential for ten to twenty more years of living. Coupled with this I routinely received 'interest' or 'favourite' hits from women who, when I checked their profiles, had specified an age range which ended way below my age. This told me that the profile holder was happy to consider me even though my age was twenty years or more above the top age range she had specified on her profile; and that age was already way above anything a typical western dating website user would seriously consider. I decided that, where I received an 'interest' or 'favourite' hit from someone in this situation, I would check the profile and, if I was interested, would respond to her with a message which queried the age specification and make my age crystal clear. Without fail this would elicit a positive response. I would receive a message along the lines of: "I am looking for love, to me age is just a number, it doesn't matter." If I was searching the website and found a profile I liked but the woman had specified forty as the top age she was interested in, I would click the 'interest' button on her profile'. I considered this to be me showing her I was interested without pestering her. She could respond if she wished and, if she did, a dialogue would start. If she didn't respond I would not follow up my interest. Where a woman specified an upper age which was above forty but below my age I devised a standard message. Basically it said that I realised my age was well above her top age limit so, if she chose not to reply, I would understand. However, if she was interested, to please get back to me. I would couple this by also clicking the 'interest' button so, whether she replied or not, I knew I had made a contact and would not bother her again unless she made it clear she wanted me to. Most of these messages elicited a positive response.

However all this contact with young women was in large part because 70% or so of the profiles I contacted were those of scammers; they would have responded with no regard to age; they would have responded whatever state I was in! However using this method to instigate a dialogue did seem to increase the numbers of genuine replies.

As I continued to use the website I quickly became aware that a member with whom I had been chatting would disappear for no apparent reason. As time progressed I understood that this reflected two types of user. The first was the scammer who had better things to do than exchange pleasantries with someone genuine. They voted with their feet so to speak and disappeared quite quickly. The other type of profile which disappeared is a little more difficult to explain. These were people who continued with their use of the website; I would see them online periodically; their profiles told me when they had last used the site. However they choose not to answer my message, or the reminder I would occasionally send to someone I had chatted with for a while. Maybe these profiles were also being used to scam, perhaps they had received a better offer, or maybe they realised just how big our age gap was. Occasionally I would get a request for money. These were forwarded to the site managers and the profile disappeared. On one occasion I did receive contact from a person who I had blocked. She claimed to have set up a new profile because she could not understand how we could have lost contact. However it did not take long before she again began talking about money so I linked the two profiles by membership number and reported this back to the site managers who removed the second profile.

Whatever the reason there were many disappearances, however one or two people stayed the course and I built up a level of trust where I would be happy to meet using the video link provided through the website. In time one lady rose to the top of the pile. We reached a stage where we were chatting face to face via video link four or five times weekly. She did not have any religious hang-ups and told me she had a degree in Administrative Sciences and worked as a supervisor in a warehouse which distributed perishable goods to supermarkets. (A Bachelor's degree awarded by a Philippine University is about the equivalent of two 'A' levels in the U.K.) The topic in which she claimed to have been awarded her degree is not one which we would recognise at degree level in the U.K., however I checked the website of her University and this subject was offered; along with a variety of other course titles with which I was unfamiliar. This led to me searching several other Philippine University websites and confirming that what she was telling me checked out nationally. Her times coming on and off the website supported her alleged pattern of work; if I checked her profile when she claimed to be at work, her profile was never in use and the time of the last use would be consistent with the time we last had a communication together; this was true also for her Facebook profile. So I was reasonably satisfied that she was not involved with anyone else on this website. I used her profile information to do a detailed search of the other Philippine based dating websites and could not find her. This had become a routine part of screening once I was chatting with someone who I felt had serious prospects. Probably half the time I found the profile and the person behind it were active elsewhere at the same time I was chatting to them, so this was another useful way of identifying and screening out scammers.

However I had now found someone where I thought there was a serious possibility of a long-term relationship.

Planning the first trip.

Whilst I am now retired and have been happily married for well over three years, the events I will recount here began getting on for twelve years ago. At that time I was working on a full-time basis. My disposable income was treble what it is today and I have never been a big saver! At that time a holiday to the Philippines was, financially, a fairly minor financial ripple. More difficult was finding a time slot in which to make the trip. I found a couple of periods when my diary was quiet and asked my secretary to keep both clear. If the first trip was a success I would probably want to re-visit to help the new woman in my life prepare for her visit to the U.K. I had checked the visa requirements for a Philippine citizen visiting the U.K. and believed, wrongly, that the issuing of a visitor visa would be pretty much a formality. What I was trying to engineer was a first visit for the two of us to meet and for me to be introduced to her family and friends. If all went well I would then want to extend the opportunity for her to visit the U.K. so that she could meet my family and friends. This would allow us to have good look at each other and have some understanding of our respective backgrounds. As part of the process I proposed to make a second trip to the Philippines a couple of months after the first one. In the interim she would be able to obtain her passport and I would gather together the documents required to support her visa application. It would also give each of us the opportunity of a second look at each other on her home territory to double check we were doing the right thing before taking things forward seriously. A visit to the U.K. would be a huge step for both of us, particularly for her as she might well have to give up her current job to make such a trip happen.

I was keen to progress this way for two other big reasons. Even though I have travelled extensively I had no previous experience of south-east Asia and the Philippines were presenting themselves as a bit of a challenge; it would be the same for her if she came to the U.K., magnified several fold. I hoped she would find the differences positive but she would be visiting a totally different world. The other reason was that two people can pull the wool over each other's eyes for a couple of weeks but, if we were under the same roof for a few months, (and the visitor visa allows up to six months), we would both learn a lot about each other and be in a much healthier position to take a measured decision on a future together.

I took a look around the accommodation websites and found a full range of options from a cheap downtown room in a boarding house to five star luxury hotels. The room option would be cheap; much cheaper than similar accommodation in the U.K. As a tourist it is still possible to find a bed for less than £10 per night in the Philippines. At the top end were the luxury hotels which charged £200 per night and upwards; similar rates to that which one finds at the quality end the market in any major city or resort in the west.

As I began using the dating website I had also begun to understand the geography of the Philippines and the area it covered. From north to south the distance is similar to the trip from London to Alicante, Cairns to the Gold Coast in Australia or Washington DC to Miami. I used the website in conjunction with GoogleEarth and, by the time I was thinking about the first visit, had a reasonably good idea of the layout of the country and its transport systems. Going any distance by road would be problematic; there are no motorways and only a handful of dual carriageways, etc. in the cities; the main options were air and sea.

As we have discussed the Philippines splits, geographically, into three distinct regions and has many airports. There are two main hub airports. Ninoy Aquino International in Manila is the country's major airport and services the northern part of the archipelago, Luzon, and surrounding islands. Mactan Airport, Metro Cebu, services the central island belt of the country called the Visayas. Manila is a huge international airport with four terminals. When I began visiting Mactan had a single terminal split for domestic and international flights. However a new terminal building on the same site opened on 1st July, 2018 which covers international arrivals and departures. It is bigger, brighter and cleaner than its predecessor, which is now used for internal flights only, and

Filipinos are very proud of it. Unfortunately it is still blighted by paperwork, a reflection on the level of technology which can be used and the addiction the Philippine government has with bureaucracy. The main airport in the south of the country, Mindanao, is in Davao City. However with the exception of the odd flights to and from Singapore, it is purely a provincial airport. The upside of this is that night flights are rare so accommodation near the airport does not have a problem with noise after dark, the downside is that it makes the south of the country a little less accessible. For the would-be Romeo that could be a bonus as the competition will be less. However, as noted earlier, it is this part of the country that, prior to anything to do with Coronavirus, the U.K. Foreign Office had warned against visiting for many years. Most areas are safe enough, but there is without doubt an added risk factor of religious friction and that has a significant impact on travel insurance and one's day to day activities.

(At the time of writing the U.K. government are slowly trying to re-open the airways having banned all but essential international travel due the Coronavirus pandemic. Once travel restrictions to the Philippines are lifted it is likely the previous exclusion areas will remain.)

The woman I was planning to meet, let's call her April, lived in the city of Bacolod, with a population of over 200,000 it is located in the Visayas. It had an airstrip to the south of the town which had daily connections to both Manila and Cebu, Cebu being the closer. A new airport has now opened to the north of the town with the same flight options. So I began the search for accommodation and flight options.

I went back to the literature about travelling and visiting the Philippines. A point most sources made was that, whilst low priced accommodation was readily available across the country, to have a reasonable degree of security nothing less than a three star hotel should be considered. That put my costs at a minimum of £30 (P.1880; €33; $38) per night bed and breakfast. The more I read the more concerned I became about the issue of security. What would happen if my cash, cards or passport grew legs? I decided I had to get serious and up my game. What I needed was to find a place which had what I wanted rather than something which satisfied a minimum requirement. Whilst money was not much of an issue, safety was. So security became the main concern. I wanted to know I could relax in my room, sleep safely whilst neither my property nor I were at risk. It would also be a plus if the room had a safe where I could set the combination. Secondly I wanted a swimming pool. Whilst the Philippines has its seasons they tend to reflect rainfall and typhoons rather than temperature. The island to which I was proposing to travel experienced a climate of which I had little experience. Across the year it was unheard of for temperatures to fall below 23°C and they rarely exceeded 35°C. The norm was around 32°C at the height of the day and 28°C in the middle of the night. For me that is hot. I enjoy swimming but a pool was more of a necessity to help stay cool than a preference; air conditioning in the room would also be an essential requirement. I was also looking for a place where I could be discreet, but needed to be close to a hub airport which meant being close to a major population centre. I finally went with a beach resort which was about a thirty minute taxi ride from Mactan Airport, Cebu.

The hotel blurb promised privacy and quality. It delivered both to Philippine standards. It was an unforgettable experience but not entirely for the reasons I had anticipated. There were several other resort hotels in the immediate vicinity and I saw from GoogleEarth that there seemed to be plenty of activity in the surrounds.

Having decided on the hotel and the airport, I needed to make reservations. There are several international airlines which fly into the Philippines but most fly into Manila, a connection then being needed to Mactan/Cebu. At the time I made these plans only two of the international carriers were able to deliver the passenger to Mactan Airport, from the U.K. without problematic transfers and stopovers. Cathay Pacific flew from London or Manchester to Hong Kong and from Hong Kong to Cebu with a maximum transfer time of eight hours but, usually, a wait of just under two hours. Singapore Air flew from London or Manchester to Singapore. The Manchester flight had a stopover in Munich. Outward bound you got off the plane and spent an hour or so in the airport building; inbound you stayed on the plane whilst local passengers disembarked and embarked and the airline cleaning staff worked around you; a bizarre experience. I understand it is a refuelling stop. There are then several direct flights daily from Singapore to Cebu with the Singapore Airlines subsidiary Silk Air or other local provider services. However the stopover time is usually 3-7 hours. The lowest cost flight from the U.K. to the Philippines was usually a toss-up between Dutch carrier K.LM. and Royal Brunei Airlines. K.L.M. will fly you from your local airport into Schiphol Airport, Amsterdam from where there is a flight to Manila via Taiwan. Royal Brunei goes from Heathrow, London via Dubai to Bandar Seri Begawan, Brunei. There is then a change of plane to fly into Manila. From Manila you are able to travel on to the regional airport of your choice. Be warned though; Ninoy Aquino Airport is an acquired taste. In 2009 it won an award for being one of worst airports in the world for passengers. There are four terminals and travel between them is much more difficult than one would expect from experience in the west. I have only been through the Airport on one return trip, in 2013 and have no burning desire to return. The flights were fine, the airport was chaotic. The recommendation was, and I think still is for Ninoy Aquino, a minimum of three hours for check-in or transfer. Somehow the suitcase that I took off the conveyor belt in Terminal 1 weighed three kilos heavier when it was checked in at Terminal 3; and that attracted a price surcharge. Nothing inside the case had changed, it hadn't even been opened. I avoided the charge by distributing the excess in various pockets and into the cabin baggage but it was a lesson learned.

Emirates now regularly fly from the U.K. to Dubai where there is a change for either Manila or Cebu. The return flight from Mactan stops at Clark which is an airport on Luzon Island which serves Angeles City and its surrounds. For the last couple of years that was consistently the lowest cost option for the economy traveller from the U.K. Immediately prior to the Coronavirus outbreak the choice on price and flight times it is a toss-up between Singapore Air and Cathay Pacific again. It is also possible to fly in direct from airports in South Korea, Japan, China and

Los Angeles. However these routes are unlikely to be of interest to the traveller based in the U.K.

A bit of housekeeping for the would-be traveller. As I began to look around for flight options I also sought medical information; my main worry was a risk of malaria.

There is a risk of malaria in the Philippines. It covers almost all of the north and south of the country. The area I was visiting was the central belt which is malaria free. That does not mean there are no mosquitos. However these mosquitos, whilst they carry other risks, do not carry anything which will give you malaria. There is plenty of insect life and a supply of quality repellent is an essential when visiting. There are many other factors to consider. In addition to routine vaccinations in the U.K. you also need, as a minimum, Hepatitis A, Typhoid and Tetanus. Depending on your activities and the type of area you will be visiting consideration also needs to be given to:

Hepatitis B (where you may have unprotected sex or otherwise come into contact with blood or body fluids);

Rabies (caught from a bite, scratch or lick from an infected animal), the risk is low but, if not treated quickly, will most likely be fatal. The Philippines is not rabies free. 300-600 Filipinos die from rabies annually. Dogs are the major risk; cats carry the virus as do bats and, once outside major conurbations there are a lot of them. A series of three injections before travel will buy you 24 hours from being bitten to getting to a hospital which can provide the necessary two further injections. Unless you attend a properly resourced city hospital facility these two serum in these injections may be based on an animal based serum. This is much riskier than the recommended human derived serum (and you may be in no position to check or ask);

Japanese Encephalitis. This is a small risk for all travellers but one that grows for the long term visitor particularly those visiting agricultural areas;

Cholera is active in parts of the Philippines. You need to check if the part of the country you are visiting has a recent history of cholera and inoculate accordingly; and,

Tuberculosis. This is passed on through the breath of an infected person. So, theoretically, should mask wearing as a consequence of the Coronavirus pandemic continue, numbers should diminish. However in the Philippines about 1 in 2,500 people are infected; there is a higher incidence where there are a lot of children around; and, once off the beaten track for the tourist, children are everywhere.

This list does not include the biggest risk which is Dengue Fever, also known as Breakbone Disease. Dengue Fever is passed on by the Aedes Mosquito found across the archipelago. It needs water to thrive and prefers stagnant water of which there is plenty. Dengue levels are high in the Philippines and rising. There were over 125,000 cases in 2017 of which the top side of 350 were fatal. A vaccination programme is being trialled. It began in 2015 amongst high-risk children and aims to reduce incidence of the disease by around 25% over a four year period. However there is no treatment available. With some similar features, including transference via insects, there is also Chikungunya Fever. This is occasionally fatal but usually debilitating and again there is neither vaccine nor treatment. With both you just have to drink plenty of clean water, give it time and hope for the best.

So, if you visit the Philippines there are issues you need to deal with around health. If you need vaccinations this should be sorted out a minimum of three months before travel. It is not something you can do at the last minute. But there is also a need to keep these issues in perspective. If you are appropriately inoculated, staying in a three star hotel or better, visiting popular areas such a tourist beaches, shopping malls and good restaurants, etc., you are likely to be absolutely fine. Just be aware of the risks and take the appropriate precautions; particularly if you intend to wander off the beaten track. It is a hot climate but if you wear a long sleeved top, trousers and socks, you may feel a bit uncomfortable and sweaty but the insects will have much less flesh to go at. The level of poverty can be obscene by western standards, take a look on YouTube, so the traveller needs to cut their cloth accordingly. If you think you may be visiting someone in a poor area or off the beaten track, be sure to get vaccinated and dress appropriately. But remember that statistically the three biggest threats to the health of a tourist are:

> motor bikes;
> water; and,
> other tourists.

What is absolutely essential is a good health insurance policy which you should carry with you whenever possible. Make sure you have a paper copy and photocopy it. One copy to carry with you at all times, the other to leave in an obvious place at your accommodation. You will not get any medical treatment unless you produce proof of insurance or cash; and that holds even if you are unconscious – so have that proof about your person. You will certainly not be asked to say "aah" until payment is guaranteed. Should you be considering a visit to part of the country where your government advises against travel, then read the small print of your insurance very closely. It is likely visiting such an area will disqualify the entirety of your insurance cover.

Whilst entry to the Philippines requires a visa that is not something you need to worry about before travel provided that, when you arrive in the country, you can produce a flight ticket which will take you out of the country within thirty days. A standard return ticket is the norm. Make sure you have a hard copy; mobile and laptop versions may be refused. If you are travelling on a one-way ticket and intend to plan onward travel whilst in the Philippines, you must attend to the visa before you travel. You will not be allowed into the country if you only have a one-way ticket. Contact the Consulate in London (or in your home country if that is not the U.K.). If you are staying for up to 30 days the Philippine authorities will stamp your passport at the point of entry to the country, i.e. Manila, Cebu or Davao Airports, there is no charge. If you are staying longer than thirty days there are two options. Apply at the

Philippine Consulate in your home country before departure. A single entry visa will be valid for 59 days from the date of issue and costs £25. Six month and annual multi-entry visas are available at £47 and £70 respectively. Alternatively enter the country with a thirty day stamp in your passport at the point of entry then visit the Bureau of Immigration office nearest to the place where you are staying. Check their location online before you begin your trip; but you will find their offices in all cities and most major towns. You can apply for the same visas at the same price. Beware of unexpected administration charges like express lane and double express lane surcharge, if you want to be processed quickly you will pay for it! Check the location before travel because the likelihood is your mobile will not work on Philippine systems, a modern western device will attract thieves, local systems often break down and stay down for a few hours and the country as a whole if prone to power cuts – locally known as brownouts.

Back to the travel arrangements. Do not make a hotel reservation directly with a hotel; it is likely to cost much more. Use the available websites. Initially I would choose one where you pay a little more but can cancel up to seven days before travel. That way, if the wheel comes off your plans, you are cutting your losses. However I would also advise that, if the meeting you have planned falls through, there will be a queue of potential suitors agreeing to meet you. Maybe you should continue your plans, arrange to meet someone else whilst you are there, and see how it goes. You might get lucky, (if you are simply looking for sex you will get lucky, the right places take little finding). If this is not your plan then a trip will allow you to pick up invaluable experience of the country. For all its faults and problems it is rare to see a Filipino who is not smiling and there are many beautiful places to visit.

All major airlines have websites through which you can make your reservation. With most you can hold a reservation for a few hours to give you time to confirm your accommodation should that be necessary. Prices vary depending on the day of the week and there are seasonal variations for school holidays and the like. These will be based on the school timetable for the west. This is not the same as in the Philippines where the main college and school holiday begins around Easter with a return in early June; not what we would anticipate in the west so be aware of local conditions.

I have sufficient knowledge of the hotels now and am happy to leave my reservation to the last minute. This way a cheapish airfare can be picked up so long as you are flexible with your travel arrangements. But the first time traveller to the Philippines would be well advised to get your flight and accommodation nailed down well in advance.

Prelude to the first visit.

When I first told April I had booked a trip to the Philippines to meet her, her first questions were: "Where will you be staying?" And, "Do they have wifi?" These are reasonable questions which I answered straightaway, but it was not the response I had been anticipating and should have acted as a warning. I was expecting more of a sense of surprise, excitement and pleasure at the fact that we would be in a position to meet in person at last, rather than two very practical questions.

My flight was to Mactan Airport, Cebu and the hotel was about half an hour by taxi from the airport. I told April this and gave her the hotel name. I held back the information that arrangements had also been made for a visit to Bacolod a couple of days following my arrival in the country. There were two reasons for not staying on the island where April lived. Firstly there were no direct flights from outside the Philippines to her local airport. The hotel I had chosen was close to hub airport from where it was convenient for me to fly to her island for a visit. At that time there were two flights a day between the two places. Secondly I wanted to meet April without disrupting her routine. She worked full-time and had told me that she struggled to get time off work. I knew she lived in a boarding house with two or three other single women. This is why the return flight from Cebu to Bacolod had been made and a city centre hotel room booked for a one night stay, (for me, not for both of us). This would allow us to meet and chat without putting her under pressure at work. If it worked out my intention was to repeat the process a couple of days later or to offer her the opportunity of joining me in Cebu for a day or two – her call.

We had been chatting online for four or five months by this time, using Skype and operating away from the dating website. I had given her plenty of opportunity to ask for support, financial or otherwise, and she had not done so. I had sent her flowers on Valentine's Day and some chocolates for her birthday. In typical Philippine style, whilst I had ordered each a week in advance, the Valentine's Day flowers were delivered around the end of February. The birthday chocs? They were three weeks late. On each occasion she had been quite emotional telling me that no one had ever treated her that way before and, on each occasion, without prompting, when our next chat following the delivery occurred, she showed me the gifts. She was twenty four years old; I knew she had had a couple of previous relationships; she knew I had been married. So we were fully aware we were chatting with someone with a bit of experience of life and love. I was surprised that no previous boyfriends had given her what for me were fairly traditional gifts in acknowledgement of special events. I was relatively new to the online version of the dating game at that point. From our respective membership numbers on the dating website I knew that she had joined around a year before me; and I had been using the site for nine months before planning a trip. She confirmed this without being prompted. Her main reason for joining the website echoed the reasons given by many Filipinas of her age. She was looking for a relationship with someone interested in the long-term. When using the website she was sick and tired of being hit on by men whose only interests were carnal. She was also tired of local men whose only interest was sex with no commitment; now where have I heard that before! In short she came across as being a normal heterosexual woman in her mid-twenties looking for a normal heterosexual man with whom she could build her life and family. She seemed to be what I was looking for; my only real concern was the difference in our ages.

Whilst using the dating website I had read the available literature about visiting the Philippines, and about meeting Filipinas. Essentially the information broke down into two types. The first and most easily accessible and readable was written by western men for western men. They made it very clear that a man making a visit to the Philippines was a target; not just for the woman they planned to meet but also her family. The advice was clear. The man travelling in from the west should never tell anyone in the Philippines he was making that journey until he had arrived in the country. They stressed their opinion that Filipino women are brought up to obey. You tell her what to do and she does it. Occasionally she might get a bit stroppy but, what's new with women?!

They were clear that the western man would find the Filipina to be compliant and uncomplaining; as they remembered their grand-mothers to have been. Not like the modern day western woman who is constantly demanding and bickers when she does not get what she wants, and often continues to bicker even when she does.

I found myself at odds with this description feeling it probably said more about the authors than the women they had met. I enjoy vigorous debate but I don't enjoy arguing just for the sake of it. However I certainly don't think it is my job to enslave someone and that was the direction of travel these writers were suggesting, at least implicitly. I respect people who will stand up for what they believe in, female or male. I also value education and what comes with that are people who know what they are talking about and will back it up with evidence. I am not frightened of re-evaluating my position or of changing my mind. I do not see that as a weakness. No one knows everything and, as more knowledge comes my way, I reappraise my opinions. These books were describing women first as a sexual commodity, to be consumed, and then as a potential domestic commodity to use and abuse at will. Of course they did not mention the word 'abuse'. But much of their rhetoric pointed that way. They went on to suggest that, until the man knew they would be sleeping together, he should never tell a woman he meets where he is staying. He should never plan to meet just one woman. Their message was that most of the women using the dating websites could not be trusted to tell the truth and had agendas which revolved mostly around money. He should meet several different women, try them between the sheets, and, maybe he will find one of them who is genuine. The same books proffered the advice that if you had not got the Filipina to bed by the third date something strange was going on and the man should drop her and move on. They also pointed out that the western man would be carrying the expense of a long trip, etc. and should maximise his opportunities. I understood clearly what they writers were saying. I also understood that, whilst they were not writing specifically for the sex tourist, they were writing for an adult male who believed that the flexing of his relative financial muscle should directly correlate with the flexing of his gusset muscles! Don't get me wrong; I enjoy a horizontal jog but see it as a healthy consensual activity in a normal relationship. These books said nothing about education, personal development, etc. and, whilst they pointed out a few differences in cultural norms, discussed these in terms of the western male interpretation of life being non-negotiable whilst all other views should be the subject of suspicion.

Was I traveling with sex in mind? I would be lying if I said "No". Was sex the reason for my trip? No. My anticipation was to meet the woman I had chatted with online, to establish if we got on together, discover if we might be compatible in the medium and long term and move that relationship along what is best described as a traditional pathway to marriage. At some point on that journey we would both decide the time was right to share a bed. When that happened I was up for it. But I also realised I was operating across cultures and across generations. I was dealing with an adult woman who was much younger than me; who lived in very different circumstances and, in consequence, would have different norms and values. The assumption of the authors of this type of book took sex as the starting point; anything beyond that was a potential bonus. They also assumed the man would either have identified potential women through a dating website before travel or would visit the seedier parts of town and frequent discos or girlie bars where women made themselves available for a price. Those were not my aspirations at all.

As mentioned earlier I was aware that a thriving sex trade exists in the Philippines, legitimate and underground. Part of the information I collected whilst using the dating website; getting familiar with the geography of the country also covered this business. I know the cities which lead in this area and have avoided them. I have visited the cities of Manila and Cebu. I have yet to get beyond the airport in Manila and have no particular desire to. I like a quiet life and am not a city person. Having flown into Mactan Airport, Cebu, I have always steered well clear of the red light district of Cebu City and have never visited any adult entertainment venue. The closest I have been Cebu City's red light area has been a visit to a nearby Robinson's Supermarket which has a kiosk which provides money exchange at a competitive rate. My money changing visit was mid-morning and the streets were quiet insofar as there was no evidence of working girls.

I understand from the literature that the way the girlie bars work is that the man will go in and buy himself a drink. There will be several women in the bar who will make it clear they can be available to him. The man can make it clear that he just wants to have a drink. He will then be left alone so far as sex is concerned. However, if he is looking for female company and finds one of the women attractive, he will buy her a drink. This will be surcharged to cover the time she spends chatting with him. If they decide to spend some time together the man then has to pay what is referred to as a 'bar-fine' to the owners of the establishment. When a girl working in the bar is privately entertaining a client, then one of the attractions of the bar has gone. Business will be less brisk. So the bar owner is charging what he considers to be a compensation payment. It is usually charged at an hourly rate and rooms are normally available on the premises where the customer can be 'entertained' by his guest. What they do together is a matter of negotiation between the couple. The woman may get a previously agreed percentage of the bar-fine; that is a negotiation between her and the bar owner before she bases herself in that particular bar. However that should not be assumed. There are plenty of women the bar owner can choose so market forces may dictate that he does not have to pay her anything. Whilst all Philippine cities and most towns have these establishments, I was not seeking a woman who, for whatever reason, generated her income that way.

I was far more comfortable with the second type of literature. This consisted of information about the country told through travelogues, memoirs and the like; it included a more academic type of read. Here I was advised that Filipinos are a respectful and rather reserved people who lean toward shyness unless with family or close friends. I was also told that when meeting a member of the opposite sex for the first time the woman was very likely to be chaperoned. This was a complete contrast to the description in the lad's books; the picture painted was of young women who were far less outgoing than their western counterpart. The importance of religion and the family were discussed in some detail.

As a child the Filipino is brought up to be respectful to all, particularly other family members, and to be sure not to cause embarrassment or dent the pride of another. Remember amor-propio? They will also be brought up not to question authority to any great extent; such behaviour would be likely to challenge the self-image of someone sooner or later. Unless there is a massive problem the Filipino is born into a family and remains a member of that family for life. The family takes decisions for her so she is also likely to avoid discussion and decision-making which, for a western man, can be very frustrating. A man marrying a Filipina will become a member of the family. All that is theirs is yours and all that is yours is theirs. Given the average levels of income we have seen for our respective countries that alone should provide some food for thought. I was informed that if I showed an interest in a Filipina within a few days of first meeting I would be expected to make my intentions clear. This would not be a simple acknowledgement that we were going to the cinema or shopping together and would see where that took us. No. What I should expect is to be politely questioned about my prospects and how I saw any relationship developing. This would go so far as talking about when marriage would happen, where we would be based, the likelihood of children and, in broad terms, finances. Not something one would expect in the first fortnight of a possible courtship in the west. Because I was a foreigner they would not expect me to do the same. However, if I did, I would be answered honestly, accurately and with respect. The second type of literature was far more to my liking. It was properly researched and sources were provided where relevant. Various different sources triangulated with each other and all were more thorough and respectful than the first set of books I had read. However both types of read proved to be useful in their own ways.

On the dating website I was asked by several young women if I was looking for a virgin. I told them that I was not expecting to meet a virgin but, if that happened, I would treat her with same respect I would treat any other woman I met. Sex for me is a consensual activity. If a partner says no, it means no. However I expect the same. If I am not in the mood I don't expect to be pestered to provide an instant erection. I suppose I have reached an age where there is more to life than sex. It is important and has its place in relationships, but it is not the be all and end all it tended to be in my youth. Given the ages of the women I was chatting with on the website this probably explains why some of them just could not comprehend that my first interest was genuinely trying to understand what was going on between their ears rather than between their legs. To most I was demonstrating a new, novel approach to online dating and one which they did not warm to straightaway. As time progressed this became another great way of identifying, getting rid of and deterring scammers.

As I mentioned at the beginning of these recollections my education was completely wrecked in my teens by a serious accident. But that did not mean I was stupid. During my youth and early adulthood various people told me that was the case. When I look back on those days I do not like myself at all; I was a horrible person and, had I not joined the police, may well have ended up in prison. I think the accident retarded and seriously confused my adolescence and I was well into my twenties before I properly grew up. This was not a move from ugly duckling to swan status, more of a shift from obnoxious delinquent to acceptable member of society. In many respects I was looking for someone who had travelled a similar path. The cause would be very different, I agree, but the consequences would be similar. The person I was seeking would likely be undereducated, but not educationally challenged; someone more likely to have been deprived of the opportunity to learn, for whatever reason. I was seeking someone with aspirations for her future, someone who might have been compelled to leave full-time education as soon as legally possible due to the economic circumstances of her family, but who had an interest in the world around her and had the potential to grow and flourish. Someone seriously looking for a genuine and potentially life-changing opportunity to which she could contribute; carpe diem. So far as sex was concerned I was looking for someone who viewed it as a normal, healthy and enjoyable part of a relationship that would happen if and when it happened.

The hotel I had booked into was on a different island to that where April lived. It was a four star beach resort with swimming pools and restaurants on site. Typical of the Philippines there were no single rooms. All accommodation was either in rooms for two people with the capacity for two more people to share, or they were family rooms. My overall trip was for eleven nights excluding travel. I told her of my trip to Cebu a couple of days before I travelled which was four days before I was due to arrive in Bacolod. She told me that she would arrange things with her boss and make sure she would be able to meet me. I told her that I was excited and looking forward to getting to know each other better. After checking there was a wifi connection, she agreed. We were looking forward to meeting up in person, progressing our online friendship and seeing where it would take us.

April.

When I reflect on the first visit I made to the Philippines my naivety of how this part of the world works, or doesn't as the case may be, shines through. Pretty well anything that could go wrong did; and, to a large extent, it was my own fault.

I am a big man. For a short haul flight in Europe I can manage in the economy section of the plane but it is better for all concerned if I have an aisle seat; if that is not available then a window seat. The middle seat is not only a difficulty for me but it becomes a problem for those sat in front of and on either side. So for the flight into Hong Kong I paid for a seat with extra legroom. However this is not my biggest problem when flying long haul; there is another practical issue to do with space. Toilets. These are a major challenge; they are tiny. Because of my overall size I can only use them whilst standing and then I have to stoop, which creates problems of balance and reduces the freedom of movement of the necessary equipment. There have been occasions where I have had to stand on one leg, bend the other at the knee and move it up the wall at the side of the loo to create space where the trajectory will hit the target. Think of a dog and a lamp-post and you will get the idea! There is absolutely no chance of a seated performance. Sorry to be so graphic; however this has meant that throughout my adult life I have had to regulate my food intake beginning a couple of days in advance of long haul travel and avoid anything which might have a loosening effect. Alternatively consume only liquids for twenty-four hours before travel. Stewards on planes do not have the imagination to understand this difficulty; without exception they claim their facilities are suitable for my use and refuse to provide any further assistance. One of the major carriers with whom I have discussed this issue mentioned they had what *they* called, a big toilet in their economy section. The sad thing about this is that the space may have been larger but the toilet itself was still tucked in a corner. Had they positioned it along the side of the longer wall instead of in a corner against the shortest wall, then they would have provided an effective facility for all. On my flight to Hong

Kong the toilet was not really an issue. I stood, stooped and did the best I could! But there were two things about the flight out of Hong Kong to Cebu which I had not anticipated. Firstly the plane seemed to have had seats fitted for the comfort of the average sized person of oriental descent. My height is about 18 inches (45 cms) above that average with corresponding adjustments for width and breadth! Secondly the water the airline provided during that leg of my journey, for coffee, was either locally supplied in the Philippines or had not been boiled; maybe both. It had a serious impact on my digestive tract. The consequence was a thoroughly uncomfortable flight into Cebu.

As we approached Cebu Island the airline staff handed out landing cards (effectively a very brief visa application) and Customs declaration cards for non-Filipinos to complete. There were a series of questions with yes and no boxes to tick. One of these asked: "Are you carrying more than 10,000 pesos in cash?" My bank, and the website I used to make the hotel reservation, both told me that my Visa debit card would be accepted without question across the Philippines. However the travel books I had read and other travel websites told a different story suggesting credit and debit card use could be a very hit and miss experience. When I arranged my finances for the trip I had worked on the basis that I might be unable to find a cash machine that accepted a bank debit card which had Visa but was issued by a small bank rather than one of the international High Street banks. I did not know if traveller's cheques would be recognised but did know the hotel expected payment in full at check-in and that I would be checking in after the banks had closed for the day. So I was carrying a large amount of pesos. When I saw this question panic set in. When I bought the currency in the U.K. there was no mention of this issue. In September, 2016, these rules changed. A person can now carry up to P 50,000 into the Philippines; any excess will be confiscated at the point of entry.

I knew I had a hotel bill to pay in full on arrival. That alone was the top side of 90,000 php for eleven night's bed and breakfast. I did not know there was a limit on the amount of cash I could carry into the country. It was only as we were approaching Mactan Airport that I became aware of this issue; it was too late to do anything about it. I had checked that there would be a safe in my room; I just hoped I would still have some cash to put in it!

By the time we landed I had been travelling for about twenty seven hours. I was carrying far too much currency, was tired, sweaty, hungry, thirsty and in desperate need of the bathroom. During the flight I had been subjected to the disgusting conversations of some North American men which I recounted earlier. Most of the other passengers were of oriental ethnicity. However, there were four of five other men who looked western and were travelling solo. There were a similar number with much younger women of Filipino descent, some with children. During the check-in at Hong Kong Airport I had been surprised by the build of the Filipinos. When using the dating website I had noticed the height of women was usually around 4'10" and weight rarely not much above 50 kilos with many members using the lowest weight level the site allowed, 40 kilos. Over months of use I had forgotten all about this issue. Just chatting with people online means you cease to pay attention to issues like height and general build but it was very noticeable when seeing a Filipina alongside her western partner. Filipinos are generally of a smaller and slimmer of stature than their Chinese, Japanese and Korean counterparts, many of whom will be found in the Philippines. However, the fact that these mixed ethnicity couples had children, did go some way to answering the question I posed early around the practicalities of baby-making. Whilst none of these men were my height they were significantly taller than their Filipino partners and children had been produced. This suggested that the appropriate parts of our bodies should function harmoniously. Perhaps if the opportunity arose I should encourage my partner to jockey so she could safely get to grips with the reality of our situation!

We landed and there was the usual rush to the border control point. I found a loo and then joined my fellow passengers. There were the usual queues as passports and identity documents were presented at the border. Six or seven lines of passengers had formed and they seemed to split: five for Filipinos, one for non-Filipinos and one for flight crew, airport staff, the military and dignitaries. Unsurprisingly most of the people I queued with seemed to be Hong Kong Chinese. The queues moved quickly enough and soon I emerged into the baggage collection area with a thirty day visa stamped into my passport and, thankfully, local cash intact. I collected my case, presented my airline baggage receipt which was checked against the suitcase and stamped; and then emerged into the Philippines; the arrival hall at Mactan Airport around 7.30pm on a weekday evening. It was a busy area and I was immediately aware of the presence of armed security staff. However I was quickly grabbed by a little girl who said: "Hello." A pause and then: "Don't you recognise me, I'm April?"

Frankly I was flabbergasted. This must have been obvious from her reaction. April had anticipated her unscheduled appearance would be a great surprise and cause for celebration. My initial response was one of shock as I looked down on a very young woman almost two feet shorter than me, skinny, good looking, who, to my western eye, looked like a schoolgirl in her early to mid-teens. For a few seconds my expression must have been one of horror. Here I was, thousands of miles from home, seriously looking for a wife, and I had found a child! I could not equate the person I was looking at with the woman I had travelled to meet. The head and face matched to the person with whom I had Skyped on many occasions and the voice sounded the same, but they were attached to such a tiny frame! In any case she was supposed to be on a different island; another flight of an hour or so was needed to get to that island, I had the ticket for that trip amongst my papers. I had expected to contact her later that evening to tell her when I would be arriving in Bacolod, I had thought it would have been me who was delivering the surprise. So who was this girl? It was April and she had turned the tables on me completely. I was utterly flummoxed. After a few seconds I began to get my act together and rallied. We had a hug and said "Hello." But the shock of her appearance had absolutely stunned me. She looked so child-like.

As we were in the taxi en route to the hotel in the Maribago barangay, I realised I could be in very serious trouble here if she was actually the age I thought she was. We would shortly be checking into a hotel together as a couple and I certainly did not want to be sharing a room with a girl aged in her mid-teens. At the check-in we would need to produce identity documents. I had my passport and asked for her identity document. She immediately produced a card which looked official and authentic. It contained her head and shoulders photo, name and date of birth. Her signature was there; there was a number and what looked like a part of an official stamp. It was about the size of a credit card and had been laminated. Provided this card was genuine then she was twenty four years old. To my eye an incredibly young looking twenty four year old. We arrived at the hotel and, when I looked at the reception staff, most of the females also looked like teenagers to me. They checked my passport and her card without comment and seemed quite content with both. I paid and was told that the category of room I had reserved was full and that we were being upgraded at no extra cost. We now had a larger room which was much closer to the beach. After a complimentary drink we were shepherded to a battery operated vehicle which drove us through the grounds to our room with a small patio area outside set with a table and two seats. The room itself was actually two large rooms. We entered from the patio into the bedroom area which contained two king sized beds with space enough for two more, beyond which was the bathroom. That was my first port of call. I had the trots, boy, did I have the trots!

What a start to a relationship! A woman who looked like a child, tiredness and diarrhoea. I looked around and found myself in a very nice split-level bathroom! It was huge, about ten metres wide and twenty metres long. I was seated on the upper level; there was a waist high screen around the rear and sides of the toilet. Facing me was a built-in double wardrobe. To the side of this were his and her sinks with plenty of space for simultaneous use, and beyond them the door back into the bedroom. Behind me was a free standing standard sized bath, a separate shower comfortably large enough for two to use and a Jacuzzi for two. Sadly it was missing a bidet and I was developing a bum like a cherry! Unfortunately, whilst the bedroom had an excellent air conditioning system, the bathroom didn't, nor was there a fan. It had a roof made of rushes and there were small spaces through which the stars could be picked out. This was supposed to keep the air fresh and circulating; an arrangement was which not up to the challenge presented.

At this point April was, happily, completely oblivious to my dilemma. However, unwittingly, she did present me with another problem which I had not anticipated. When I returned to the bedroom she was sat on one of the beds with her back resting on the pillows, legs akimbo and completely naked.

Welcome to the Philippines. Acute diarrhoea, smelly, hungry and thirsty in company with a young women demonstrating a strong desire to fully express her sexuality. Newton's third law of motion needed some serious consideration here: every action has an equal and opposite reaction. If I girded my loins and thrust I could well receive similar pressures and pleasures in return; usually a most uplifting experience. The air conditioning in the bedroom was working and, were I to take April up on her offer, the proverbial was likely to literally hit the fan with some force! Her opening gambit to me was: "Hello Daddy, come here, I want to say thank you for the flowers and chocolates." This triggered the unexpected and unlikely response of: "Not a chance. Any sudden movement from me is likely to lead to disaster."

As an aside by presenting herself this way I was immediately aware that April removed all body hair. For me this raised the issue of age again. Yes, she was an adult woman; she was in her mid-twenties (although to my eye she had the physique of girl in her mid-teens); she was at ease with her own sexuality and proud of her body. Rightly so. For me I associate pubic hair with maturity. How a woman deals with this is her call. But, in these circumstances, April's youthfulness was dramatically reinforced. Using the word 'Daddy' when speaking to me was also a shock. Was I receiving an implicit message? Was she telling me that Filipinas associate older western men with paedophile sex tourism; and she was role playing her part in a Daddy daughter scenario? From what I had heard on the flight into Cebu that was a distinct possibility. It was not a place where I put myself and these thoughts put me right off any idea of sex; just the opposite of where her mind had wandered. Was I guilty of over analysing the situation? Was my imagination running riot? Whatever, these were issues I needed to get my head around. Thank heavens a loose bowel provided a ready-made excuse. Not what either of us had wanted or anticipated.

So began a most peculiar week for two disparate souls in search of love and romance. April told me she had managed to get a week of holiday from her employer and had decided to join me in Cebu to make the most of our time together. It was also a very effective way to ensure I did not have the opportunity of seeing her in her home or work environments. Nor did I get the opportunity to be introduced to her family, friends or colleagues. Nor was she chaperoned! For a Filipina considering a long term relationship this was strange indeed according to the serious literature I had read; but just what the doctor ordered from the perspective of the lad's books. Having seen her room in the boarding house through Skype I knew it was much as one would expect. But I could not check that out. For all I knew she could be sat in someone else's room; she may not have been in a boarding house at all. But, as far as building a relationship together was concerned, we were where we were. I cancelled my flight to Bacolod and hotel reservation and we shared a room for a week, after which I had four days alone. I knew within the first couple of hours that she was unlikely to be the woman of my dreams; in all probability she felt just the same way.

However I had a more immediate issues to deal with. I had to establish what had caused the sudden digestive issue. All had been fine until leaving Hong Kong. On the incoming flight to Mactan I had drunk a couple of cups of coffee. So everything pointed to the water. At Mactan Airport I had been a little loose, once checked into the hotel room the situation became dire. In between times the only substance to pass my lips was the complimentary drink provided at the hotel reception.

Our hotel had four restaurants. One was in an area close to the entrance and was used by people attending the conference block. I never used it and don't know if it was used full-time or just for specific events. A second was on the end of a pier built out into the sea. This was primarily a fish restaurant. The quality of the food and service were high; so were the prices, but it provided both a beautiful and an intimate setting, pleasant during daylight hours, very romantic during the evenings. The other two restaurants were the ones which guests would routinely use, one being an annex of the other. The main restaurant was in the centre of the site. It was here that the breakfast buffet was served. It was possible to eat indoors or outside where there was a small stage area for evening entertainment and the resort's main swimming pool; also a bar. Next to the bar was the annex, a small area which doubled as an Italian restaurant, however, if you wanted anything beyond pizza and cappuccino you were out of luck.

After our initial parlay in the room we dressed and strolled to the main restaurant. The time was about 9.30pm. It was quiet, maybe two other tables were occupied. We ordered something to eat from a restricted menu as the kitchen had just closed. I needed something which would need little digesting and tried a local dish called halo-halo. This is an ice-cream based desert containing rice. I thought the rice might help provide a little internal stability! However, it also contained a variety of unexpected treats, mostly but not exclusively, fruit based. This one, for example, contained beans amongst pineapple, papaya, mango and melon. The cost of the food and drink within the hotel was similar to that which one would pay in a similar establishment in the west. I now know that by Philippine standards the prices were astronomical. What I found really peculiar was how few guests there were around. This was a beach resort hotel in the middle of the evening. A restaurant which would comfortably seat sixty of seventy people had five or six in it. The kitchen was closed. The cabaret area was empty. The bar, which was a good twenty yards long, had two waiters, several bar stools but no customers. The Italian restaurant was empty; closed.

Following the food we took a few steps to the bar. At that point I was still drinking alcohol but with considerable moderation. My food made its presence felt and there was another trip to the loo. We had a cocktail each and then retired. I needed to keep visiting the bathroom. Everything

I ate or drank went straight through. It was a horrible situation for both of us. I knew about local water being a likely problem and had a supply of Loperamide to cover that contingency. But it made no difference whatever. For breakfast I had coffee and some rice. The result was just the same. April left the site and returned with a local medication. I looked at the ingredients and they were virtually identical to the tablets I had. I took them but the impact was the same, nil, or at best very negligible. In temperatures constantly around 30°C I was in a position where it was important to maintain a good intake of fluids. I asked the hotel staff on several occasions if the water they used was bottled. They assured me that all the water they used and served was mineralised and filtered. I only began to see an improvement when I bought bottled mineral water off site. It took me a few days to realise that the hotel staff were perhaps being more than a little economical with the truth.

On the plus side, from my perspective, this situation did provide the opportunity to take a good look at April. I do not mean physically, in private getting her to keep her clothes on was the challenge; she was a liberated lady; good for her. I mean looking at each other in terms of any shared interests or ambitions, if we were being truthful with each other, in essence, if we had the makings of a good match. What I quickly discovered was that she enjoyed T.V. She had an addiction to Pinoy Big Brother, a programme which coincided with our trip. When this could not be found on any of the hotel T.V. channels or her laptop, it would be soap operas, a never ending stream of them. Now, in terms of light entertainment, if there is anything I can't abide it is reality T.V. and soap operas; historical dramas come a close third. We had discussed our TV likes and dislikes on Skype. What she had told me then was that she enjoyed a bit of drama, the Discovery and History channels, some sport and some comedy. But whilst I was with her it was back to back Big Brother and soaps; perhaps she considered soaps to be drama. I asked her about her work, the conversation did not take off, all I got was warehouse supervisor. She must have had some work to afford the flight to Cebu and to have her own laptop. She must also have had some autonomy to be able to free herself up for a week having only received a couple of days warning. I enquired about her education; she eventually told me that she had finished High School but had not attended University. April was a very attractive and affectionate young woman. She did remarkably well to deal with a man well over twice her age with barely controllable diarrhoea. But it became apparent quite quickly that during our online chats she had been telling me what she believed I wanted to hear. The reality was somewhat different. She came across as being a pleasant and genuine person but she did not have an enquiring mind; she had no interest whatever in further educating herself and her social horizons were extremely limited. Coupled with this it was very difficult to prise her away from the TV. Except at meal times, which she did her best to plan around the TV schedules, she was glued to it. Our room was about twenty-five yards from the beach. We visited it together once. She went offsite to shop twice; once for Loperamide, and was only away briefly on each occasion, no more than fifteen minutes. There was a small art gallery in the hotel; she showed no interest in visiting it. Each evening the hotel laid on a cultural event, music, dancing or local folk lore, etc. She only attended one of these and that occurred on a Sunday because the Pinoy Big Brother schedule had changed! She would probably make similar negative remarks about me. She would have every right to. My time was largely spent between the patio, where I could read without disturbance from the TV, and the bathroom. We were both looking for love; we were both prepared to deliver, but the other baggage we each carried would have made life difficult for both of us. I very quickly knew this relationship would be going nowhere. April did not seem to notice this; or maybe she did not want to do anything which might become an issue of self-esteem, for either of us. Amor-propio, again. Perhaps she considered she would be jeopardising a few days of luxury living. There were occasions during the week we were together when there was intense intimacy, but we had to negotiate those occasions very delicately. For much of the time it would have been foolhardy in the extreme for me to have engaged in any vigorous activity. I did manage to provide April with one new and enjoyable experience. We regularly showered or took a Jacuzzi together. We both found the experiences pleasurable, stimulating and satisfying. But, for the most part, we needed to be sensible. We did what we could when we could, enjoying what we could of each other. For me, even a visit to the sea or one of the swimming pools, needed to be taken extremely gently. At the end of the week, when she departed, we agreed I would visit her home island a couple of months later. I went along with this as I enjoy travel, had kept my diary clear and thought she might be a bit different in her home environment. We both acknowledged that I would be much better company once I had recovered full health. In retrospect I think her agreement to this was probably an effort to avoid any difference of opinion and to avoid any embarrassment, either way. On my part I was also thinking this would be an opportunity to arrange to meet someone else should April and I decide we were non-runners in the marriage stakes.

I learned a couple of things as a consequence of my experiences with April. Firstly it is not unusual for a Filipina to refer to her partner as Daddy. It is a term of affection sometimes used by established couples who have children. Once married with children it is not uncommon for a Philippine man to refer to his partner as 'Mother' or similar. It is also a statement of what a Filipina expects her lifetime partner to become; the father of her children. However, the first time I came across it, it just reinforced my concerns around the differences in our ages and worries that the word Daddy fed into some kind of fantasy around sex between the young and old.

The second regards the sex act itself and is reinforced by Philippine experiences beyond April. Earlier we flagged up possible concerns that a Filipina may have when presented with a western man. She might worry of a potential risk given their natural differences in body size when this is translated to the bedroom. Might the western man be too big for the smaller Filipina body; or too heavy? The size of the male erection is something I have never researched or had discussions about. With lovemaking I grew up believing in a general principle of one third in, one third out and one third going in and out. As men will differ in size adjustments will need to be made as appropriate to the element which remains out! This, of course, assumes all women are the same size; they are not. From my very limited experience I would suggest that a Filipina and a western man making love together need to proceed with caution initially. They will need to negotiate this issue and discover what is appropriate for them. There may be some minor concerns around length particularly if the man engorges further immediately prior to ejaculation. However that is only a part of the story. There is the issue of girth and that will not be so easily dealt with. Initially it is important to ensure both parties are very well lubricated and that care is taken until the bodies adjust to each other. Whilst this issue will not be resolved overnight, even a very hectic night, in time a mutually comfortable resolution to the issue will develop. From a male perspective one needs to keep in mind that the female body has evolved to create life and the birthing process creates far more significant issues around dilation, etc. than accommodating a man ever will. The experiences I have had around oral and anal sex suggest that the former presents no problem; the latter has never been attempted.

There are a couple of other issues in this area that a man travelling to the Philippines needs to consider. Firstly, sex education in the Philippines seems to be non-existent. The Filipinas I have met and chatted with have no more than a baseline understanding of anatomy and physiology. The link between a pregnancy and periods stopping is about as far as knowledge in this area goes. The women I have met have all been in their twenties; some have had previous relationships, some haven't. None of them knew anything about contraception. The concept of sexual health care is an unknown and, if I raised the issue, something which they backed away from quickly whilst demonstrating shyness and ignorance in fairly equal measures. They may be quick to learn but their starting point is very basic indeed. Unless you are finding a partner in a bar and paying for the experience then, whilst you may find a willing partner, don't expect to find someone with much confidence and certainly don't expect her to take the lead in the bedroom.

Finally the man needs to be aware that, just as he may have concerns over the genuineness of his Filipina girlfriend, so she will also have concerns about him. With significant age difference comes concern about the ability to perform horizontally! Future family is very likely to be an important issue for her and the last thing she needs to deal with is

Mr. Floppy! Whilst she is likely to show a great deal of naiveté, she will want to find out, simply put, that the man she is considering as a husband is able to deliver in the bedroom. Some unfortunate chaps can't, which could be the reason for him travelling so far. So, if she is treating her older boyfriend seriously, she will want an answer to this question; particularly where the age gap is significant and she considers the risks to be higher.

> "Water, water, everywhere, nor not a drop to drink."
> (S.T. Coleridge: The Rime of the Ancient Mariner.)

I think the problem I faced on the first visit to the Philippines deserves a fuller explanation perchance other travellers experience similar difficulties. I am happy to announce that, after many visits, I have the solution to the issue. The cause of the trouble has been identified and a solution put in place which has been tested and works. When I visit the Philippines nowadays I am the proud owner of a pretty reliable digestive tract.

As initially identified the issue is water. However it is an issue that extends much further than one might imagine.

When the Philippines gained their independence from the U.S.A. in 1946 they were bequeathed a public water system begun and developed by the Spanish colonisers which the U.S. colonisers maintained. It was a system which, only thirty years earlier, had been described as a disaster. Doubtless there have been many major improvements. In the seventies the water supply system was privatised. When you visit the Philippines nowadays you will find there are three kinds of water available for public consumption. There is the privatised system which delivers the regular water supply; tap water, etc. This should still be used for nothing beyond washing, showering and flushing toilets. It should never be consumed in any way and avoided whenever possible. The World Bank Report of 2005 tells us that, in the Philippines:

> Water quality usually does not meet the standards set by the national government, especially in urban areas. As a result, waterborne diseases remain to be a severe public health concern in the country. About 4,200 people die each year due to contaminated drinking water.

If the system creates 4,200 deaths per annum consider how many illnesses it will be responsible for causing and how many life years will be lost. There are reasons for life expectancy rates in the Philippines being so much lower than they are in the west and this is one of them.

15 years later the www.water.org website tells us that:

- Out of 105 million Filipinos, nearly seven million rely on unimproved, unsafe and unsustainable water sources and more than 24 million lack access to improved sanitation.
- Those without a sanitary toilet facility at home face a number of unattractive choices, including venturing out at night or suffering the embarrassment of asking to use the toilet of a neighbour.
- While about 75% of surveyed Filipinos expressed an interest in a water and sanitation loan, previously few banks or microfinance institutions offered loans specifically tailored to this purpose.
- In 2014, water.org expanded WaterCredit … We now work with 25 different microfinance institutions, providing philanthropic and technical support to build their capacity to provide a variety of water and sanitation solutions in urban and rural communities.
- From 2015 to 2017, partners conducted research, trained staff, designed their loan products and executed lending pilots.
- We are expanding our partnerships, and by the end of 2019, we aim to reach more than three million people with safe water and sanitation.
- In addition, we are developing innovative approaches to working with municipal water utilities and developing new toilet models, so even more low-income Filipinos can enjoy safe water and the dignity of a toilet.

I visited my G.P. within a couple of days of returning home from the first trip. She told me that Loperamide was the only known cure and that it might take a week or two back in the U.K. before my system returned to normal. It actually took three weeks and I was in the process of having samples analysed before my system recovered of its own volition. I had continued with the Loperamide throughout that period.

When I asked my wife what happens at her family home when the toilet is needed she told me it would be same as when she lived there ten years ago – you make sure you choose a spot where there are some big leaves!

Given this is the state of play you may wish to consider the likely issues around hygiene and hotels and restaurants in the Philippines. They are the places you will use and will stay at; however their staff will be drawn from the local community and share the prevailing norms and values of that community along with its attitude towards hygiene. On our last visit to the country we stayed at our usual hotel for twenty nights. The hotel pool was closed on three separate days. The reason was the same each time. Local people, using the hotel facilities for a day or half day, had taken their unnappied babies into the pool for 'selfies' and the baby had pooped in the pool. It is very unlikely anything like that would occur in a western hotel. If it did there would be much apology and embarrassment and it would not happen a second time. Here it meant the pool being closed for cleaning and the introduction of chemicals into the water which needed to be left overnight to properly sanitise the water.

Let's get back to the drinking water supply issue. You will find there is bottled mineral water. This should be the only type of water you drink and use for cleaning the teeth and rinsing out the mouth. Even then, if you drink from the bottle, you will be taking a risk as you will know nothing about the chemical content of the plastic bottle or how it has been manufactured. The risks of drinking from plastic bottles are becoming better known in the west. The current evidence suggests these risks to be modest. But you are not in the developed world so expect manufacturing standards to be different and the risks to be different. Not only that but you should be sure to buy from a reputable source and to open the bottle yourself. The reason for doing this is to check you are getting a genuine, new and properly sealed bottle of mineral water. This is a poor country. You need to protect yourself from the individuals who will take an empty water bottle, refill it from goodness knows where, and screw the top down tightly. They want to give the impression it is factory sealed. It is very simple to check this provided you know that is necessary. If you buy water in a shop, restaurant or bar be sure you ask for it to be served with the cap intact.

There is a third source of water. Locally this is referred to either as mineralised water or filtered water, terms I had not previously encountered in this context; the Philippines are full of surprises. As the consumer you need to make sure you are getting mineral water, not mineralised water or filtered water. I suspect the word 'mineralised' has been adopted because it is so similar to 'mineral', the intention being to suggest they are one and the same thing. They are not. But, to the unknowing, no difference will be anticipated. You have to check. Mineral water is plentiful. You will find it at any general store, even at roadside stalls, and you can find brand names which you recognise. What makes this situation more challenging is that the mineralised water is also plentiful and can be obtained from most of the same suppliers, where it is stacked on the same shelves and priced similarly. You have to check the label even if you buy water because you recognise the brand name as being a product you are familiar with. I have not seen any reports to date of forged labels being placed on bottles of water but it would not surprise me. It is your body the water is entering so it is in your own interest to be certain you are getting proper water; particularly if you have children to consider. You are in a place where false claims are common place and often not illegal.

Take the issue of a pharmacy. In the Philippines there are two types, each equally legitimate and above board. Following the name of the store it will say either 'pharmacy' or 'generic pharmacy'. The latter provide medications at much lower prices. However, whilst there are some excellent generic versions of many prescription drugs, there are also thousands of sham copies. How can you spot the difference? You probably can't unless you are a pharmacist.

Probably the easiest relevant example to provide here is the internet trade in pills to help the male erection, Cialis, Levitra, Viagra, etc. If you buy online you are likely to find you are dealing with a website in one part of the world but, when the tablets arrive, they come from a supplier in another part of the world. They are unlikely to be in a box and equally unlikely to provide an S.P.C. (Summary of Product Characteristics), which is a legal requirement in the U.K. Visually the tablet will look identical to the genuine version of what it purports to be; they will need to be viewed side by side with a genuine pill before any difference can be spotted. It is only when, having taken the tablet and discovered it has had no impact, that the purchaser will realise they have no idea what they have actually taken. The likelihood is that you have taken a sugar pill or something similarly innocuous, a more appropriate word for innocuous in this instance might be impotent! But, whatever the contents, they were not fit for purpose. To whom are you going to take your complaint? So, when in the Philippines, stay with the proper pharmacy. Pay a bit more and get want you need rather than gamble on your medication being useless.

Back to the purveyors of mineralised water. Their TV and magazine advertising will tell you their product is of a higher quality than mineral water. They claim to have supplemented their product with a selection of additional minerals which will give you that extra zip; will add zest to your life, etc., etc. Don't let them fool you. From the limited information I can track down, mineralised water is just a very basic naturally occurring water which the manufacturer *should* purify before supplementing with the mix of minerals which give their product its unique raison d'être! Oddly, beyond the information put out by the manufacturers, who will have a significant bias, verifiable information is scarce. I suspect that mineral water is water that has been processed properly and guaranteed genuine whilst mineralised water is mineral water which has not received the same level of validation. What I do know from painful personal experience is that when I am told an establishment uses mineralised water or filtered water I consume their produce at my peril. Half an hour or so later I will begin to feel minor twinges in the lower part of the abdomen. That means the clock has started; I have about thirty minutes to go before swift access to a bathroom will become necessary, access which will need to be maintained for the following two or three hours at least. It is also a reminder to ensure you have packed a stock of Loperamide for your trip.

When you are operating in a country where you cannot trust the domestic or business water supply you have to take charge and make every effort to ensure your water supply is safe. If you don't it is you who will carry the consequences. There is a cost to bottled mineral water but it is modest, maybe 10p-20p per litre; a few pesos/cents.

I suspect the cause of my problem does not lie with way the establishments I have visited use filtered water; rather my system has an acute reaction to something which the filtration system does not remove. The likelihood is they will bulk buy what they consider to be the lowest cost safe option. The difficulties I have had probably reflect the sensitivity of my digestive tract. If that were not the case then the problem would be much more widespread. Or maybe this is a subject which rarely gets such an in-depth analysis! I have had more contact with local people than tourists during my trips and have never heard anything negative said about filtered water; if anything the locals seem to be proud of their product. However I needed to accept that this was my problem and I needed to deal with it. The problem did not just manifest itself at the hotels I used, and I have visited many now from unstarred up to luxury, the problem manifests itself wherever there is water, which means being vigilant everywhere.

Dealing with it is very simple. Only use bottled mineral water which you have sourced for yourself. However living your life this way places major limits on how you operate in the Philippines. The problems which can be created when you are unable to identify the source of your water are serious and the uses of water which you either don't think about or are unable to do anything about are many. Anything you eat with or off or drink from will have been washed in water; it should be properly dried. This raises two issues. Firstly, the quality of water used to wash it; secondly, the drying process. You are in a tropical climate so cutlery and crockery will dry naturally in a matter of a few minutes, so it may not be wiped dry. This means there will be a residue of substances left when the water has evaporated off. Should a tea towel be used to dry these items, the tea towel itself will have been washed in local water. The risk is small but it is there. Any food which contains a sauce or gravy will contain water. There is some fresh cow's milk available in the Philippines but not much. North and north east of Manila the farming of buffalo for milk is happening, but most of the milk used is imported into the country in powder form. To reconstitute it water is used. When a Filipino refers to fresh milk they will usually mean powdered milk which has recently been reconstituted. So, every time you use milk, the likelihood is that you are consuming water which you cannot source. This means no cereal at breakfast time. No beverages is a given; even if you do not take milk in your tea or coffee, they are made from water which you cannot source. It means no complimentary glass of water with any meal. Rice in the Philippines is ubiquitous; the Filipino diet consists of rice (bugas) and/or noodles (pancit) with everything. These are the major staple foods of the country. How are they cooked? They are boiled in water and absorb some of it; again water which cannot be sourced. This is a country where the climate to westerners is hot and humid, a nice refreshing iced drink might be the order of the day, but think again. Ice is frozen water and you do not know where it has originated; the purpose of the ice cube it is melt into your drink and chill it. It could well also see you running for the bathroom. There is water content in ice cream which was reinforced to me on a recent trip. Salads and fresh fruit are washed in water. Now I am not saying that all these various exposures to water will create digestive problems all the time. What I am saying is that so much of one's normal diet involves the use of water that, if you are susceptible to the local water, you will continually have problems. All the above have given me a difficulty at one time or another. It has only been by rigorously controlling sources of water that I have been able to get on top of my digestive tract issues. As you have seen in the beginning it was a major source of trouble, apart from being highly embarrassing. I have now taken a position where I will buy my own water and only eat food that is thoroughly baked, i.e. pizza, or is fried. These are not traditionally thought of as healthy options in the west where my usual diet is full of fresh fruit, salad and vegetables but, for a week or two, what would be generally thought of as the unhealthy option becomes the safe and, ultimately, the healthy option.

Before leaving the subject of water and protecting your health I will give a brief mention to other instances where water based problems may develop. The obvious one, as mentioned in passing earlier, is the swimming pool. The hotels in which I have stayed and visited all seem to have plenty of pool staff. They take a pride in their work and generally do a good job. This means tending to the needs of their guests and looking after the pool. They will regularly clean the surrounds collecting any debris. Most of the pools I have used have trees around them and there is plenty of bird and animal life around. Any leaves, twigs or wildlife poop which fall into the water will be cleared up quite quickly and effectively. However, at the beach hotels I have used and visited, after early morning, before the pools are open to guests, I have never seen anything being done to check the safety of the water in the pool. I have only seen checks during the day at an airport hotel I have used and at a place close to the family home of my wife called Lalimar which gets discussed much more later on in this story. Whilst the people using the pool tend to behave well, very few will shower before getting in. These are pools in beach resorts. A lot of games are played in pools; there are also a plethora of excited children jumping around and having a whale of a time. Accidents must happen. When I visit the Philippines I tend to spend quite a lot of time in the pool. Apart from enjoying swimming it is a matter of staying reasonably cool. There have been a couple of occasions when I have picked up ear infections; so has my wife. This has never happened in the U.K., where we will use local swimming pools from time to time. I can only put these infections down to a lack of pool hygiene. You also need to bear in mind that if you get an ear infection it is likely to give you some serious pain during your flights home. Ear infections and changes in air pressure do not sit well together.

A further exacerbating factor is the clothing Filipinos and holidaying Orientals wear for swimming. In the U.K. a man will wear the traditional trunks or shorts and a woman will wear a purpose made one or two-piece swimming costume. The Philippines tourist industry is targeted at Japan and South Korea. These tourists and the local people know about the power of the sun. Some will wear what we westerners would view as traditional costumes. However many will make sure they are well covered; particularly children. The tourists and more affluent locals will wear rash guards which consist of a full bodied top, shorts and sometimes, a hat. The overall effect is something like a frogman suit with short legs, but a little more colourful. Away from the main centres, particularly in the more rural areas, they cover up with normal clothes. In consequence the swimming pool can become something of a place where local people wash their clothes whilst wearing them. Once outside the main tourist areas a hotel with a swimming pool is likely to attract people who will get in and play or swim without changing at all. Afterwards the high temperatures will dry them out fairly swiftly. But this practice seriously heightens the risk of swimming pool water becoming contaminated. It is also rare to find the local people showering before getting into the pool. The result is that it is like swimming in water which looks and feels as though it has been discharged from a washing machine.

It is important to fully consider the implications of water so, before leaving the subject, I will conclude with a few comments on sea-water, rivers, wells and aquifers. If you leave your hotel these are issues you need to be aware of, particularly if you are a sea swimmer or diver.

To begin we need to cast our minds back to the state of our country a couple of hundred years ago. Public health as a science had yet to be discovered. To state the obvious, water flows downhill; it is a matter of gravity. Two hundred years ago all of the rubbish, including human waste, (here we go again!), created by the people living at the top and on the slopes of hills would be buried. It would then break down gradually over time and leach into the water supply. Water did not receive the treatment it does today. As it made its way downwards it would flow through whatever was in its path; fields, other housing, maybe an early factory, farm or church yard. During its downward journey debris from various sources would be collected and join the stream. As the water from one hillside joined that from others streams were formed and then rivers. Rivers which, in those days, were the direct providers of energy to power the mills of the industrial revolution. Population density was much higher in valleys than on hillsides because that was where the mills and therefore the work was located. Towns and cities developed. With them came an increased demand for water; in those days this was, by and large, water that had not been treated. A working example of the consequences of this can be seen in the village of Haworth, West Yorkshire, the home of the famous Brontë family. The Parsonage, where they lived for many years, is located close to the top of one side of the Worth valley. Below the Parsonage is the church and its graveyard, then the top of the village with a population density increasing as you get closer to the valley floor where the textile mills used to be. This might explain why the Reverend Patrick Brontë, outlived his literary children. They were more outgoing. Whilst he stayed on top of the hill, evangelising and excreting above his flock, who were in the factories and homes below; this was also where his family would be active. It was also where people were routinely consuming the pearls of wisdom he wittingly and unwittingly delivered. The likelihood is that he routinely consumed water with far fewer contaminants than his offspring who shared the risks of most local people. A look through any graveyard will demonstrate how quickly life expectancy rates increase once a community/society gets on top of diseases delivered through water born viruses, etc. carried in rivers and streams.

In the west there have been major improvements in hygiene led by the sciences of health promotion and public health. I grew up in a small suburban town in an area where textiles were manufactured. Two rivers met close to the town centre. We walked to school over bridges which crossed these rivers and saw that their colour changed daily. Of course what was happening was that the upstream factories, which had originally been built by the riverside to utilise the water flow as a source of energy, were also finding the river to be a very convenient means of disposing of dyes and goodness knows what else; discharging directly into the river. As kids we found this amusing, we used to play guessing games about what colour the water would be. One of the rivers would be bright orange one day and the other purple. Within a few yards of their confluence was a waterfall which quickly mixed the colours together. As the river left the town it became a peculiar muddy greyish colour. The next day one of the rivers might be blue and the other yellow creating a river flowing out of town which was coloured green. This was the reality in our developed world going to the early 1970s. It demonstrates how recently we have begun to get our act together in the west. The state of health promotion and public health in the Philippines is way behind this.

The family of my wife live in a tiny village of around five hundred people; less than a hundred homes when the size of the Philippine family is accounted for. It is close to the top of a significant mountain range. There is only one road leading into it. That is unsurfaced; impassable when it rains and can only be accessed by scramble type motorbikes and, possibly the more adventurous/reckless drivers using four wheel drive vehicles. When I visit I apologise because I will not touch any of their water or food. I know that by turning down their hospitality I am being rude but I also know that members of the family will periodically disappear around the back of the building. I assume that is the toilet area. There is no sewage piping in the village, there is no access road which could be used for a vehicle which might service septic tanks. So I ask myself, where do the waste products go? The answer is that they don't go anywhere very quickly. They will gradually sink into the ground where they will break down and are very gradually either absorbed into the earth where they will become food for local plant and animal life; or they flow downhill. To visit their home means a journey of two to three hours on the back of a motor bike. The journey may only be thirty miles from the nearest main town and hotel, but all bar a couple of those miles are on unmetalled roads, in most places these are little more than dirt tracks. Part of the terrain is so poor one usually has to walk. I do not like appearing discourteous to my in-laws, but saying 'no' to their hospitality is preferable to a return journey of two to three hours over uneven surfaces with a loose bowel and only the roadside as a toilet. I also prefer not to share their food as it is a relatively scarce resource and they can make far better use of it than by fattening up an already overweight son-in-law!

A women I met a few years back lived in one of the poorest parts of Cebu City, Mambaling. When I visited her home I found it to be poor but clean and tidy. The family had a pride in the place they lived. However, waste was discharged directly into the streets. There was nowhere else for it to go. It was the same principle as slopping out in a prison. Only instead of flushing human waste away it was thrown onto waste ground from where it flowed directly into watercourses and into the sea a few hundred yards away. A few open areas of waste land acted as open sewers. There was a lot of homelessness. Accommodation was in tin huts and the population density high even by Philippine standards. The local river was called the Jai Alia. It carried with it the waste discharged from about five miles of the city including some slum living as it made its way to the sea. People live by the riverside when it is not in flood. They live beneath the bridges that go over the river. Twenty or thirty people will co-habit beneath a road bridge because it provides shelter from both sun and rain. After Mambaling is the sea; the industrial and port area of Cebu City. I am no expert on sanitary engineering but have yet to see any evidence of treatment plants or any attempt to clean this water. Waste products drain directly into the river which, in the case of Cebu City, means water courses which very quickly drain into the sea. You may think I am describing some kind of hell. By western standards that may be the case. But there are positives. Do a quick search on YouTube for Mambaling. You will find what appears to be a fairly happy community; you will also see some of their daily problems. They too have issues with the water; given the conditions they live in it is hardly surprising. Up to 20% of their lives are likely to be spent with diarrhoea; it is part of life, get used to it! These are normal living conditions for millions of Filipinos. In such conditions consider also the pointlessness of teaching children to wash their hands after a toilet visit. All that could be on their hands has already passed through their bodies. The risk of picking up a health hazard from water sourced externally is much greater than the risk in not washing ones hands at all.

To conclude this section the point I am making is simple and obvious. Look for water everywhere; it does not just suddenly arrive in your body; it has a source and you need to very carefully check that source before drinking it. Carry plenty of Loperamide. It will work for the occasional disturbance, if you routinely consume local water, knowingly or unknowingly, it will not be effective and, in the medium to long term, your health is likely to seriously suffer.

From April to May.

April's flight back to her home island left Mactan Airport around four in the morning with final check-in being an hour earlier. I took her to the airport. We kissed goodbye and confirmed I would travel to her island a couple of months later. I then returned to the hotel. There were four days and three and a bit nights before my flight home to the U.K. departed; four days to have a look around the area and to try to get my digestive system prepared for a long haul flight back to dear old Blighty!

I have to admit that it was April's departure which allowed me to have four good days. Good in the sense that I could inject a bit of selfishness into getting my health back in order. There was no need to be so sensitive to the needs of another; using the bathroom and the associated rigmarole assumed a relatively minor status. Following her departure also meant my daily routine was freed from the diktat of TV schedules. If Big Brother or one of her soaps was showing, April would not leave the room, she would be glued to the set the only breaks being meal times (swiftly and reluctantly) and sleep (whilst the housemates slept). For different reasons I had also been stuck on-site. However by the time she departed I was beginning to get a handle on what was causing the problem and had eliminated some of the more obvious sources of filtered/mineralised water from my diet. That said I still did not know about the powdered milk and maintained a false assumption that, provided water had been boiled, drinking tea and coffee would be safe. It wasn't. Either there were contaminants in the water which were not killed off by boiling, or, much more likely, the water was not boiled properly. However I had gained sufficient trust in my system to risk leaving the confines of the hotel more regularly. To some extent the way in which I began to take care with my diet happened by accident. For two or three days before April's departure the only water I had drunk came from a local shop outside the grounds of the hotel, and that had led to a significant improvement. Immediately outside the hotel was a small but busy village which had developed in large part to service the tourist trade; it was really little more than a ribbon development alongside a hectic but quite narrow two lane highway, with no footpaths, which provided access to around a dozen hotels from zero star to luxury with plenty of good quality and some sleazy room lets in the neighbourhood. The hotels were almost all beach front, the room lets were wherever they could be squeezed in. There were fast food restaurants and a few bars along with the local type of small shop known as a sari-sari store; we would call then a corner shop, maybe, a small general store, but often they were very small, barely a kiosk. Oddly to my western eye there were no night clubs or discotheques, nor anything directly comparable with what one would find in the typical western holiday resort. It all had a strange feel to me. I was expecting a thriving night life but in this particular neck of the woods it just did not happen. There was a Karaoke Bar frequented by one of two local ladies who dressed very skimpily, but it was rare to see many people there. The biggest attractions appeared to be a very large screen TV and the services I thought the ladies might offer. I never went inside so I cannot be more specific. Of the restaurants; well, similar to what we discovered inside the hotel, they were closed by ten in the evening. A few bars stayed open well into the night, but the ones I went into were just that. Bars. They played some contemporary music, served drinks and provided bar snacks. The staff, whilst mostly young women, were certainly not a part of the sexual services sector. A ten minute taxi ride away was a busy shopping area, Grand Mall, Mactan, (which is a grand name for a modest sized Mall), but even here there was no evidence at all of any kind of night-life. Everything was geared to services for local people, because this was the real Philippines where the local folks conducted their routine business and did their day-to-day shop; at a modest shopping complex based on the traditional U.S. style of mall. It had three levels. The experience was fairly similar to the U.K. weekly shopping experience. A place designed for the regular citizen, not the wealthy or the tourist. I was still drinking alcohol at this time and discovered that I could buy a 1½ litre bottle of vodka or gin for the same price that I was paying for a single shot at the hotel. I bought a 70mm bottle of each along with mineral water, branded cola and orange drinks, (orange pop is known locally as Royal; I have no idea why; perhaps it is the local brand name!) I had avoided drinking much alcohol whilst with April. The trots were bad enough, I did not want to risk anything which might further impede the horizontal jog and certainly did not want to give the dreaded brewer's droop any encouragement! But I also thought there was a possibility that alcohol might kill off any germs that had collected in my gut.

From the mall supermarket to the Mooon café (yes, that is the correct spelling); which has now become a familiar haunt, a great little restaurant, part of a local chain specialising in Mexican food, and then to the taxi rank outside the Mall. On returning to the hotel security stopped the taxi and looked inside, asked to see my key; they then allowed me through. The taxi dropped me almost beyond the reception area, I retrieved my shopping from the boot, and headed to the room; now a huge space occupied by one person. I expected to need the loo. I did, but the feeling in my gut was trivial compared to past days. I was not back to normal by some way but was much improved. Things were looking up.

Amongst the eateries close to the hotel was an excellent restaurant, the Maribago Grill. The first evening following April's departure I ate there. They sat me at a table next to a fence which provided the boundary between the restaurant and the road through the village. This meant that locals outside the restaurant were able to try to engage me directly in conversation. The first was a young lad who looked about ten or eleven years old. He asked me if I wanted his sister for the night. A quick reminder of the realities inside and outside the hotel. I shifted table and returned to my room an hour or so later digestively hopeful but anticipating tummy trouble. At the Mooon I had consumed some nachos and a beef taco washed down with cola without ice. In the evening all I had eaten was some chicken with fried rice. When I returned from the Mooon I had drunk a lot of mineral water and fizzy drinks but no alcohol. Before the evening meal I had had a large vodka and tonic with more of the same during the meal. On returning to the hotel their bar was empty as usual except for the staff (most peculiar at nine in the evening) so I returned to the private stock in the room. The impact on the digestive system of the evening meal was much the same as at lunchtime. By the time ten o'clock arrived I was feeling much better than I had done for the past week, slightly merry after the vodka and tonic; I was on holiday and ready to boogie. Well as ready as you tend to be at my age! These days being turned off can be as exciting as being turned on! I decided to visit a bar I had spotted opposite the Maribago Grill. This was open air and could seat around fifty people comfortably. When I walked in I saw three young women working the bar and eight or ten customers.

I know earlier we have discussed bar girls and paying a bar fine to get their personal attention. Whilst this bar had rooms for rent it was not that kind of bar. (The Karaoke Bar I described earlier served that purpose and was located between this bar and the hotel entrance; I was routinely cruised as I walked between the two, except during the mornings. Either activity the night before prevented this or the ladies had discovered there was little call for the alleviation of early morning stiffness.)

This was a regular bar at the back of which the owners had a few rooms which were available for rent to tourists. They served drinks and light snacks, played music and effectively ran what was a fairly quiet bar. The measures they served were at least twice the size of those provided at the hotel and their prices were around half the price. I guess this explains why it was so rare to see anyone drinking at the hotel bar. As in the rest of the world drinks off-site were much cheaper than in the tourist hotel and the atmosphere was better. I had two or three drinks and returned to my room for a good long night's sleep. The best I had had since leaving home.

The following morning I had breakfast and was back to the bathroom within half an hour.

It was at this point that I began to seriously question the hotel's attitude to water and the information it was providing to guests; or at least to this guest! That morning and preceding day I had consumed breakfast and, within half an hour, was struggling. At lunchtime the previous day I had consumed fried food at the Mooon café and plenty of non-alcoholic liquids sourced outside the hotel. During the evening I had a meal off-site and plenty of alcoholic liquid, none of which was sourced at the hotel. Apart from breakfast time, whilst systems had not returned to normal, there was a significant improvement. So the problem had to be breakfast. The next morning I stayed with processed hot food, avoided liquids completely, and had no problem.

During the remaining days I used the hotel internet to check April had made the trip home and that all was well with her. I took a couple of trips to major shopping malls in Cebu City. I am a typical male shopper and was as excited about the shops as I was about Pinoy Big Brother. I really made the trips to alleviate the boredom, to see what the attraction was, to experience local transport and to generally begin to understand the lie of the land. Big city malls were the same as the small one near the hotel; the only difference being one of scale. However they were fairly obviously pick-up spots as I got a lot of eye contact and the occasional "Hello" from local young women, something which would never happen in the local Sainsbury's or Tesco! This had not occurred at Grand Mall. Maybe it was too close to home or maybe it is too small a venue to generate sufficient numbers of potential partners!

What I did regularly see when visiting these Malls were couples where the man was much older than his female partner. Whilst all the women were Filipinas in these significant age-gap relationships, only around a quarter of the men were local. A good half appeared to be western, the remainder being Oriental but not Filipino. I also saw a few western women well into middle age accompanied by Filipino men who were much younger. The first time I noticed the age-gap phenomena was when I saw a tall man who I think was Korean. He was well into his sixties and was walking away from me with a girl I initially took to be his grand-daughter. My initial thought was that she was a teenager. They were holding hands as they strolled through the Mall pushing a pram. When they turned back and walked towards me I saw the woman was probably a similar age to April, early to mid-twenties, they were wearing the rings to indicate marriage and had a little boy of eighteen months or so doing his best to trot alongside them; presumably their son. When I first saw this it looked very odd. But, over the years I have now been visiting the Philippines it is something I have seen so frequently that it has ceased to merit comment. However it is something I cannot remember ever seeing in the U.K. I thought about the implications of this for me and any future partner when we lived in the U.K. I have to say my anticipation was we would get a few negative comments. Whilst this issue does not merit comment in the Philippines; back home we would continually be seen by British people who had never previously witnessed such a significant age-gap in a relationship. However, as I look back, we may get the odd glance but that has been it apart from one curious incident. I have involvement with a couple of voluntary groups. Both organise meetings with speakers and one holds a monthly social. Those regularly attending the social event are mostly young adults; mid-thirties and younger. That includes the age of my wife. When she first arrived in the U.K. I was keen for her to meet people of a similar age to herself and to make a few friends and saw this group as being a logical place to take her. However, on the three or four visits we made we were generally ignored. On the last occasion we attended, the 12-15 other attendees did not acknowledge our presence at all. We were completely ignored by everyone. After a drink we got up and left having been there for around half an hour. I had expected more enlightened behaviour from a group of supposedly well educated people mostly in their twenties and early thirties. However this has been the only occasion where we have felt deliberately excluded.

The taxi rides from Maribago into the city took me through the suburbs and many different housing areas. The type of housing was rarely more than tin huts or small wooden shacks. The ones near the edge of the sea were really crammed in, some constructed on top of poles and actually built out over the sea. What really struck me was the number of people on the roads and streets. Until late in the evening and from early morning the numbers of people just chatting or walking back and forth was massively more than I have experienced anywhere else in the world. I began to recognise elements of Philippine life which I had read about. When several people live together in a hut the only way to find any space is to go outside. Once there it is likely you will socialise with those around you. It was quite normal to find a child of ten or eleven looking after two or three younger siblings. Initially I was sure a parent would have been around and it was obvious that the older child was in charge and the younger ones knew their place; nowadays I am not at all sure about this. It is considered the job of older children to look after siblings whilst parents generate income or are otherwise occupied. Around the hotel there were beggars everywhere. Immediately one left the hotel gates someone would hit on you. And immediately means just that. It was not a matter of seconds, it was the second you were off the grounds of the hotel! It did not matter what you said or did they would persist. After getting a bit wound up by these people refusing to take 'no' for answer I took to ignoring them altogether. Some saw this as a challenge and would walk alongside me constantly twittering questions around their perception of my needs and offering the solutions they could provide, before backing off. As they did this I realised that, as they lost sight of their own home territory, they were effectively handing me over to someone else, so, during a walk of a mile or so, I would be hassled by four or five different people; a process which would be reversed during the return trip. Perhaps there is a code amongst the locals that you stick to your own territory. The surrounds of the hotel formed a ribbon development and you only got clear of beggars once you were clear of buildings. Even then youngsters would appear from out of the undergrowth; however they were more interested in who you were and why you were there. They usually had a smile on their faces and a few words of English but, if you engaged in conversation, it would normally end with a hand being held out. Whatever the reason you were pretty well guaranteed to have company if you are walking alone and they would see you as a potential source of income. As a man the usual offers were women, transport and laundry services, in that order. I didn't want any of them.

As my trip drew to an end I packed my bags, returned to the airport and made my way back home. On balance it had been a very strange trip but I had, without really realising it, been on a steep learning curve.

Once back home my diary was cleared, another flight booked with an online reservation at a hotel in the town where April lived; well, close to the town. Whilst she had recommended a town centre hotel with a small swimming pool on the roof, which was close to her room, I preferred a place just out of town which was on the coast, on a sandy beach and had a large swimming pool and on-site amenities for the tourist. I confirmed this to her and she disappeared.

I was in the U.K. and she was in the Philippines, so what do I mean 'she disappeared'? Well, subsequent to my return home, we had exchanged a few messages on the dating website and had a chat on Skype as I was planning the next visit. Then her profile disappeared from the website and her Skype contact no longer functioned. I knew she used Facebook as we had, very occasionally, chatted there. That profile was being used, there was not much posted, but the sidebar on my Facebook account told me that April's account was being accessed four or five times a week. After a couple of weeks I sent her a message on Facebook asking if she was okay. I was immediately blocked.

I was now in a position where I had a return flight booked from the U.K. to Cebu and accommodation reserved at a beach resort just north of Bacolod, on a different island an hour or so fight away from Cebu. The only reason for visiting Bacolod was to meet April, her family and friends; no April meant a pointless trip. Whilst the flight to Cebu had been booked and paid for, the onward flight to Bacolod had not been purchased. Fortunately, when reserving the accommodation, it was done through a website that allowed free cancellations until seven days prior to travel, so there was wriggle room there. I went back to the dating website and had a serious look around at the profiles again. Amongst them I found a profile which contained April's photographs but now under a new name and a new city. Rightly or wrongly I immediately assumed that, not only had April duped me, I had also been scammed for a week of good living; if that is the right term for watching soaps and Big Brother at someone else's expense. On reflection it is possible someone copied her photos from the website and re-used them to support a fake profile; but, with everything else that had happened, that does not seem very likely. In any case I did not want to be in a relationship with someone more interested in the TV than anything else. My head told me I had been taken for a fool, my heart still wanted to believe that we had met each other as genuine users of a dating website and decided we were not a good match. We just used different ways to say goodbye. On reflection, whilst April definitely received her Valentine's and birthday gifts; when using Skype she had showed them to me; and produced the right identification when we checked into the hotel, I had no real idea who she really was; where she was from; or, what she was doing.

But there was learning to be had from this experience. It was necessary to be more careful. Being Mr. Nice Guy and treating all those who I met online with respect and dignity was the right way to behave, but I also needed to treat myself the same way. I went back to the lad's books. I didn't like them much but they did cover ground on which I was active and getting caught out. Their focus was principally upon sex and relationships in relation to their author without devoting much time to the breadth of the environment in which the 'action' took place. A book which really did turn out to be useful was from the Marshall Cavendish series of international guides under the title of 'Cultureshock! A survival guide to customs and etiquette'. Perhaps unsurprisingly this was written by Philippine academics, (now based in Australia). The difference showed!

As you will remember when using the website attracting people to my profile was not an issue. The issue was differentiating between the genuine, the time-wasters and the scammers. Having caught a cold once, I did not want to go down the same path again. That said I did not have time on my side. There were fifty-five days between returning home from the first visit and embarking on the second. The time taken for the contact with April to end was on the top side of three weeks, during which period my digestive tract was able to fully return to normal. I needed to take a decision. Whilst I could cancel the accommodation without charge, there was definitely a cost to cancelling the flight. My diary had been cleared. The planned trip had been fairly brief, eight nights plus overnight travel each way. So I decided to continue as planned with the flight and to re-book the accommodation. The same hotel, thirty minutes by taxi from Mactan Airport was available, so I reserved it. Better the devil you know! I also knew I would feel more comfortable in a place I had previously visited and would benefit from the experience of the first trip.

The dating website allowed me to search in specific areas. For example I could set the parameters for Metro Manila; a search would return thousands or profiles, so I could break that down by age and by area within Metro Manila for example 33 year olds in Pasay City or 25 year olds in Parañaque City. That would bring the numbers down to far more manageable proportions.

So the search for a date restarted. It was possible to restrict the search to just Cebu City or for the parameters to be set to flag up the profile of any member whose location was within fifty, a hundred or two hundred miles of the city. I took the fifty mile option because I now knew that Metro Cebu was the generic name for four cities and their suburbs all comfortably covered within a fifty mile radius. Metro Cebu is formed by Cebu City itself, Mandaue City, Talisay City and Lapu-Lapu City. The latter is where Mactan Airport is located. The city is named after a famous figure from Philippine history, General Datu Lapu-Lapu. He was the chieftain of Mactan Island when it was attacked by Portuguese explorer and adventurer Ferdinand Magellan in 1521. He killed Magellan thus postponing the full impact of colonisation by the Spanish for a further forty-three years. The city which has developed in this area was renamed in his honour and forms all of Mactan Island except a strip of land in the south which is called Cordova. That seems to be the most deprived part of Mactan Island. Perhaps in consequence it also has a reputation for child prostitution and cybersex with underage girls. Grand Mall, Mactan is close to the border between Lapu-Lapu City and Cordova. I have not been there but, on the approaches to Grand Mall, have seen street posters and advertising warning young people to avoid engaging in this type of behaviour. Mactan Island lies a few hundred yards off the east of Cebu Island and is so close it is joined by two road bridges with a third currently nearing completion and a fourth in the preliminary planning stages. This third road will link Cordova with the southern end of Cebu City and will be a toll road. The existing routes provide a road connection directly into Lapu-Lapu from Mandaue City.

Mandaue City merges into Cebu City to its south and south-west; to the north are the towns of Liloan, Consolacion and then Danao City. To the south of Cebu City is Talisay City. There is a bit of a coastal greenish belt separating the two, but it is a bit. A bus ride going south from Cebu city centre will take an hour before any countryside is seen and that is well beyond Talisay City.

With regard to making a second visit Cebu the most important question for me was whether or not there was sufficient time to meet someone online who might be genuine before setting out. My initial thoughts were probably not, but, being an optimist, I would give it a go. In that first week back online I meet several young women, all aged between twenty and thirty; all claiming to be single, not concerned about my age, all living in or within close proximity of Cebu City and willing to consider a long term relationship based in the U.K. However I was a little wiser now. I had also had my fingers burned very recently. So I began to ask more pertinent questions of the women I was chatting to. The first of these was: "Do you have a passport?" I soon dropped this question. The answer was almost always: "No." On the couple of occasions where the woman said she had a passport my next question was: "Please can we use the website's Instant Messenger system so you can show it to me." That led to their disappearance from my Inbox! Anyone visiting the Philippines or dealing with a Filipino needs to quickly understand that the word 'yes' can mean yes. It can also mean probably, perhaps, maybe, I'm doubtful and no. I have lost count of the number of times I have taken the Filipino 'yes' to mean the same as a western 'yes'. Furthermore, with the exception of bedroom manoeuvres, 'no' does not always mean no. My guess is that this all links to the concept of not wishing to offend. The meanings attributed to many words are highly negotiable and the Philippine 'yes' is notable amongst these.

After losing contact with people as a consequence of the passport issue I reverted to the more traditional type of informal interview format; asking about likes and dislikes, domestic circumstances, did they have work or work experience, level of education, ambition; variations on the traditional interview question of: "Where do you see yourself being in five/ten years' time?" The responses were interesting and began to show ambiguity with some site users. The more I probed the more the chaff was separated from the wheat. Scammers who realised they were not going to get very far without spending time they could more profitably spend elsewhere. I also began to notice how regularly certain profiles were in active use. For some it was a full-time occupation.

I decided for my second trip to try to find one person who I would arrange to meet but maintain a dialogue with two or three site users who I could contact quite quickly should the initial meeting nor pan out. And this is what happened. We will call her May. We met on the dating website within a couple of days of my new search beginning. Her profile told me she lived in Mandaue City. She did not have a passport. Her education had finished when she was sixteen as there was no money available to send her to college, but that was what she would like to do if it were ever possible, I pressed this point. I wanted to provide her with ample opportunity to ask me to fund her college. Several other members of the site had done this. May did not. She had had some casual work but that was around looking after the children of neighbours when their parents found some work. When she talked of her likes and dislikes she talked about things I quite enjoy; music and art. Her profile told me she was twenty years old. I considered this to be a bit on the young side even for the Philippines but our dialogue continued in a positive way. Given her age I thought the music she would be into would be totally different to that which I enjoy. However, whilst she liked the love songs that most young Filipinas go for, she also mentioned music I liked and, when she suggested song titles I had not heard of, I found them on YouTube. Whilst there were a few I would turn my nose up at, many I was very happy with. She made similar comments back to me about music from my era. One major thing which drew me to May was that, although it was obvious she had very little money, she never asked me for anything. When we chatted on the website video link we always had to pre-arrange because she did not want to be spending twenty pesos (about 32p in the U.K., €0.35 or $0.41) for half an hour at the internet café if I was not there. She was never online unless we had arranged to chat and everything she said was consistent. I told her of my visit the day before I travelled. She took that in her stride and asked if I would like to meet her. I said that she was the only reason for my trip and that I would love meet up. She told me that we needed to arrange a venue. Now Mandaue City is a big place with an official population approaching 400,000 and plenty of unauthorised squats, but I knew she liked pizza so I found a pizza restaurant online which was in her city. I sent its name and the address. She said that was about ten minutes' walk from where she lived and would be okay as a place to meet but pointed out that it was unlikely to be open at eleven in the morning; the time we agreed to meet. She was being sensible, another good sign. She then asked if she could bring someone with her. Again this was a positive signal. The Cultureshock book had told me to expect all Filipinas to be chaperoned for the first few occasions on which they met any man; even the lad's books grudgingly acknowledged this possibility. I would land at Mactan Airport in the evening and we agreed to meet for the first time the following morning.

May.

So I flew into Mactan for the second time and back to the same hotel arriving around eight in the evening. Checking in alone felt like an old friend returning and enjoying the usual welcome drink. I was taken to my room; this time there was no upgrade but it was still a sizeable room, although the bathroom, whilst perfectly functional, was a bit on the small size. A man travelling alone does not take long to unpack. I used the hotel complimentary internet to send a message to May telling her I had arrived and would meet her tomorrow morning at eleven. Why not phone her? Well the main reason was that my mobile phone will not function in the Philippines so I don't take it with me. Secondly, whilst private calls could be made from the hotel, by the time I had sorted myself out it was getting a bit late for the normal Filipinos. May was part of a large family group, I knew this from the messages we had exchanged, and she had told me they had a small place in which to live. So I was aware that, if I called, I could well disturb several people. After sending an e-message to her using the dating website I headed straight for the bar. I had been on the road for over twenty-four hours with no sleep so did not consider going off site. It would be a nightcap and then an early night. The hotel bar was adjacent to the main restaurant area. A couple of tables were occupied by guests finishing off their meals. There had also been some form of entertainment as the artists were being paid off before moving on either to their next gig, or home. Other than staff there was no one else present at the bar; I was their only customer. I ordered a cocktail and knocked it back pretty quickly. I ordered a second and, whilst I was drinking it, felt that awful feeling at the lower part of the stomach. Back to the bathroom – here we go again! However this time I could immediately diagnose the problem. The last food I had eaten was at Deco's restaurant, Hong Kong Airport; it had been excellent as always, and had given no digestive problem. I had completely avoided any liquids from leaving Hong Kong Airport four or five hours earlier and had had nil by mouth from then until arrival at the hotel. When I arrived everything had been fine in the digestive department. Since arrival all I had consumed were the complimentary drink at the check-in and a couple of cocktails. The only thing it could be was the ice in the drinks; or local water if the drinks had been watered down. I would have to stop consuming the local water in any form. That would do the trick, hopefully. I returned to the bar and asked for a fresh cocktail but without ice. Obviously this was an unusual request as the bar staff questioned why. I told them my problem. The response was a cross between politely confrontational and immediate denial. Once again they insisted their water was in perfect condition; it was mineralised, they used nothing but properly mineralised water. That was what the ice was made from; it could not be their fault. Quite an odd response given that I was not seeking to blame anyone, but there you go. I was not going to argue but had to insist they either served me the cocktail without ice or I would be moving on. The cocktail arrived; eventually. I had a couple and then retired for the night. I had taken the precaution of buying mineral water en route from the airport to the hotel, so I was able to safely keep the liquid intake up.

When booking a hotel in the Philippines the website blurb is likely to tell you that bottled mineral water is provided in the rooms. It is; a 0.3 litre bottle per person per day; the smallest commercially available size, sufficient for the cleaning of teeth, twice daily at a push, but nothing more. You could of course buy mineral water at the hotel, each room had its own refrigerator and bar with the prices comparable with hotels in the west. Many Philippine hotels from three stars upwards will charge corkage on anything you bring into the hotel with the exception of soft drinks; and they do check you and look through your bags. During my first trip I got away with this as the only occasion on which I brought alcohol into the hotel it was in bags in the boot of a taxi. The taxi was checked by hotel security as it entered the hotel complex but my shopping bags remained in the boot, unseen. I had been dropped beyond the reception where the concierge staff did not see me unloading. However the rule was that anything purchased outside the hotel, with the exception of soft drinks, was surcharged. So if you ordered a pizza or carried in a bottle of cognac you had to pay a fee which reflected the difference between the local price outside the hotel and that charged by the hotel. I found this practice intrusive, not least because I was a heavy drinker on holiday and wanted to bring in my own supply of booze. The issue of corkage is often not mentioned by either the company selling you the accommodation package or the hotel itself, except perhaps in the small print of documents many customers will never look at; it is an issue which came to a head during the third visit. It was not difficult to bring alcohol onto site. After all a bottle of sparkling mineral water looks just the same once the water has been consumed and replaced with vodka or gin and tonic! A partly consumed two litre bottle of cola with 0.7 litres of Bacardi mixed in will pass muster. Whisky and brandy are more difficult as there are no local sales of shandy, Irn Bru or anything of a similar colour. However hotel security were rigorous, some were armed, but when they checked supermarket plastic bags all they were interested in was checking that the colour of the liquid matched the label on the bottle and that the bottle was plastic; alcoholic drinks came in glass bottles, non-alcoholic drinks in plastic bottles. Their thought processes did not extend beyond that, thankfully. I got a bigger buzz from smuggling the stuff in than from the actual drink!

An early night led to an early breakfast. This was just as well. I had a cooked breakfast with coffee and again had stomach trouble. However this did not last long and it again reinforced the local water problems. No ice in future nor any tea or coffee. I went to the hotel reception and asked the concierge to get me a taxi. He asked where I was going so I told him Mandaue City. He said he needed the address. I asked why. He looked surprised but told me it was hotel policy, a measure which helped them to look after their guests; if I did not return they would know where to start looking. That was a new one to me; a line that had never been peddled to me previously, anywhere. I don't know how genuine their concerns were; it sounded like a load of old bull to me. Having paid their bill in full on arrival I thought the likelihood of the hotel showing concern was minimal; maybe I was doing them a disservice. Whilst this was another practice that seemed intrusive, I provided the address of the pizzeria outside which May and I had agreed to meet. This did prove to be necessary as the first two taxi drivers said they did not know where the address was. I had been on GoogleEarth and written down the road names. I did this because I suspected the taxi driver would try to run me all over town before arriving at the chosen destination. The third driver agreed to take me but made it clear that, if he was unable to find the address, it would be my problem. I found this peculiar but am confident and have a tongue in my head so I told him to get me there. Hotel security staff check everyone out and back in. They do this by asking to see the room key which was on a fob bearing the hotel's logo. (A far better security option would be to request the guest to hand in their key whenever they to leave the site.) When departing by taxi the concierge will also give you a pre-printed slip of paper on which they write the registered number of the cab. The idea is that, should you be dissatisfied or think you have been overcharged by the taxi driver, you complete the slip and send it to the address provided from where any complaints will be followed up. I found it quite common for taxi drivers, once they left the hotel, to try to talk me into going to a different place which would give them a better fare. Some would assume the passenger had no idea where they were going and go the long way round whenever they thought they could get away with it. If you tell then to go by a particular route they will take notice; this also creates the impression that you know your way around. They regularly ask if you have visited their city before; this is not chit-chat or polite enquiry; they are evaluating their chance of literally taking you for a ride before delivering you to the requested destination. Not all are like this but, in a country where taxis are a cheap and regular means of getting around, you will come across them quite frequently. Their interest is in finding out whether you know the layout of the streets.

Philippine law around taxi fares is quite clear and much the same as it is in the U.K. They have a standing charge. This is fixed at P40 for a regular cab and P70 for a yellow airport cab to cover the hire and first few hundred metres. During the journey there is a charge based on the distance you travel. In late 2017 an extra charge of P13 was added per kilometre driven and P2 per minute waiting time (provided it is a short wait; anything beyond ten minutes should be negotiated before you leave the cab). This means that the meter does not advance evenly. What the user must look out for are the switches on the meter itself which the driver can activate to charge at premium rates, i.e. the higher rates charged at night or during public holidays, so the passenger needs to be careful they are not in a cab where the meter is running fast. If you think that is the case, tell the driver. All speak some English. If they refuse to reset the meter or begin to debate, tell them to stop. Get out, pay the amount shown on the meter, and find another. I understand there are over 7,000 registered taxis active in Metro Cebu. Unless you are well outside the city limits and in the middle of the night there are plenty around. Taxis will wait for you but it is important to agree the charge before you leave the cab. Failure to do this is likely to mean they will reset the meter for the return journey which means you are paying two standing charges as well as an inflated waiting price. Compared to the west taxis are very low priced. A drive of an hour through city traffic will cost around £12, (P750; €13, $15).

We finally made our destination with a couple of minutes to spare. The taxi driver indicated that he was willing to wait but I paid him off and away he went. I found myself on a busy urban road. The pizzeria was closed but I was at the right place, the name and street number checked out. It was two minutes before eleven.

Whilst the pizzeria was closed life was going on all around me. It was a hot day, or should I say a typical day for Mandaue City. The street gave an overall impression of tattiness and being run down. The car fumes were more noticeable than back home, unpleasant now and then, but not overpowering. People were coming and going in all directions. I spotted a couple of places where they were repairing tyres, several garment workshops, two or three mechanics or engineers workshops, a laundry, a couple of kiosks selling cheap food and drinks. Most of all I found there was no shelter from the sun. I kept an eye open for May. I had seen five photographs of her and we had chatted a few times using Skype, but, in a mass of people, she could be difficult to pick out. Whilst I had a contact number for her I did not have a mobile phone. Fifteen minutes went by and then thirty. The hustle and bustle around me continued unabated. Every couple of minutes an opportunistic taxi driver would slow down or stop to offer their services. Two or three locals asked if there is anything I would like. "No, thanks," I replied, "just waiting." I decided I would wait up to an hour and then move on. After around fifty minutes I saw two young women walking towards me on the opposite side of the road but looking in my direction. They were pushing a pram with a baby in it. One of them could be May. As they got close May waved to me. I crossed the road and we said: "Hello." She introduced me to her sister who was acting as her chaperone. The baby was her sister's, a little boy approaching two years of age. As the pizzeria was closed I suggested we got a taxi to a shopping mall. They suggested what is often said to be Cebu City's best mall; Ayala.

A ten minute taxi ride and we were deposited at Ayala Mall. I expected the sisters to know their way around but they seemed to be as unfamiliar with the area as I was. We went through the security check and entered the mall area. For me that was straightforward, I was in a sleeveless T shirt, shorts and sandals and carrying nothing. The ladies had their bags searched and there was a perfunctory check of the buggy. Then off we went. Row after row of shops, restaurants and cafes. I asked what they would like to eat and their preference, despite all the choice available, was to select a rather insignificant looking purveyor of pizza; they recognised the brand name from their own locality.

We ordered. I had a ten inch pizza with a bottle of mineral water. The girls asked if they could share a big pizza and a large bottle of cola. I agreed. The prices were about a quarter of what I would have expected to pay at a similar venue in the U.K.

As an aside pizza is a cheap way of filling up several people. In Metro Cebu there are pizzerias which offer the 36" family pizza which is square shaped rather than circular. So, if you order a large pizza anywhere, be sure to check the menu first as you may get substantially more than you bargain for!

The food arrived and I tucked into my pizza; the girl's giggled as they shared a slice from theirs with the little boy and shared a plastic cup of cola from the two litre bottle which had arrived. We chatted away happily for half an hour. By that time my pizza and drink were long gone. Theirs was minus the one slice and a couple of inches had been consumed from the cola bottle. I asked if everything was okay with their food and drink. They assured me it was. The sister then announced that she and her son had to leave. Would I have a problem if they took the remaining pizza and drink with them? Of course I wouldn't. She told me that May had a curfew and was expected home no later than 8 pm. How many twenty year old women in the western world would accept that?! I promised she would be home by then. They left and I picked up the tab. I was surprised that the chaperone had departed and wondered if May had had anything to do with this. Once her sister had departed May wanted to get closer and was keen to hold hands. We looked around the shopping centre together. She told me it was the first time she had been inside the Ayala Centre. As I mentioned earlier I am not a great one for shopping. We had a good look round. On the top floor we found a cinema complex. I asked if she would like to see a film. The look she gave me was one of absolute delight. She had seen films on TV but had never been into a cinema before. So we watched one of the Bourne series of films which had just been released in the Philippines. It included a car chase supposedly set in Manila. I put my arm around over her shoulders and she very happily snuggled up to me. I can't say that we enjoyed the film very much. It was too much fantasy and special effects for my liking and too much of a boys film for May. But she had her popcorn and seemed to enjoy what was a completely new experience. I enjoyed her closeness and trust. I also enjoyed seeing how she was enjoying herself. It was obviously a new experience and she was alive to everything all the way through.

After the film had finished it was still afternoon, we had the best part of four hours before May's curfew became active. I suggested she might like to visit the hotel I was staying at. Just to have a look around, nothing beyond that, and a promise that I would be sure to get her back home in time. She was happy with this.

So began my first jeepney ride. The jeepney is ubiquitous in the big towns and cities of the Philippines. It is based on the jeep which the U.S. Army used during World War II with the area behind the front seats completely cleared out and bench seats provided down each side, the back door is removed and a metal roof supported on each corner by metal struts; any glass or Perspex has been removed from the side windows which are open to the elements and there is a single step at the back as the entrance. The benches will seat at least seven Filipinos on each side; on busy routes it is not unusual for one of two people to grab hold the sides of the vehicle or ride on the back step. On the outside these vehicles are painted in all sorts of bright colours by their owners. Within that design the route the vehicle plies will have been painted onto its side. The driving tends towards the insane but, thankfully, they are not capable of any great speed; 20 mph is doing really well. But they get you there; they are cheap and other motorists know better than to argue with a jeepney driver. I am around eighteen inches taller than the average Filipino and have the build to match, so getting into the back of one of these vehicles was something of a challenge and of great amusement to the locals. Once in, it was physically impossible for me to sit up straight. If I were to keep my back reasonably straight I would need to bend my neck so it and my head were pressed against the roof. With the state of some of the roads, and the antics of some of the drivers, this would be courting disaster so I have to slide down in the seat a bit to reduce the risk of injury. However this means having to negotiate space for a lot of leg. From my perspective it is a thoroughly uncomfortable but effective experience. The only positives I can say about it are the price and that it is a definite step up from airplane toilets! For the locals it was more than a little amusing. I took up the space of at least two Filipinos so, from the perspective of the driver, I was not a good economic option! In the front there is a single seat available alongside the driver and I now aim for that seat whenever possible. The upside is that I have plenty of headroom, the downside is that the legroom is pretty tight.

We needed three jeepneys to get us to the hotel. The final stop was about fifty yards from the hotel entrance. As we walked into the hotel together security stopped and asked to see the key. I showed it. They told me to visit reception to check my guest in. At reception I was asked if May was checking in to stay with me. We replied – no. They then advised that there was a P1,500 day rate for guests; this equated to £24; €26.50;

$30.50). We were now in late afternoon, about five o' clock. I pointed this out to the reception staff advising we would only be on site for a couple of hours and would not be using any of the hotel facilities. They asked if she would be eating or swimming; I said "no" to the food and pointed out that she did not have a costume with her. After a debate the reception manager agreed to waive the fee *on this occasion*. So we took a walk around the site. We began with the gardens and a well-stocked fish pond, then to my room. We stayed there a few minutes. As we sat on one of the beds we shared our first kiss; lingering and exciting, lips brushing, tongues gently exploring. When we came up for air we were looking rather pleased with ourselves. After that it was time to walk around the grounds. We walked around one of the swimming pools; it was beginning to go dark now but there were still a few people in the pool. From there we walked through the accommodation block I had stayed in during the first trip, on down to the beach. We paddled along the shoreline for half an hour or so, chatting, fingers linked, getting to know a little more about each other. Then a stroll through a small copse of palm trees and back up the side of the hotel to reception. Time had moved on. I asked for a taxi and got May back home with about twenty minutes to spare on her curfew. The place I left her was outside a small boarding house on a busy road close to the centre of Mandaue City. We arranged we would meet outside the boarding house at ten the following morning. She would then introduce me to her mother and family. Her father had lost his life in a motor bike accident when May was a small child; she told me she could not really remember much about him. Her Mum had subsequently had boyfriends and more children, but there was no 'man of the house' for want of a better phrase.

I went back to the hotel feeling rather pleased with myself. May was a lovely young woman; she did not have an in-depth command of the English language but she was able to make herself understood and we seemed to understand each other most of the time. What she said and her body language and tone of voice were in synch; I knew she had enjoyed our time together as much as I had and was sure she was looking forward to what the morning would bring. A couple of drinks and then to sleep.

The following morning May met me as I alighted from the taxi. We walked about forty yards down a wide unmetalled road which led off the main road by the boarding house where the taxi had dropped me. We then stepped between two buildings onto a very narrow footpath which was actually a dry drainage channel. I remember walls close to each side. I had to walk sideways and, even then, felt my bum brushing the wall behind me at regular intervals whilst making sure I did not catch my nose or chin on the tall building to the front. That was for the first fifty metres or so. This drain then became a fairly narrow path with passing places here and there for around a further eighty metres. Throughout this distance we were passing between tiny homes, some with other homes precariously perched on top of them. Effluent from these houses drained directly onto the path; most of this was dirty water with some evidence of detergent here and there. The smell was that which you get from manually washing clothing; I had begun to expect the smell of human waste but did not detect that at all. I don't know how sewage was dealt with but it certainly wasn't discharged directly into the narrow paths and drains where I was walking. There were children everywhere. They chattered until they saw me and then stopped and gazed upwards. I don't think they had ever seen someone my size before; they just looked amazed; as soon as I had passed the chatter resumed; occasionally one would follow us for a few yards. May acknowledged one or two people as we passed. The path narrowed and she disappeared into a small opening on our right. I stooped and had to bend almost double to follow her. She had actually entered home. 'Cultureshock', the book, did not prepare me for the culture shock I received. Her home was about eight metres by three, much smaller than my hotel room and tiny compared to the room I had had during the first visit. The walls were of bare breeze block and the roof was tin sheet. A small area was curtained off. That was a changing area; it may also have contained a bucket toilet. If not then there was no toilet. There was certainly no shower or bath, just a sink with a single tap and poor water pressure. It was normal to kick off footwear when entering the house. I stayed right next to the door for two reasons. The first was that I would have been unable to stand upright anywhere indoors. The second was that we were met at the door by three children and I could not easily get past them. When my eyes adjusted from the bright sunlight to the gloom I saw that inside there were four adult women and three more children. May, her mother, the sister I had met the previous day and another sister who had two children. Beneath a table at one end of a room were two bundles of clothing which turned out to be two teenage youths who were sleeping. These two and the three remaining children were May's brothers and sisters. Apart from May and the elder sister I had met the previous day no one else spoke any English. Of the two May had the better grasp of our language. I was offered a small plastic chair to sit on, the type you might find used by a six or seven year old at school. I indicated that I would probably flatten it, so I then got an upturned crate. It did the job.

We chatted as best we could. One of the children, a girl of about five insisted on showing me a bandage on her arm. One of the women told me she had hurt herself but, within a few minutes, the child had unfastened the bandage and was running around holding the end of it in her hand and making the rest fly behind her. It was quickly put back on but, as she played energetically with the other children, she removed it again and seemed to be in the peak of fitness, all limbs working fine, doing handstands and generally jumping and running all over the place. The temperature was hot; I was melting and had nothing with which I could dry myself. After about fifteen minutes I told May I needed to do something about this. She said there was a shop nearby where I could get a small towel, so, a few minutes later, when her Mum was ready, off the three of us went with three of the children in tow. After a few hundred yards we walked past the municipal building close to which was a small shopping mall. As we approached I saw a boy, probably in his mid-teens, lying on the pavement directly in the sun. To me he appeared unconscious. I made a move to check his pulse and see if he was okay. Before I got near enough May and her Mum pulled me away. May said it was probably glue but maybe alcohol or drugs and I should not go near him. We went up the steps into the Mall. On the third floor I invested in a piece of towelling about a 30 cm square foot square, similar in size to a large flannel. I had seen some Filipinos carrying similar and had wondered why. Now I knew, it was a sweat collector, and I was now the proud owner of one of my own! It proved to be a shrewd investment. Each night it was thoroughly washed and was dry, clean and ready for action the following morning. When we came back to the ground floor we passed a Jolibee; that is a Philippine owned fast food chain, equivalent to the burger bars we have in the west. Her Mum wanted to talk and this was as good a place as any to do it. So in we piled. Drinks for all and an ice-cream for each of the children. What May's Mum was after discovering was what my intentions were towards her daughter. As we have discussed whilst this would be very unusual in western culture it was something I was prepared for. So, using May to interpret, I told her that my intentions were determined to a large extend by what May's intentions were towards me. I would not be getting her involved in anything unless it was what she wanted and I certainly did not want to create any difficulties for her with her family. She asked about my work. I don't think she understood my answer but did understand that I had the financial wherewithal to look after May. May then told me that her Mum had a friend who spoke good English who would join us later. We left the Jolibee and returned to her home passing the same young man still lying in exactly the same place as he had been when we had arrived the top side of an hour earlier, still looking unconscious; still with people walking around him and stepping over him; doing anything but help him; still lying uncovered in a fierce sun.

Mum and the small children went ahead. May and I took our time. I bought a bottle of mineral water from a kiosk and we followed back to her home. By the time we arrived the translation service was already in situ. She was a big woman by Philippine standards, she was also loud, self-assured and spoke a pigeon American-English, badly, with a strong deep-south accent. At some point she had obviously been exposed to the delights of W.C. Fields as she continually referred to me, affectionately, as 'her little chickadee'!! (She did not get an offer to 'come up and see me sometime!')

They sent May on an errand and got straight down to business:

Question:
Will you be marrying May?
Answer:
If all goes well when the time is right I will do the right thing.

Question:
What the hell's that supposed to mean?
Answer:
It means that if we get on well together and are both in agreement then I have no problem at all with marriage. I am ready to re-marry if I meet the right woman.

Question:
(Roaring with laughter) How many babies you gonna give her?
Answer:
Whatever the two of us decide. I don't want a house full but have no problem with children.

Okay. We need to get something to eat. I know the right place.

End of interview.

When May returned around eight of us left the house; May, her mother, the interpreter and myself with four different children tagging along. They jumped into a jeepney; I followed, and paid! It took us to a different but still nearby shopping mall which I now know was Pacific Mall. The interpreter said she wanted to find a specific restaurant and marched us through the various levels of the mall, up and down, until finally admitting defeat. Back outside she asked passers-by. We were eventually pointed to a place across a minor road to the back and side of the mall. It was closed, thankfully. It was a fish restaurant and, from the look of it and menus displayed, a fairly exclusive place to dine. Instead she had to settle for a sandwich bar. Drinks and butties all round.

In both my visits to May's home I had been expected to feed several people. It didn't worry me as the prices were low and I had the cash. But I was very aware that I was being taken advantage of. I also knew that this was a big family whose only incomes were from taking in washing and renting the two rooms next to the one in which they lived. I fully understood that money was scarce; I also knew May and I could become very close.

During the meal May asked if she could come back to the hotel with me. Her mother let it be known that the 8 pm curfew stood. She also wanted to know where her daughter would be and asked the interpreter to go with us to check out the suitability of the hotel. Mum and the three children returned home with a substantial doggy bag. The interpreter, a boy of eight or nine, May and I got into a jeepney and returned to my hotel.

Hotel security were not impressed and accompanied us from the gates to reception. The boy and May stood back. As I was advising the reception staff that May and I would be staying for a few hours but the other two were just looking round, the interpreter engaged another member of their team in conversation. It quickly became heated, loud and animated. The interpreter's version of the conversation was that the hotel were thieves and their prices absolutely ridiculous. She told me I should move out straight away; she would get me a good deal at the boarding house close to May's home. The version the receptionist later gave me was that the interpreter had been told of the charges the hotel made for day guests and had used some colourful language to tell them, in no uncertain terms, that they were a gang of thieves, telling them very bluntly where they should stick their charges. This was not typical Philippine behaviour and probably represented the class divide within the local culture, a divide through which May was trying to raise herself. In any case I had paid for the hotel on arrival; I certainly had no intention at all of moving into the boarding house! I agreed with reception that May would wait in the reception area whilst the interpreter and little boy would visit my room to see what it was like. I would then return to reception with them and sort out how we would deal with May's visit. Twenty minutes later the interpreter and boy left the hotel. I checked May into the hotel as sharing a room with me. The hotel agreed that this would be in order whether or not she stayed overnight.

At last May and I would have a few hours to ourselves at the hotel. We bought her a swimming costume at the hotel shop and returned to our room; we were well overdue a kiss and a cuddle! We both had the same thought because, as soon as the door was closed we hit the bed. A twenty odd inch difference in height becomes so much less relevant when horizontal. We kissed and caressed each other. The way in which May wrapped herself around me and thrust into me encouraged my hands to begin to wander; not that much encouragement was necessary. One thing led to another and soon we were naked together for the first time. As we progressed towards the mating ritual it became apparent to me that this was something new to May. She was excited and encouraging but things were happening within her that were unanticipated, exciting, involuntary, unexpected and seemed to be very new to her. As my fingers fondled her breasts and my tongue massaged a nipple her body shuddered violently and she groaned ecstatically. As I gently parted her labia and brushed across the hood of her femininity she was unable to control herself. It was as though multiple electrical impulses were rushing through her. As my fingers approached the entrance to her body I understood why. This was her first time. She was with a man she had only known briefly for two days and was prepared to give up her virginity. I continued to stimulate her and the writhing continued until she finally asked me to stop; we were exhausted.

After showering we changed into our swimwear and hit the pool. We paddled around for a while just enjoying being together. We talked of how much we were enjoying each other and how we might be able to build a future together.

I had not taken May's virginity. Whilst the opportunity had been there, May had seemed to be in such ecstasy without penetration that I savoured her total abandonment to the physical experiences she was enjoying, seemingly for the first time. I wanted to excite her again and again. For me it was the first time I had encountered a woman who was still intact. The way she allowed the new feelings she was experiencing to take over her very being was a wonderful experience for me also; it was a privilege to share her ecstasy. I was sure we would soon be together on a more permanent basis. All in good time. We dried off and lay on the bed whispering sweet nothings and touching each other intimately, but we both knew the curfew was approaching. It was important that family and cultural traditions be respected. So we dressed, strolled to reception, ordered a taxi and I got May back home. This time I gave her enough money to get a taxi back to the hotel in time for breakfast. We agreed to meet in the reception area around eight in the morning.

I am going to take a slight diversion at this point in the story to talk about May's sister. This was the young woman who acted as chaperone the first day we met. She was twenty three years old and had a son approaching his second birthday. On both the days I had met May other members of her family had informed me, through her, that the father of this boy was an Australian. Their story went that he had been in Cebu for a few months, they had dated and gone out together most of that time. He left during her pregnancy but came back for the birth and stayed for the best part of the first year of his son's life. When he was around he covered all costs for himself, his girlfriend and their son. When he left he said it was because his visa had expired; he promised to send money and to return once a new visa had been issued. He had also promised to marry his girlfriend and that they would relocate as a family to Australia. By the time I arrived on the scene the best part of a year had passed and May's family had heard nothing more from him. From a practical point of view this meant there was another mouth to feed and the opportunity for May's sister to find a foreign man for marriage had been reduced somewhat. But this was also an issue which was at the forefront of my mind with May. We had known each other online for three of four weeks and in person for two days. Whilst getting lovey-dovey was very pleasant I definitely did not want to leave her pregnant. No penetrative sex gave me that guarantee. As a good catholic she used no birth control and, when we chatted about this, she did not really have any knowledge of what might be available to her. Condoms occasionally fail and using no birth control was reckless. So, whilst I might at one level have been gallant in not taking her virginity, at another level I was just being pragmatic.

Furthermore I had heard stories about western men being trapped through pregnancy. They would have sex with their girlfriend whilst in the Philippines and, a few weeks later, be contacted with the news they were going to become a father and asked how they proposed to deal with the situation. Some of these stories suggested that the Filipinas were so desperate to escape their country that, following sex with a tourist boyfriend, they would have sex as often as possible during the few weeks following his departure in the hope they could maximise on their chance of conception. They would then tell the tourist boyfriend of their pregnancy and that he was the only man who could be the father. I have no idea how true these stories are but was not going to allow myself to fall into that trap. May would not have behaved in that way but that does not prevent contraceptive failure. April may have taken that path and her idea of good contraception was withdrawal a split second before ejaculation. Of the other women I have visited in the Philippines to date, only April and perhaps the fourth lady I met may have even considered that path, (not likely, but possible), but I don't think any of the others would. Just like their western counterparts most Filipinas are decent, respectable and honest women. There may be a handful who would practice this type of trickery, but that is something which will be found across cultures and genders wherever you are based.

I also noted that the Australian man who fathered the child of May's sister had departed using the excuse that his visa needed to be renewed. This is quite bizarre. Why would an Australian return to Australia to obtain a Philippine visa? A visa would be issued on behalf of the Philippine government at their Ministry of Immigration offices; they had an office only a couple of miles from May's home. Perhaps they were giving me a confused message; maybe it was his passport which was close to expiry. International travel with a passport which has less than six months to run gets complicated. But that would have been swiftly handled by the Australian Consulate without him having to leave the Philippines, so I smelt a bit of a rat; my belief was that he was using the story of an expired visa or passport as a means of escape!

Back to breakfast on day three with May. She was already in reception when I arrived and we walked to the restaurant area, found a table and tucked in. She told me that her mother wanted to meet me again with the interpreter and they had agreed a particular fast food outlet inside Pacific Mall at two that afternoon. That was about a thirty minute taxi ride away. So we had the best part of six hours together. After breakfast we strolled around the hotel site, down to the beach and then called into the small art gallery the hotel provided. It was probably just a means of using a modest sized outbuilding and exhibited around thirty works of a local artist. I enjoy art and we spent some time looking around. The works were largely abstract with bright colours having been scattered and positioned running together and forming a variety of patterns across the canvas; some patterns repeated other didn't. It wasn't everyone's cup of tea but I enjoyed it. May made the comment that some of the pieces bore a resemblance to the works of Jackson Pollock. I was dumbfounded. How did a twenty year old from a poor part of Mandaue City, who had had to leave education at the earliest opportunity, have that sort of knowledge? Whilst Pollock is an artist of some repute but perhaps something of an acquired taste, like him or not, it was very surprising that someone in May's position had even heard of him. I asked her how she knew about the works of Pollock and she told me that she liked drawing anime and cartoons. When she had the opportunity she would search the internet and look at the works of different artists. She enjoyed this but it also acted as an inspiration to her providing ideas of what she might sketch. Her work was all done with pencil on whatever paper or card she could find on the streets. We were beginning to realise that we shared some similar interests and found that very encouraging. We got back to our room and changed for swimming; this took a while as we took the opportunity for an affectionate encounter. I discovered that we shared identical concerns with regard to possible pregnancy so we agreed what we would do together and what we wouldn't, and then got on with it! Later we swam and then repaired to the room for some drying off and more mutual grooming before setting off for Pacific Mall.

We arrived to find we were far from alone. Mum, interpreter and six children were already seated with a waiter ready to take the order. I was buying a meal for ten then! We sat down and I realised that this was to be their meal for the day. In fairness they did not go for the top priced items on the menu but they did eat well and also made sure they had a decent doggy bag to take home. As the meal finished I was manoeuvred to be next to the interpreter whilst May's Mum took her aside. I saw her Mum give May a large plastic bag which appeared to contain some kind of material. The children had moved off and were amusing themselves out of earshot.

The interpreter told me that she and May's mother thought I was okay and that her mother had brought a bag of clothes for her. They had decided that May would be returning to the hotel and to the U.K. with me. There would be a one-off payment of 15,000 pesos, (about £240; €263; $304), cash. She went on to say that, once payment had been made, I was free to do whatever I liked with May.

To say I was surprised by this turn of events would be an understatement. It is rare that I am at a loss for words but for several seconds I was.

"Is there a problem?" she asked.

"Damn right there is!!"

The position they had outlined to any rational person was insane, it was also completely untenable. I didn't go to the Philippines to buy a person. That was a crazy thing to suggest. However the offer had been made seriously. I asked to see May's passport. I was told that she didn't have one but they knew how to get one. There would be a cost of etc., etc., to get the papers together and to get it issued quickly. I pointed out that no matter how quickly they could get a passport issued we could not think about their plan. Once she had a passport May would then need to apply for a visa which had to be issued by the British authorities within the Philippines. Without a visa the airline would not let her get onto a flight out of the country; if they did they would be saddled with the cost of returning her when the U.K.V.I. refused her entry into the U.K. To get a visa she would need to submit her passport with various other documents to the British Consulate who would consider whether or not they would issue one. I would have to provide most of those documents and had no access to them whilst in the Philippines. Even if I'd had all the papers with me it would take a minimum of three weeks, but probably longer, to get a response to a visa application; and there was absolutely no guarantee that a visa would be issued. It could very well be denied. In any case I would be leaving in five days' time.

The interpreter's response to this was that I would have to get the papers sent across to me and stay until the visa was issued.

Apart from this being a completely hare-brained scheme, these women obviously had no conception of international travel. I told them I would discuss all of this with May. We got a taxi back to the hotel; went through security and headed for our room. During the journey May was very, very quiet. What I did not know at that point was that Mum, interpreter and six children were following us in the first jeepney they could find. I later discovered that security had turned them away.

It was around half past four in the afternoon when we sat down and had a serious talk about what had happened. May was very tearful. On our dating website chats she had made it clear she was looking for love with a foreign national and wanted to leave her family and live in his country. I had made it clear I was looking for a similar outcome and that, whilst I would help make it happen when I found the right person, I would not be supporting her family. Once married I would be happy to review that decision and, if and where we could, I would be happy to support her in supporting her family in the Philippines. I made it crystal clear that I would support, facilitate and finance her move to the U.K. and our marriage, but I would not be taken advantage of. She knew I had first-hand experience of scamming for money and that I would have nothing to do with it; and that I was likely to immediately terminate whatever relationship I was in should efforts be made to use me as a source of income. My view is that once a request for financial support is made a decision has to be taken. If you chose to provide that support you are just opening the door to similar requests being made again and again. Word will get around and various members of the extended family will be coming to you with their tales of woe and requests for this and that. So I had been very clear in specifying the parameters within which I was prepared to operate.

May knew this and was frightened that the request made for money through her Mum would mean the end of our relationship. However what I did not know was that whilst the interpreter had been telling me the terms and conditions for *taking ownership* of May; her mother had given May a plastic bag containing all her clothes and said, in essence: "We think you have found a good man who will pay us a good price for you, go to his hotel and then back to his country. Have a nice life!"

May had a bit more about her than her mother and, like me, knew that she had not got a passport and would need a visa. So she had told her mother these things. This had not matched mother's vision for May's immediate future and some harsh words had been delivered. However the outcome was that May was with me in a hotel room. We both knew that after four more nights I would be returning to the U.K. If May had had a passport I would have been happy to apply for a visa, explore the possibilities of fast-tracking this and brought her to the U.K. at the earliest opportunity. May's belief was that, whilst she desperately wanted to join me on a permanent basis, she had been put in a 'no win' situation. Her mother's expectation was that May had now left home, permanently. After four nights at the hotel May knew that I would be returning to the U.K. We both knew that it was impossible to pull together the paperwork which would allow her to travel with me, even if a flight ticket were available. Her mother believed that May had left for good and was embarking on life with a man who would soon be her husband. The interpreter knew she would get a percentage of whatever could be screwed out of the situation.

What a mess.

We had a very emotional and lengthy discussion about how we might be able to build our relationship in view of what had happened. May was upset and angry with the attitude of her mother and thought she would be in trouble if she went back. I had talked about her needing to keep her links open with her Mum firstly because they were a mother and daughter which was a link they should strive to preserve. Secondly because, if we continued to try to sort out the paperwork, she would need somewhere to stay until all documents were in place, especially as May's understanding was that she had no documentation at all. Any papers which did exist were held by her mother! So remaining with her family would be the obvious option.

May then told me that the woman I thought was her mother was actually her stepmother. She had no idea who or where her real Mum was. A reverse situation of the man getting the woman pregnant and then disappearing. Her Mum had delivered the baby and then disappeared. When her Dad and stepmum originally met May was around two years old. Her stepmum had two girls already; these were the elder sisters of May who I had met. They were actually step sisters. Her Dad and stepmum had a child; the elder of the teenage boys I had met. Not long after his birth her Dad had died in a motor bike accident. Her stepmum then had the other children with different men. May took the view that if she could get out of this situation she would do. We were beginning to talk about how she could apply for a passport. Once that was issued I could then send papers across to her so she could apply for a visa. We left the room and went to the I.T space provided by the hotel. This was close to the hotel reception area and within sight of the entrance. The idea was to go online and find out how she would apply for a Philippine passport, how much it would cost and the paperwork she would need. However, as we were walking through the reception area towards the guest computer, we heard shouting from the entrance area and saw the interpreter had pushed past security and was running towards us. May's stepmum was following with various children in her wake and security, whilst doing their best to contain the situation, were failing miserably.

To cut a long story short we met the women and, once again, they were after money. They claimed that the little girl with the bandaged arm, who I had met on my first visit to their home, had suffered a serious relapse of the arm injury and had been taken to hospital. Her life was in immediate danger and they had to pay P15,000 before the hospital would begin treatment. May and I looked despairingly at one another. This straw was going to break the camel's back; we both now knew there would be no Cinderella story here. I had seen this little girl take the bandage off her arm. There was no visible injury whatsoever and she had been playing with the other children, waving her arms around, pushing each other about. She had even been doing handstands! How could a relatively minor alleged injury to an arm be seen as potentially fatal?! I knew there was nothing wrong with her arm. May knew that I knew. She translated the message to them. I could see from the expressions on the women's faces they knew they had been rumbled. They did not argue.

This marked the end of what could have been a wonderful relationship which May and I had begun building very positively; but it was torn apart by the actions of her stepmother and interpreter friend. May left with her plastic bag and the interpreter. They collected her stepmum and the six children at the entrance of the hotel. Sadly, that was the last I ever saw of her.

If it had been possible I would have checked out of the hotel with May, got her a flight and returned to the U.K. immediately. I would have had no second thoughts, but I knew that border control staff would refuse her entry to the U.K. In the circumstances I am describing they could do nothing else. Her only possible way into the U.K. would have been to claim political asylum at the point of entry to the country, i.e. my local airport, and that would have been as nonsensical as the attempts made to sell May to me! I will not try to place the blame for our position on border control officers. Their job is to enforce the law as it stands and, on a daily basis, they are dealing with people who are trying to circumvent it. However the issues created by the process of administering the border control regulations meant that May could not travel with me. That meant she had no choice but to stay in her own country. The only place she had to stay was with her stepmother and family. It was that stepmother, and her interpreter friend, who were making constant and significant financial demands. I had met May on each of the first three days of my trip. Each day I had purchased food for the family, or parts of it. For three people on the first day, six on the second and ten on the third day. Where would this end? Had May and I been together in the U.K. and been told that P15,000 was needed for medical treatment for a life and death issue involving the five year old, how would we have reacted? Either I engaged with them or I didn't. What could have developed into a great relationship was abandoned after less than seventy-two hours because of the need to survive on one side of the world and the bureaucratic process on the other.

Had I known then what I know now about the Philippines I would have considered a different course of action. I am sure May herself was genuine. Everything she said and did linked together. The only thing that might be considered a lie was telling me that her stepmother was her mother. Her knowledge of the English language was limited and explaining that difference had been difficult for her when she told me. In any case, given the circumstances under which we met, it wasn't particularly relevant. I had not queried the relationship with her; it was information she volunteered when the wheels began to come off our situation. She had not lied to me or told me anything remotely ambiguous. Her words, tone of voice, body language, everything pointed to her being an honest young woman. I now know it would have been relatively cheap and simple to rent a room for her for a few months whilst she got a passport and we sorted out a visa. However I also know that she would only have been able to get the identification documents to apply for a passport and visa with the active support of her stepmother. Would this have happened? To the stepmother May was a commodity with a price on her head. Had the Australian man who had a child with

May's (step) sister discovered the same? I can understand the reader thinking that I was abandoning May. I felt that way too. I felt dreadful about the situation. However I also knew something about the bureaucracies in both the Philippines and the U.K.; not as much as I know now but I was aware how incredibly difficult it would be for May to get a passport. Even if she managed that there would be major challenges in obtaining a visa. Application processes are quite complex and can be very challenging, particularly if he applicant's knowledge of the English language is limited. So I hope you will reserve criticism of my actions until you have read through that part of the story.

Whilst I felt a bit upset for myself, my main concerns were for May. She had been mercilessly used by her stepmum and interpreter friend as a means to try to scam me. Very likely the same thing had happened with her stepsister and Australian boyfriend. As soon as they had left the hotel I went online and blocked her on the dating website. When I got home and logged onto the dating website there were two messages from her; she had set up a second profile. I considered my options. This was a woman I had been falling in love with and the feelings were obviously very mutual. I was now back in the U.K. If I responded to these messages I would be re-opening a situation which had been effectively closed. Furthermore, I had no way of knowing if May's new profile would actually be her acting alone. The fact that I had received these messages told me that May had been able to create a new profile and get back online so I could reasonably assume she was at least in a position no worse to that which existed when I had first met her online. Given the antics of her next of kin my thoughts were that any attempt at continuing to build and develop a relationship could only happen if they were directly involved. They controlled all May's access to the papers she would need to apply for a passport or visa. Furthermore, as she was still under twenty-one years of age, she had to have the written support of her stepmother before an application for a passport would be considered. This created further issues around proof of identity. To apply for a visa, as we shall see in a later chapter, I would need to provide comprehensive information about myself, my finances and my identity. These papers would have to be delivered to May as she would have to make the visa application in person. Given May's domestic situation this was akin to delivering these documents directly into the hands of May's stepmother and interpreter friend. The necessary papers included full details of my bank accounts, savings, salary and tax returns. Other papers, such as certified copies of my birth certificate and passport, would make it very simple to copy my identity. I considered I would be putting myself at an untenable level of risk. These were the thoughts going through my mind when I received the new messages from May on the dating website. I could not see how it would be possible to take things forward with May safely, for both of us. I deleted her messages unread and blocked the second profile. A few months later whilst using the website I checked her profile a saw that it had been dormant for over three months. I hope May is thriving but will never know. I wish her well and am very, very sorry for the hurt she suffered. Whilst I cannot put that right I realised the need to do my best to make sure nothing similar would ever happen again.

Following May's departure I still had a few days left at the hotel. It was around this time that I noticed the hotel was still providing women for western men. I spotted two women who had also been present on my first trip a couple of months earlier. So I concluded that either the hotel was providing women for male guests or pointing those guests in the right direction at check-in. At another hotel I stayed at it was fairly common in the late evening to see working girls arrive at security, be searched, walk through the lobby to the lifts and then re-appear ten to thirty minutes later and depart. I am sure this goes on in hotels across the world, it just seemed to be a bit more obvious on my Philippine trips. What I found really annoying was that the hotel I was staying at allowed this to happen but, when I wanted to bring some company onto the site, despite having paid in advance for a room for two people, further payment was demanded.

From May to June (and five highly forgettable ladies).

May had inadvertently provided me with a salutary lesson. Whilst I didn't want to get hurt I knew I was far better placed than any genuine Filipina I might meet on the website to deal with such feelings. Whilst I owed it to myself to be careful the last thing I wanted to do was create any sort of domestic problem for genuine women I might meet. I had seen the circumstances in which many Filipinas lived. Whilst I was at an age where I had seen a lot of life, been knocked down a few times and brushed myself off and got on with it; these women, the ones who were genuine, were just embarking on life's journey. Many were having a difficult time, certainly by western standards. I suppose this might also be a toughening up process producing a fairly robust individual, maybe more resilient than her western counterpart. However, from the women I have met, I would say they seemed to be content with what most of us in the west would consider to be the bare necessities. They also knew what life was like without them. When you have little or nothing that is the norm; it was their reality. A person in my position needed to respect that. Just because someone seems to be in a position of relative weakness does not give me, or anyone else, a right to take advantage of their situation.

However it took a few weeks before I started searching the dating website again and thinking about another trip. The end result of that second trip has stayed with me.

July to December is broadly the typhoon season in the Philippines. It is not a time to plan a visit and, in any case, I had a backlog of projects to catch up on. So there was a lull in my internet dating activity. However, as time progressed, I did plan a third visit, to the same hotel, early the following year, about eight months after the second trip.

I was learning the ropes. I knew that I would find someone to meet by using the dating website and that I could have two or three other site members in reserve. However I thought I would try a different approach. This was motivated initially by the experience with May. I did not want to be used as a mechanism through which a third party could abuse a young woman who was genuinely looking to improve her opportunities in life. I had looked at some specialist tour operators who were marketing a 'find a bride' type of visit. However it was apparent from the first glance at their websites that these operators were, at best, setting up a good time for the lads! Their offerings, alluring, glossy and colourful as they were, were barely a single step removed from sex tourism and prostitution. Images of young women lined up in scantily cut swimsuits, or of several girls provocatively draped over an ugly fat westerner in a night club. Not what I was looking for at all.

What I did find was a Philippine based agency offering tailored services for *the discerning male* who was looking for marriage. The images on that website were more in keeping with what I had in mind, even though their testimonials had an air of fiction about them.

I liaised by e-mail with company and did a Skype interview. The end result was that we agreed a fee for which they would find five dates for me. The women would be as close to what I told them I was looking for as they could find. However they did comment at the outset that finding a woman with no children aged between twenty and thirty-five who was interested in a long-term relationship with a man approaching sixty could be a challenge. They also made it clear that they were operating a legitimate introduction agency. They were not providing women who were available for sex. Their clients all had long-term interests in mind. That suited me just fine. Over a period of a month or so they e-mailed to me head and shoulders photographs and brief descriptions of a couple of dozen potential candidates. Through a variety of questions and answers by e-mail we whittled this list down to five and I agreed to meet them on consecutive days following my arrival. This would maximise the time I had available to develop a relationship with one of them should things go well. The company's representative would bring the women to the reception area of my hotel, the same hotel I had used for the two previous trips. She would give me details of a reservation they had made for a meal at a hotel or restaurant where we would have our date. It was then up to me to arrange the taxi and pick up the tabs we generated.

Following the initial meetings an agency representative would meet with me to discuss if I wished to take things further with any of their clients. The women I would meet were in the uncomfortable position of knowing I was judging and assessing them against their counterparts. It was the agency's policy to make this known to them, not mine, a situation I was unable to influence. However it meant the women knew they were in a competitive environment but it would be a few days before they knew if they were going to get the call for a second date. They were given strict instruction not to exchange any personal contact details with me and I was given strict instructions not to ask.

When I left the U.K. for trip number three I was expecting to meet the five ladies provided through the introduction agency. I had also met a young woman on the dating website. We had chatted for a couple of months using both the website and Skype. I knew she was studying at a university in Cebu City; I was able to check out the course online and also see her name on the list of candidates entered for finals exams which, co-incidentally, she would complete a few days before my trip began. She was one of seven children and twenty-three years old. She had a much younger sister still at home and three teenage brothers. Her two older sisters were married with children but lived close by, (as is typical with many Filipino families). Around about the day I arrived in Cebu was a big event for her family. Her Dad, who was working abroad, (he had a seven year contract to do building work in connection with football's World Cup being held in Qatar, 2022), had a six week holiday and was coming home. He had earned this having reached the mid-point of his contract. It was the only holiday he would have during the seven years. The only other contact he had with his family was via Skype and similar. I did not tell her of my trip as I did not want to do anything which might have an impact on her studies; I also wanted her to enjoy her Dad's return, and, who knows, I might hit the jackpot with one of the ladies I would meet using the introduction agency. Were that to happen I would be politely closing down my website activities and concentrating on her.

My third trip was for seventeen nights plus overnight flights each way. I had to be back in the country to sign various financial documents off at the end of the financial year so it was early in March when I drove from home to a workshop where my car would be serviced during my absence: I had arranged for a taxi to collect me there. The previous day we had had snow; the local airport had been closed for a couple of hours which was very unusual. There had also been a heavy overnight frost. I had packed light clothing in my suitcase but, on leaving home around four in the morning, needed to wear clothing suitable for a temperature of minus five Celsius for the journey to the airport where I arrived at five on a Tuesday morning. All went smoothly. Just before noon the following day I had the Philippines visa stamped into my passport at Mactan Airport and headed for baggage reclaim. I then heard my name on the tannoy and went to the enquiry desk to be advised that my luggage was still in Hong Kong. It would be delivered to my hotel once it had arrived. That would be on the airline's next incoming flight made from Hong Kong; on Friday evening. In the interim I should go into town and buy some clothes!

My height is distinctive in my own country; in the Philippines I look something of a freak. At home no High Street shop carries clothing which is long enough for me; I can only buy clothing and footwear using websites catering for the outsize man. I knew there would be nowhere in the whole country which would sell clothing anywhere close to my size. Placing an online order was not an option because of the delivery times, even express delivery to the Philippines would be three to five working days. So I had been up and about from around 3 am on a Tuesday morning, in clothing appropriate for a frosty morning in England, and arrived in Cebu around mid-day on Wednesday. Even allowing for the time difference I had been travelling for over twenty-four hours and would have no ability to change clothing for the best part of a further two and a half days. The estimated time my case would arrive at the hotel was 10 pm on Friday evening. To further compound matters I had dates arranged through the introduction agency on the first five evenings of the trip. So the first three ladies I met would find me becoming increasingly aromatic and hairy. I was not a happy bunny. All I had with me was a briefcase containing wallet, travel documents and an electronic book reader.

I did not do myself any favours. When I walked from arrivals hall to the front of the Airport I was bombarded by the usual chancers wanting to carry my hand luggage and find me a taxi at a good price. Yes, a good price for them! I was feeling tired and damn stroppy. I knew the taxis I would be guided to at the airport charged about double the price of the street taxis so decided to walk to the nearest shopping centre, Marina Mall, about a kilometre away. By the time I arrived my irritations had been replaced by the realisation of the serious error I had made. I was dressed for the British winter and had stormed out of the airport ranting to myself about the iniquities of life only to be hit head-on by the midday sun in Lapu-Lapu City which was blazing down, no breeze, the sort of fumes you would associate with an international airport and a midday temperature well into the thirties Celsius. I was quickly vaporising. As I strode down the final few hundred metres to the Mall, sweat pouring off me and dripping onto the road surface, I received some strange looks from the locals; even the cockerels, which were tethered at intervals down one side of the road, seemed to be casting disdainful glances my way! I called into a café to cool down both literally and metaphorically. Once I was seated the sweat continued to pour off me to be absorbed in the only clothes I had! I drank several bottles of mineral water, remembering to open them myself, and had a bite to eat. After the best part of an hour I was ready to move on. Marina Mall houses a supermarket which has a decent money exchange so I changed some cash, bought non-alcoholic drinks and picked up a taxi off the street going straight to the hotel. I checked in, paid up, turned down their complimentary drink as I remembered only too well the impact it had had on me the last time and retired to my room just in time to deal with the after effects of the café. Part of the snack had included boiled rice; the water absorbed during cooking was making its presence felt!

The clothing situation presented a problem but, in all honesty, was not too bad. I was wearing shoes, socks, underwear, denim jeans, and a fairly thick 'T' shirt. I had a winter coat with me. The problem was straightforward. After travelling for so long my clothes needed to be washed, and so did I! The hotel had a laundry and, nearby, were several places which would wash my clothes. However, once I took these clothes off, I had nothing else to put on. The complimentary dressing gown provided by the hotel was for the average sized Filipino. Once the cord around the waist was knotted the slightest tilt in any direction would have provided an eyeful to anyone nearby. So I set to and washed my pants, socks and 'T' shirt. That meant staying in my room until they had dried; there was no iron available so I put the 'T' shirt on a hanger to drip dry. After the journey I was tired so I showered and then had a nap.

I was awakened by the phone in my room ringing. It was reception. They told me there were two women at reception asking for me. I checked my watch. It was seven o' clock; the nap had extended longer than intended. My clothes had dried in the heat. They didn't smell but were fairly crisp. So, dressed cleanly but for the British winter, off I trotted to reception where the introduction agency representative introduced me to my date for the evening. I paid their fees in cash, got the receipt, then the two of us went out for a meal.

These dates can be dealt with in a couple of sentences. Two of the five women made it very clear from the outset that their only interest in me was as the provider of a bite to eat and a drink. The other three were pleasant ladies but did not press any buttons. I met one of them for a second date but she was shy and reserved. Conversation was challenging and mostly one-way.

The final date had taken place on a Sunday afternoon with a woman in her late twenties who probably found me as boring as I found her. We were both interested in marrying if we found the right partner. My main interests leaned towards the arts and my work; health and environmental issues, and music which, from her perspective, was from a bygone era. She was interested in fashion. A feature of all the women to whom I was introduced was this love of fashion and making the most of one's appearance. That should not have come as any surprise to me as the leader of the agency claimed to be a former international model.

However, as you may have gathered, my focus is not particularly on appearances. I've been around long enough to know that actions speak louder than words. I am interested in what someone does, not what they say they will do. When it comes to appearances, I am interested in what somebody thinks and says, not what they dress themselves up as. So long as they are clean I'm not bothered what they wear. All the con artists I have met over the years have been well groomed; they have also been thieving so and so's. In any case most of the women I have met in the Philippines have good looks in abundance; or maybe it is just something about the Filipina which gives me a buzz.

My luggage arrived as promised on Friday, late evening, I collected it as I returned from date number three. It was a relief to unpack, get my toiletries and shave and shower properly rather than making do with the limited materials provided by the hotel. But to be able to get into a pair of shorts and sandals was wonderful.

Whilst the five dates I had had were anything but memorable, they had taken me to five places I had not previously visited. The Airport Hotel, two good quality restaurants in an upmarket area of Cebu City and two of the top beach resorts; Shangri-La and Imperial Palace, now refurbished and called J-Park. I had minor digestive problems with all except the Airport Hotel. So keeping a close eye on the water was reinforced but I also became aware the water problem did not simply present itself at the hotel I was using and its immediate surrounds. That said life there was becoming increasingly unpleasant.

When I stay at a hotel I am a paying guest. If it were not for its paying guests the hotel would have no business and close. So, whilst I neither want nor expect to be waited upon hand and foot, I do expect a reasonable standard of treatment from hotel staff. At Philippine hotels security is an important issue. Where I was staying was an area of considerable poverty; however it was far from being the worst I have come across in Metro Cebu or even Lapu-Lapu City. That said, in the last three years there have been four murders which is a high rate of return for a village with a population which is probably well under ten thousand excluding holidaymakers. Two of these occurred in a dispute between the owners of a restaurant, the other two were related to drug dealing. Had there not been twenty-four hour armed security guards at the hotel, I dread to think what would have happened. Stepping from inside to outside the hotel grounds was stepping from first world to third world; in a single step. So I have no doubt that security was both necessary and important. The problem was that the security guards did not differentiate between guests and potential infiltrators. They treated us all in the same way. It was not quite as bad as visiting someone in prison but they searched all bags and, if there was something large in a pocket, would ask to see it. Even though they knew me I was not allowed out of the hotel until I produced my room key. On returning I would not get back in without repeating that process even though it would often be the same person doing the check. There was a single entrance to the hotel. It was ungated but staffed by at least two security guards 24/7 and one or both would be armed. During the day there would be anywhere up to a dozen uniforms around. This entrance/exit would take two cars side by side and was located in a rear corner of the grounds, exiting onto an unmetalled road which joined the main road through the resort after about thirty metres. The remainder of the rear of the property was protected by a wall, the backs of hotel buildings and fencing. One side of the hotel directly joined the hotel next door so they provided each other with an element of security. But the other side was bordered by a rough track which ran down to the sea. The hotel formed one side of that track, the other side contained several clumps of small tin rooved makeshift homes. There were even efforts to deter sea swimmers going from one hotel to another. Each hotel had constructed a rough type of pier of rocks and wire, unsafe to walk on, which went out around a hundred metres into the sea. Whilst these obstacles made a clear demarcation between the hotels and the public land, had anyone been seriously considering an unlawful entry to the site, it would not have presented much of a challenge.

As I mentioned earlier the hotel security staff were zealous in their duties. With the exception of the suitcases one had on arrival, all bags carried into the hotel were checked. They were after the corkage. The hotel bars also charged top dollar for their drinks. I needed plenty of water and non-alcoholic drinks and brought those onto site without a problem. I found it very annoying when the security staff insisted on rummaging through the bag or bags I carried every time I entered the hotel. However I also knew that, to some extent, I only had myself to blame. At the back of my room was a solid fence which was at least ten feet high and had barbed wire running along the top. Beyond that was the publicly accessible dirt track running down to the sea. However, whilst the fence had been fitted flush with the ground, there were small gaps here and there along the base. Literally rat runs. This was a poor area and rats, though rarely seen, could be heard quite often. However these rat runs also provided a space sufficient to take a bottle. My third trip was for seventeen nights. Given the amount of booze I was knocking back at that time, I would have had one hell of a bar bill had I paid the hotel rate for each drink consumed. Whilst on the public side of the fence it was a rough path, on the inside of this fence, on the hotel side, was deep uncut grass and undergrowth. Every few days I would push a few half litre bottles of spirits underneath the fence and into the deep undergrowth on the hotel side. I would then go through security, be cleared, and collect on the room side of the fence. There were plenty of waste bins throughout the hotel and I disposed of the empty bottles using them, avoiding the ones closest to my room. The empties would, of course, have been found. I am pretty sure they knew it was me bringing these in. Maybe they went through my room when I was absent, who knows. If they did the issue was never raised with me; amor-propio, perhaps? But I suspect this was the reason for the fairly rigorous searches I got. Looking back I now understand this concealment activity is very typical behaviour for an alcoholic. At that time the use of that word to describe me was something which would have horrified me, although it was undoubtedly correct. For me a major part of dealing with alcohol has resulted from accepting that it was controlling me rather than the other way round. A couple of weeks ago I had a major success when, whilst dining at a friend's home and being part-way through a trifle dessert before realising the sponge had had some sherry soaked into it, I completed the meal and have not thought about the incident until now. If it were not an issue I would not have remembered such a minor incident and that tells me I need to be careful. I am still recovering from alcoholism and will be doing for the rest of my days.

Returning to the hotel and its search policies; a couple of days before leaving I deliberately came through the entrance carrying two bottles of spirits. Security were delighted they had caught me red handed at last. Two members of the gate security team actually physically took hold of an arm each and I was frog-marched to the reception desk where I was told in no uncertain terms that, when I checked out, there would be corkage to pay. However I had got these as gifts so, when I checked out, had the same bottles with me, unopened. You could hear the crests falling!

I also handed them a towel.

This related to a separate issue which had occurred the day after my luggage arrived at the hotel. In front of my room was one of the hotel's swimming pools. Once I had swimwear I was keen to use it. Complimentary towels were provided; normal practice for most hotels. At this one they not only required the production of your key to prove the room number before they would issue a bathing towel, they also required that it be signed for. Perhaps it was just me being a grumpy old fart but I felt that being asked for a signature was a step too far. It suggests the default position of the hotel is to assume its guests will steal their towels. So, when I returned the towel, I took my own piece of paper with me and asked them to provide a signature to acknowledge its return. This threw the pool staff completely. They could think of no way in which to deal with my request. I pointed out that when I signed for the towel I was accepting responsibility for it. If I were to return it and not get a signature, the hotel could claim I still had the towel. A member of the management team was summonsed. He also choose not to understand the point I was making. It was simple:

> I sign for a towel.
> The hotel provides me with a towel.
> My signature proves I have the hotel's towel.

> Your signature will prove its return.
> Do you understand?
> No. We don't do it like that.
> Fine, then you don't get your towel.

I took to using the towels provided with the room; they were changed every day and the staff worked on the basis of double occupancy. The original bathing towel, for which they refused to give me a signature, was returned as I checked out for the final time.

However the real driver of my stroppiness was the attitude of the hotel in making it difficult for me to entertain guests on site. The hotel billed me for a double room knowing it was for single occupancy. There was no price reduction; everything they did assumed two people in the room. Two large beds so you could sleep together, separately or mix and match, two bottles of water, two toothbrush mugs, two chairs on the veranda, etc. Payment also included the provision of two breakfasts which was a joke as most of the food they provided gave me the trots as I had learned from bitter experience. I took my own water to breakfast. However, on the day I arrived for this third visit, the lady from the introduction agency also arrived with my first date. The reception staff had called the room to notify me of their arrival. I did not know who these women were. When I reached reception, instead of the staff pointing me to my guests, they told me I needed to pay 3,000 php (about £48; €53; $61), to cover the P1,500 pesos per guest charge they made for the use of hotel facilities, (an issue I came across with May and her family). Four hours earlier, when I had checked in, the same members of reception staff had insisted on full payment for single occupancy of a double room. That was charged at P8,400 per night for seventeen nights, a total of P142,800, (£2,277; €2,500; $2,887). I had paid this in cash in full and the next thing they were doing was asking for more.

I told reception that I had agreed to meet the ladies at reception but one of them would be leaving shortly and that this would be happening for the next four evenings. They did not like the sound of that at all. I took the view that, as I was paying for a room with joint occupancy, there should be no question of a second person being able to join me if I wished; irrespective of whether or not they stayed over. But no, any guest I had would only be allowed beyond reception if the lady signed in as a co-habitee. If I checked a second person into the room, that was fine. However if the second person was not sharing the room overnight they were categorised as a day guest for which a premium was charged to cover their use of hotel facilities; whether or not they used them. Furthermore, that premium had to be paid before they would be allowed beyond the reception area into the grounds of the hotel.

I had been intending to ignore the venues suggested by the introduction agency for the dates they had arranged preferring to wine and dine all five dates at the hotel restaurant where we could relax, dine and enjoy the cabaret which was provided each evening. If things went really well we would have the option of a private room to move on to; ever the optimist! But the hotel created a situation where I decided I could not take this option. The cost of a meal for two, with wine, at hotel prices would have exceeded P1500 per head cover charge, so they actually lost business as well as goodwill by their attitude. For each date I ensured we left the hotel within a few minutes of their arrival.

An issue which probably relates to this I mentioned earlier and noted again during the third visit. The hotel seemed to be making Filipinas available to western men for the duration of their stay. I saw at least one of the women I had noticed on my two previous trips with another western man; and a couple of others who seemed to be providing personal services. Perhaps what really upset the hotel was that I was not in the market for prostitution; if so, they would have been in a position to help and presumably profit from the arrangement. But a man trying to find a woman without their collusion played no part in their game plan.

On my previous visits to the hotel I had used the concierge to get a taxi when I needed one; however around half the taxi drivers tried to take advantage. On my third visit this occurred with the first two taxis I requested, one of which was with my first date. So I took to walking off the hotel site to the main road and finding my own taxi. Again this created friction. The concierge staff lost the opportunity to ask me where I was going, they may also have lost an opportunity to receive a few coins from the taxi driver as a thank you for finding him a fare. (I use 'him' advisedly; I have yet to meet a female taxi or jeepney driver in the Philippines). However the security staff at the entrance still insisted on asking where I was going every time I left the site. I told them it was none of their business and they disputed this saying their job was to keep me safe and, to do that, they needed to know where I would be, blah, blah. For the sake of a smooth exit from the site I told them all sorts of rubbish. However, so long as they had a location, it did not seem to matter. They were happy and I escaped!!

This would definitely be my final stay at this hotel. I was not exactly fighting a running battle with the staff but my reactions to their actions created a fairly unsavoury atmosphere both ways; it was not a pleasant experience. Whilst I do not agree that the customer is always right, from a business perspective it is as well to give this impression wherever one can. Such a principle was lost on the staff of this hotel group. They worked by rote – these were the rules and that was that. Sorry, but I don't work that way.

So, having disposed of dates with five highly forgettable ladies, let's move back to June. I contacted her through the dating website following my fifth date. The family reunion had gone well, her university studies were now complete and she was awaiting the result of her final exams. I had an announcement to make to her. I was in her area and gave her the name of my hotel. I had no idea whereabouts in Metro Cebu she lived. It could have been up to almost a two hour taxi ride away. But, as luck would have it she was within walking distance of the hotel, less than two kilometres away, in a village called Dap Dap, co-incidentally also the location of the main prison for Lapu-Lapu City. I asked if we could meet at the local mall; I did not want her thinking I was trying to get her into the hotel for any nefarious purpose, (nor did I want to provide the hotel any further opportunity for financial opportunism). She asked when and where so I suggested the Red Ribbon coffee shop on the ground floor of

Grand Mall, Marigondon, a ten minute taxi trip away. She said she would try to meet me. We agreed 1 pm the following day.

One o'clock came and went but, whilst the place was milling with customers, the only people I had seen who could have been looking for a pre-arranged date were two young women who had cruised my table a couple of times giggling. About twenty past they came close again and I made sure they knew I was aware of their cruising; I gave them plenty of eye contact. They moved closer but I didn't recognise them: "Is one of you called June?" I asked.

"No," they smirked as if to say: "We know what you're after!" Then moved off.

A few minutes later another two young women walked by and one of them did look like June so I asked again. I was right. A couple of her friends had had a look at me first and reported back. We went up to the Mooon café where we shared a coffee and had a chat for an hour or so. It was a good job June had her friends with her as she was quite withdrawn and shy with me whilst chatty with her friends. When it seemed a logical time to bring the events of the afternoon to a close I asked June if she would like to have something to eat together that evening. She agreed but said she would need to be chaperoned and would also have to get the permission of her parents. We had established she had access to a computer at home and agreed she would send me a message through the dating website to confirm our planned date. Confirmation duly arrived and she told me she would have two people with her. Her younger sister who was nine or ten years old and a friend of her mother who spoke good English. My thoughts immediately went back to May and her mother's English speaking friend! I need not have worried. Well, not about the same things. This woman could speak English fairly well and, from the dialogue we had, was obviously acting in the best interests of both parents and daughter. She also believed that, having eaten good food, it was polite to acknowledge this with a series of loud belches! A trait I discovered was shared by other family members. The questions this woman asked were sensible and, whilst they were more detailed than I would ever have expected back home, I had been here before.

I outlined my ideal situation to Mum's pal. It went like this. Firstly I did not want to involve June in anything unless she had the support of her family.

Big smile!

What I hoped could happen would be that, if we got on well during my visit, that June could visit me in my country. The only visa which would allow this would be valid for six months. However, that did not mean she would be expected to stay for six months. It meant she could stay for a single day or up to the full six months, whatever she wished. That would be her choice. The house had five bedrooms so she would have her own room in a house which we would share. We both needed to know if she could settle in my country. We also knew that we could not decide if we were perfect for each other during the ten days we were enjoying at present in her country.

Big frown!

I knew that I could not settle in the Philippines for three reasons. My work would not allow that and, once retired, the state pension element of my income would lose its index linking were I to live outside the country. (I now know this is wrong as the U.K. and the Philippines have a reciprocal arrangement around this issue.) Secondly I had some minor responsibilities to an elderly parent which, over time, could grow. (My father died around 18 months ago so this reason would no longer be valid.) Thirdly how could I live permanently in a place where the slightest hint of local water did terrible things to my digestive tract?

An air of inscrutability.

I had around ten days left for this trip. We knew that, if June was to make a trip to the U.K., the first step was for her to obtain a passport.

For this there were some papers she needed to gather together and a form that needed to be submitted with payment. Total cost, less than £20; peanuts; my 50% contribution was not requested but welcomed.

During the remainder of my stay June and I spent time together on all days but one. Whilst shy for our first two or three meetings she began to open out a little. I was introduced to her family and friends. This included her father. He was about fifteen years my junior, as was her mother. They seemed to accept me. I attended one of the several get-togethers celebrating her father's holiday during which June prepared a meal which we shared together. This had been encouraged by her family as it allowed her to demonstrate her culinary prowess. Whilst I am a firm believer in equality in a relationship and the kitchen and bedroom are places to share, I did see this as an encouraging sign in that her family were supporting her in this new relationship and she was doing what a Filipina would naturally do in her position in these circumstances. I invited her family to join me at a local restaurant but her father declined, three or four other family members joined us. A good time was had by all. We visited the cinema together and made two or three trips to shopping malls in Cebu City where we would chat over a drink or a snack. The Cultureshock book which I read had mentioned the protective environment in which traditional Philippine families keep their daughters which results in a distinct lack of experience of building and developing personal relationships, and how these young women can be very reticent towards anything new. This seemed to be the case with June. The closest we got to a physical relationship was holding hands in the back of a taxi and an arm across the back of her seat whilst we were sat in the cinema. As my departure approached she did begin to touch me, but in a way which showed affection whilst there was no hint of anything which might be described as sexual. She would rest a hand on my forearm, link arms or lean against me if we sat together. I got the distinct impression that such contact was completely new for her, she was like a teenager with her first boyfriend, which may well have been the case.

When I returned to the airport we had agreed that, once June received her passport, we could then consider applying for a visa. Online meetings using the dating website and Skype were also put into diaries. Having taken three days to get my suitcase to me on the outward leg of the journey, the airline improved slightly on the return trip by taking two days. At least they were consistent!

About a month after my return I received a message from June. Her father had returned to Qatar. Before departing he had given June his support in her relationship with me. However he had attached two conditions. The first was that we married before we lived under the same roof together; the second was that, like her elder sisters, the roof we lived under must be close to her current home.

So, that marked the end of my relationship with June. It was not as abrupt as that; we chatted for a week or two through the dating website but we both knew that she would not disobey her father, nor would I encourage her to, but he had, in a very Filipino way, scuppered any likelihood of his daughter entering into a long term relationship with me; or having the opportunity to travel.

July? (Well, Julia actually!)

From my perspective it was back to the drawing board; or back to the dating website.

Whilst I was not progressing very far in finding the long-term relationship I sought, I was gaining a fair bit of experience about life in the Philippines and the pleasures, perils and pitfalls which came with it. However, up to that point, I had been seeing life along a strip of land about two miles long with tourist hotels dotted along it. Added to that I had visited the sort of places Filipinos wanted me to visit. Shopping malls, restaurants, etc.

I decided to persist with my search but, for the next trip, would stay at a different hotel. I felt I had been treated shabbily at the beach resort and, whilst I may not have helped my own cause much, had no wish to put any more business their way.

So whilst I was looking at the dating website I was also looking for a different hotel base. Having dealt with an airline that had managed to separate me from my baggage on both legs of a flight, I also looked around for a change of carrier.

Before moving the story forward there are a few cultural issues worthy of mention. Setting a time for a date is viewed differently in the Philippines. In the west I would not be surprised if a date arrived ten or fifteen minutes late. I would probably get a text to explain she was running late. Do not expect that in the Philippines. Time has a different momentum and, from a western perspective, there is a definite air of serendipity to the Filipina. Being late does not happen for the Filipina. For her (and her male counterparts) time does not occur in the linear way it does in the west. If the lady is an hour late it will hardly merit comment on her part and there will certainly be no apology. The same holds for online dates so expect to wait. It is not an attempt to wind you up, it is a way of life for her. The Spanish concept of mañana is also deeply embedded in day to day life. If something can be put off until tomorrow, it will be.

Another thing I have found disconcerting but also occurring consistently is the attitude to gifts or presents. Don't expect a 'thank you'. It is not likely to happen. With a physical gift it will probably be taken away to be opened at a later time when the lady is alone. This links to 'amor propio'. She does not want to be party to a situation which could cause her, you, or anyone else around her, any embarrassment. Operating in this way means that, whether the gift is above or below expectation, no one will have a problem because only she will be present when she reacts to the gift. There will be no prying eyes and no opportunity for comparison. Similarly if you advance in a relationship to where you are sending financial support prior to your lady visiting your home country, do not expect to be thanked for your donation. It may occur occasionally but no acknowledgement means there is no place for embarrassment or any other issue. Everyone can be happy as there is no risk of anyone losing face.

A further issue is around telling the truth and lying. The difficulty on each side is that for the Filipino, once a statement has been made as a truth, whether true or false, for the sake of amor propio they are socially pressured to stick with it. So, even when it becomes patently obvious to all that an untruth has been told, there is a likelihood of no backing down, no losing face and neither apology nor acceptance that anything untoward has occurred. I would link this to another socio-cultural difference. If I am asked a question I will try to answer it. If I don't know the answer I will say that I don't know. If I am not sure, I am likely to be clear that I am not sure or caveat my answer with conditions. The Filipinos I have met and heard chat do not do this. If a question is asked, an answer is required. I suspect this can lead quite quickly into situations where, having given a wrong or inappropriate answer, the Filipino is then stuck with social pressure not to lose face or cause anyone else to. So they stay with their initial response. This is likely to lead to them ending up in an untenable position. Within their own culture the issue will not be pursued because the whole of society understands the problems of causing someone to lose face and how the communications game is played. In their own communities a person will never be put in a position where they are deliberately made to squirm or feel some element of shame. However when Johnny Foreigner comes along (s)he will continually force these issues with the result that the Filipino will lose face and might well become very upset with their questioner. However, subliminally through culture, (s)he has learned not to cause offence to others so they are unlikely to challenge or complain. The likely result will be silence, maybe some muttering and a hanging of the head. When this happens between a couple a bout of 'tampo' (a very Filipino type of sulking) may result. (More on this later.)

Filipinos, particularly women, also communicate with each other by way of what is called 'eyebrow talk'; literally the way one moves ones eyebrows up and down. Dependent upon the strength of the message this may also link with other facial expressions and the turn of the eye. This, for her, is part of day to day life and the process has been carried across to the U.K. by my wife. On returning from a trip to visit a relative I made a comment to my wife which, to a British contemporary, would have got a reply. I got silence so I repeated the comment. Still silence so I asked her if she had heard me. "Yes," she said. I raised my eyebrows. When driving down a motorway eyebrow talk does not work! However this has happened before so maybe I should have guessed.

I spent much of my early working life dealing with people who continually told lies. With their words came tone of voice and body language. Over time it became relatively straightforward to understand with some confidence when I was being lied to, whether it was clients or former colleagues doing the lying. It was much the same situation as a parent finds themselves in with a young child who denies eating all the chocolate when their face is covered in it.

There are a couple of other significant issues I wish to flag up here. Firstly the body language of a Filipino is significantly different to that displayed by people in the west. There are overlaps here and there but much of the time there are major differences. So reading body language accurately is tricky and making mistakes common place. This is true both ways. A Filipino reading western body language is bound to make the same mistakes. They too will assume the westerner makes the same gestures and expressions as the Filipino. The difficulty for both parties is that it takes some time to realise these errors are occurring and this can very quickly lead to distrust. Secondly do not make assumptions based on the tone of a Filipino's voice. There are major contradictions with western norms here as well. My wife will often end a phone call to family or friends and I will have no idea it has ended. There are none the traditional tones around farewell.

Finally irony and sarcasm seem to be lost on the Filipino. My limited experience had stopped me using either as they routinely seem to be confused with mockery and ridicule.

April, May and June had passed but, on the dating website, things were much the same as usual. Around 70% of the replies I received were from would-be scammers or people playing games. Of the remainder most of the exchanges I had would last for a couple of weeks before we realised we were not really much of a match for each other. One or two members stayed longer and we would chat for a while before moving onto video chatting. This was another area where one could anticipate a dropout rate. The woman would see what I really looked like and that I really was the age and the size I claimed to be. I would also see her, warts and all; although I have to say there are few Filipinas I find to be physically unattractive, and I have yet to find a wart! But I was looking for intellect over physical beauty, whilst trying to discover both! I hoped to find someone with potential. Someone with a good enquiring mind who could use it.

So the chats continued and I was confident that, whenever I booked the next trip, there would be a few people from the website who I could arrange to meet. After the first visit I had changed my way of thinking about these trips. Initially they were for the sole purpose of finding that special relationship. However I had lightened up considerably and took the view that I was going on holiday to a tropical island where I could meet a few local women amongst whom I might find the right one for me. But, if that did not happen, what the heck. I would at least have enjoyed a good holiday. I still held the view that I would not arrive to play the field nor did I avail myself of any adult services. I had taken the view that I would arrange a meeting with one specific woman whilst having two or three alternatives in mind perchance things didn't work out, and I stayed with that plan.

I decided to return to Metro Cebu. I knew my way around the area a bit now and did not want to spend time in Manila. Across the metropolitan area were the owners of thousands of member's profiles so finding someone to meet would not present a difficulty. When I came to reserve my flight the best financial deal I found was with Royal Brunei Airlines. The downside was that there were several stopovers and changes of flight. I needed to go from my local airport to London Heathrow. From there I would fly to Bandar Seri Begawan, close to Darussalam, the capitol of Brunei, with a stopover en route in Dubai. At Bandar Seri Begawan I would need to collect baggage from my flight from Heathrow then check-in again for a different plane with the same operator to reach Manila, where there would be another change of flight and operator and collection of baggage along with a change of terminal. Then on to Mactan, Cebu. (There is, of course, the ethical issue one now has to deal with. Brunei in an islamic state which has tightened up its application of sharia law. Now openly gay people and anyone guilty of adultery can be sentenced to death by stoning. This hard-line should be kept in mind if considering travel through the state of Brunei.)

I gave some serious thought to the hotel. I did not particularly want to stay in a city centre hotel. The beach hotels were okay but they were really for couples and families. They were also restrictive, partly because of security issues, partly due to their location, but mostly because the owners wanted to keep a captive audience on site. So I sat down and made a list of what I was looking for. I then checked that against the offerings of the various accommodation websites which cover The Philippines.

I did not want to be in a place where there were hundreds of traditional holidaymakers people milling around 24/7, but neither did I want to be isolated. I wanted a place which had good transport links and was secure. It was important that my personal property would be completely safe when I left the hotel. I also wanted a place which had a good wifi, a swimming pool, air conditioning and food I could eat. I settled on one of the places I had visited whilst using the introduction agency during my third trip; the Waterfront Airport Hotel. (Not to be confused with the Waterfront City Hotel in downtown Cebu City – same hotel group but different hotel.)

One of the dates arranged by the introduction agency on my previous trip had been to a restaurant at the Waterfront Airport and the food had been well above average. (What a terribly English way of saying things! Why don't I just say: "good"?) Also, despite it being located very close to an international airport, I could not remember having heard any aircraft noise; in fact I hadn't even been aware of the airport. On the accommodation websites I looked for feedback and comment from former guests. They were generally favourable; where noise was mentioned it was usually in the context of it being surprisingly quiet. It had a decent size of swimming pool and a variety of room options. A very big plus was that, after a twenty-four trip, I did not want to be doing battle with locals trying to make a few coins by getting me into the taxi of their choice. I knew where the Airport Hotel was; just across the road from the Arrivals Hall, a short walk of two or three hundred metres from plane to hotel check-in. The complex also housed the Mactan Casino. Whilst I am not much of a gambler and have never used a casino, this did mean that security would be high and the general public would not be all over the site. So I took the plunge and made my reservations.

By the time I was packing my bags and ready to travel I had been chatting for a couple of months with a woman we will call Julia; (to call her July would be far too pretentious!) She told me she had recently finished a relationship with a French guy. He had returned to France; contact had become minimal and then stopped altogether. She was twenty-five years old and did some work in the family sari-sari store.

The day before I travelled I told her of my trip and we agreed to meet on my first evening at an Italian restaurant on the Marina Mall complex about a ten minute walk from the hotel. After the experience of my third trip I hoped I would have some clothes to wear!

The flight was enjoyable but weird. It was like being on a long coach trip. Forty-five minutes then change plane. Six hours and then off the plane for refuelling and back on again an hour later. Off after another five hours, change plane, a couple of hour's flight and then Manila. The best part of four hours to get the visa stamped into the passport, collect my luggage, and then change terminals. Argument over how my suitcase had managed to increase in weight by three kilos between the terminals; spreading the alleged excess across hand luggage and into various pockets, etc. to prevent local baggage surcharges. Ridiculous. All this followed by a further ninety minute flight into Cebu.

Royal Brunei is the only islamic airline I have flown with. It was unusual to me to have a constant reminder of where I was in relation to Mecca. There was no alcohol available on the flight. I was still drinking at this stage but, for many years, had avoided alcohol whilst on a long haul journey; the two just don't mix. The Royal Brunei experience was good; Manila Airport was anything but. By the time I came out of Mactan Airport I was glad to have a reservation at the Airport Hotel. I crossed the road, checked in and was taken to my room which was considerably more than expected.

Whilst the bedroom was smaller than that provided by the beach resort it was big enough and had plenty of storage space. The bed was a queen sized double. The bathroom was not big but had a bath, toilet, sink and two showers, one built into the bath space, the other a separate unit. However the big surprise was that I also had a short entrance hall and lounge with a three piece suite. It was not the world's most comfortable, of a wicker construction, but it was certainly fit for purpose. Both lounge and bedroom had a television. The lounge had views in two directions, one of which was across the metropolitan area of Cebu City to the mountains beyond. There was a safe in the bedroom but the lock didn't work; however the hotel offered a safety deposit box service located as a part of reception services; this was very secure, accessible 24/7; absolutely ideal. (In May, 2018, I discovered that the safes in the rooms are now fully functional.)

I arrived in the early afternoon, just in time for the 2 pm check-in. Once unpacked I found the swimming pool. It was about thirty metres by twelve and just over a metre deep throughout, with a small circular area separated off as a paddling area for young children. At one end of it, at ground floor level, were rooms used by the hotel staff and a small gym. Above these were several guest rooms. At the opposite end were the toilets which doubled as changing rooms and an area in which to shower. The hotel bordered one side of the pool, the other side were gardens with a couple of water features. (A recent change has seen the gym moved to the hotel side of the pool, its former location being returned to guest rooms.) For me it was ideal. I like to swim lengths for exercise.

Poolside was really the only integral part of the hotel where aircraft could be heard; even then it was not a problem. The hotel is adjacent to but on a small rise above the main airport buildings. The runways were on the opposite side of the airport buildings to the hotel, about a kilometre away at their closest. Coupled with that the main noise associated with take-off and landing are towards the ends of the runways. These would be at least a further kilometre or so away. My room was on the fifth floor and there was no aircraft noise at all there, just an occasional faint vibration as a large plane landed. The lobby and reception was a large area facing the airport and ran into the bar and main dining room area. If it was quiet and you were listening carefully the noise of aircraft was just about audible when sat in reception. For travellers who are looking for a posh hotel at which you can strut your stuff and pose amongst fellow travellers, flashing designer labels, etc. this will not be the place for you. But it suited me fine. It was a hotel used by business people and travellers. There was a distinct lack of posturing by fashion obsessive bimbos parading around which had been a hallmark of the beach hotels. Overall I considered I had made a good choice. I returned during my next three trips and several times subsequently and would recommend this hotel for anyone travelling into Cebu. It is not a logical first choice being next to an international airport and surrounded by a lot of light industry. But being so close to the airport and sharing the site with a 24 hour casino means there are a regular supply of taxis at very short notice. These taxi drivers know they have to behave themselves, to do otherwise would be cutting their nose to spite their face. Jeepneys service the airport and are available a short walk away. They will take you to Marina Mall, the nearest shopping centre, just under a kilometre away for seven pesos, about twelve pence, from where you can get jeepneys to destinations across the metropolitan area.

There are cash machines on site which take most international credit and debit cards. There is a charge per transaction and, whilst you can withdraw up to the limit your account sets, these machines, and the ones in Cebu's shopping malls, only allow P10,000 [£160; €176; $203] per transaction. If you need more than P10,000 then you need to make more transactions so there are more local cash machine charges.

The hotel itself is clean and well maintained. Some of the fittings could be described as tired; I would prefer charming. There is live music in the lobby lounge on the three weekend evenings. Generally the food is very good but, on occasions, I have experienced much the same difficulties with the water, so my diet and liquid intake are still somewhat inhibited. I have found all the staff hard working, competent and helpful, keen to make my visit a good experience, most spoke good English and they were far superior to most of the staff I came across at beach resorts. As it is an airport hotel very few guests stay for more than one night. They check-in, sleep, have breakfast, check-out and move on. So, if you stay a few nights, the staff get to recognise you and you are able to build up a good rapport. One thing I did appreciate was being told at the first check-in that the corkage system was in operation. It did not come as a surprise but it was good practice on the part of the hotel to make sure guests understand these ground rules. The beach resort staff only advised me of this once they believed I was transgressing! Whilst the hotel food is high quality and well presented, if you are looking for a cheaper option the airport is only a couple of minutes' walk away with a variety of small cafes and snack-bars. On my first couple of visits there was a local Sitio shopping centre up the side of the airport where snacks and drinks were available at a very low prices. However this was demolished as terminal two of the airport, international arrivals and departures, was constructed. The domestic terminal now occupies what was the terminal for both international and domestic flights. The international terminal is now an additional 500 metres walk away. There is a complimentary bus service available between the terminals. With baggage the walk can be a sweaty experience. It is also possible to arrange for a hotel car to meet your flight. However it is still only a short walk from the airport to the hotel.

Julia was an interesting lady. She had the best command of the English language of the women I had dated so far and we had an enjoyable meal. Over a couple of hours we shared a few experiences and agreed we had similar aspirations and goals. We separated around 10 pm and agreed she would meet me at the hotel the following afternoon.

We had a swim together and some drinks at the poolside and continued chatting. She brought up the subject of the former French boyfriend. They had apparently been together for around two years before his return to France. I asked why he had not returned to Cebu. She hesitated and then told me that he had not kept up his side of a deal they had. I asked if that deal was of any relevance to me; if we decided to become a couple did she have some kind of arrangement in mind. Again she hesitated and then said that the deal she had with the Frenchman was that he paid the rent on the house they lived in with her family; it was 5,000 php per month, [£80; €88; $101.50]. This was a house they had lived in with her parents and three siblings, so it would have been more than a single room with cooking and W.C.; it also incorporated a small sari-sari store. There was a lull in our conversation. I then asked her how she saw our relationship developing. She responded: "I will love you so long as you keep paying the rent on my parent's house." I thought that was what had been coming; however I flushed out further just what she had in mind. She was offering to build a relationship together, move to my country and live with me, get married, and have children. None of this presented a problem to her so long as the rent was paid on the family home here in Cebu City. That gave me pause for thought, further emphasised the importance of family to the Filipinos, and further exposed the differences between our respective realities and cultures.

We had a meal together and she left the hotel around nine that evening; we had made a tentative arrangement to meet two days later as she had to work in the sari-sari store the following day.

This gave me a little time to think through what she had suggested. Again I found myself in the realm of being asked to buy a person only in this case she was renting out her own life and ambitions; or, more accurately, was marketing herself as a long-term investment at £80 a month. This would include the full suite of domestic and bedroom services! Provided her family home was paid for she would marry and continue life as a normal married woman. From a business perspective it was a pretty good deal! Even if we married, were we to hit hard times, she would leave if the rent on the family house went unpaid. How would that play in any financial settlement around divorce proceedings?! The way in which Julia was framing the arrangement that would not be an issue; if the rent stopped she would be on the next available flight home. Her job was to make sure the rent got paid; if she had to marry and make babies to do that, she would. As soon as the monthly rental ceased, she would be off to find someone who would pay the rent! It was a concept I found quite abhorrent. Not only does it mean I would be demeaning a woman I wanted to love and marry, I would also be demeaning myself.

> Q. Are you in love?
> A. Yes, it costs me £80 per month.

I used the dating website to send Julia a message. Effectively I thanked her for being so frank and honest with me but told her that I did not think this was the best way to manage a relationship and suggested that, whilst it was really none of my business, she should consider finding some other, legitimate, means of paying the rent. I wished her well. She replied a few hours later thanking me for being sufficiently honest to tell her this at the outset rather than move her into the hotel as a bed-mate for a couple of weeks before discarding her. To think in that way I think she must have experienced that sort of behaviour before. We parted amicably enough but it gave me a further insight in the realities of life for a Filipina and how, even those dating site members who were not obvious scammers, could have their own agendas which were likely to include finance in some way, shape or form.

Had I known the price of rental property when May's mother and interpreter asked for money, I would have seriously considered renting a place for May for a few months whilst she applied for her passport and we sorted out a visa application. Another example of the wonders of hindsight!

Given the huge difference in the economic realities of life for a western male able to take early retirement and a young adult Filipina starting out on life, this should be hardly surprising. However the difference is not just financial. Let us briefly revisit current Philippine reality. A national election for a new government and President took place on 9th May, 2016. There were five presidential candidates one of whom was the mayor of Davao City, the main city on the island of Mindanao in the south of the country, a man called Roberto Duterte. Just to the north of his island is Negros Island, split politically into the states of Negros Occidental and Negros Oriental. The capital and major town of Negros Oriental is Dumaguete City, home to the oddly named Silliman University! The weekly newspaper issued in this city is called The Negros Chronicle. On page five of the issue of 1st May, 2016, in a section titled Reader's Views, I found the following letter. It was submitted by Cecilia Hofmann of GWAVE (Gender Watch against Violence and Exploitation) and related to an article concerning Duterte which had been published in the issue of the same newspaper the previous week. It neatly portrays a cameo of current cultural realities for Filipinas. Publication was under the headline:

Rape joke: a moral squalor.

Anyone, seeing the lifeless body of a murdered woman, her throat slit, after the torture of gang rape, would be engulfed with horror and pity, and an infinite sadness at her personal fate. But not a Presidential candidate [Duterte] who said that the thought that came into his mind was sexual – he should have had the privilege of raping her first.

The large audience listening to this statement laughed, delighted with their candidate's "joke". What they call humour, we call moral squalor, on the part of one seeking the highest office in the land.

It is disheartening and even frightening to witness the continuing devaluing of women, the trivialisation of women (how Filipinos adore pageants of near naked women – what's been called a "glammed-up meat market").

How often have we heard the domestic violence law tagged as "biased" or GAD [gender and development] measures as a mere nuisance and waste of resources, or complaints that there isn't an International Men's Day when there is one for women?

The[se] ends so much more constitute evidence of peoples' continuing educational and moral underdevelopment as regards many things, but in particular, as regards the half of humanity that are women.

Rape is a deadly weapon on the war on women, GWAVE sees daily how rape devastates lives, and diminishes us all as a society. GWAVE never laughs [about rape].

It does not auger well for us that political leaders and great swathes of the population think it is a mere laughing matter.

Duterte won the election by a landslide. A contradiction? Well, as Mayor in his home city for around twenty years he has fought a war against drug running and the organised crime which goes with it. It has to be acknowledged that his efforts have met with considerable success. So far during his term of office the government accepts there have been over seven thousand extra-judicial killings which are widely accepted as a nationwide extension of Duterte's policy in Davao City. Human rights groups put this figure in the tens of thousands. There will be those who see this strategy as state sponsored murder. That may be an accurate description. However, in drug and crime ridden cities in the Philippines, this hard-line policy has generated a lot of support. Furthermore he is responsible for forming special police units to deal with the issue of child prostitution and exploitation. These units are also meeting with success. His methods may not be seen positively by many outside the Philippines; some of his opinions are lurid, but he is getting positive results when tackling some of the most noxious crimes one can imagine. So there is a definite contradiction. A President who has allegedly supported gang rape is running on a high-tide of popularity because of the measures he has taken to combat narcotics, serious sex crimes against children and organised crime generally!

About six months after Duterte's election, the Inquirer, a national Philippine newspaper, had this article on its website, (photo, advertising and Philippine language content removed):

Duterte tells law graduates how he spanks female cops

By: Leila B. Salaverria - Reporter / @LeilasINQ
Philippine Daily Inquirer / 12:16 AM November 27, 2016
http://newsinfo.inquirer.net/848251/duterte-tells-law-graduates-how-he-spanks-female-cops

President Rodrigo Duterte speaking at the San Beda College of Law Alumni Homecoming. —From an RTVM video

There are too many prohibitions in these "modern times," President Rodrigo Duterte said on Saturday.

He said he is the kind of person who likes to joke around even with members of his female security staff, who he playfully spanks in the rear.

Mr. Duterte made the observation after saying in jest that San Beda College should have allowed female students during his time so that he would have done better in class, especially if the women were pretty.

"The problem in these modern times and the living past, everything is prohibited," he said in a speech before San Beda law graduates.

He said he is a person who likes to joke around.

I like to joke around. The police women, I spank them on their bottoms in Malacañang [the official Presidential residence in Manila] if I'm ill-tempered. I get my folder and tell them, you're part of the problem," he said, demonstrating how he spanks them with a folder.

He said western mores have gone too far.

Our lives now are no longer fun," he added.

But he said he is aware if sexual harassment is taking place.

Not only is he aware of sexual harassment, by general western standards he is sexually harassing these women and happily discussing it with the media!

When considering the actions of the Filipinas I have met keeping this sort of information in mind is important. The Philippines can be a tough place. What I consider reality for women may or may not be right, but it will reflect my understanding of issues in the west. It is a false understanding when considering the situation of those in the Philippines.

There will also be an impact upon how the Filipina sees herself and her position within her society. For her to make the shift to a western society will also present major challenges as she will not have any experience of the freedoms western women, rightly, have. Nor any realistic conception of the struggle for equality which is still being fought.

Post Julia.

I had made a reservation at the Airport Hotel for seventeen nights. Before going to sleep on the second night Julia and I were history. I was glad I had maintained contact with two or three other members of the dating website. I wanted to enjoy a holiday but I also wanted to maximise my opportunity of meeting Miss Right.

I thought I would also visit the bar which I had frequented when staying at the beach resort. The three young women who staffed it were all good lookers and would have friends. They flirted with customers but it was a very gentle flirting. I had never seen them leave the bar area with a customer and thought they would probably have their boyfriends. The latest I had ever been at that bar was around 1 am and I knew it claimed to stay open until 4 am. So there may have been things going on that I did not know about. That said they also had a dozen or so rooms for rent to genuine tourists and I knew that staff hours rotated as they had to provide breakfast for guests. Nonetheless it would be interesting to let them know the reason for my trips to see if they might make any suggestions.

There were also many women working at the Airport hotel. I found most of them attractive Whether or not they had any interest in me was something I would never discover. Most of my late evenings were spent in the lobby bar and, at that time, I was drinking like a fish. In a country where the typical female body size was a fraction of mine, my consumption rate would have seemed absolute lunacy to them; ultimately it also seemed that way to me. That said I was not an aggressive, noisy, amorous or badly behaved drunk. Alcohol was more likely to lead to my nodding off to sleep! My experiences with drink have only pushed me towards violence when I have been consuming whisky. For some reason I quickly turn nasty if I consume whisky. It goes to my head very quickly; something I have never experienced with any other form of alcohol; and there are few I have not tried. When drinking whisky I would actively look for a fight and find myself in the frame of mind to argue about anything with anybody. Having realised this I stopped drinking whisky during my early twenties. I had knocked beer and lager on the head by my mid 30's; they made a significant contribution to weight gain and also created the most awful flatulence! During a normal working week I would never drink on the evening before a working day which normally translated into being sober from Sunday afternoon until Friday evening. But on Friday and Saturday evenings I would make up for lost time. When on holiday, whilst rarely drinking during the daytime, in the evenings I did not hold back. The hotel staff were aware of this. I would happily sink a couple of litres of wine or the best part of a bottle of spirits. That was my normal consumption from the bar whilst staying at the Airport Hotel. I also made sure I had my private stock in the room. Whilst I paid their prices and tipped well I would definitely be seen as someone they would keep at arm's length. So much so that one of the waitresses, whilst serving me double vodkas or gins, I don't remember which, told me I was drinking far too much and asked if I was trying to kill myself! The lady was very polite and what she said did stick with me. One of the excuses I made to myself was that alcohol helped to ensure a good night's sleep, particularly in a strange bed. The reality was that I was anaesthetising myself! Since I have stopped drinking I find my sleep is far better than it ever was whilst drinking; and so are a variety of other things!

However, I digress. I returned to the dating website and contacted the other three women with whom I had been chatting. I agreed to meet two of them on consecutive days around mid-day at specific locations of their choice in shopping malls. I made sure I was there in good time and waited an hour beyond the agreed meeting time. In both instances no one showed. On my return to the hotel on each occasion I sent messages to them through the dating website. One didn't reply, the other said she had been detained on unexpected business but declined to meet when offered a second opportunity. Either they were not using the website seriously or, more likely, they had weighed me up from a distance and thought to themselves: "thanks, but no thanks!"

The third woman told me she worked and could not easily take time out. Despite her profile on the dating website describing her occupation as 'student', her work was as a waitress at a bar restaurant a few kilometres from the Airport Hotel. I asked her if there were any quiet times during her working day. She suggested I visit the bar/restaurant around six or half past in the evening, so I did.

When I arrived at her place of work I found there were around thirty tables outside but, despite good weather, all were empty. Indoors there were plenty more tables and a thriving business was operating. Five or six of the tables were occupied by groups of diners. Some tables had been pulled together and were occupied by fifteen or twenty male ex-pats. They were full of themselves. I asked at the bar for the woman I was hoping to meet and was pointed to someone I did not recognise. This woman was busy attending to a man who seemed to be of western origin and in his mid-seventies. He either had a fairly serious mobility problem or, more likely, was blind drunk. She was trying to walk him from the main body of the restaurant towards the toilet area at the rear. As I approached I could see she was the right person. I could also see that her dating website profile, on which she claimed to be twenty three years old, of slim build weighing in at forty kilos, as well as being a student, was in some serious need of refreshing. She looked at least ten years older and at least double the weight. Nor had life been particularly kind to her. This was emphasised as one of the ex-pats walked towards her and took hold of one of her breasts which he began to massage through her clothes. "Have you come to meet our ...?" he asked. Whilst it didn't have the look of a girlie bar and was well away from that part of town I wondered if I had walked into a brothel.

Showing a complete lack of gallantry I replied: "If she is a college student in her mid-twenties then I've got the right person". Conned once again, I thought to myself.

At this point the elderly man began to slide from her grip. She grabbed him and hauled him off towards the bathroom. The ex-pats offered me a place at their table. They communicated in English; loud and crude

English. Their accents, and the occasional word picked up from their native tongues, suggested them to be a mixture of Scandinavian, German and Slav. They tried to sell me women, young, old or in between, accommodation, passports and/or visas and sexy trips into the city. I took the easy way out; through the front door; quickly.

My visits to the bar close to the beach hotels became more interesting. The women working there knew me from my three previous trips. I told them of the website I used and two of the three of them claimed to be members of the same site. Why had I not seen them online? Well, they tended to surf during their working time when it was quiet. That translated into mid to late evening Philippine time which was the middle of the working day in the U.K. so we would have generally been using the site at different times. However the main reason was that when specifying their location on the website they had used their home town or city. There is a lot of mobility amongst the young Filipino population as they move around the country to find work and opportunities. These young women, all in their early twenties, gave their locations as the town and island on which they were born and where their families lived. So their website accounts did not link at all to Metro Cebu and they would never show up on a website search of that area or in a Metro Manila search because they had not bothered to change their home base details on the website. That is why I had never seen them whilst using the dating website. Once they knew I was a member of that website they moved to a different part of the bar and chattered amongst themselves but I could see them scrolling their mobiles and having the occasional giggle. The upshot was that two or three days later I received an 'interest' on my profile from a woman who worked at this establishment. I had seen her but she was not amongst the bar staff. She would occasionally appear in the bar area but to either serve food or to tidy up. Usually she was in the kitchen area which was well away from the bar itself. She was a highly attractive young woman whose profile told me she was twenty-two years old.

We exchanged a few messages and I asked if she would like to join me for a meal. We discovered that the only time she had free during my stay was a couple of days before my return flight was due to depart. We agreed we would have a meal together away from her place of work although that would be where we would meet up.

Our date was still about a week away so I continued searching the dating website. As the meetings, perhaps better described as non-meetings, with dating website members were taking place I had received an 'interest' and a brief message from a site member who called herself Tina. I followed this up. Tina's profile told me she was twenty one years old and a part-time student from Leyte Island. Leyte is quite a large island and the fastest ferry trip from Cebu would take two hours each way. We began to chat online. In one message I told her I was in Cebu City and asked if she would meet me if I travelled to Leyte. She replied that Leyte Island was where she had been born but she was currently living with her parents and siblings in Cebu City. So, the next day, we met at the Mall closest to her home.

Whilst chatty online when meeting in the flesh she seemed happy enough but was quite reserved. The time passed quickly as I got answers to the questions I asked her, but she did not ask many in return. That said she was attractive and clear in her intentions. She wanted to find a foreign husband and would like to leave the Philippines and live in his country. We enjoyed a coffee together and I asked her if she would like to meet the following day. She agreed but said I would need to meet her parents first and she would need to be properly chaperoned and would have a curfew. I asked why she had not been chaperoned today to which she grinned and said her parents thought she had just gone for a walk to do some window shopping at the local Mall. In effect that was just what she was doing; I was in the shop window. On asking her if there was any place she would particularly like to go her immediate response was Mountain View. I had never heard of Mountain View and asked her where it was. I got the predictable answer: "Somewhere in the mountains." Cebu Island is 122 miles (195 km.) from north to south and 20 miles (32 km) wide at its broadest. Running down the centre is a spine of mountains rising to around 3,300 feet, (1,000 metres). Mountain View could be anywhere.

We agreed a landmark close to her home where we would meet at 2 pm the following afternoon. When I got back to the hotel I asked about Mountain View. I was told it was fairly local and an oft visited beauty spot in an 'out of the way' location. It would take around an hour to get there by taxi. There was no taxi rank at Mountain View, transport was essential, so the taxi had to be retained. The concierge staff with whom I spoke told me it was a viewpoint high in the mountains overlooking Cebu City and Mactan Island. If the weather was clear the view was fantastic. They also suggested that I consider visiting at night, particularly if I had female company, because the view across the city with all the lights twinkling and then onwards and out over the ocean was very romantic. They suggested that a price should be negotiated in advance with a taxi driver which needed to include the entry fee which was 50 pesos per person (including the driver). The return trip from the city with a wait of one hour should be somewhere between 1,000 and 1,500 php, (£20 ± 15%, €22; $25). Not bad for a trip out.

Tina and I met at 2 pm as planned. The spot where the taxi driver dropped me off was a very busy narrow street with shops and commercial premises on each side. Whilst smells of the local cafes and businesses were noticeable they barely concealed an unpleasant background aroma. There were people everywhere. When Tina met me she was with two other women who were introduced as her mother and her younger sister. The sister may have been a couple of years younger, she was also significantly pregnant. They led me down a series of 20-30 badly eroding steps at the edge of the road into an area of shacks and sheds which ran into each other, through each other, across each other, over and under each other, etc. It was a chaotic place; within a few seconds I was completely lost. Most of the paths were narrow but walkable; others provided drainage and, from the aroma, what was draining was everything produced by thousands of people whose circumstances forced them into communal living on the edge. This was my first real experience of the slums of Cebu City. I had thought that May's home in a poor part of Mandaue City was challenging; this was something else altogether. After a few minutes we emerged from the gloom and stench of shacks tightly packed together onto a piece of rough communal ground around forty metres square which had a gap in one corner sufficient to allow a small vehicle in. There were bits of grass here and there and a couple of straggly trees, plenty of moped tracks and several tethered up cockerels making their collective presences felt, testament to cockfighting which is still a major sport in the Philippines. There were children everywhere. All smiling, all happy, all noisy, all pretty normal children. The women acknowledged them as we walked quite briskly along one edge of the rough ground and disappeared into a corner where, after making three 90° turns, we entered a small house. The outside smells were left behind. It was clean and tidy but there was little by way of furniture. The settee unfolded to make a double bed and that was the only bed the family had.

For Tina, this was home. But why did everyone call her Joe? She explained that Tina was the name she used for the dating website; her real name was Joanne. That was a relief; I think; or could I have fallen for a ladyboy whose real name was Joseph?!

I had the usual chat with the family – what are your intentions, etc. which I explained. They seemed okay with what I was suggesting but I did not know how much English they understood. After the best part of a couple of hours we made our way back to the main road, found a taxi and off we went to Mountain View accompanied by the pregnant sister and a cousin, a young girl who would have been seven or eight years old.

Because of it closeness to the equator, daylight and night time in the Visayas each last about twelve hours varying by around half an hour over the course of a year. Around five thirty in the morning dawn is breaking and around five thirty in the afternoon dusk approaches. The change from daylight to darkness is also quite brisk, fifteen to twenty minutes. Hotel staff had told me how the Mountain View aspect changed between day and night so I made sure it was around four when we got into the taxi. We arrived about quarter to five, whilst it was daylight, and arranged with the taxi driver that we would leave no earlier than 6 pm.

The idea was that we would take in the view in both daylight and darkness. We managed this and it was definitely worth the effort. The daytime view showed the entirety of Metro Cebu. From the north we could see the southern end of Consolacion, Liloan, Mandaue City, Cebu City and the northern part of Talisay City. Beyond Mandaue City was Lapu-Lapu City, the Airport and the whole of Mactan Island was laid out before us. Beyond that was a haze peeping through which was the west coast of Bohol Island and between Bohol and Mactan Islands were a plethora of other tiny islands and rocky outcrops. It really was a spectacular view. We spent a little time picking out different places. It began to go dark and, by the time we left, was absolutely dark. The view changed and was again stunning. Joanne's choice of a place to visit was a big hit. We held hands and she snuggled up to me in the taxi. I decided that if this continued I would have to make sure she was really a Joanne and not a Joseph!

She could not see me the following day as there was work to be done for her family. For me that was something of a relief because, aside from the gender issue, the next evening I would be taking the woman from the Maribago bar out for a meal.

We had agreed to meet at 7.30 pm and I arrived with some chocolates and a red rose; an optimist with high hopes. My date did not show. I asked her colleagues working the bar if they knew where she was. One agreed to call her. She returned with the message that she was coming but: "she is shy, very, very shy."

She arrived an hour late and we took a taxi to a nearby shopping centre which offered several choices of restaurant. The lady decided to stay with local cuisine. That was fine by me. We chatted amicably and enjoyed our food. After about an hour things were drawing to a natural conclusion in the restaurant. Somewhat impulsively I asked her if she had been to Mountain View and she said she had, just once, during the daytime. I told her it was a very romantic place to visit once darkness had fallen and asked if she would like to make the trip together. After a slight pause for thought she agreed. So, a taxi was found, a price negotiated, and off we went. My intentions were to try to build a friendship and, if all went well, a little romance. We continued to chat. Once at Mountain View we joined many other couples who were 'admiring the view'. Some holding hands, some arm in arm, some kissing. I was not aware of anything happening beyond that and would have been surprised if anything was. This was a place very much for young Filipinos, and some who were not so young; it was not a place frequented by the ex-pat community. I may well have been the only non-Filipino there; I certainly did not see anyone else of obvious western origin. I am not suggesting that young Filipinos are not sexually active, they definitely are, but they are also very sensitive to the impression they may give to those around them. The ex-pat Lotharios whose paths I have crossed are just the opposite, the concept of discretion is not part of their vocabulary at all! Whilst love was definitely in the air, this was a busy place. Al fresco sex was highly unlikely particularly where amor-propio needed consideration! There were upwards of a hundred couples 'admiring the view' in one way or another.

And it was a view that was fantastic. We were sat on the edge of a wall overlooking the homes of over two million people. Way below us we could see the flickering lights of the metropolis, to each side of us the silhouettes of mountains, the distant sound of a waterfall; over twenty kilometres to the east were the distant lights on fishing vessels as they went about their business. Nocturnal creatures were flittering around; the air was heavily scented with the local flora; bougainvillea and jasmine? I reached for her hand. As soon as she felt contact she pulled away. After a couple of minutes I moved my arm, intending to put it around her shoulders. She stood and said: "We must leave now. Take me back to the bar." I knew that her home was two or three kilometres from the bar so I told her I would take her home instead as I wanted to be sure she was safe. A young woman walking home alone was a risk I did not want her to take, particularly on my account. This elicited a panicky response telling me we must go to the bar. A drive of over an hour followed with barely a word being exchanged. I tried to make conversation to begin with but got nothing by way of reply, not even acknowledgement. I did not understand what had caused this. The physical contact I had tried to instigate was absolutely minimal. Had I done or said something sexually suggestive I could have understood but nothing remotely close to that had occurred. As soon as the taxi pulled up at the bar she was out and away. I paid up and went in. She was nowhere to be seen.

So I had a couple of drinks at the bar and asked the staff if they knew where she was. They pointed towards the kitchen area and asked me what had happened; so I told them. They suggested that the physical contact, hand to hand or the attempted arm to shoulder, was perhaps too much for an unchaperoned young woman on a first date. Given what I understand of Philippine culture I understood that, however she had agreed to take a romantic trip with me in the darkness; she had also chosen to be unchaperoned. But I accept that her actions and my interpretation of them might reflect something of a cultural and/or generational difference.

However, when I next visited the bar, less than a year later, they told me that she was now married with a baby. At the time of our visit to Mountain View, unbeknown to me, she was engaged and her wedding took place about a month after I departed for the U.K. When we had shared a meal and visited Mountain View, she knew she was in the first trimester of her pregnancy. It was good to know I had done nothing compromising, although, had the offer been made I'm sure I would have risen to the occasion, (or made every effort too). It would not have taken much tempting. I was more relieved to know I could not be held responsible for the pregnancy; and, whilst acknowledging this was trickery yet again, understood I could easily have been tempted into a far more problematic position.

So, back to Joanne/Joseph. The day before returning to the U.K. we met. I had two or three hours with her at her home and invited her family to join us for a meal at the Airport Hotel. My motives were two-fold. I wanted to be friendly towards her family and demonstrate I was a decent man with whom they could trust their daughter. I also wanted to get to the bottom of my ladyboy worries, (not an accidental choice of words). She did not look at all male, but nor do ladyboys! I succeeded on one front; a good meal was enjoyed by all. The closest I got to a sex test was a goodnight kiss where I managed to place my leg between her legs. I did not feel anything unusual or get an unusual reaction; but it was hardly a scientific test!

The realities and stupidities of bureaucracies.

After returning to the U.K. Jo (Joe) and I maintained regular contact online. We used the dating website, also Facebook and Skype. We were getting on well together and chatting for an hour or more several times a week. When we used Facebook we tended to chat by exchanging text messages which was absolutely fine. However, when we used a video link, making conversation often became hard work from my perspective as Jo did not encourage conversation that much; often her input would be monosyllabic; a simple yes or no, with little effort, or ability/confidence to keep the conversation going. She seemed keen to visit the U.K., had the support of her family and I was happy for her to join me for a visit. It also made sense to progress that way. We both knew that, were things to progress as far as marriage, we would live in the U.K. It was important before that for Jo to spend time in my country to establish how she felt when here. It would create the important opportunity for both of us to discover how the British public would react to a relationship with such a big age difference. We would also be able to spend some time together before considering whether we were really a good match for each other or if, in our own ways, we were both chasing rainbows. But first we needed to know if Jo would be affected by the state of the U.K. as much as I was by the state of the Philippines; and I was an experienced traveller who had visited many different parts of the world. She was a young woman, so I believed, not much beyond adolescence, who had travelled between two large islands within the same country and always lived within her extended family. I also acknowledged that she had never experienced a temperature below about 23°C; being in the U.K. from June to November would be a major challenge for her, (and for me when the heating bill arrived)!!

I was also still in the position where I thought she was a Joanne but acknowledged a small risk that she could turn out to be a he. So, planning a visit would be a straightforward way of killing two birds with one stone. To visit she would need a visa. To get a visa she would need to apply for a passport. To get a passport she would have to produce official documents to prove her identity. Those documents would provide evidence of gender which would be incorporated into the passport. If gender was indicated as anything other than female I would need to make my apologies, etc.

For a British person applying for and receiving their first passport is a relatively straightforward matter. Complete and submit the application online with the payment or submit by post and pay at an enhanced price. Either way add the cost of secure postage. The process involves the completion and submission of an application form; signatures and counter signatures by a *responsible person*; send to the passport office with your birth certificate and that of one of your parents or with their passport. A few weeks later your passport will arrive along with the identity document provided by your parent; premium services being available should same week or same day service be required. I accept that for a young person making their first application this might be a bit of a test but that is due to their relative inexperience in dealing with bureaucracy and paperwork. However this is nothing compared to what occurs in the Philippines.

We may curse our bureaucracies from time to time but they are wonderful compared with the administrative nightmares of developing countries. The italicised information copied below came from the website http://passport.com.ph/requirements This was the official web link provided by the Philippine government to support its citizens when applying for their passport at the time when Jo(e) applied. There have been substantial and significant changes and this link no longer functions. The new link is: https://www.passport.gov.ph/requirements/new-application-adult The new process is a little more straightforward but much of what is discussed below still applies.

In brief, very brief, when a Philippine national applies for their first passport they need to make a personal appearance at a local office with a printed copy of the application form they have submitted online, a letter of invitation generated during the online application process, their birth certificate and a minimum of three additional specific identification documents, one of which must contain their photograph. The dreaded small print follows. Many abbreviations are used. I have written these in full and put them in [...] type brackets.

There are three elements to satisfy when a Filipino pulls together their first passport application. The first is called 'General Requirements'. The website told Jo(e) and I the following:

GENERAL REQUIREMENTS
Personal appearance
Confirmed appointment
For NCR [National Capital Region] - based applicants, present your printed application form downloaded from DFA [Department of Foreign Affairs] Appointment System
Birth Certificate (BC) in Security Paper (SECPA) issued by the Philippine Statistics Authority (PSA) or Certified True Copy (CTC) of BC issued by the Local Civil Registrar (LCR) and duly authenticated by PSA. Transcribed Birth Certificate from the LCR is required when entries in PSA Birth Certificate are blurred or unreadable. (Report of birth duly authenticated by PSA if born abroad)
Valid picture IDs and supporting documents to prove identity (Please refer to List of Acceptable IDs and List of Supporting Documents)

I will include the 'legally adopted' section of the advice here because, technically, that was the position May was in and the process she would have needed to negotiate to be issued with a passport.

Legally adopted:
Original and Certified True Copy (CTC) of the PSA amended Birth Certificate
Certified True Copy (CTC) of the Court Decision or Order on Adoption and Certificate of Finality
DSWD [Department of Social Welfare and Development] clearance for minor applicant, if traveling with the person other than the adopting parents

In case the applicant is for adoption by foreign parents:
Certified True Copy of the Court Decree of Abandonment of Child
<u>PSA Death Certificate</u> of the child's parents or the Deed of Voluntary Commitment executed after the birth of the child
Endorsement of child to the Inter-country Adoption Board by the DSWD
Authenticated Birth or Foundling Certificate

Provided you held a genuine birth certificate and access to a computer, and the skills to use it, then fulfilling the General Requirements was straightforward enough. But remember Table 2 in the Website Shenanigans chapter earlier, where the U.K. and the Philippines were compared? Only 40% of Filipinos were using the internet when these events occurred; and that information came from a 2016 report. In the west there will be very few people applying for their first passport who are unable to access and use online websites. That was not the case in the Philippines; levels of computer use amongst young people are fairly high compared to the rest of the population but still a long way from being universal. Access to computers and internet cafes also change dramatically when shifting from urban to rural communities. The applicant needed to go online, click on the link to the passport application form, and complete it. Once completed the document had to be printed off. Having done that the applicant then identified their local passport office and made an appointment. This process would automatically generate a Letter of Appointment which also had to be printed off and produced on arrival at the Passport Office. When making the appointment the applicant had to remember the need to provide further evidence of identification from a list of acceptable identification documents, (ids), and supporting documents. A further three documents as a minimum were required so there was no point in making the online application until the applicant had physical possession of these documents.

In the west most people have access to a bank account of some sort and a credit or debit card. Again that is not the case in the Philippines. If we think back to Table 1 of the comparison between the U.K. and the

Philippines we will remember that, whilst the number of electronic payments made across a year in the U.K. was in the teens of thousands of millions, in the Philippines it was too small to measure. If you are using a system which requires payment online you have to have an account and card. I have not asked around much but know that none of the women I met had this facility. As I write, in 2020, online banking is beginning to be seen in the Philippines, particularly in the major cities, but it is the province of the wealthy and the educated.

Going back to the General Requirements which need to be satisfied to submit a passport application and taking June and May as examples, I know that June had no difficulty with any of this; I was with her when she submitted her application. May would have had big problems. Whilst she was able to use a computer that was contingent upon finding the cash to use an internet café. There would then have been the issue of being able to remain online long enough to complete and print-off her application form. But that would have been the least of her problems. Her stepmother had put a price on May's head. Her birth certificate and any other documents, if they actually existed, would only come at a price; and that price would be determined by the stepmother. Adoption papers, or lack of, would be another issue.

The only mention May made to me with regard to her natural mother occurred the last time we were together. We talked of how she might apply for a passport and I asked if she knew where her natural mother was. She said that, so far as she knew, following her birth they had never met. A strange situation to be in. Immediately following her birth she had been looked after by her father. Until we were discussing the crazy situation of her leaving the Philippines with me I had believed her stepmother to be her natural mother. She had told me her father died when she was around three years old. If her birth certificate was not in the possession of her stepmother, or if her stepmother refused to release it, May would need to obtain a certified true copy from the Local Civil Registrar. That is fine if you know where you were born because you will then also know which Local Civil Registrar you need to approach. Did May know this? Did her stepmother know this? May was sadly in a position where her natural parents could not tell her. She could approach the Philippine Statistics Authority but would need to provide them with the information necessary to trace her. Again we are back to having to know where she was born. She did not know this and her stepmother was unlikely to tell her either way.

The bottom line with May was that she may have been able to obtain her birth certificate but it would mean either paying her stepmother or embarking on a journey through government bodies to get an acceptable copy. That would have been time consuming at best and, to a twenty year old who has not dealt with such organisations before, a daunting challenge. As I was originally writing this I tried on three occasions to access the website of the Philippine Statistics Authority; each time Google told me it could not be found. (Not an electronic glitch as other e-transactions occurred during the time these attempts were made.)

The next requirement for the passport application was an already existing identity card which contained a photograph. The government website provided the following information:

LIST OF ACCEPTABLE IDS (At least 1 of the following):
Government-issued picture IDs [Identity Documents] such as the following:
Digitized SSS [Social Security System] ID
Driver's License
GSIS E-card [Government Service Insurance System; its website tells us that: "The GSIS eCard is, by far, the most innovative government-issued identification card today. This is because the eCard Plus is not just a GSIS membership ID Card, it is also a GSIS transactional card, disbursement card, ATM Card, VISA debit card, hospitalization discount card, medicine discount card, and tuition discount card, among others." To apply for this card you need to produce evidence of identification; unsurprisingly the accepted types of identification are the ones which are also needed when applying for a passport!]
PRC [Professional Regulation Commission] ID; [according to its website the PRC "is the instrument of the Filipino people in securing

for the nation a reliable, trustworthy, and progressive system of developing professionals whose personal integrity and spiritual values are solid and respected, whose competencies are globally competitive, and whose commitment to serve the Filipino nation and the whole community is strong and steadfast." Again production of identification is part of the application process to obtain this form of ID.]

IBP [Integrated Bar of the Philippines ID. [To apply for the IBP card an applicant must provide two valid identification cards, a government-issued ID and a secondary ID; in other words this card can only be issued to someone who has already provided proof of their identity.]

OWWA [Overseas Workers Welfare Administration] ID. [The biggest export from the Philippines to the world is people. This organisation represents those who work outside the country. However, before the Filipino can work abroad they will need a passport and visa so this form of identification is of no use to the first time applicant.]

Digitized BIR [Bureau of Internal Revenue] ID. [This is almost universally referred to as the TIN card, TIN being the abbreviation for Taxpayer Identification Number. It means you are part of the visible economy and pay your taxes.]

Senior Citizen's ID

Unified Multi-Purpose ID [According to Wikipedia the Unified Multi-Purpose ID (UMID) is a Philippine identity card which was introduced in 2010. The card was developed as a single card for the relations between several government-related agencies. The agency responsible for implementation is the Social Security System (SSS). The Government Service Insurance System (GSIS), Philippine Health Insurance Corporation (PhilHealth) and the Pag-IBIG Fund (Home Development Mutual Fund) use the card. The card is also suggested to be used as voter's ID.]

Other acceptable picture IDs such as the following:
Old College ID
Alumni ID
Old Employment IDs

Looking down this list of documents one can begin to get a feel for the endless bureaucracy contained within the Philippine system. Having said that I may be doing the country a disservice as I do not understand the system in much detail. However I do know that many Filipinos do not have regular work and much of the work which does exist forms part of a burgeoning invisible economy. In consequence many people accept the type of employment arrangements which mean they remain unseen to the official system. So if we look at young women such as May or June, who was awaiting her University result, we find people who cannot possibly have most of the listed documents/cards as they had never formally been in employment. So they could not have the Digitised SSS, the GSIS e-card, PRC ID, IBP ID, OWWA ID or the Digitised BIR ID. In June's case she did have her College ID which she used in the application, but May would have none of these documents.

I hope you are getting a flavour for the love of bureaucracy which pervades any transaction in the Philippines. For someone who left school at sixteen, or earlier, had intermittent work on a cash in hand basis and family who have operated in the same way, i.e. many young Filipinas, providing these documents will rank somewhere between a major challenge and nigh on impossible. It is easy for you or I sat in the west to suggest they should: "open a bank account and get a debit/credit card." To do that means having to go through a very similar process of establishing identity insofar as the bank account is concerned; for a credit card you need to establish a good credit record and that takes time. Neither can be used as Acceptable ID as neither will contain a photograph of the account holder.

Recently my wife and I have been discussing bringing her parents, and two children (their son and grand-daughter to the U.K. for a 2-3 week holiday. It took them three months to get all the paperwork together to make a passport application and to then submit it, with payment. They attended their scheduled appointment. This entailed finding someone to look after their business whilst away; making the 2-3 hour trip from home to the nearest bus stop; taking a three hour bus trip; staying overnight in the town where the government office was; then returning home the following day. Not straightforward. The outcome has been that the children and my father-in-law now have their passports. However my mother-in-law's application was rejected on the grounds that her birth certificate did not make clear what her gender is! She now has to go through the process of getting the Local Civil Registrar to re-issue the document. Once that has been done she has to visit a Public Notary to swear the authenticity of the new birth certificate which is then sent to the Philippine Statistics Authority. Provided the new document is accepted by the P.S.A. they will notify her in writing and she is then able to re-apply for her passport. This process is likely to take around six months and my mother-in-law has to pay for each part of the process. Payment for her original application will be forfeited and, when she re-applies, a further payment will have to be made. This does seem unfair. She would have been a few days old when the original document was issued; it is not her fault that the word 'babaye' (female in Cebuano) cannot be clearly read or assumed by the official dealing with her passport application. Her gender is patently obvious.

We had originally discussed bringing the children across for their school summer holiday period. However the paperwork associated with that made it impossible. The grand-daughter's natural father is stated as unknown on her birth certificate. Whilst her Mum, my sister-in-law, was happy for the child to make the trip, Philippine law states that, because consent of the father has not been provided, the Department of Social Welfare and Development must consent to the trip. They advised us that they required we swear an oath before a High Court judge stating we will properly look after the child's welfare. The time and legal cost involved in doing this led to extending our invite to my in-laws as well. It was simpler. Also, as the children will be ten and eight respectively when they make the trip, having parents with them is probably a more sensible way forward.

Getting back to Jo(e) and her passport application we need to acknowledge that the person we are helping will need a lot of support. That support has to be on hand continuously. If it does not come from a supportive family and, in fairness to them, they are unlikely to have the experience or ability to provide the level of support necessary, it has to be delivered by the boyfriend/husband-to-be at a distance. I can testify that this is a very challenging, frustrating and wearing proposition. The woman might ask: "Can I get a Postal ID card and use that?" Insofar as the documents listed for the passport application are concerned, that one is not mentioned. So your response would probably be negative. However the Postal ID is a photo ID and perfectly valid for passport applications. But it is only when dealing with the system one realises this. It will also become apparent that the Postal ID may also present a potential difficulty. As indicated by its name the Postal ID provides proof of postal address. This means that all the other documents produced during the application must relate to the same address. So, if your girlfriend is one of the hundreds of thousands of women who move from the islands into the capital or other cities to find work, her Postal ID will be good for the address where she lives in that city. This means that, if the other documents she uses to support her application are from her family home on the island, they will not match and the application will be knocked back. There are all sorts of anomalies and pitfalls an applicant can unwittingly fall into.

Having obtained a valid photo id the applicant was then required to provide two additional supporting documents; the website advised the following …

LIST OF SUPPORTING DOCUMENTS (Old documents issued at least one year prior to date of application that show correct name, date and place of birth, picture and signature of applicant, At least 2 of the following):
PSA (Philippines Statistics Authority) Marriage Contract
Land Title
Seaman's Book
Elementary or High School Form 137 [This is a Department of Education form which shows the subjects taken by the holder and the grades achieved. It must be produced by the school or college attended by the form holder and needs to have the school or college stamp and be signed off by the appropriate staff member, i.e. the Head] or Transcript of Records with readable dry seal
Government Service Record

NBI [National Bureau of Investigation] Clearance [NBI Clearance proves someone is cleared from any liability, case, offence, crime or bad record covered by NBI.]
Digitized Postal ID
Readable SSS-E1 Form or Microfilmed Copy of SSS-E1 Form [This is the Social Security System Registration Form].
Voter's Certification, List of Voters and Voter's Registration Record (please attach receipt)
School Yearbook

Barangay Clearance [www.philpad.com advises that - This document is issued in the Barangay Hall or Municipal Office of the town of the requesting applicant. This certificate is usually requested for employment requirements, ID application, supporting documents in application to government agencies, supporting documents to medical certificates, affidavits, and whenever any office requests or requires it. Barangay Clearance is a document certifying that the applicant is of good moral character and good resident of a given town or barangay. It also proves that the applicant has no bad records or immoral background. In a nutshell, the certificate simply states that the person stated has a good standing as a resident. The certificate is signed by the Barangay Captain. Stamped and sealed with the official Barangay Seal.]
Barangay Clearance Requirements are as follows:
Recent Cedula (Community Tax Certificate)
Application Form
Application Fee (price varies depending on the Barangay) [On both the occasions I am aware of the cost was 100 php]

Police Clearance [Police Clearance simply proves someone is cleared from any bad record in the police department or PNP (Philippine National Police) station and its affiliates. The requirements in getting Police Clearance are:
Application Form (they will give you one)
Barangay Clearance
Recent Cedula (Community or Residence Tax Certificate)

P100 [payment of 100 php]
Make sure you bring the original and photocopy of the documents listed above. No need to bring pictures since they will capture your photo and signature in the PNP office. State your purpose in getting a Police Clearance. (...) make sure your signature is similar to all your signatures on your IDs and other documents. Police Clearance may expire after six months or a year it has been issued. www.philpad.com]

(I have separated out and provided a good deal of detail over the processes involved in obtaining Barangay Clearance and Police Clearance. That is because, if you are trying to assist a Filipino in obtaining a passport, these are two of the most straightforward ways to do it. The procedure may be tedious but they are both do-able by almost everyone. They will work with a Postal ID because that can also be obtained relatively easily.)

Once she has the identification documents your girlfriend can then go online and make her passport application.

This was the process three women I dated went through. During 2016 the issue of Philippine passports was outsourced and has been significantly simplified. However it is still a more tedious and time consuming process than that which we have in the U.K.

Once the papers have been collected together they need to be photocopied and taken to the local Passport Office. At that time there was a payment of P950 (£15.15, €16.62; $19.20) for routine processing in fifteen working days or P1,200 for express processing within seven working days.

Postal i/d supported by Barangay and Police Clearance are the easiest and quickest way to deliver the documents needed to apply for a passport under the old system and, I understand, can still be used under the new system. They all reflect the current status of the Filipino in their own country. From the westerners perspective they also prove address and give the applicant a clean bill of health so far as crime and social issues are concerned.

Yolanda.

So Jo(e) and I reached a point where she agreed she would like to visit the U.K. and had the support of her family in doing that. By this I mean moral support; financial support is not a matter for consideration. We have been here before. If, as a westerner, you propose to bring a Filipina to your country, you pay. But think of it this way. All things being equal she will still be counting years of life to come whilst you are more likely to be counting, or considering, years left. What you are really doing is quite selfish; you are making an investment in your own future. If she settles and you marry you will have a woman from a traditionally hard working background who is very family oriented and affectionate; and she is likely to be with you for the rest of your life. There is also the fact that, if you marry in the Philippines, there is effectively no divorce. Should you marry in your own country the 'no divorce' maxim will have been firmly pressed into your wife's subconscious. A lifetime marriage is what she wants and expects. If it works out that means you will have someone with you who will be bringing in an income for the rest of your life and who will look after you as your health declines. No more worries about being kept in hospital because their risk assessment says you are not safe to be home alone; no more worries about having to sell your home to pay for residential care. If you have chosen well there will full commitment and a lot of love and fun along the way. And we should also acknowledge that she is also investing in her own future. As a western man you will be offering a better future coupled with financial security. Better options than she is ever likely to be able to realise in her home country. On the downside you are likely to leave her with children, middle age and either loneliness or the job of finding a new partner. Her contacts with family and friends back in the Philippines will have become distant by then. Your estate may help offset these issues.

I digress. The next job for Jo(e) was to make her passport application. As we have seen the costs are minor. As a gesture of goodwill and support, although she never asked me for money, at this point I used Western Union to send £50 cash across. The exchange rate was close to 72 pesos to the pound at that time so she would have received around

P3,600; P100 each for barangay and police clearance, P950 for the passport, the rest for the hassle of getting a certified copy of her birth certificate and a lot of running around to tend to the demands of the good bureaucracy. In my mind I was making a positive gesture and acknowledging that she would have to do a lot of chasing around. It turned out to be a lot more complicated and expensive than that, in more ways than either of us could possibly have imagined.

To begin with Western Union will only hand cash over to someone who can prove who they are. That makes perfect sense. All Jo had was the copy of the receipt I had received from Western Union which I'd e-mailed to her. She had no documentation at all which proved her identity. So Western Union refused to hand the cash over.

No birth certificate I hear you ask. No. The reason she and her family were living in one of the poorest parts of Cebu City was because several years earlier the place in which they had lived on Leyte Island, which had also been in a poor neighbourhood but rural and surrounded by family rather than a city slum, was subjected to a flash flood. Almost all the property belonging to the family had been destroyed. Please don't think: insurance claim! In a country where under 6% of adults have health insurance, house and contents insurance is far more the exception than the case and never happens in the types of community in which Jo had grown up and lived. Her parents had been running a fishing business from home; which probably meant they bought from the catch of local fishermen and then sold this on locally. When their hut was written off in the flood, so was their livelihood and everything else they owned.

They had relocated to Cebu City where some distant relatives lived and tried to survive doing the same thing; with intermittent success. The family were familiar with having one meal a day, some days that would just be rice, other days there was no food at all.

I liaised with Western Union and the outcome was them returning the £50 to my bank account and me re-sending it but, this time, to Jo's mother. She had a motor bike driving licence and Western Union agreed that would be an acceptable form of ID. No member of the family had a bank account; everything was cash in hand; and in their world there was no such thing as social security.

Jo told me she received the cash from her mother but would need to return to the Barangay where she was born to get a copy of her birth certificate from the appropriate Local Civil Registrar. She was preparing to make the trip when Bohol, the closest reasonable sized island to the east of Cebu Island, was hit by a 7.2 Mw earthquake; the equivalent power of 32 Hiroshima bombs exploding simultaneously. Whilst the epicentre was close to the town of Sagbayan in Bohol the effect was felt throughout the Visayan Islands. Cebu Island and City were relatively close by. When Jo and I had looked out from Mountain View we had seen Bohol in the far distance and it would have been the area close to Sagbayan we would have been gazing towards. In Bohol there were two hundred and twenty-two dead and eight people missing. Around fourteen and a half thousand buildings were totally destroyed and over five times that were damaged. Across the sea in Cebu the strength of the earthquake was slightly less and buildings in the cities were a little more resilient but Mactan Airport was damaged and closed temporarily and there was some damage to the Airport Hotel. Across Metro Cebu twelve people were killed, five of these in a stampede, and there was significant damage. Thankfully there was no tsunami. Overall the event impacted on just under two million Metro Cebu residents, almost all of them, in one way or another. Needless to say transport and communication systems were thoroughly disrupted.

Fortunately none of this had a serious impact on Jo, her family, or the property in which they lived. But it delayed her travel by ten days or so. Instead of visiting family in Leyte in the middle of October, her trip was put back towards the end of the month. The two hour ferry journey from Cebu took her to Ormoc City on the western side of Leyte Island; she then needed to take a 2-3 hour bus ride to the home of her grandparents in Mayorga which was on the east side of the island about ten miles south of Tacloban, the island's main town and administrative centre. Before she left Cebu we had a long chat online. She told me that she would be visiting grandparents and various uncles, aunts and cousins who she hadn't had contact with for a while. She was really looking forward to the trip. Her intention was to return to Cebu during the first weekend of November. Mayorga had no internet café and very poor communications links so she would only be able to pick up messages from me and chat if she went into a large town or commercial centre.

So, off she went to Leyte.

I received a very short Facebook message from Jo on Saturday 2nd November saying she had tried to catch the ferry home but, because of a small earthquake in Cebu, (probably an after-shock from the major earthquake in Bohol), shipping had not been allowed to leave the port that day. I acknowledged her message and went online. News centres in the Philippines confirmed there had been a modest tremor in Cebu that had not caused any serious issues. I also picked up a report that a broad low pressure weather system was developing in the Pacific Ocean thousands of miles to the east of the Philippines. However, if it maintained its current trajectory and developed it was likely to reach the Philippines on Thursday or Friday of the coming week. As the days progressed the news items became more serious. This was going to be a full blown typhoon massive even by Philippine standards. I messaged again and sent an e-mail asking her to try to get back to Cebu as quickly as she could; if that was not possible to get to high ground and/or to a place of safety which would not be flooded or blown away in the coming storm. I heard nothing from her but continued sending messages.

Just before 5 am on the morning of Thursday 8th November, 2013, Haiyan, or Super Typhoon Yolanda as it is known in the Philippines, hit land at Guiuan, Eastern Samar, on the extreme eastern edge of the Philippine archipelago. This town of 40,000 lies on the western side of a fairly flat spit of land stretching south from the main body of Eastern Samar. The eastern side meets the Pacific Ocean. Sometimes Guiuan is referred to as an island but, technically, that is not the case. However there are no road linkages between this narrow peninsula and the rest of the island. Having wrought havoc across Guiuan Yolanda crossed the narrow spit of land and entered the Gulf of Leyte which divides Eastern Samar from Leyte Island. Once the typhoon entered the Gulf it found water in a relatively confined space. At the head of the Gulf of Leyte is the city of Tacloban, the capital of Leyte Island. Whilst Tacloban is on Leyte Island, it and the island of Eastern Samar are separated by a channel only a few hundred metres wide in parts for a distance of around twelve miles. (19 km). Whilst there are some large mountains on both sides of this channel each also has a significant and well populated coastal plain. The power of this typhoon was immense; one of the largest ever recorded anywhere across history. The high winds devastated properties across the Visayas but Eastern Samar and Leyte Island got the brunt of it. Guiuan was decimated and the eastern sides of those islands got the full force of the typhoon's initial landfall. This was where Jo was. A surge of water the height of a two-storey building was pushed up the Gulf of Leyte into Tacloban City.

The Disasters Emergency Committee is a U.K. umbrella organisation for thirteen charities which act in concert when a decision is taken to provide humanitarian aid into a disaster zone. Their synopsis of this event was as follows:

Typhoon Haiyan - known locally as Yolanda - hit eastern Samar Island at 8.40 pm GMT on 7 November 2013 (4.40 am 8th November local time).

It caused a storm surge – a wall of water – that was 25 feet high in some areas, including in the town of Tacloban.

Reports regarding Haiyan's wind speeds vary but the Philippine Atmospheric, Geophysical and Astronomical Services Administration – the relevant government authority - has said that when it made landfall Haiyan had sustained winds of 147mph and gusts of 171mph.

If the figures from the Philippines government are correct then Haiyan was not the strongest tropical storm to ever

> make landfall but it was the deadliest Typhoon in the history of the Philippines, a country hit on average by more than 20 tropical storms a year and prone to both earthquakes and volcanoes.
>
> Over 14 million people were affected across 46 provinces.
>
> The city of Tacloban, home to more than 220,000 people, suffered more loss of life than any other area of the Philippines.
>
> Five million people saw their homes severely damaged or destroyed (550,000 houses destroyed and an additional 580,000 houses were severely damaged).
>
> The Government of the Philippines said the storm resulted in over 6,201 deaths with over 1,785 people reported missing (14.01.14).

The Economist magazine of 13th November, 2013 reported that:

> In Tacloban (...) Haiyan flattened nearly the whole town of several hundred thousand people; one aid worker described it as "worse than hell". Five days after the typhoon, there is still little in the way of food and clean water, and few medical supplies are coming in. As a consequence, thousands have been trooping to the wrecked airport outside the city in the hope of getting out. Day after day, most are disappointed. Meanwhile, the risks rise of typhoid, cholera and hepatitis breaking out, thanks to an absence of sanitation or clean water. Bodies are rotting in the streets, and the hospitals have been all but wrecked. The survivors' misery is compounded by yet more rain from the next in a train of tropical depressions.

Survivors also fear looters and criminals, some of whom are reported to have broken out of jail. In many places law and order broke down after Haiyan struck. Police forces and local-government officials suffered in the typhoon as much as anyone else. In Palo in Leyte province, only 34 of 983 local policemen are reported to have shown up for duty after the storm. There are reports of food convoys and warehouses being sacked by armed gangs—as well as by desperately hungry people. More police and troops are flying in.

Amid the carnage, questions have been raised as to why a part of the world so prone to terrible storms could have suffered so much. Surely the authorities could have done better, especially with nearly two days' notice of a spectacular storm on its way?

(...) Yet some authorities in the Philippines deserve praise, too, for their immediate reaction to the storm warnings. About 1m people were evacuated, usually to buildings that were considered to be safe. The trouble was that the typhoon's sheer force overwhelmed any preparations. Take Tacloban, where thousands got to a big indoor stadium, considered to be storm proof. Sure enough, the specially reinforced roof stayed on. But people were killed instead by a 5-metre (16-foot) high surge of water which flooded the structure. In Tacloban the storm surge was like a tsunami. Nobody seems to have foreseen that it could do so much damage.

When Haiyan landed at Guiuan, gusts hit 315kph, [197 mph], which some consider to be the highest ever recorded.

The official death toll was the equivalent of 2-3 World Trade Centres. Most of the deaths in Tacloban occurred as a consequence of the storm surge. Thousands of homes were just washed away with their occupants in them. I knew Jo was not in Tacloban but I also knew she was only a few miles away. The village in which she was staying was the first land mass the typhoon would hit excepting Guiuan and the narrow spit of land forming the opposite edge of the Gulf of Leyte. I also knew of the carnage wrought by the typhoon and that communications systems were down in much of the Visayas; as were transport links. Initial media coverage showed a large area by the sea which had been washed clean of all buildings; there was some evidence visible of where roads had been. The occasional battered tree stump was visible but the only other things in shot were a couple of ships which had been lifted out of the sea and dumped the best part of a hundred metres inland. The port was not usable but, after a couple of days, the airport was able to receive aid flights. Some roads into the area no longer existed, they had been washed away, others were impassable; bridges had collapsed; trees had blown across them, they were covered in thick silt and mud. I kept calling Jo's mobile not expecting an answer; and I didn't get one. After three days I was really worried and used Facebook to contact her sister and brother. Their knowledge of English was poor but they conveyed to me that they had heard nothing from any of their family on Leyte Island. They were worried but had no means to find out what the situation was. They did not have transport and told me that, because of the disaster, what ferries there were had increased their prices as a response to the increased demand for travel into the area by relief agencies. It was pretty well impossible for people not involved and financed by the international aid community to make the trip. It was good to know that capitalism was still alive, well and thriving in the guise of humanitarian action!

I thought about how to handle this. It would have been easy to back off and disappear but that would have been a dreadful way to behave. I took the view that Jo's parents were both from Leyte Island. That is where their parents and all their close family lived and much of their extended family. Their daughter was also there. Whilst I might be concerned for Jo's welfare, they must have been out of their minds with worry. I contacted Jo's sister on Facebook and arranged that, if I sent some cash across via Western Union, her mother would collect it and they would use it to go to Leyte and find out how their family had fared.

So that is what happened. The typhoon struck early on the morning of Thursday 8th November, Philippine time. By Monday 12th they had collected a few hundred pounds equivalent in cash and on Tuesday 13th began their trip paying inflated ferry prices and using a motor bike. I finally got a Facebook message on Friday 16th telling me that they had been found. All properties, crops, communications systems, etc. had been decimated but the family had made the local storm shelter and survived with a few bumps and bruises. The main problem had been water and food. The only water they had been able to consume was what they had been able to collect when it rained. They had had no food at all for around six days until Jo's family arrived.

It took a couple of weeks before I met Jo face to face on Skype. She explained to me how she was lucky in many ways because so many people had lost their lives and loved ones. Hundreds of thousands of people were homeless because the storm had blown their homes away completely or damaged them to the extent that they could not be lived in. For a few days she thought she would be joining the dead and was amazed when her parents rode into town on a motor bike with food and liquids. No aid effort had reached their village and they were only about a half hour drive from Tacloban, under normal conditions. But the situation was far from what could be described as 'normal'! What aid was available, and certainly all the media attention for the first few days, was directed at Tacloban. I mention the media because they put a lot of pressure on local systems and policymakers to show some results from aid efforts. However reporters would have had great difficulty in getting anywhere more than a couple of miles from the centre of the city. In consequence this was where the whole humanitarian effort was initially targeted; where it could be filmed and photographed for global consumption. Interestingly within two weeks of the typhoon passing, a memorial to U.S. General Douglas MacArthur, which had been damaged, (one of seven statues had been blown over), was repaired. I wonder why that was given such a high priority when people were dehydrating and starving, the dead could not be buried and related diseases were beginning to be recorded? The infrastructure of the area was almost completely written off. Kow-towing to the U.S. and developed world aid audience?! The governor of the town had heeded the advance warnings of Yolanda and retreated to Manila a couple of days before the typhoon struck. But he was back a couple of days later, empathising with his electorate and was filmed directing traffic, of which there was very little. Image over responsibility!

The few vehicles available were needed to support the relief effort and could not travel any distance as the roads were so badly damaged. A further problem initially was a lack of fuel. The result was that any community beyond walking distance of Tacloban was effectively cut off, and anyone arriving in Tacloban would be joining the clamour of people trying to survive. Stores were looted and then those doing the looting would be at risk of being mugged. Jo and her family, whilst fairly close to Tacloban, could not really make that trip because most of the land and communities in between now formed a wasteland; similar to their own community. I don't know if Jo's parents were the first outsiders the villagers saw after the disaster but they were certainly the first who brought any help to Jo and her family.

When we chatted on Skype and Facebook I gave her as much time as she wanted to talk about these events. However she was not a big talker and preferred to discuss the future. She had got the certified copy of her birth certificate a week or so before the typhoon struck. Once those events kicked in she began to fear for her life and believed we were unlikely to ever see each other again. However she had kept the document safe and, once back in Cebu, got the papers together and submitted her passport application.

Christmas arrived and, online, I managed to track down a takeaway in Cebu City which would deliver food to Jo and her family to celebrate Christmas. That might not sound like much. Here in the west we have a whole industry geared up to support food being delivered from restaurant/takeaway to the home. However, at that time, (and I have not checked since), the idea of home delivery was not so strong in Cebu City. But there were certainly plenty of restaurants and takeaways to choose from. The difficulty was one of trust, both ways, and the takeaway having the facility to process an international payment. If I placed an order and paid for it online and the money went through, then the restaurant would be happy enough, but I had plenty of previous experience of things in the Philippines not always being quite what they should be; where my trust had been abused. My worry was I would paying in advance for something which would never be provided. How many U.K. takeaways would accept an e-mail and online payment for a buffet meal for ten to be delivered in the late evening of Christmas Eve if the person placing that order was in the Philippines and paying with a credit card issued through a Philippine bank? But we got there. Jo acted as local liaison and, rather than send a card or presents, which could well be delayed, stolen or lost in the post, I was able to provide them with a Christmas meal to remember, and to have it delivered.

In the third week of February Jo's passport arrived. She proudly showed it to me on Facebook and sent me a copy of the information page. Next to gender I saw the word 'Female', and was both relieved and delighted.

Visas and Jo(e)

If the level of bureaucracy a Filipina has to follow to obtain a passport is challenging, that is something she needs to deal with, with your support. However, your turn is to come with the visa. Yes, it will be her visa and it will be stamped into her passport, and the application must be made and paid for from within the Philippines and in her name. She will need to submit the application electronically and, during that process, pay the fee electronically. This means she must either have a bank account in place and a payment card or access to someone else's bank account before the visa application process commences. It also means she has to know how to use that card to make an electronic payment. This is something young people grow up with in the west. It is not the case in the Philippines. We saw the World Bank statistics earlier. The number of electronic payments made in the Philippines in 2012 was too small to measure. Eight years on things have changed a little, but not too much. Assume the person you are working with, whilst doing the best they can, is dealing with a system of which they has little or no experience. Furthermore it is unlikely they will be able to get help from family and friends as they will be in just the same position. It would be a case of the blind leading the blind.

This chapter discusses the barriers a westerner will meet when trying to get a visa stamped into his would-be partners passport which will permit her to leave her own country and enter his. It is a process which is far from straightforward.

Within the Philippines this has led to the development of an industry of fixers who claim to *know* the system and, for a fee, will sort the paperwork out for you. Not just for passports or visas but for anything which requires knowledge of how the government systems (national and local) work. This could well create a difficulty for you. Your girlfriend will know of these agents and may have previously used one of them. From amongst her family and friends she may receive well intentioned recommendations for a particular agent; someone they have used successfully in the past. I suspect the agent system will encourage the buying of documentation, greasing the palm of the appropriate official. But I have to say that this is only speculation on my part. What we can be sure of is that there will be good and bad agents. They make their money by keeping the work flowing through and building their reputations locally. On the one hand working with a client to successfully apply for a visa to visit a western country will enhance their reputation; on the other hand, once that visa has been issued, that client will move on. That moving on, relocation, means the agent is unlikely to get any further business from them directly. The agent will appraise the client standing before them and, in our case, quickly conclude they are dealing with a young woman with plenty of ambition but little or no real experience of life. When the agent knows their client is being sponsored by a foreigner they smell opportunity and profit. Experience suggests they are likely to quote ridiculous prices and will do their best to pressurise you're the lady into using their services. They are also very likely, as part of the process, to tell her she needs things which are not necessary. They are following the money and your girlfriend is likely to be naïve in these matters. That means, if an agent is used, you should expect the worst and to pay top dollar for it. They have a client who is ripe for exploitation. Whilst your girlfriend may put you under pressure to allow her to use an agent, which you will be expected to pay for, this is something you should do your best to resist. However, in doing so, you are putting her in a position where you will be the only person she can turn to for support. You are in a tricky position. When it comes to visas there are so many different types issued by each country that few people without legal experience or a lot of training can legitimately claim to be an expert. Use an agent and you are very likely to get ripped off financially and, unless what you are wanting is very simple, you are unlikely to get a positive result. Refuse to use an agent and you are dealing directly with a complicated system on behalf of your girlfriend who, with the best will in the world, is unlikely to be of much help.

It has to be acknowledged that applying for a visa to enter the U.K. (or any other country in the developed world) is far from straightforward. To begin with the application form and the guidance which comes with it are written in the language of the country which will decide on whether or not a visa will be issued. In our case this is English. Whilst this is logical it is an immediate barrier for someone who is not a native English speaker. Many of the visas which are issued to visit the United Kingdom require the applicant to take a test to prove their understanding of the English language. Frankly this is little more than an earner for the authorities. Any applicant who can complete the application form correctly is demonstrating a level of knowledge and understanding of the English language way above the basic levels set by the various tests. The guidance provided to assist completion of the visitor or short stay visa comes at the end of that particular application form. An e-link to the form itself is provided in Appendix 1, but the guidance section, copied below and retaining the font size and colour of the original, runs to the 515 words, about two-thirds of a printed sheet of A4 size paper:

> **8.1 If you are not a national of the country in which you are applying, what permission do you have to stay in that country?** Please provide evidence of your immigration status if you are not a national in the country where you are applying, e.g. a residence permit, visa, green card.
> **8.2 Are you travelling with anyone?** Answer Yes/No. If 'Yes' please provide the full name, date of birth and nationality of the people you are travelling with. If you are travelling in a large group please just give the details of the group leader.
> **8.3 Do they already have a visa for the UK?** Answer Yes/No/They don't need one.
> **8.4 What will you do in the UK?** If you have a planned itinerary please submit a copy of this with your application.
> **8.5 Do you intend to work in the UK?** Answer Yes/No. This includes voluntary work. If 'Yes' you are filling out the wrong form. Please refer to your local visa application centre guidance to check which visa you should apply for. Further guidance and information can also be found on the UK Border Agency website: www.ukvisas.gov.uk
> **8.6 Do you intend to study in the UK?** Answer Yes/No. If 'Yes' you are filling out the wrong form. If study is your main purpose in coming here, you should apply as a Student Visitor. If your purpose is to come here for a holiday or to visit family but you may also study for no more than a month, you can use this form.
> **8.7 Where will you stay in the UK?** Please provide the full address, telephone number and email address of all the places where you will be staying during your visit, including hotels.
> **8.8 Do you have any friends in the UK?** Answer Yes/No. If 'Yes', please provide the full name, nationality, address, telephone number, their permission to stay in the UK and explain how they are related to you e.g. "My mother's brother's son"

Definition of a family member
A "member of the applicant's family" is any of the following persons who is permanently settled in the UK"
- *Spouse, civil partner, father, mother, son, daughter, brother or sister;*
- *Grandfather, grandmother, grandson or granddaughter;*
- *Spouse or civil partner's father, mother, brother or sister;*
- *Son or daughter's spouse or civil partner;*
- *Stepfather, stepmother, stepson, stepdaughter, stepbrother or stepsister; or*
- *Unmarried partner with whom they have lived as a couple for at least two of the last three years.*

In addition, children adopted under an adoption order recognised in UK law are treated as if they are the natural children of the adoptive parents.

8.9 Do you have any relatives in the UK? Answer Yes/No. If 'Yes' please provide details of all your relatives in the UK in the space provided including name, nationality, exact relationship to you and their permission to be in the UK. If you require more space please use Part 9 – Additional Information. If you have no other family members in the UK please state 'None'.

8.10 Do you intend to visit any of these relatives? Answer Yes/No.

As guidance, is this adequate? I ask rhetorically; no one can answer this question until they have experienced the system applicable to their own country. However, government guidance provided to the U.K. Visas and Immigration staff, who manage the visa process, is to be found in what are called the 'Immigration Rules'. When Jo made her application just the index to these rules runs to 1,748 words and can be found as Appendix 2. The index to the Rules is almost three and a half times the length of the text used to guide the applicant, (which is inconveniently placed towards the end of the application form.) One could be forgiven for thinking that the application form itself is geared up to assist the application to fail. In 2014, whilst Home Secretary (Minister for Home/Internal Affairs), Theresa May, who went on to become the British Prime Minister, actively encouraged the development of a 'hostile environment' for anyone seeking entry into the United Kingdom. The application process provides significant evidence of this.

The only mention of the Immigration Rules on the application form is to be found in the advice on the submission of documents in support of the application; in the small print towards the end. I have copied the paragraph below and highlighted this in bold print but it is still very easy to miss and there is nothing to indicate how it is absolutely essential that the applicant operates within these rules. Furthermore this advice is found towards the end of the twelve page application form when it would be far more appropriate for it to be at the top of the first page.

The section in the application form reads as follows:

> Please ensure you submit all the relevant original documents that you want the Entry Clearance Officer to see when considering your application. The UK **Immigration Rules** make it clear that it is your responsibility to satisfy the Entry Clearance Officer that you are genuinely seeking entry to the UK for the purpose and duration that you have stated. Submission of particular documents does not guarantee that your visa will be issued. It is your decision how you satisfy the Entry Clearance Officer that your intentions are as you state in your application. It is your choice which documents you submit. Further guidance on supporting documents can be found on the UKBA web pages.

The importance one needs to accord to the Immigration Rules hardly leaps off the page at you; and this is representative of the general tenure of the application process. The best general advice I can give is that the applicant should assume their application is not wanted and that the authorities will do everything within their power to refuse it. From the point of view of protecting our borders in the U.K. one can argue that such a robust approach is absolutely right. However, when trying to legitimately bring a would-be long term partner into the country, you are likely to find the Immigration Rules to be, at best, a nightmare. I will caveat this statement. For an educated Filipina with no financial concerns and a good working knowledge of the English language the process will be fairly straightforward. However most Filipinas are not in that position; and those who are will be unlikely to be applying for a visa to spend time with a potential husband in his country to establish if they are a good match.

Anyone considering sponsoring a non-European national to visit this country, for whatever reason, needs to familiarise themselves thoroughly with the Immigration Rules. Unless you have employed a specialist lawyer, based in your home country, it is you who will be directly responsible for guiding the application process and paying for it. Furthermore you will find that part of the terms and conditions of doing business with a law firm around a visa application will state they cannot be held responsible should the visa application not be granted whatever the reason(s) given.

As regards the Visitor and Short stay visa there is no longer any right of appeal against a refusal to issue. That was not the case when Jo applied; the rule change came in during 2014. The situation now is that you pay your money, £85 then, £95 now, and, if the authorities say 'no', it has gone and no explanation which can be challenged has to be provided. The reasons for refusal may be debatable and spurious, but, legally, the only challenge which can be made is on the grounds of a breach of human rights. As we will see later 'no right of appeal' can lead to the authorities taking a very cavalier attitude to a legitimate application. So it is important that you acquaint yourself with the visa application process and the Immigration Rules as it will be you who will have to guide your girlfriend/fiancée through every step of the journey.

You also need to be aware that these rules are being constantly updated and changed. Ostensibly this is to react to changing circumstances; in practice it is an exercise undertaken by politicians, through their civil service lackeys, to close or tighten any perceived loopholes.

I have put the index to the Immigration Rules into an Appendix to make this part of our story easier to read. There are seven pages of them and the contents are the handbook of the person who will be considering whether or not a visa should be issued to your Philippine friend. The seven pages is just the index! On the U.K.V.I. website each line of the index is provided as an e-link to that specific section of the Rules. Not all rules apply to all visa applications but, as U.K.V.I. will constantly remind you, it is the responsibility of the applicant to submit the visa application correctly; so it is also up to the applicant to be aware of and submit their application within these Rules.

Any phrase or sentence in the Immigration Rules can be used to generate a reason for refusing an application. As you will be paying for this application and the person who is making the application is likely to have a very limited understanding of the English language, it is very definitely in your own interests to be sure the application is submitted correctly. Don't be talked into allowing an agent to work on your behalf unless that agent works for a bona fide law firm with a good and verifiable pedigree.

What follows relates to the Immigration Rules for entering the U.K. only. In the English speaking world Australia and the U.S.A. receive greater numbers of visa applications from Filipinos than the U.K. Then there is the rest of the developed world. What agent is going to be an expert in dealing with such complexities? They will all claim to be up to the job but common sense has to prevail. The overwhelming majority are shams and spivs who are living on their wits and by exploiting the relative ignorance of those around them. I had the dubious privilege of meeting a table full of these jokers in a Cebu bar after discovering Julia was available at £80 per month!

The U.K. Immigration Rules comprise in total of several thousand pages. Whilst the main body of these rules are fairly constant, the nature of the system is one of flux, so any reader who is going to progress an application must use the live website and follow the up to date guidance. For instance a recent change has done away with the Visitor and Short stay visa. It has been replaced with the Standard Visitor Visa. The U.K. government website applicants:

> Apply for this visa if you want to visit the UK on holiday or to see your family and friends, do business, take part in sports or creative events, or receive private medical treatment.

Just to give a flavour of how confusing and/or ambiguous the website can be the same page then goes on to advise that this visa should be applied for also by seeking a:

> Short term study visa
> Visa to pass through the UK in transit
> Permitted paid engagement visa
> Marriage visitor visa

Parent of a Tier 4 child visa
Visit the UK in a Chinese tour group

Let's get back to the application Jo would make. What is discussed here reflects the Rules as they were when Jo submitted her application. Any sentence or phrase within those rules could be used to deny the issue of a visa. On the plus side when using the U.K.V.I. website each element is clickable straight to that section of the Rules on the website.

Mentioning visa authorities also throws up another issue which one has to deal with. This relates to language. In normal day to day life we can often misinterpret what another person specifically means. Confusion can follow. This issue is more extreme when you are supporting someone who does not speak good English in making their application. You would be well advised to spend a few days scrutinising the Immigration Rules. They are written in the English used by officials and bureaucrats and have to be read and understood that way. They are what they say; Rules. They are written by those lucky people who live in a world without ambiguity; with no shades of grey. This creates a problem for applicants who are dealing with the reality of day-to-day living which is choc-a-block full of shades of grey. They are not written for a skim read or a quick check on some point. Where you need to refer to the Rules in your application, be thorough, and have a good general understanding of the various sections. For example there is a section called: 'Private Life'. You cannot possibly know if this section applies to your circumstances until you look at it. In this case 'Private Life' refers to settlement in the U.K. and has nothing to do with applying for the initial visa. However, you cannot know that until you read the appropriate section of the Rules.

With a view to establishing what lies within the Rules here is an example chosen at random.

Immigration Rules Appendix P: lists of financial institutions.

Clicking on the hyperlink in the index led into this Appendix. It contained thirteen links, two of which are pertinent to Philippine applicants and their sponsors. The first listed the financial institutions that do not verify their financial statements to the satisfaction of the U.K. visa authorities. In lay terms this means that the U.K. visa authorities will not accept information provided by these banks. The second lists those whose information will be trusted,

If your girlfriend has a bank account, or you are considering opening one with her or for her, it is important you scrutinise these lists. At the time of writing they show sixty-two institutions whom the British visa application authorities will accept. More to the point they also show 757 (seven hundred and fifty-seven) financial institutions which will not be accepted. Again, many pages of text to work through, but user friendly as they are presented in general alphabetical order. Checking this list prior to opening her bank account could save you from depositing money in what you believe to be a genuine account where that may not be the case. It will also ensure that, should you need to use that account in some way to support a current or future visa application, you are dealing with an institution which U.K.V.I. will recognise. Check the list before you open an account, it does change. The good news is that the current list contains many more financial systems than it did when Jo applied. Then it was twenty-two.

A word of warning that applies across the Immigration Rules is that you should never expect them to be fully comprehensive. The writers of these rules will always ensure they have what experts in human communications call plausible deniability. This means they consistently ensure there is always sufficient wriggle room to manoeuvre their way around any challenge made to their decision(s). As regards the lists of financial institutions which are acceptable and not acceptable, there is nothing anywhere in the rules to tell us the criteria used to distinguish between the two. Interestingly Western Union does not get a mention on either list. They must not have been around long enough to convince the authorities of their legitimacy and high standing. Any challenge on which list an organisation should be on, or whether it should be listed at all, would be a debate on the specific meaning of a few words. The writers of these rules have a strong preference for what we might call 'establishment' organisations; anything other than that is likely to get short shrift.

And that is worth bearing in mind for the documents or evidence submitted to support any visa application. Link your application to what the visa authorities know and understand; it is the only realistic way forward. It is limiting and will limit you; but you are dealing with a heavily blinkered organisation supporting a government which, in the case of the U.K., is explicitly trying to reduce the number of immigrants it receives and politicians who are hell bent of making sure the media know that the only foreigners acceptable to them must have very deep pockets. The authorities will not make assumptions on your behalf, you have to state the obvious and, if you use information to support the application that comes from anything other than what *they* consider to be a blue-chip, secure source, forget it. You must assume these people are dim-witted and malevolent. In reality they are neither; they are 'just doing their job'. But, as the applicant, making such an assumption will guide you into submitting an application which has a decent chance of acceptance.

An issue when dealing with someone whose first language is different to your own is the need to be constantly vigilant with your foreign partner around language and misunderstandings. Mistakes come often, easily, both ways and can have a funny side. I remember the first (and probably only) time my first wife and I watched a cricket match she asked: "Why do they keep shouting cat shit?" The actual words, of course, were 'catch it'. However, more seriously, you need to be sure the woman you are working with understands she is likely to be paying for her visa using Visa. Obvious to you and I; a complete unknown and potentially very confusing use of words for a young Filipina with no experience of dealing with border controls, finances and bank accounts.

I have been involved in the opening of two bank accounts in the Philippines. On each occasion we went with a well-known bank which had a presence on the Philippine High Street. Each appears on the U.K.V.I. list as it stood at that time. I guess to some extent it is a case of using a bit of common sense. However, if you meet a Filipina who lives in a rural environment and reach a stage where you are thinking of a bank account, the choices could be very restrictive and you would do well to check dear old Appendix P before taking any decisions.

As an aside in comparison with banks at home, do not expect the same levels of information to be provided to you by any bank you use in the Philippines. A couple of years back I returned from a visit to a fairly remote part of the country. I took British bank notes with me as they generally get a far better exchange rate than any currency dealer will offer on an electronic transaction. That proved to be the case on this occasion. In Cebu City I obtained P63.8 to the £. However, once we reached our destination, well away from the financial centres of the country or even those on that particular island, we found that the only bank offered P58 to the £ and a local finance broker, with an eye to a fat profit, offered P49 to the £. This made me very reluctant to change the cash I was carrying particularly as I knew I could make an ATM withdrawal and get the normal daily rate from my own bank. This would come with a charge £1.25 (€1.37; $1.58) from the U.K. bank but still provided a far better deal. However, what I did not know until I checked my bank statement online after returning home, was that the banks in the Philippines are now also making an automatic service charge of P200 (£3.19; €3.50; $4.04) per transaction for all foreign currency transactions. The amount you are requesting from the 'hole-in-the-wall' can also be ambiguous when in the Philippines. The maximum amount of cash which can requested from the ATM in the Philippines, so far as my experience goes, is P20,000; however the only machines I can find nowadays are programmed with a P10,000 maximum per transaction. The first ATM transaction I made on this particular trip brought these issues home to me. I keyed in a cash withdrawal request for P10,000, (£160, €175; $203). I was surprised when the ATM only gave me P100. The problem was that the machine had given no indication that it assumed a decimal point and had read my request for P10,000 as P100.00. I was charged at both ends of this transaction so ended up paying bank charges of £4.44, (€4.87; $5.62) for the privilege of obtaining £1.60, (€1.75; $2.03).

Let's get back to discussing the issue of the visa application! Make sure you frequently check the Immigration Rules as they seem to be in a constant state of flux. That said the website itself will highlight major changes. Either the small print does not get updated or the owners of the website, i.e. the government, do not draw attention to such trivia. The U.K.V.I. is, of course, the arm of government which will decide which changes will be highlighted.

There are a variety of types of visa. It is the responsibility of the applicant to choose the correct one. Most of the visa choices for the U.K. are for specific and fairly obvious purposes. To visit to work or study; to visit as a sports person or entertainer; to visit to get married. And this is where the nub of the problem lies when it comes to romance. When I visit the Philippines it will be for a few days up to a maximum of thirty. The reasons for this originally were work related. It was impossible to take so much time away from one's work. Since retirement my reasons are still basic. I have no intention of ever living permanently in the Philippines; due to issues around diet; also my banking is all U.K. based. From a practical point of view staying for no more than thirty days pre-empts the need to consider applying for a visa to stay longer.

Now, a short time frame of up to thirty days does not really give the opportunity for a couple who have only met recently the time to understand if they are in love or in lust or, hopefully, both. It is possible to hide the 'true you' for such short periods of time. What is really necessary are a few months under the same roof so one may love and lust to ones heart's content whilst getting properly acquainted, warts and all. This is a sensible way forward rather than an alternative of 'marry in haste, repent at leisure!' However the U.K. visa system prevents such an approach. When Jo considered her visa application, two options were available. She could apply for a Visitor visa, also known as a Short Stay visa; alternatively we could announce our engagement and apply for a Fiancée visa. We discussed how we should progress and decided that honesty was the best policy; there is no point in trying to con the visa authorities. Even if you were to succeed first time around, that false application would remain on record, be consulted when further applications are made, and, were it identified at a later date as a false statement, the applicant would not just be returned to their own country, (s)he could also be barred from returning for a period of years.

At the point when Jo and I were considering this we had met each other several times over a five day period in Cebu. Following that we had maintained regular online contact using the dating website, Skype and Facebook and we had worked together to resolve a major problem created by Typhoon Yolanda. There had been some money sent across by me and the provision of a Christmas meal. We had a friendship and, whilst together, had the beginnings of the hots for one another. We needed time and space to understand if this was a passing phase or something which could develop into a solid, long term and meaningful relationship. We did not plan to marry first and discover our suitability for a long term relationship afterwards. That would be crazy. So we submitted an application for a Visitor visa. We were clear throughout that the reason for the visit was to understand if we had a relationship which would lead to marriage. Should a successful application be made for a visitor visa it comes with some serious and necessary conditions. The applicant cannot work; nor can the applicant study (except under fairly limited circumstances). The applicant must have a place to live and be financially independent of the host country welfare systems and provide evidence of that. They cannot draw on public funds. I agree with these conditions. Jo would not be visiting to work or study although it is obvious that living in a new country and culture would provide a steep learning curve. There are no Cebuano speakers in the area where she would be living, so a dramatic improvement in her understanding of the English language would logically occur. She had no finances so it was up to me to demonstrate I had sufficient resources to evidence she would not need to draw on public funds; also that I would ensure she had a roof over her head, clothing, food and drink.

A visa application generally has to be made within the country of the applicant. This means that the woman you are dating will have to make the application. You cannot do it for her unless you take a trip out to visit. Even then it will be submitted in her name and it is she who has to attend the appropriate offices in her country for interview if required and for biometrics to be obtained. She has to go online, register, chose the correct application form, complete it, pay online, make an appointment at a centre within her country, and then present herself at that appointment with a signed printed copy of her application and all the supporting documents. If you try to do this from the U.K. the website recognises your location and refuses access to the options necessary to make and submit an application. The U.K. Visa website asks that applicants submit applications within three months of their proposed date of travel. For someone with little experience of dealing with bureaucracies this can be quite a challenge.

I downloaded a copy of the correct application form, completed it leaving gaps where I did not have the information, and e-mailed it to Jo. She added the bits where I had no answer and suggested changes here and there. It went back and forth a few times. Within a couple of weeks we had the application ready for submission. The difficulty then was for Jo to identify someone she could trust who had a bank account. The payment had to be made electronically during the electronic submission of the application. I had had to send cash across to Jo's mother before. However Jo now had a passport so could collect cash herself. Unfortunately she did not at this point have a bank account, nor did any of her close family. Jo had told me that, whilst her mother was always honest with her on the issues of money, she, (her mother), had chatted with the local relatives, in fact some of them had shared the Christmas meal, and those relatives were putting pressure on Jo's parents to pressure Jo into begging from me. She never did this but told me it happened. What she needed was a trusted friend who would accept the money I sent across being paid into their bank account and then spend time with Jo, as she got the application ready for submission, so that they could pay for it when the electronic request was made. She did not have such a person in her group of friends. Apart from immediate family the only people she trusted were family members back on Leyte Island. Given the carnage wreaked by Yolanda help from them was impossible. I bit the bullet. It would be a further test of trust. I was on Skype with her as she went through the submission process and, when the financial information, etc. needed to be entered onto the application form, I passed this to her verbally on Skype so it could be paid directly from my bank account. The payment went through and I forewarned my bank I had an increased level of risk. We kept a very close eye on my account for the next couple of weeks but, apart from the payment for the visitor visa, £85, ($112, €100), no other Philippine or potentially fraudulent transactions were attempted.

I was then somewhat reckless. In anticipation of Jo's visa being issued I bought a return flight from Cebu to my local airport in Jo's name. We had specified the start date for the visa as 1st June. That was six or seven weeks away. The website told us the visa decision would be taken in about three weeks, so this gave us a bit of wriggle room. She received an electronic ticket from the airline and we began to plan her trip.

Three days later I met a very tearful Jo on Skype. She told me the visa application had been refused. She copied the letter to me which explained the reasoning for refusal. At the time there was steam coming out of my ears but, on reflection, we submitted a terrible application. It would have been a travesty of the system had a visitor visa been issued.

Several reasons were given. The three principle ones were:

> we are not satisfied that the address provided exists; if it does, we are not satisfied the applicant has any incentive to return to it when the visa expires; and,

> whilst the sponsor has provided a letter and comprehensive supporting documents, the application provides no hard evidence that you have ever actually met; and,

a six-month visit to the U.K. will have a damaging impact on the continuing education of the applicant.

Let us take these reasons for refusal one at a time.

Firstly the address. In the west there are few people without an address. Given the amount of poverty and living on the margins that occurs throughout the Philippines the situation is very different. There are many homeless and many more who have a roof over their heads which should not be there; these unofficial shanties do not have formal addresses. Coupled with this the youth population is highly transient as they move in connection with their job or actually finding work of some sort. This is also likely to be the case in much of the rest of the developing world. The rooms in which Jo lived did not have a number or name; it was part of an unofficial barrio in a densely populated slum area. The address we supplied for her application was in two parts. The first was a description of the location of where the building in which she was living was located; that was close to being an address we would recognise in the west. It had a post code. However a Philippine post code is simply a four digit number. That would get you to a city or island but not to a specific district or road within that city. However the postcode was accompanied by the name of the city and the name of the Barangay (area of political administration). That advances us to something akin to Hackney, London; 4th or 5th Arrondissement, Paris; or, Hoboken, New Jersey. However the Barangay is broken down into smaller administrative units called the Sitio or the Purok. That is a specific area within a Barangay. The Sitio or Purok can then be further broken down by using a number to identify a small group of buildings. So, whilst this was not what we in the west understand as a complete address in our traditional sense, it was close. It brought the location of the building down to a handful of buildings where only a few families would be living. It was good enough for the Philippine authorities to issue Jo with a postal id; for the local authority to issue her with Barangay clearance; and for the Philippine National Police local office to issue police clearance. It was sufficient for a takeaway restaurant to accept as a viable address to which they would commit to deliver a takeaway meal. As part of her application Jo had submitted her police and barangay clearance to support this address. These documents were less than a couple of months old and had also been used as part of her passport application. The second part of the address we supplied was what we would call Poste Restante or a P.O. Box; however in this case it was for the family (that is immediate family; parents and siblings only). We drew attention to this issue in the application. Jo had no other documentation to prove an address and you cannot supply evidence of something that does not exist. That was the position Jo, and millions of others in the Philippines and across the developing world, are in. So what we are seeing with this issue is that it indicates cultural difference. What we provided was fine by the Philippine authorities but definitely unacceptable to the British authorities. Whilst I have some sympathy with the position of the U.K.V.I. on this, if they refuse a visa on these grounds then the number of visitor visa applications they will be able to issue is automatically slashed dramatically. So this, to me, is also an indicator of the Home Office enacting Theresa May's 'hostile environment'. However, in fairness to U.K.V.I., we should ask how many genuine applications for a visitor visa to the U.K. are going to be made by someone in Jo's position? Probably not that many.

U.K.V.I. were also telling us they considered Jo had no incentive to return to her home address, even if it did exist. What they were meaning was she did not own property and had no regular source of income to return to whilst, if she remained in the U.K., they considered her opportunity to generate an income would be much greater. This is a value judgement made from the perspective of a U.K.V.I. officer. In the letter covering the application we were clear that, should a visitor visa be issued, there were three possible outcomes. The first, and one which probably gave Border Control the most concern, was that if we decided we were not compatible with each other, Jo would return home. U.K.V.I. would be concerned she would disappear into the invisible economy in the U.K.. They may well have considered, given our age difference, that we had no intention of building a relationship and that the visitor visa application was no more than a ruse I was using in an effort to bring a vulnerable young woman into the U.K. where she would be exploited in some way. Moving on, if we felt we did have the makings of a permanent relationship then Jo would return home from where we would plan a wedding. If that occurred in the Philippines, after the nuptials, we would apply for the appropriate visa allowing her to return with me to the U.K. as my wife. The third option was that, once back in the Philippines, we would apply for a fiancée visa to enter the U.K. and then marry here.

The issue of demonstrating that we actually knew each other was the major failing of our application. On reflection it is common sense that we should have generated and supplied plenty of evidence of this and I was very naïve in not doing so. We had spent a fair bit of time together over five days. Generating such evidence would have been a very straightforward process. We could have been photographed together at Mountain View and again, as a full family group, at the meal we shared at the Airport Hotel. We could have been photographed as a family group inside and outside their place of residence which would evidence I was fully aware of Jo's circumstances; and could have given some reassurance that her address did actually exist. This is something I should have thought about but didn't. So my advice for fellow travellers is to make sure you thoroughly document the time you and your girlfriend spend together. Have photos taken of yourselves together with different people, on different days, wearing different clothes. Have photos with different members of her family, in as many different places as you can. Provide documentation on every conceivable situation; yes, even if you are in bed together. U.K.V.I. want to know your relationship is genuine. A photograph of the two of you sharing a bed, obviously not in any sexually explicit position, indicates you know each other a little better than a photograph of you sat next to each other in a restaurant or taxi! If it is at all possible try to generate these images with a date on them. That way there can be no argument as to their authenticity. It is best to produce too much evidence to U.K.V.I. than to risk sending too little. U.K.V.I. will consistently tell you it is the responsibility of the applicant to prove to the U.K. visa authorities that a relationship exists and is genuine; they will not make any assumptions on your behalf, nor should they. Just because your girlfriend has copies of her sponsor's birth certificate and passport certified by a solicitor in the U.K. along with bank statements, tax records, council tax statements and utility bills, etc. does not mean you have physically met; you have to prove it!

The third reason related to the potential negative impact U.K.V.I. perceived a visit to the U.K. would have on Jo's education. They stated a visit would either prevent her education continuing or prevent her earning sufficient in her own country to be able to continue her education. Is that the business of U.K.V.I.? I would suggest not. It is the right of the individual to decide how they wish to spend their time. In this instance, even were the applicant to spend the full six-months away from study or generating income to pay for study, surely that is her business. It is not the prerogative of an official acting on behalf of a foreign government to determine how the applicant should act so long as what they are doing does not create an issue for the U.K.

This was probably the most worrying of the reasons given as it is not covered directly by anything I can find in the Immigration Rules. At the time Jo made the application she was studying a degree level course in I.T. at a bona fide Cebu further education college. The course was inexpensive in western terms; about £600 (€660; $760) per annum. However, in her circumstances, this was a difficult sum to raise. What she had been doing for four years was working for six months to generate the income to pay for the next college semester and then attending the college and studying the next modules for a six month session. In the Philippines this is not an uncommon phenomenon. It would mean her degree would take twice as long to complete but also meant she was consistently on top of the payments; a very sensible practice. One might argue this to be better financially than the current system in the U.K. where most students will run up debts well into five figures and may spend many years paying them off. At the time Jo made the visa application she had completed four of the eight semesters necessary to allow final examination and award of a degree. So she was in a six month work period but having difficulty in finding any kind of employment. U.K.V.I. cited a reason for not granting the visa because to do so would have a negative impact upon her education. If she were to visit the U.K. for up to six months, (and that could mean anything from an overnight stay up to the full six months), either her studies would be delayed or her ability to pay her college fees would be affected. Resulting in a negative impact on her education. I understood the point but felt a very high-handed attitude was being shown.

Whilst I would not claim to be an expert on the Immigration Rules I have certainly had to spend some time finding my way around them. Nowhere have I found anything which suggests the granting of a visa can be refused because there would be a negative impact on the education of the person making the application. Normally travel is believed to be a great way of broadening ones horizons and growing as an individual. Reading between the lines their thinking may have been that Jo would find a way of using her U.K. visit to quickly generate some income to pay for her continuing education. But, if she did that, she would immediately put herself in breach of the visa, if it were issued. Her actions would be illegal. Given the documents and letter of support I had to provide that would also have made me complicit in her activities. However, even if one were to argue that this was a genuine cause for concern, surely there would be a need to produce some evidence. To cite this as a reason to refuse the issue of a visa is to assume Jo and I were conspiring to deceive U.K.V.I. and create some kind of advantage for ourselves. All we wanted was an opportunity of living under the same roof for a few months. Nothing else. The actions of U.K.V.I., in practice, made assumptions on the state of mind of the applicant, Jo, and her sponsor, me. Were such allegations made publicly in the U.K., they would be libellous. Not only does this make a mockery of the Immigration Rules, it is also a demonstration of a government body placing itself above the law. It is solid evidence that U.K.V.I. took the Home Secretary's instructions to create a 'hostile environment' for would-be immigrants very seriously indeed.

If U.K.V.I. genuinely considered that Jo would behave in this manner then it was incumbent upon them to support such an allegation with some evidence. They could not do that because such evidence didn't exist; we can be certain that had they discovered the tiniest shred of evidence they would have used it. Not to do so would have placed the member of staff in a position where they were neglecting their duty. If they felt the application was suspicious then it is something which should be followed up as part of the process of considering the visa application. If no evidence is found but suspicions were still aroused then it would become a matter for U.K.V.I. staff in the U.K. to follow up once the applicant arrived. If Jo, or anyone else in the U.K. on this type of visa, was discovered working, then they would not only be immediately returned to their country of origin with the visa cancelled, but their passport would be endorsed to that effect and a further application to visit the U.K. (and probably many other developed countries) would be refused for a number of years. They would also be in a position to take action against the sponsor, i.e. me.

Removing the right of appeal against the refusal to issue some visas worsens this situation. Not only can there be poor decision-making, bias is also arguable. There is now no way to challenge these decisions. In the case of Jo to even comment on the education issue was completely unnecessary. Our failure to provide information of knowing each other was plenty good enough to deny the application.

So Jo had a ticket but no visa. More experience paid for; the cost of the visa lost and also a fairly small cancellation fee for her flight ticket. It seemed quite bizarre that because the ticket was issued in Jo's name the only person the airline would deal with for refunds/cancellations was Jo. They would not allow me to cancel the ticket. The issue for Jo and I here was that the closer one is to the date of the outbound flight, the higher the cost of cancelling the ticket. So Jo had to make her way to the airline office in Cebu City, prove who she was, and make the cancellation. The cost of the ticket was then returned directly to the account which paid for it, minus a percentage for cancellation charges. The cancellation charges had increased as it had taken her three working days to find out where the airline office was and to get there.

Whilst I had lost money, somewhere between £150 and £200, on this project, Jo had lost confidence in the system and was upset that our plans had, seemingly, been scuppered. To re-iterate a point I made earlier, with no visitor visa we had lost the opportunity to spend a few months getting to know each other properly. We had two alternatives. One was for me to spend much more time in Cebu with Jo and her family, get to know each other better, gather evidence that we knew each other, and then re-apply for a visitor visa. Or we could apply for a fiancée visa.

As was made clear, provided you could read and understand the small print, the information an applicant puts forward for a visitor visa to be considered is entirely up to the applicant. We have also seen that, whilst U.K.V.I. staff will rightly turn down applications which are not strong enough, they are also willing to use reasons for refusal which would probably not stand up to much scrutiny, particularly now the right to appeal has been removed, i.e. potential negative impact on education.

I took the view that, given the keenness U.K.V.I. showed in turning down the visitor visa application; it took three days whilst their website claimed that ninety-five per cent of applications would take three weeks to be processed, Jo and I should seriously identify our intentions. Whilst I would have liked six months under the same roof I was prepared to take the plunge and marry, a compromise by a month or two was acceptable. We chatted about this and agreed that twenty weeks or so together was likely to be sufficient to make a decision on whether or not we should marry, and that opened up the possibility of applying for a fiancée visa.

As an aside, whilst I have problems with the idea of living in the Philippines, this is a situation I may review in light of current cultural developments in the U.K. and the election of a U.S. President who seems rather gung-ho to say the least. When I married a Filipina I automatically qualified for a Philippine passport. That could be useful should the current rise in racial tensions in the west continue. However, before such a passport could be issued by the Philippines authorities, I would need to refute my current nationality. As part of the process I would have to specify that I would become solely a citizen of the

Philippines. That would satisfy current Philippine law. In the U.K. I would still be able to assert British nationality. However I suspect that if the Philippine authorities discovered this, Philippine citizenship would be withdrawn. Where this would leave me with international law, I don't know.

Back to the issue of a visa to enter the U.K.. The big advantage to applying for a fiancée visa was that the Immigration Rules were very clear about what an applicant must show before this type of visa would be issued. This also meant that, provided the applicant fulfilled that criteria, U.K.V.I. will be on very shaky ground if they refused it, as their judgement on this type of visa application is open to appeal.

The Immigration Rules as they existed when Jo made her application can be found using Appendix 3. They show that, instead of a nebulous criteria which could be opposed at every turn, we are now presented with a checklist. There was a glimmer of light at the end of the tunnel!

Let's go through these requirements point by point:

Rule 289AA:
Both parties need to be at least 18 years old.

No problem, Jo's passport and other documents all proved she was over 18 years of age.

Rule 290(i):
Need to prove that the visa would be issued to allow marriage to a person settled in the U.K.

Not a problem. Get the paperwork in place to prove a wedding has been arranged. Then produce my passport along with certified copies of the information pages which could be retained by U.K.V.I. in the Philippines.

Rule 290(ii):

The parties have met.

This told us that I would need to make a second visit and that we should consider hiring a film crew to cover our activities, 24/7! Okay, so I am still miffed at not getting the visitor visa; a camera and/or selfies would suffice!

Rule 290(iii):
We need to prove that we would live together after the wedding.

Dependent upon the person scrutinising our application, this could be a bit of a grey area. However my work was in the U.K. and I had no intention of leaving it. There were also contracts in place proving that the work existed and U.K.V.I. were in a position where these could be straightforwardly checked and verified. For Jo, she would have no difficulty in proving that she did not have work. The refusal of the visitor visa was a part of the evidence of this as U.K.V.I. had provided a comment that they doubted that she had work. Effectively they would be hoisted by their own petard.

Rule 290(iv):
Adequate maintenance and accommodation until the wedding.

Not a problem. I am the owner and sole occupant of a five-bedroomed property in which we would live. At that point there were a few years of outstanding mortgage to pay off. I could evidence regular payment over many years with annual statements from the various financial institutions which, from time to time, had held the mortgage. I could also evidence monthly income at a level more than adequate for us to live on and savings to cover off emergencies.

Rule 290(v):
Adequate accommodation after the wedding.

See at (iv) above. The same situation would prevail.

Rule 290(vi):
Adequate maintenance after the wedding.

See at (iv) above. The same situation would prevail but, once married, Jo would then be in a position where she could obtain employment.

Rule 290(vii):
The applicant provides an original English language test certificate in speaking and listening from an English language test provider approved by the Secretary of State.

This relates to an English language test which a Philippine fiancée visa applicant must pass unless she ticks one of the boxes which exempt her from this requirement. Jo was not exempt. The answer was fairly straightforward. Whilst the system around testing has now changed, at that time she could enrol to take the test at a local college. As she was not very confident with her English we chose an option where the test was taken following a four week course.

She passed.

Rule 291:
Provided we satisfied the above criteria and a visa was stamped in her passport whilst she was still physically present in the Philippines then, on arrival in the U.K., she would be admitted.

Rule 292:
If a visa was not stamped into her passport then, on arrival in the U.K., she would not be allowed entry

One could be forgiven for thinking that, in the section of the Immigration Rules titled Fiancé(e)s and proposed civil partners, one would find *all* the requirements listed. I hope my commentary to date has led you to being equally sceptical!

In the paragraphs above there is reference to 'adequate' funds being available to the applicant. There is a financial figure within the rules to tell you precisely what 'adequate' means in terms of annual income. In the case of Jo and I the figure was set at a minimum income of £18,600 per annum, (P1,166,405; €20,404; $23,585). Where children are involved the minimum income level increases. What is also not mentioned is how the 'adequate funds' criteria will continue after she arrives in the U.K. A successful applicant will arrive in the U.K. and, to maintain her legal right to stay, must marry the person named on the visa. She can then take up residence, settle down, find employment and build her family. However the adequate maintenance figure will be used for each subsequent visa application until indefinite leave to remain in the country has been granted. Logical and sensible one would think. I would agree up to a point. What was not made clear when Jo applied was that the income generated by the visa applicant, once married and able to work in the U.K., could not be assumed to as a part of this figure. The same situation applied when my wife of three years first visited the U.K. on a fiancé visa and also when she successfully applied for her first visa to remain as a married woman. There have been interpretations of the Rules concluding that the financial figure relates solely to the income generating capacity of the sponsor.

In such circumstances what happens if a sponsor loses their job and becomes reliant on benefits? What happens if a sponsor retires? What happens if the sponsor becomes ill and is unable to work? The one which concerns me most is: What happens should a government, hell bent on getting immigration figures down, decide to raise these threshold figures substantially? The answer to all these questions currently is that any visa renewal can be refused on the grounds of inadequate finance and the applicant returned to their own country whether or not they are legally married to a U.K. citizen and having followed all the Rules. This could even be the case where the applicant has become the major wage-earner of the couple. This effectively prevents the sponsor from stepping back from income generating activities to concentrate, for instance, on rearing young children. Whilst at the initial application stage this is something of a distraction, it is something which must be carefully thought about. There has been a recent case discussed in the media where the sponsor had chosen to become a house husband and was not generating any income whatsoever. However, his wife, the visa applicant, had a legitimate job, which paid almost four times the threshold figure, she was a head teacher. The visa application was turned down on the grounds that the sponsor, the husband, was unable to deliver the financial element.

Not mentioned at all in the 'Fiancé(e)s and proposed civil partners' section of the Immigration Rules was the requirement of a test for pulmonary tuberculosis (TB). There is a lot tucked away in the Immigration Rules and Appendix T is a section which covers TB screening. However there is nothing whatever in the fiancé(e) section of the Immigration Rules to signpost an applicant to this. It is almost as though the Rules were written with a view to creating a gap in the fiancé(e) application which will then allow its refusal. Even if the applicant notices towards the end of the Immigration Rules index that there is a section relating to TB and opens it, all they will find is a lengthy list of countries which includes the Philippines. It is still far from explicit around the type of visa application where TB clearance is necessary. All it said above the list of countries was:

> Any person applying to enter the U.K. as described in paragraph A39, Part 1 General Provisions of the Immigration Rules, must present at the time of application a valid medical certificate issued by a medical practitioner approved by the Secretary of State for these purposes, as listed on the Gov.uk website, confirming that they have undergone screening for active pulmonary tuberculosis and that such tuberculosis is not present in the applicant.

When you try to locate paragraph A39 the index itself is still far from clear. It is only when the 'Medical' section of Part 1 is accessed that one will find:

A39. Any person making an application for entry clearance to come to the U.K. for more than six months or as a fiancé(e) or proposed civil partner applying for leave to enter under Section EC-P: Entry clearance as a partner under Appendix FM, having been present in a country listed in Appendix T for more than six months immediately prior to their application, must present, at the time of application, a valid medical certificate issued by a medical practitioner approved by the Secretary of State for these purposes, as listed on the Gov.uk website, confirming that they have undergone screening for active pulmonary tuberculosis and that this tuberculosis is not present in the applicant.

With information to hand regarding the financial requirements and TB screening we are now making progress and can see a much fuller picture. However those who write the Immigration Rules are fully cognisant of the limited level of understanding and knowledge applicants have, otherwise why would they insist on English language tests as a condition of being able to apply for a visa? On the one hand the Immigration Rules accept that applicants will have a limited knowledge of the English language; and when one sees the level at which the current A1 Life Skills test is pitched one can see this requirement is incredibly basic. Yet, to apply successfully for a fiancé(e) visa the applicant (for it remains the responsibility of the applicant to submit an application completely and correctly) is expected to wade through the Immigration Rules which would confuse many people who are native speakers of the English language. The matter gets further complicated because, once in the U.K. and married, she then needs to apply to extend her fiancée visa into a family visa, something discussed in more detail later. Without going further into the Rules are you, the reader, confident of being able to distinguish between fiancé(e) and civil partner in the way the Immigration Rules do? Could you reasonably be expected to understand about border clearance of a partner under Appendix FM without a further journey there? What is EC-P?

As the person holding the purse strings, losing £150 to £200 because I failed to realise the importance of proof of having met, was annoying. At the time Jo applied for her fiancée visa the cost was £845, just for the visa; almost ten times the cost of a visitor visa. Now, six years later, it stands at £1,202.20. As the visa element of that is currently £1,033 politicians may argue that the cost of the visa has been reduced as it stood at £1195 in early 2019. However there are costs associated with other essential elements of the application.

There is £150 to renew the English language test requirement. The tests are valid for two years and, surprise, surprise, a family visa extension will be valid for no less than 2½ years. This means that each time an extension to a visa is applied for, a new test needs to be taken, and passed. The test can only be taken at a Home Office specified centre. To confuse matters further there are two levels of testing as the level of knowledge of the English language differs dependent upon the type of visa which is being applied for. Again it is the responsibility of the applicant to wade through the Immigration Rules, discover these requirements, and work out which test they need to take.

For U.K. based applicants there is also a fee of £19.20 to attend a centre, which again must be Home Office approved, for collection of biometric information. The Home Office has actually outsourced this function to a private company, Sopra, whose main aim appears to be selling the applicant further services. The U.K. equivalent of the agents we found plying their trade in the streets of the Philippines.

These essential elements of the application mean there has been a small price increase, not a reduction. Coupled with this, and in keeping with creating a hostile environment for applicants, the applicant has to make two trips, to a different centres, to fulfil the requirements, language and biometrics, before the application can be submitted. There is no way around this.

In addition to this there is now a health surcharge. This began in 2015 but did not exist when Jo made her initial applications. This payment allows visa holders to use NHS services. I wish it had been available to Jo as you will see when we come to discuss insurance.

To have a fiancée visa application turned down due to a failure to provide evidence of a TB test would be infuriating, especially when the section of the Immigration Rules written specifically to guide those applying for such a visa make absolutely no mention of it. And, to compound matters, those Rules need digging into thoroughly before this requirement will be unearthed and fully understood. The issue does not stop there. Can the applicant visit their own doctor or local hospital to get evidence they have been screened for TB? The Rules very clearly state that the person or organisation doing the testing must be approved by the Secretary of State. So the answer is an emphatic 'No'. In the whole of the Philippines the Secretary of State has seen fit to only specify one testing centre.

How likely is it that an applicant, with a limited understanding of the English language, is going to fully appreciate the implications of Appendix T?! Again we are driving the applicant into areas where their knowledge of the English language is likely to be insufficient for the task they are being required to perform. It is very likely the applicant will not fully appreciate what they need to do. This is a further example of what politicians want when telling bureaucrats to create a 'hostile environment' for applicants.

For a Filipina to get TB clearance the only one venue in her country which the U.K. government will accept as being valid is located in Makati City, the business district of Metro Manila; probably the most expensive area in the whole country. An appointment has to be made online, which will be a challenge for the percentage of the population who do not use, and/or have no access to the internet. If the applicant lives in the Metro Manila area then the TB test might end up as a relatively straightforward day trip. For people who live outside that area it is a visit that needs to be planned. To put this into context the population of the Philippines is around 35% higher than that of the U.K. and the land area is between twenty and twenty-five per higher overall.

However the land itself comprises of thousands of islands spread out over a much greater area; and that is where the difficulty lies. Remember the geography of the Philippines from earlier? The distances we are talking about are as follows. The Philippine Islands run north to south a distance similar to Edinburgh to Marseilles, Seattle to Los Angeles or Paris to Cádiz. Compared to these routes there is also a minimal transport infrastructure. Imagine if we residents of the U.K. needed to prove we were clear of a particular disease before we could apply for a visa to visit a foreign country and that the only place the government of that country would accept as providing a valid test was located in the most expensive place in the country. That is the situation the Filipina can find herself in; like a Shetlander being sent for a medical check on Harley Street, London!

For the Filipina from the central and southern islands of the Philippine archipelago and those in the north outside Metro Manila needing TB clearance, flying into Manila Airport is the logical choice of transport. From there it is a fairly short jeepney or taxi ride into Makati City. Internal flights are fairly cheap, particularly if travel is off-peak and reserved two or three weeks in advance. Jo had never flown before and had never been to Manila. Nor had her parents. The experience she had of travelling was as part of a family group and moving between two relatively quiet islands, Leyte and Cebu. Her most recent travel experience had dropped her into the deadliest weather system her country had ever experienced. To this background we planned her TB test. There would be no point in her studying for and taking the English language test were she to be positive for TB so that needed to come first. Were the test to indicate she was a latent carrier of pulmonary TB then she would need to take a six-month course of medication and then present herself for testing a second time where the outcome was very likely to be clear; if not, repeat the process at six monthly intervals until the test is passed. As we will see the system has recently changed and sorting out the language test should now be the first priority. I decided to encourage Jo to travel with her mother. There were several reasons for this. She was a very inexperienced traveller; so was her mother, but together they would be good support and company for each other. I considered she would be vulnerable if she travelled alone. She did not wear spectacles but had told me that was because the family could not afford to have her eyes tested or to buy them; (something we sorted out when I next visited). She did have poor eyesight. Maybe that was why she found me attractive! Being with her mother would demonstrate I was working with her family, albeit at arm's length, and allow them to share a new experience together. Were anything untoward to occur, two heads are better than one in dealing with it. In Makati City it was impossible to reserve a single room in a hotel, as in the rest of the country double occupancy was expected, so there was no additional cost for a second person sharing a room. The accommodation package would include a buffet breakfast so the women could have a huge meal at the start of the day if they chose to. That would also mean a much reduced need to spend on food later in the day. I also considered that the parents would see that I was acting responsibly and could be trusted to look after their daughter, just in case they needed any more convincing. Having experienced some of what the Philippines can throw at you; unexpected delays, queues, unpredictable weather, appointments changed at the last minute, etc. I felt it best to fly the ladies to Manila on day one, for Jo to take the test on day two and for them to fly back to Cebu on day three. I also had more disposable income at that time; it was not something I would do now. Jo reserved her test for a date three weeks away and I was able to pick up return flights very cheaply. The return trip for them both cost less than £250, (P 15,680; €275; $317), all in. I bought the flights and three star hotel accommodation online and sent some cash across to cover sundries such as airport tax, which they had to pay at check-in for each leg of the journey, transport to and from the airport to their accommodation and the equivalent of £42 (P 2,635; €46; $53) for the test itself. The accommodation was within easy walking distance of the TB test centre.

A word of warning when making internal flight reservations online using airlines in the Philippines. At every stage the company may use a default to include something within the ticket which you have not requested but which has a price attached. If you do not remove these items as they crop up your flight costs will escalate dramatically and you will get services you don't want; like a two course meal on a 45 minute flight. For a simple return flight from Cebu to Manila I had to deal with the following items which were all added to the flight cost automatically.

>baggage fees (you are billed on the assumption you are carrying baggage; you have to check to ensure the default charge is accurate, and for the correct baggage weight);

>fees for allocating seats (they will be allocated automatically at check-in);

>in-flight meals (these are a real pain; you cannot just say no to an in-flight meal, you need to click into the menu and remove everything that has, speculatively, been ordered for you); and,

>insurance.

On a recent visit to the Philippines I booked return flights from Cebu to the city of Bacolod to link in with our return flights from the U.K.. These were paid for in full at the time of booking. The booking system allowed three options. Flight only; flight with baggage; or, flight with baggage and meal. Until you have paid you are not advised that the weight limit for your baggage is 20 kgs. This was a problem as our international flight gave us a weight limit of 30 kgs. If you buy a flight only, then before you pay for the ticket, you are asked to specify your add-ons. These include not just baggage but the ability to choose from several weight options up to 32 kgs. Doing it this way solves the problem but you cannot possibly know this until you hit the difficulty and try to find a solution. As luck would have it, (or mismanagement on the part of the airline), we got a solution to this issue. Following the purchase of two return flights we needed to purchase four single flights from Bacolod to Cebu on the return leg of our flight. This all happened in September. Before Christmas the airline sent me an e-mail advising that our flight from Cebu to Bacolod, originally scheduled for take-off around 4 pm had been rescheduled. It would now leave Cebu Airport at

3 am the same day. I took the option to cancel. A couple of months before travel a second e-mail arrived advising that the flight from Bacolod to Cebu had also had to be rescheduled. A 6 pm departure had now been put back to 10.35 pm. As this meant we could leave our hotel at a more reasonable time to travel to Bacolod Airport we kept the flight. However it did mean we had two very tired young children travelling with us. When we got on the flight the extra legroom seat I had paid for had already been taken by other passengers and was only available to me if I separated myself from the rest of our party of six (me being the only English speaker) and broke up the party which had taken the seat. We found that all safety announcements and information on the flight were provided in English, which was no use to my fellow travellers. When the safety announcement was made it was spoken quickly by a Filipina speaking English with a strong local accent. I couldn't understand a word that was said.

So, back to Jo and her TB test. All went smoothly and she passed. This was in mid-April. I immediately reserved her English language test and paid the fee and tuition fees for a four-week course in preparation, together costing around £70 (P 4,400; €77; $89). The course really consisted of two sessions a week at college which lasted an hour with plenty of work being taken home. In mid-May she took the language test and, two weeks later, at the beginning of June, received notification she had passed. I had remained the optimist and kept the second half of June relatively free in my diary. On the same day we received the language test result I reserved a flight from my local airport to Mactan and secured two weeks accommodation back at the Airport Hotel. I packed a large bottle of Tia Maria, a digital camera and the original documents needed to support her application for a fiancée visa. This included, before travelling, getting copies of my birth certificate and passport certified as authentic by a solicitor and, through my local registry office, booking a wedding and taking the original document with me whilst leaving a copy at home. So, off I went intending to make a trip that was so well documented that no one in their right mind could claim that Jo and I didn't know each other. The Tia Maria was for both of us. She had never previously consumed alcohol but wanted to try and loved chocolate and coffee flavours. For me, I used to enjoy a Black Russian cocktail; vodka, Tia Maria and coke, and, in my younger days, found it acted as a bit of an aphrodisiac. Ever the optimist!

Ongoing negotiations.

It was a very busy two weeks. The first thing we did was open a current bank account for Jo with the Bank of the Philippine Islands. Well, almost the first thing. Having booked into the Airport Hotel it was a walk of around three hundred yards from arrival lounge to bed. So, on the sexual side I discovered within an hour of arrival at the hotel that Jo was very definitely female. She was keen and enthusiastic in the bedroom but the experience bore marked similarities to that with May. After an extensive and enjoyable foreplay I moved towards penetration. As soon as I made contact with the entrance to her vagina she winced and pulled away. I asked if this was her first time and she said it was and that she did not want to feel pain. So, rather than try to force the issue, we reached mutual satisfaction with non-penetrative sex. We did not spend every night of the fortnight together but Jo stayed over around half of the nights. So the first and third things we did were located in the bedroom; disturbed by the opening of her bank account.

We felt it was necessary to quickly get an account opened as this would allow Jo to pay for her visa using her own bank account. This would indicate to the person examining the application that she was sufficiently well established in her own country, as well as in her relationship, to be managing such responsibilities. Impression management. Whether it made an iota of difference we will never know! We also took the opportunity to get Jo's eyes properly tested. This resulted in the purchase of a couple of pairs of specs.

The second time Jo stayed over she decided to try the Tia Maria. As I have discussed I have had an unhealthy relationship with alcohol for much of my life. Prior to this trip I had been drinking at weekends only, never before a working day. Jo had never had the opportunity to consume alcohol before. I told her that Tia Maria was a liquor with a flavour somewhere between coffee and chocolate and that it was stronger than beers and wines, including most sherries and ports, but not as strong as vodka or whisky. Hindsight suggests this information meant little or nothing at all to her. Before I realised what was happening she had downed a tumbler and was part way through the second. The third one she mixed about half Tia Maria and half coke. As she knocked that back she began telling me how lovely it was. Judging from the reaction she had to it I think the first two must have been mixed same way. Within ten minutes she was into her third tumbler. During that next ten minutes she became extremely randy, there were ten minutes of frantic and unrestrained horizontal activity before the impact of the alcohol kicked in. She then spent two to three hours vomiting and consuming water and followed this with a solid fifteen hours of sleep. When I checked the Tia Maria bottle she had shifted the best part of a 70cc bottle. The downside of this episode was that she had a blinding hangover for a couple of days, needing to rehydrate and get her system back up and running. The upside was that, whilst we were together, I was only aware of her touching alcohol on one other occasion.

To convince the visa authorities that we were genuine and knew each other we decided to collect as many photographs as we could with the two of us and various members of her family. To achieve this we needed to visit her family so, whilst her sister and new baby stayed with the boyfriend and his family, Jo, her parents, her brother and I made the two hour sea crossing from Cebu City to Ormoc City on the west coast of Leyte Island. Leyte is the eighth largest of the Philippine Islands. It is about 110 miles from north to south and forty miles across at its widest, (176 x 64 km) . The total population is around two and a half million, Tacloban being the largest town. The records showed Tacloban as having a population of 220,000, in the aftermath of Yolanda (Typhoon Haiyan) it was probably down to around 210,000.

On disembarking, the impact of Yolanda was immediately apparent. Walking from the vessel to the Ormoc quayside we saw plenty of unrepaired storm damage within the terminal. As soon as we exited the port we saw the market and bus station. Parts of the roof of the latter had been torn off. On the waterfront close to the port was the Ormoc City Superdrome. The large letters around the stadium's upper level spelling out its name had suffered storm damage; some were missing, others hanging off.

We had reserved two rooms at a quayside hotel, one for Jo and I, the other a family room for her parents and brother. Once we had checked-in phones were tapped on and talked into and friends and relatives began arriving. During the course of the afternoon and evening around fifteen people dropped in and I think the family room housed seven or eight overnight. Jo's father had arranged transport for our trip in a mini-bus which arrived early the next morning with driver and guide. We were met at the hotel from where we found a café for some breakfast before filling the tank and heading out of town on roads to the north. Our first stop was to be the home of Jo's maternal grandparents. We left Ormoc City travelling north-east reaching the small town of Kananga after about ninety minutes. From there we continued climbing into a mountainous rural area. The road provided for two-way traffic, it was quite narrow in most places but well maintained. Outside the towns there was very little traffic about. A couple of hours away from Ormoc City we pulled up on the grass verge outside a small hut. This was the home of the maternal grandparents. Word of our trip and its purpose had been sent ahead. There was a large reception committee, around sixty people, well over half of whom were children. Whilst evidence of the typhoon had been around us everywhere in Ormoc City its effect here was more subtle. Countryside areas are much poorer than their urban counterparts across the Philippines. It is also naturally emptier and access to food, potable water, power, communication systems, everything really, is much reduced. The impact of this, which had been exacerbated by the outcome of the typhoon, was evident. As we have described the typical Filipino is small and of slight build compared to their western counterpart. Here people were of slight build compared to their city Filipino counterparts. Whilst Yolanda had caused major damage to their communities seven months earlier, they had done their best to rebuild. In remote settlements such as this they knew no help would be coming so, once the weather had settled, they gathered together the branches, rushes and general debris left by the typhoon and used then to patch up the damage to their properties. Where trees had been uprooted by the storm, they had been chopped up and used in the rebuild. The fields were mostly rice paddies worked manually. There was little evidence of any mechanisation. There were a few head of cattle about. It is possible they could be used to help plough, etc. but I got the impression they were mostly for meat production. I do not know what breed these were. Philippine native cattle tend to be small and only the male has a lump of fat at the back of the neck. These were too large to be the native cattle and all (three I think) had a lump of fat/muscle at the top of the spine behind the neck. Nor were they Caribou which one finds in the Visayas as there was no evidence of horns. They were probably Ongole or Zebu; visually they were similar and these are breeds native to south-east Asia.

We spent a couple of hours with Jo's maternal relatives and took a walk through the village. The municipal building was akin to a big shed; a similar size to the hut one would find at a village cricket club in the U.K. There were religious shrines by the roadside marking where deaths had occurred and a small sports field equipped with aged basketball hoops. Beyond that there was very little; perhaps thirty occupied properties in total, most of which were single storey huts. The reception committee we received was most of the village with the exception of those out working in the fields and the elderly and infirm.

Everyone was warm and welcoming with the exception of a little girl who was barely two years old. She looked up at me and the wails started. I don't think she understood what I was. She had certainly never seen anyone remotely my size before. No matter how we tried to pacify her all that worked was to keep us well separated. In the couple of hours we were there no more than a dozen vehicles passed on the road; certainly nothing that would count as public transport. There was no evidence of any cars or vans in the village itself; just a few ancient motor-bikes.

When we left our mini-bus was full. Several locals hitched a lift with us. We had a drive through the mountains and some spectacular scenery before descending to a place called Carigara. We stopped briefly, lost three or four people and gained a couple more before following a coast road for a while and then climbing back into the mountains before finally descending back to the coast on the outskirts of Tacloban close to San Juanico Bridge. This is a fairly new highway which connects Leyte Island to the island of Eastern Samar by road. Here I got an odd flavour of Filipino culture. The San Juanico Bridge is similar in purpose and structure to the M4 and M48 motorway crossings over the Bristol Channel. It is nowhere near as busy the comparison solely being one of size. It is an impressive structure. The road across the bridge between these islands does climb, nothing dramatic but there is a definite summit. Our driver went over the highest point and then 'U' turned parking close to the summit itself. By the time Jo and I had alighted I saw that the driver, the guide and Jo's Dad had walked up to the summit. They were stood apart from each other but were taking the opportunity of relieving themselves off the bridge into the sea seventy or eighty metres below. Whilst we were there a bus party stopped and several men got out and took the opportunity to do the same! Whilst these men moved away from the group they were with, there was no further effort to conceal what they were doing. They were almost treating it as a spectator sport. The others shrugged their shoulders and just treated what was happening as normal and natural. No comment was made. The reactions of all simply marked this as typical everyday behaviour; but likely to be a bit of a surprise for anyone sailing beneath!

From the San Juanico Bridge we drove south into Tacloban City. As we approached there was much stronger evidence of the impact the typhoon had had. We were driving on main roads in a large town and saw plenty of structural damage to buildings and one or two areas where something had obviously been but was now gone, yet to be replaced. Some repair work was underway but it was clear that to get back to normal would take years rather than months. I remembered on the TV seeing a boat which had been beached by the typhoon and asked the guide if we could drive by that spot. He did better than that. We stopped and took a look around. This was the piece of land by the side of the Gulf of Leyte into which a two-storey high wave of seawater had surged, pushed by the typhoon. The TV reports had shown a desolate area in which the surge, coupled with the ferocity of the typhoon, had pretty much wiped the landscape clean. All that had been left was the outline of a few tracks, well rooted bits of undergrowth and the footings of a couple of buildings. Into this a ship had been dropped. Seven months on any ideas about desolation were long gone. We had parked on what would have been a ridge about a hundred metres from the water's edge overlooking the sea. But very little of the sea was visible. The area was fully occupied by makeshift huts and shelters. As we walked into the area we saw a homemade sign telling us we were entering Yolanda Village. Never has a village been so densely populated. There were thousands of people about. We actually passed two beached ships. The one I was able to walk around and look into typified the chaos and serendipity of life on the edge in the Philippines. It presented a bizarre situation. It was obvious this vessel had become home to several dozen families. There were people constantly coming and going, some with babies and quite young children; makeshift walkways had been erected to provide access. At the same time there were gangs of workers busy dismantling the vessel. Blow torches and saws were being used to remove any bits they could get at; it was slowly being cut up. None of these people had any sort of official status, they were just using what they could as best they could to help them get on with life. For one group it was home, to the other it was a ready source of scrap metal from which they could make a few pesos. At a very practical level it was the ultimate in recycling.

We passed a Robinson's Supermarket on the Tanauan National Highway. It seemed at first glance to be business as usual. It was only at second glance we saw that some signage was yet to be repaired and, down each side, we could see piles of debris from fallen buildings and flattened tracts of the urban landscape. That was the pattern in the central area of the city. Whilst the main roads were relatively clear of debris we would see clear evidence of the ferocity of the typhoon, but it was only by looking between buildings and beyond the major thoroughfares one could really understand the devastation that had been wrought.

We continued south for two or three miles arriving at the MacArthur Monument in the town of Palo, or what was left of it. The monument is in a park area on the sea front. This had all been tidied up. We spent a few minutes there before continuing our journey southwards towards the home of Jo's paternal grandparents. Next was the town of Tanauan. It had been built next to the sea on a flat and fairly level plain two to three metres above sea level. It had ceased to exist. It had been a town of around 10,000 people, around 2,000 were either confirmed dead or missing as a consequence of Yolanda. All I could see was a large tented area, and an awful lot of empty space. In the far distance I spotted a single row of new houses which appeared to still be under construction. There was nothing else but thousands of people milling around.

The conversations I had with people in Tacloban, Palo and Tanauan were very limited both by time and the lack of a common language. But what I was told was that the local government were not releasing details of the numbers who had died or been injured or were missing. There was a strong belief that, whilst a major disaster was acknowledged, the true extent of it in terms of lives lost would never be known. What I did find very irritating was the amount of visible advertising being done by the charities in these areas. Their flags, banners and posters were everywhere. But there was very little evidence of any useful work being done to feed and house the thousands of people whose lives had been wrecked by the disaster beyond the provision of tents and food stations. More annoying still was that almost all of these charities were branded with the symbols of one religion or another. From the limited amount I saw my suspicions are that, whilst collections were made, the distribution to those who were really in need was questionable. There was a very definite emphasis on these organisations shouting out their presence but there was little tangible to show for their efforts; and this was seven months on from the typhoon striking.

This was confirmed when we reached the home of Jo's paternal grandparents. The coastal village of Mayorga, south of Tanauan, was a thirty minute or so drive from Tacloban. Yolanda had caused major damage to many structures in the village and decimated the agricultural base of their economy. Apart from well-built brick and stone buildings, of which there were few, the village had been almost flattened. That said they had also been extremely fortunate. Whilst Mayorga is a coastal village it is separated from the ocean by a tract of land about a kilometre wide. This land is dense with well-established undergrowth which had protected Mayorga from the wall of water as in advanced up the Gulf of Leyte. The village had not flooded. It was up this channel the flood waters which had wiped out Tanauan and went on the kill thousands in Tacloban had been building up steam.

Seven months on they were beginning to rebuild but the only aid they had received came from the local government. The media had not visited and there was no evidence of any charity organisation activity. The typhoon had occurred in November. Jo's parents had arrived six days after the event to find utter devastation and desolation. Local support for this community had been restricted to some timber being delivered to the villagers in April; six months after Yolanda had struck. The villagers had been told to get on with the rebuild themselves. This was progressing whilst I was there in mid-June. Their biggest worry was that the next typhoon season, July to January give or take a week or two, was almost upon them. Whilst they had been able to construct load bearing pillars which took the weight of a roof, they were still busy constructing external walls. This work was taking place alongside getting their agricultural activities back up and running. It was literally a matter of life and death. They needed shelter before the next typhoon season hit and they needed to be able to feed themselves across that season. Again there was a lot of cheerfulness and many smiling faces. Life was to be enjoyed despite the events they had suffered and the poverty in which they were living. In management-speak this would probably be referred to as 'resilience'; but it is resilience at a level no one in the developed world will ever have to display. Maybe this attitude builds into the serendipity of the mind-set typical of Filipinos or maybe the smiles were window dressing the tears of a clown. However, everywhere and everyone was clean and there was undoubtedly a sense of pride.

I enjoyed my brief time with this arm of Jo's extended family. Staying longer was impossible given the schedule we had. At the practical level it would also have been challenging. There was not enough space and the only place where I could have slept would have been on the floor.

There was a distinct lack of bedroom furniture and no room which would have been long enough for me to lie in!

To give the reader an idea of how slow development projects can be in the Philippines I have copied the following brief extract from the online edition of the SunStar newspaper for 9th April, 2017:

> *Since 2014 until last month, the DAR (Department of Agrarian Reform) has already approved the conversion of 41 hectares for Yolanda housing at various sites in Tacloban City, Basay, Samar, and the towns of Pastrana, Carigara, Mayorga and MacArthur in Leyte. A land use conversion certificate from DAR is one of the requirements needed to set up relocation sites. The NHA (National Housing Authority) intends to build 205,128 houses for the affected areas in the central part of the country.*
> (http://www.sunstar.com/tacloban/local-news/2017/04/04/yolanda-housing-developers-told-secure-clearance-deadline-534815)

In lay terms it had taken 2½ years for one arm of government to provide another arm of government with permission to build.

From Mayorga back to Ormoc City was a further drive of the best part of three hours. It had been a very long day. When we got back the mini-van driver stopped at the petrol station, filled up and presented Jo's father with the bill. A debate ensued during which he paid. I discovered from Jo that her Dad had not understood that he was expected to refill the vehicle for them. He had reluctantly paid up after a few words, for the sake of amor-propio, but he was now almost without funds. I had thought the price he had quoted for the vehicle, driver and guide for the day was ridiculously cheap; 3,000 php (£48; €53; $61); so I was happy to give him a further 2,000 php. to cover the fuel costs. That represented the hire of a fifteen seater vehicle for the day with driver and guide; and it was a twelve hour day. For the experience we had this still represented incredible value for money for an affluent westerner who did not have to worry about having a roof over his head during the next typhoon season, or worry about there being enough food to see him through that period!

Once we were back in Cebu City work on the fiancée visa application began in earnest. We now had hundreds of photographs of the two of us in many different locations with various members of Jo's family. The day following our return we selected an engagement ring which we collected the following day after it had been correctly sized; a gold band with diamond setting. The day after that we had a meal at the Maribago Grill which was effectively our engagement party. Jo and I were accompanied by her sister, boyfriend and baby, the young cousin who had visited Mountain View with us, Jo's parents and her maternal grandparents who had returned to Cebu with us. The event was well documented especially the presentation of the ring. Over the next couple of days we pulled together the visa application, selected the photographs we would use, paid up and took the earliest opportunity we could to visit the U.K. visa offices in Cebu City, located close to the Ayala Centre.

At this point it is important that I am clear about my intentions. I was with a young woman I had known for almost a year. We had applied for a fiancée visa for her to visit the U.K. and get married within six months of arrival. I had bought her an engagement ring and we had had a celebratory party with members of her family. However during that year we had only actually been in each other company for around eighteen days and eight or nine nights. We had been together online for much longer, we had sorted out some pretty difficult situations, we had confidence in each other, but we had physically shared each other's company for less than three weeks. The only way we had of spending more time together was to plan a wedding. It was a weird situation for both of us. Was I in love with Jo? At one level I certainly was. I was in lust with her and thought there was a good chance that love would quickly develop. The signs were all positive. However there is much more to any marriage, civil partnership or long term relationship than finding someone physically attractive. This was why we had first applied for the visitor visa. What we really needed was to spend time together under the same roof to see how things developed. But the only way we were able to do this was to seriously plan our wedding.

It is an expensive way to enjoy a courtship which could end in marriage but could equally end in pieces. Whilst it focuses the mind it is also a confusing thing to do. To be able to spend some time together we had to arrange marriage and prove we were in love when the reality was that we could reach that point but were certainly not there yet. The visa system forced us into a position where we had no alternative but to make these arrangements as it was the only means of allowing some form of courtship to happen which was both legal and practical.

Perhaps it is worth a mentioning a few more practical issues around the visa application process which may not be anticipated. My bank account is in Pounds Sterling. Jo's bank account was in Philippine Pesos. Whilst she made her application for a visa to enter the U.K. in her own country, the Philippines, the visa authorities insisted in taking payment in U.S. dollars. This meant my account had charges for converting funds from Sterling to Pesos which were then accepted into Jo's account; and her account was charged for changing Pesos into Dollars. A crazy system and another reasonable opportunity to dispute the religious texts. Jesus may have thrown the moneylenders out of the temple, but they landed on the High Street and have been screwing the public ever since. Online and telephone banking are still in their infancy in the Philippine provinces so we needed to allow time for these transactions to take place.

The requirement to pay in U.S. dollars I suspect reflects the second point. That is that the application, whilst electronically submitted in a form which can be accessed by the Entry Clearance Officers employed by U.K.V.I., once printed off and signed is actually physically handed over to the organisation to whom U.K.V.I. sub-contract much of this work, V.F.S.. They also take biometrics on behalf of U.K.V.I.. This means that the visa applicant will only see a Border Clearance Officer if they are called in for interview. This happens very infrequently. An interview will only happen if there is some doubt as to whether a visa should be issued. Most applications are open and shut cases; either a visa is issued or it is refused. So most applicants will never have seen a Border Control Officer until they appear in the U.K. at their point of entry into the country.

During Jo's application the third party international organisation to whom the U.K. Border Control subcontracted this work was V.F.S. Global. It was founded in India in 2001 and is, according to Wikipedia, part of the Kuoni Travel Group. From records filed at Companies House, U.K., there is some evidence of V.F.S. and Kuoni sharing Directors. This relationship, between what is generally regarded as a top of the range tour operator and the system which manages visa applications, is curious to say the least. V.F.S. operate as a visa application screening service for many different governments.

(V.F.S. is an abbreviation for Visa Facilitation Services. More to the point it also stands for Very F...... Slow!)

The pre-nuptial agreement is also a subject which can get an airing here. Given the huge disparity in age, income, investments, etc. between Jo and myself it is an issue to which I had given considerable thought. Given the circumstances in which I was placing myself, common sense told me a pre-nup would be essential. However, as it concerns what will happen when the relationship fails, it is one of the least romantic things to think about when starting out together. At the time of writing I was thinking it was something I would not pursue. Why?! Well a non-European citizen entering the U.K. needs visas; as we have seen these cannot be taken for granted and, if anything, the system is being tightened rather than relaxed. Without the visa a Filipina is in the country illegally and can be removed. This would put Jo, or anyone else who came to the U.K. and married, at a huge disadvantage. From her perspective, should marriage fail, her visa will terminate. This situation prevails until she has a permanent right of residence and obtains a British passport. Unless the woman holds a degree recognised by the U.K. education system, it will take a minimum of seven and a half years from the time she marries and could take as long as twelve and a half years before she is able, legally, to get these documents in place. My thinking is that this situation buys me enough time to know if I have a genuine person with me or the ultimate scammer. Why go through the stress and expense of a pre-nup in these circumstances? A scammer is likely to be long gone before the seven and a half year mark arrives. I also considered how valid a pre-nup would be after seven and a half to twelve and a half years. Would it retain any value? A further consideration is language. A pre-nup written in legal English may be understood and signed off at a superficial level by a Filipina new to the country but, should it come to enforcing that document, it would be very easy for her Counsel to argue she could not be expected to fully understand the implications of such a document.

I returned to the U.K. and, three weeks later, Jo notified me that the fiancée visa had been issued. The next job was to reserve Jo's ticket and get her from the Philippines to the U.K. Once we had the ticket reserved we discovered we had some Philippine bureaucracy to sort out. I had thought, at that point, that Jo would just have an airport terminal fee, then P550, (now P850) to pay as she exited the country. I was wrong. There is also Philippine Travel Tax; a government tax charged on all Filipinos leaving the country on a Philippine passport, and chargeable every time they leave the country. The cost is dependent upon whether the passenger is travelling economy, P1,620, or business or first class. However it does not end there. What we had not been told and discovered almost by accident was that a Filipina leaving the country for a period which could extend beyond six months, i.e. marriage, had to take a half day course to prepare her for life outside the Philippines. There was a notional charge for this of P400 as I remember. This course is administered and delivered by the Commission of Filipinos Overseas. Jo had to register with C.F.O. and take various documents with her. Her passport and a photocopy of it; a secondary form of identification which contained a photograph; her visa and a photocopy of it; a copy of the booking form for the wedding; a completed C.F.O. registration form and two passport sized photographs. Getting this together was a nuisance but do-able. The problem lay in being able to get a seat on the course. At that time they took place twice a week in Cebu City, had twelve spaces only, and were allocated on a first come, first served basis. When we discovered this Jo was two weeks from planned departure. This course is a sensible and good thing. It tells the Filipina what to do if things go wrong. How to contact the Consulate, what to expect from the police and support services in the U.K. etc. When completed the course leader would stamp and sign the traveller's passport. Without that stamp and signature the airline, but more likely Philippine Border Control, could and probably would, refuse Jo permission to depart. Jo got a place on one of these courses. It ran from 8 am to 1 pm. She had to start queuing at 3am. in order to secure her place. Even then she was seventh in the queue. The first time she tried she arrived at 6am and there were already over twenty people waiting. Late arrivals will try to push in; some will try to buy a place from you, others use it is a money making opportunity and will queue with no intention of doing the course but to sell their place in the queue to the highest bidder. However Jo stood firm and completed the course.

The evening before she travelled I received a panicky e-mail from her. She had closed her bank account but, as she walked home, had been mugged. Her handbag was snatched with all her money in it. Fortunately her passport and travel documents were at home so she could still travel. Cash was sent out via Western Union so she would be able to pay her airport and personal travel taxes.

Jo's flight landed on time at 6.30am. 26th August, the day after a Bank Holiday in the U.K. She had checked in at Mactan Airport, Cebu, around 5 pm the previous day and flown into Hong Kong where she had had a stopover just short of three hours. One thing we had not considered was any requirement a Filipino might have for a transit visa in Hong Kong, part of China; thankfully that was not necessary. The long haul leg of the flight took around 12½ hours allowing for a seven hour time difference. So she had a seriously lengthy journey, something of which she had had no previous experience.

Whilst I am by nature a glass half full man we had done a lot of chasing around to get the visa issued. I expected the worst. So, I made myself visible and available in the arrivals hall expecting a border control officer to tap me on the shoulder or to hear my name on the tannoy. I need not have worried.

There is a supreme irony in all this planning, applying for visas and having concerns about Border Control staff. In the U.K. much action is being taken, rightly, in an effort to prevent forced and arranged marriages. Most of these occur when a parent or guardian of a vulnerable girl or young woman send her from the U.K. to a developing country for marriage. The girl may not know what is happening until she arrives by which time it is too late for her to do anything about it. Coupled with that she will be struggling with a language and culture with which she is unfamiliar and will have no trustworthy familial infrastructure around her.

Jo lived in a poor part of a developing country and, to create the opportunity to spend time with a man who could become her husband, in the U.K., his country, she had to arrange her own marriage in that country before she could make any visa application. She was then subject to a rigorous checking process on arrival. Coupled with that, once she arrived, she would be struggling with a language and culture with which she was unfamiliar and have no familial infrastructure immediately around her.

Our government recognises the danger girls and young women are in if they leave this country for an arranged marriage. However it has designed a system which requires a young woman to be party to arranging her own marriage if she wishes to visit a boyfriend based in the U.K. Concomitantly it has designed a system in which young women from a developing country can be brought into the U.K. for exploitation. My intentions were wholly honourable. However, once Jo had arrived, there was nothing to stop me behaving abusively towards her, passing her on or selling her. I had no intention doing any of this. However the system as it stands makes in very simple for that type of abuse to occur. The aim of our law is laudable. It endeavours to prevent young women and girls from the U.K. being abused in a third country. This is morally and legally the right thing to do. However, when a young woman or girl from a third country comes into the U.K. there is, at best, very limited protection for her. Perhaps this is a system which needs some rethinking. A good start would be to provide her with an e-mail address/emergency contact phone number when her visa is issued, or at the point she enters the country. This would allow systems to be set up where she would receive messages at set intervals asking her to confirm her well-being. Failure to respond to these measures should set alarm bells ringing. Having a contact phone number would mean that if she needed to cry for help she could be heard. These are far from being flaw proof ideas; just an attempt to get the ball rolling, to get some thinking done in this area. The means to do this already exist; we just need to find the right way to join everything together.

Back at the Airport Jo cleared Border Control walking straight through and into my arms with no problem. From the looks we received from people around us, whilst Jo and I had no problems, others had. I had taken a ladies coat to the airport as I thought she might feel the cold; even in August, but Jo said she didn't need it. I took her suitcase and we made our way to the car park, en route paying by card for the parking to provide a demonstration of how different things are here. Such a transaction was completely new to her, as was the concept of having to pay to park a car, or having routine access to a car.

Once she arrived there were a number of things Jo and I had to do quite quickly. One of the most important was to establish an electronic link between Jo in the U.K. and her family and friends in the Philippines. On the way home from the airport we called at a major computer retailer and purchased a good quality laptop. I had been planning to buy one for several months as it would be very useful when travelling, but had held back as I knew Jo would be in the U.K. sooner or later and would likely be the principal user of it. Delaying the purchase was to give Jo the opportunity of choosing it. I wanted to instil a sense of belonging and of being wanted from day one and felt that encouraging her to share these decisions would be a good start. It was also a way to demonstrate I was delivering on supporting her links back to home. We bought one which came with an onsite familiarisation course. Having purchased the laptop the store required 24 hours to set it up properly. We killed two birds with one stone by arranging Jo's familiarisation course at the time of collection. Just over a day after arrival she had access to a desktop and a laptop computer but, at that time, whilst we did have broadband, it was not supported by a fibre optic link.

Between selecting the laptop and collecting it we visited some clothing stores to get Jo properly clad for the British climate. It was late August but she did feel a chill, not surprising given the climate she came from. She also needed a hair dryer. This was something she had never used before. In Cebu she washed her hair, towelled it off, and ran a brush through it as it dried naturally in the humidity.

During her first fortnight we hit two major practical problems which could not really have been foreseen. The first pertained to broadband. Perhaps using two computers on the same broadband link was too much for the router. Having been working perfectly the wifi spluttered from the second the laptop was linked to it. Within three days is stopped working altogether for both computers. For Jo this was a major issue as she ceased to have 24/7 contact with home. I liaised with our broadband provider who was adamant that their equipment could not have failed and refused to replace dysfunctional equipment when it could not possibly be either malfunctioning or their responsibility. For a fee, they were prepared to send out an engineer to demonstrate why we weren't using it properly and show us how to set it up properly. However we did have limited online success when a neighbour allowed us to access their wifi; the solution to this dilemma was ultimately solved by visiting our local library where a desktop computer could be reserved in advance and there was no charge. So this is what we did. Library membership also provided Jo with immediate access to a range of reading materials which she could use to incrementally improve her English language skills. We discussed what we should do with regard to the dysfunctional broadband and decided to place the telephone and broadband account with a separate supplier. However this did create a problem in that twenty eight days' notice was demanded. So, for a few weeks, we had to pay for a service which did not work. Once the new supplier sent their equipment normal service immediately returned for both computers. In the interim this was a problem as Jo would have benefitted from access to a 24/7 link to her home community.

The second problem arose as I had arranged a trip to the continent in late September/early October. However, because the U.K. is not a party to the Schengen border agreement, (and is in the process of leaving the European Union altogether), the visa permitting entry to the U.K. was neither use nor ornament for Jo when using the Folkestone to Calais Eurotunnel service. What we needed was a Schengen visa. First we needed to determine which country in the Schengen area we needed to apply to for issue of the visa. We would arrive in France. However we then had a four to five hour drive which would take us through Belgium and Luxembourg before finally arriving in Germany where we would stay. Did we apply to the country we first entered or the country in which we would be staying. It turned out to be the latter. Jo had to present herself, her papers and her application in person at the designated offices of the country which would issue the Schengen visa.

Surprise, surprise, we were back in V.F.S. Global territory but they were now operating in the U.K. on behalf of the German government for the issue of Schengen visas. As we hoped to travel within four weeks a personal visit to their offices was imperative. This meant a trip to the V.F.S. offices in London. At that time they were located by the side of the Grand Union Canal close to Paddington station in west central London. The cost of the visa was modest but, on our first trip, they refused to accept the papers claiming they were incomplete. Their concern was two-fold. They claimed to not have sufficient proof that the hotel accommodation, which I had reserved for two people in my name four months earlier, included Jo as the second person. At the point when I made the reservation Jo had been refused her U.K. visitor visa and we were in the process of planning the application for the fiancée visa. The difficulty V.F.S. claimed with the reservation was, to me, strange. When reserving hotel accommodation previously I have never been asked to, nor found any need, to specify with whom I would be sharing a room.

Who I sleep with is my business. This was a first for me. However, we were where we were. I e-mailed the hotel, which I have been using for many years, and asked for written confirmation on a document containing the hotel letterhead and logos, that the room I had reserved was for two people, they understood the second person would be my partner and that I was a known and respected customer, etc. They replied to this within a couple of minutes of me sending the request.

However V.F.S. were also dissatisfied with the information we had provided of my finances. Despite there being six months of bank statements which showed all incomings and outgoings and a substantial balance which did not shift significantly from one month end to the next, they claimed this was not good enough for a seven night visit to Germany! They required the production of payslips to back the entries shown on the bank statements. As I am in receipt of pensions and a pay slip is only issued when the net monthly payment shifts by more than £10, this meant returning home to collect two pension pay slips, each issued in April and covering a pension payment unlikely to shift over the course of a year. So we had two four hundred plus mile return trips. On the return leg of the second trip my car broke down with a significant engine problem. The recovery insurance ensured that, after a wait of a couple of hours, we were towed back home with the car. One of the pistons in the engine had stopped working and needed to be replaced. The car was seven years old but an obscure model. To get the part and a slot at the repair shop would take two weeks. So, for two weeks we were without a car and had no broadband. Such things are sent to try us, and they did!

Things were also a little trying in the bedroom. We slept together as soon as Jo arrived. I respected Jo's right to retain her virginity but felt myself in a seriously weird position. We were sharing a bed and we both slept naked. We would cuddle up together and she seemed very happy to give and receive physical contact digitally and orally but as soon as any contact was made which hinted penetration might follow she winced and pulled away. She told me again this was a fear for losing her virginity. Perhaps her younger sister's unplanned pregnancy had proved a salutary lesson. Maybe she was worried about our relative sizes; that penetration might be painful. If that was the case it was not mentioned. However she had no problem at all with contact to the labia, clitoris or anywhere else on her body. Being male I have to admit my knowledge of that part of female anatomy is somewhat limited, but I had opportunities to look closely and could see nothing unusual. I was aware that if I put a little pressure on the outer lips of the vagina they would part naturally. From my perspective there was no sign of a physical problem. Possibly, because I was being gentle, the vaginal entrance itself remained closed. In short I believed she was still a virgin and was being very clear that she wished to remain that way. I felt this was a very strange position for us to be in. I also believed that I had to respect her wishes. I was certainly not going to force myself on someone who did not want that type of attention. I had to respect that she was nine thousand miles away from friends and family and at the beginning of a new relationship in a totally different culture, probably feeling extremely vulnerable, so I fully respected her wishes.

But I can't in all honesty say I would have been as supportive had we been of similar ages and from similar backgrounds. By that I do not mean that I would have considered non-consensual sex, in effect raping her; such a thing would not cross my mind. But I do mean that the 'me' in my twenties or thirties would have probably exerted more psychological pressure on Jo. Given the circumstances, had she continued to refuse sex whilst sharing a bed, naked, it would not have taken long before a suggestion would be made that we get it on or go our separate ways. For me, sharing a bed, means a willingness to engage in intimacy. The halfway house which developed drove me nuts; nuts and all!

The fiancée visa is very clear that the person to whom it is granted cannot use public funds for support. This means that, if medical assistance is necessary, it must be paid for. As the person responsible for Jo that meant that I would be paying, so medical insurance was essential. Prior to travel I had promised Jo that, as soon as she arrived in the U.K. I would register her at our local General Medical Practice and ask for a medical. We did this on the day she arrived. Early the following week she attended her medical. Whilst that showed she was of general good health the examining clinician did ask her to return for blood tests. These were taken at the end of the same week. Jo then received a letter from the practice. This asked her to make an appointment to see the clinician as the results of the blood test had thrown up the need for further examination and further tests. I asked her what this was about and she told me she didn't know specifically but it was gynaecological, she believed it was to do with the positioning of her fallopian tubes. Whilst this might provide a logical explanation for her reticence in the bedroom, I can't imagine how it might link to the results of blood tests. But then I am not medically trained. However I also discovered that, whilst in the Philippines, she averaged a period every seven months. I do not know why. Perhaps diet, or a general lack of food, had a part to play. However, on a practical level, this re-enforced another issue the two of us needed to deal with. Medical insurance.

We had briefly looked at Philippine travel insurance policies prior to Jo making her trip. The difficulty I found was two-fold. The main one was that I did not trust that the policies would be honoured. Maybe I am doing Philippine insurers a disservice but I have little faith in the insurance business when presented with their policies etc. in the U.K. and written in English. Even when I can understand every word of their policies and small print that is a lay understanding. Were a dispute to arise I am sure the insurer would have me tied up with red tape and firmly knotted very quickly. The idea of purchasing a policy which was written in Tagalog or Cebuano and would, in the case of dispute, be interpreted through the Philippine Courts, did not appeal at all. However an alternative was hard to find. There were plenty of regular U.K. based companies willing to sell a health care policy to us. However they all included a line in their small print which meant that, whilst I might buy the policy in good faith, they would never pay out on it. That line stated simply that the insured party must have been registered with a U.K. General Practice for a period of at least six months before the commencement of the policy. I checked this directly with the companies explaining our specific circumstances. They had nothing to offer. The only company I could find with an appropriate product was B.U.P.A. I found their website rather ambiguous over what would be included and excluded from their policy but they had a product, B.U.P.A. Worldwide, which would provide health cover. It did not come cheaply. In brief, to cover circumstances where hospitalisation was necessary, the policy would cost about £2 per day; for full cover; when adding in G.P. and dentistry services, the price rose to around £5 per day. For a six month period this worked out at £366 (P 22,950; €400 $465) or £915 (P 57,375; €1,000; $1,160), respectively. The requirement to be registered with a General Practice in the U.K. was still there but it did not have the proviso of having had that registration in place for six months prior to commencement of the policy. However it was clear that known pre-existing conditions would not be covered so anything which the G.P. discovered from Jo's initial blood tests would not be covered by this insurance package.

This brought up another issue. My understanding, rightly or wrongly, is that in the U.K. if a person is admitted to a hospital as an emergency they will receive immediate treatment. If that is the case then it was an aspect of health care I would not need to insure against. What I needed to identify was when the 'emergency' element of treatment would end because that was when either I or an insurance policy would need to pick up the costs. I wrote to my local Clinical Commissioning Group posing this question. I got no reply. I phoned them twice and was told on each occasion that they had no one available with sufficient knowledge of this subject. On getting the same response a third time I asked who I should speak to and was told to try N.H.S. England. When I called N.H.S. England I was told this was a decision which would be taken by my local Clinical Commissioning Group.

As a stop gap we took out the £2 per day policy. B.U.P.A. advised that they would only communicate with the policyholder. The fact I was paying for the policy which was for a person who could only speak elementary English was, to them, irrelevant. Health information is personal and subject to data protection law. Agreed. I did not want to discuss her health issues with anyone. However, because of the language issue, the policyholder had no conception of health services in this country and what the insurance would and would not cover, it was pushing the boundaries of common sense to exclude a fluent English speaker who could assist directly with interpretation. Unless, of course, the company considers it preferable to deal with a client who cannot fully understand them! More competition has now come onto the market and some policies have removed the requirement of being registered with a GP for six months.

Whilst all this was happening Jo, who was quiet at the best of times, became almost mute. She made no effort at all to make conversation, showed no interest in T.V., music or radio, and, although we visited the library regularly; at least once a day; showed little appetite for either contacting family and friends or for looking at library books. I felt it was quite a bizarre situation. I tried to find out if she was just completely overwhelmed by the situation she found herself in. I gently asked about her experiences with Yolanda (thinking of possible post-traumatic stress or similar). Was she suffering home sickness? I did not know and I did not get any answers. Whilst we would visit places together, go shopping together, take walks together, she remained silent and provided yes/no answers to any questions and minimal acknowledgement of anything else said by me or others.

As was mentioned briefly earlier there is a well-established aspect Philippine culture called 'tampo'. This relates to a type of behaviour we would find very unusual in an adult in the west. It is a word which does not translate effectively into English. A literal translation would describe behaviour somewhere between sulking and displeasure but, culturally, it goes far deeper than this. It is something ex-pats in the Philippines find frustrating and discussions about this can be found very quickly using YouTube, etc. At the time of Jo's visit I had not heard of tampo. It was drawn to my attention a few months later. This is what Wikipedia has to say on the subject:

"Manifestations of Tampo

Tampo usually is manifested in the withdrawal of affectionate or cheerful behaviour, and its expression is almost entirely nonverbal. These manifestations may include:

resisting expressions of affection
not talking to the person concerned, or to people in general
being unusually quiet
locking oneself in his or her own room
refusing to eat
not joining friends in group activities
withdrawing from the group
simply keeping to oneself.

There are usually efforts to get the offending party to make amends, and if these behaviours do not work, one might choose to escalate them, perhaps to foot-stamping, door-slamming, or muttering.

Cultural context
While these external manifestations may indeed sound like "sulking" in the western sense, the underlying cultural reason for them is what sets *tampo* apart. While sulking has strong negative connotations in western countries, *tampo* is quite acceptable among Filipinos. In fact, *tampo* has positive connotations for the Filipino, quite aside from the obvious negative ones.

As a cultural behaviour, *tampo* springs from the non-confrontational nature of Philippine social interaction. *Tampo* offers an acceptable means of expressing hurt feelings in a society in which direct expression of anger or resentment is discouraged. The withdrawal behaviours of tampo are indirect ways of expressing hostility. *Tampo* may also be seen as a means by which Filipinos "save face", as direct confrontation is usually a threat to the "smooth interpersonal relationships" deeply valued in Philippine society.

Responses to person manifesting Tampo

The basic expectation of one who engages in *tampo* is that the offending party will woo or cajole him or her out of the feeling of being unhappy. The Tagalog word for this is *amuin*. This wooing and cajoling is done in a loving and tender way, a gesture called *lambing*.

For the offending party, the typical Philippine way of dealing with *tampo* is to respond to the offended party with friendly overtures or expressions of concern, after a short "cooling-off" period. Not to do this may cause relations, especially romantic ones, to deteriorate. In most instances in which *tampo* is engaged in, healing the inner, emotional relationship between two people is usually more critical than resolving the issue itself.

(...) tampo "is a mild behavioural reprimand that verges on role-playing. Tampo is mild and controlled and is the direct result of some perceived offense of a minor nature. It is short in duration. Apologize for your bad behaviour. Whether or not you're guilty of the perceived 'crime' is irrelevant. The important thing is that your girlfriend or wife desires to be consoled. She has been wounded emotionally and requires emotional solace. Intellectual objections will have little effect, and may actually aggravate the condition. After you apologize, allow the Filipina to lift the tampo slowly, at a respectable pace. Do not expect instant results. Do not continue apologizing, again and again, in an attempt to speed the tampo's demise. This will only make you look foolish, and it won't work. Keep your dignity, and let her keep hers. Similarly, don't accuse a Filipina of tampo – that will embarrass her, and would be a breach of etiquette on your part. Her job is to execute the tampo as best she can, and your job is to play along and make her feel better. The old standbys are still effective: a romantic card, chocolate, jewellery."

I mention tampo because of the way in which events unfolded. Having arrived on 26th August, Jo announced on 8th September, the morning her passport was returned in the post containing the Schengen visa, that she had to return to Cebu City. I am still searching for the reasons for her decision.

The event occurred like this. We had eaten a silent breakfast following which I had not seen or heard her for the top side of an hour. I wandered upstairs and found her in bed crying. I put an arm around her and tried to comfort her. I asked what was wrong and she said she was missing her family terribly and she had to go back to Cebu.

Now, being frank, I was finding her silences, general lack of interest in what was happening around her, lack of ambition and enthusiasm, reluctance to communicate with her family as well as me, a turn off. I had begun considering how we might work together so she could be supported through what would inevitably be a tricky period of adjustment as she familiarised herself with British society or, alternatively, bring our relationship to an end. So, when she raised this issue, whilst I made an effort to persuade her to re-think and to not be too hasty, it did present an opportunity to resolve what was becoming a two-way issue.

When she arrived it was with a return flight ticket. For her journey into the U.K. she arrived on a flight where the ticket could not be altered but, for the return leg, an extra fee had been paid which allowed the changing of the date of the return flight provided it was for a seat in the same price range. The reservation had been made that way perchance any difficulties arose but principally because, once we were married Jo's name could change; her visa would need to be updated and this would mean changes to both the ticket and when she chose to use it.

Not having a return ticket is likely to present an issue for a visa holder arriving in the U.K.; Border Control staff are likely to take the view that the traveller on a one-way ticket intends to remain in the country once the visa has expired, legally or otherwise. On this basis entry is likely to be refused; a return ticket was the only way of protecting against this. The return ticket was also a means of giving Jo confidence that, if things did not work out, she was able to get back to her family fairly easily. Furthermore, purchasing a single ticket for a flight from Cebu into the U.K. can be more expensive than buying a return ticket. It is also usually the case that the return flight from Cebu to a U.K. airport will cost more than a return ticket from a U.K. airport to Cebu.

Back to Jo. I asked that we visit the library so she could go online and discuss her decision with her family; reluctantly she agreed. I also made it clear that if she did return it would mark the end of our relationship. She eventually acknowledged this inevitable conclusion but asked me two or three times to return with her so we could live together in Cebu.

Within ten minutes of arriving at the library and logging onto the computer, whilst I was checking my e-mails and under the impression Jo was chatting with her family, she sent me an e-mail saying her decision was final. I replied asking when she wanted to return. She replied that her preference would be the day we returned from Germany. "Cheeky mare!" I thought. However, as we walked back home from the library she said she had changed her mind and would like to return as soon as possible.

So I set this up and, within about three hours of broaching the subject she had been booked on an early morning flight back to Cebu on 22nd September. That she tried to persuade me to return with her to live in Cebu suggests that I was not the problem. The date she left was the day before she was due to discuss the results of her blood tests with the G.P.; perhaps there was some fear attached to this. It may also have been tampo. She exhibited all the symptoms mentioned in the Wikipedia article in spades.

We will never know if this was tampo followed by amor propio, (feeling her self-esteem was under threat), i.e. having taken offence at something relatively minor which she perceived I had done, (but that I was unaware of), she escalated. If she believed I was ignoring her tampo then an escalation would, culturally, be the logical next step for her to take. I was certainly unaware of having done anything to upset or annoy her so, from her perspective, there would have been no hint of an apology. In fact no acknowledgement whatever that I had transgressed in some way. What I did do, and if she was expressing tampo my actions would have come as a bit of a shock for her, was to arrange her flight back to Cebu at the earliest opportunity as she requested. Perhaps before she realised she was being treated with absolute seriousness the changes to her schedule were made. Whilst she was not on her way home immediately there was no doubt that would be her fairly imminent direction of travel. At that point the concept of amor propio would very likely have prevented her from doing anything akin to backtracking; for fear of losing face. These events may also link to the feeling of serendipity which some Filipinos seem surrounded by; a sort of 'what will be, will be', mentality. Perhaps a throwback to the days of Spanish colonisation and 'que sera, sera'!

Between 8th and 22nd September she moved to a different bedroom; said very little, ate little, and communicated with no one. I did try to chat with her but she remained monosyllabic. We maintained our visits to the library which were eased by the return of my car, now repaired, but, whilst there, I saw she did not use any video link or chat facility. I received messages from her sister and brother on their own behalf and on behalf of her parents asking me why I was sending Jo back. My reply was that I wasn't sending her back. She had told me she had to return and the only explanation she had given suggested she might be suffering from home sickness.

A couple of days before she left Jo got plastered again on Tia Maria and coke. During this time she handed me a note which explained she felt very guilty because she was not a virgin. She had had a relationship which ended a year or so before she met me. When I met Jo whether or not she was *virgo intacta* was of no concern to me. It was something never discussed in any way; it was not my expectation and it certainly wasn't any requirement on my part. With anyone I have met, online or in person during my life, the subject has only been discussed if the woman herself has raised it. I am long past the age where there could be any expectation of meeting a woman who had never had sex; I would find that quite peculiar. My concern is that I will remain as the next person she will sleep with; her history is her business and private unless she chooses to discuss it.

As a teenager I spent about two years living away from home. That experience was nowhere near as isolating as that which Jo would have experienced in the U.K. Mine was work related. I was able to return home on my days off. I also had regular telephone contact. That said, whilst the first three months were exciting, the second three month spell was difficult; I fretted constantly and was phoning home every evening without fail and occasionally during the day. However I worked through that. Looking back I view it as a rite of passage; part of growing up. I explained this to Jo but to no avail.

At face value Jo decided after less than a fortnight that she had had enough and, a couple of weeks later, was on a flight home. Now, because of the silences and other irritations, I cannot say, hand on heart, that I made every effort possible to persuade her to stay. I didn't. But it did make me think about what I could have done to anticipate how Jo's visit might pan out. From her perspective she endured an unpleasant experience but was back home in less than four weeks having travelled and seen another culture (and presumably not liked it very much). For me it had been an expensive waste of time. I was trying to find a wife and ended up with someone whose onsite commitment lasted a few days before deciding to give up and go home.

What did not dawn on me until a few weeks following Jo's departure were the influences from her own culture which would be a deeply entrenched part of her mind set. She knew she was not a virgin but also knew she had told me, twice, that she was. She also knew she had consistently backed that up by refusing any kind of penetrative sex. This would be a very difficult position for her to negotiate whilst retaining 'face'. For the future I needed to learn that I would have to open conversations like this should a future would-be partner behave oddly. For me virginity or otherwise is insignificant; its only consequence is of how I behave towards her in bed. But she didn't know that. My worries concerned who she might sleep with in the future and anxieties around age and the potential for future equipment failure on my part. Who she had slept with before meeting me was, from my perspective, a complete inconsequence.

I contacted B.U.P.A. to cancel the health insurance and get a refund. I was told that I could not do this for two reasons. Firstly it was not my insurance; it could only be cancelled by the policy-holder. Secondly the two week cooling off period had ended so they would not cancel in any case.

Interestingly, about a month after Jo's return, there were very heavy rains in the Cebu City area to the extent that getting on for half of the city flooded. The area in which Jo and her family lived was on some of the lowest lying land in the city. I received Facebook messages from her sister and brother telling me that Jo had caught some disease as a consequence of this event and was so weak that her father had to carry her to hospital. They needed money straight away to pay for her treatment. I advised them of the B.U.P.A. policy. They told me that B.U.P.A. refused to accept the claims they were making. As I was not the policy-holder I could not intervene! How much truth there was in their claims I do not know. What I do know is that at Christmas Jo contacted me again and asked if we could try a second time; she realised she had made a mistake and wanted to return to the U.K. I suggested she needed to get on with her life as I had. I was glad to know that she was okay. Little did she know that three weeks later I would be back in the city in which she was living. A further eighteen months passed and I received an e-mail from her again apologising and asking if I had found another girlfriend. I told her that I had and received a second message telling me that she understood but she would always be there for me. I let her have this as the last word and have heard nothing subsequently.

One step forward, one step sideways!

In truth I was back to the drawing board before Jo left. Whilst she may have taken a while longer to realise the situation which had developed, I was clear. I still held the same ambitions and, time had shown, that I had made a poor choice, again!

Whilst still wanting to keep open the option of starting a family I have to add that the traditional symptoms of age are now slowly creeping up on me. I have clicking joints, stiffness in the wrong places, getting put onto G.P.s lists for various check-ups, nodding off to sleep after any meal other than breakfast; and, on a much more positive note, pretty good health, despite a constant battle to keep the weight down. I know I have early onset macular degeneration; this is hereditary and was initially diagnosed around twenty years ago. The diagnosis meant there was a likelihood that in twenty years or so I will have lost much of my sight. However my most recent eyesight test, whilst confirming the macular degeneration showed it to be in a part of the macula which was unlikely to impact on my sight. Good New indeed. Also in my family history is dementia. Both sides of my family have a history in that area. Statistically this is something I may also have to look forward to! There is also a need for me to admit that in the bedroom I am no longer the young buck I once was. Having had recent experience of women in their early twenties (and I don't suppose many men my age can say that, and many probably wouldn't want to) I have to admit that I struggle to keep up with them. That is a situation unlikely to improve as the years roll by. In my sixties I may be able to satisfactorily look after the needs of a woman in her twenties, may be! The only person able to definitively answer that question would be the woman herself. However I ask myself what will the position be like in ten years' time? As a man in his seventies, how will I fare with a woman in her thirties?! Having worked in health promotion I have seen the literature and know that, insofar as quantity of sex is concerned, the average male peaks in his late teens. The heterosexual male in his late teens and early twenties is not particularly discriminating and likely to jump into bed whenever the opportunity occurs with whoever makes him an offer. In terms of quantity of sex women tend to peak around the age of thirty and often in the context of a settled relationship. Now I have to ask myself a very serious question. If I meet a young Filipina, marry and breed, which is my intention, when she is at her sexual peak it is likely she will be working full time and I will be retired with significant child-care responsibilities. At one level that is absolutely fine as we will have no worries about mortgage payments or childcare and work which are big issues for most couples with a young family. However children, on a good day, wear you out; often they are exhausting. After providing childcare for the day, how am I going to cope when dealing with the needs of a randy wife in her prime?! This is something both us will need to be aware of and deal with to prevent it becoming a problem. As an eighty year old I will be with a woman who is half my age who has every right to expect to have her expectations met; whatever those expectations might be. Life should have many positives but, if I make my nineties as my father and his father did, the bedroom may not be one of them.

So, after a brief health check, you are invited back to the dating website where little had changed in a practical sense. Whilst I renewed my membership of the site and took a good look around I did not try to make contact with anyone or respond to any attempts at contact until I was happy that Jo was back in Cebu. However, as soon as I got back onto the website I found there were still many Philippine women claiming they would be interested in a long term relationship with an older man in his country, etc. etc. No surprises there then. I was retired and time was very different so I decided to book a return flight for my longest visit yet, four weeks; well, twenty-six nights in the Philippines and one night travelling each way. My travel dates were from the third week of January to mid-February. I would be in the Philippines on Valentine's Day. What I had not realised was that I would arrive twenty-fours after a papal visit; and as the festival of Sinulog, the biggest most spectacular religious festival of the year on Cebu Island, was drawing to its close. I had enjoyed my time at the Airport Hotel so I reserved the first and last week there whilst leaving the remaining twelve nights open. Whilst I was happy to return to Cebu I was not intending to restrict myself solely to women based in the Cebu City area.

Once Jo was confirmed as being safely back with her family I began to look at the website with some serious intent. There were a variety of members showing an 'interest' in me and sending messages. I followed these up and ended up in chats with three young women. In terms of keeping communications open one of these contacts lasted a couple of weeks, one a couple of months and one, Rosa Beth, who preferred to be called RB, became routine and continuous. This lady and I have now enjoyed our third wedding anniversary and been together approaching five years. It is now getting on for six years from Jo's departure. So let me bring you up to date.

Within a week of Jo leaving I met RB on the website for the first time. That is my recollection; RB thinks it was three or four weeks later. She is probably right. However it would have been late September or October, 2014, close to the date of her twenty-first birthday; an event which went uncelebrated. (I wasn't aware of this until well after the event.) We exchanged a few standard messages and contact was maintained to the extent that we tried to chat on Skype. This was a very hit and miss affair for several reasons. RB possessed a very basic mobile phone which could be used for calls and texting only. There was also the issue of 'load'. This is a common term in the Philippines and it relates to buying access to a network which allows usage. It is similar to a pay as you go type phone here. The major difference is that, instead of paying for an amount of usage, in the Philippines, you are buying a period of time over which the phone can be used. So, to access social media, either by phone or computer a payment is needed. An internet café, of which there are thousands, will charge a fee for a set amount of time. At home 'load' has to be bought to go online using a computer, a mobile phone or similar device. Alternatively access to domestic broadband has to be negotiated. RB had work as an au pair/nanny and, whilst the house in which she was based had broadband, that was principally the preserve of her employers. As we have commented, bandwidth is narrow, so, for an employee, access is unlikely to be encouraged. To use social media RB needed to borrow the mobile of a colleague. She had no access at all to any computing equipment and had very little experience of using any I.T.

Let me give you an example of how advanced I.T. was in the Philippines in 2014. To use simple I.T., i.e. to surf or to send and receive e-mails, was straightforward provided you had wifi/broadband access. Receiving e-mails with large attachments would take much longer than one would anticipate in the west.

Whilst in the Maribago bar one evening I was chatting with a group of North Americans. They told me they were working at Bigfoot Studios. (These TV studios were situated midway between Mactan Airport and Maribago. I'm not sure if they are still a studio but some of the site has been turned into apartment type accommodation.) We chatted about what was possible and impossible in the Philippines when it came to the live streaming of a concert. This topic came up as, on a largely informal basis, I have worked off and on in the music sector over the years as rhythm guitarist and support vocals in a band and as a solo singer/guitarist. I've deejayed, produced a couple of albums, appeared in musicals and done a little low level recording. For a couple of years prior to this conversation happening I had sat at my desk in suburban U.K. and performed music online to an audiences in western Europe; charity events. I was enquiring if it would be possible for me to play live in the U.K. and stream this as a live concert to a venue in the Philippines. The conclusion of the discussion was that, whilst it would certainly be possible for me to perform and live stream material out using acoustic guitar and voice only, (no backing track or anything of that nature), the systems in the Philippines had a bandwidth so narrow that it would be challenging to download live audio/visual files simultaneously at a speed sufficient for the transmitted material to retain its integrity. At best the performance would be disjointed. The likely outcome would be that, whilst the sound of the guitar, the sound of the voice and the image of the performer would be received it would not be possible for local I.T. systems to download them simultaneously. The likely result would be a heavily pixilated image coupled with layers of sound routinely overlapping each other. So voice and guitar would not be in synch and the image would be very poor quality. The guys with whom I was chatting were professional film-makers. They knew of nowhere in the country where a concert could be live streamed in the way I was describing; not even a simple one person acoustic event. They speculated that the national government may have access to a decent broadband width but, if that was the case, they were keeping very quiet about it. Which they would do because their usage would be geared toward state security, not entertainment. Six years on there has been some significant improvement. Bandwidth is not a lot better but there are many more access points reaching into all towns and cities. In rural areas there are still serious difficulties. Greater access to broadband in impoverished communities has now created a secondary problem of the internet being used to generate income illicitly; live sex shows for private consumption, etc.

However, when RB and I tried to chat using Skype or Facebook, we experienced some difficulties due to the low level of the technology available at that time. Whilst she was working and living in Metro Cebu a Skype audio chat was possible without too much difficulty provided we chose a time of day away from peak usage times. Once she left Metro Cebu it was normal for us to get a connection on Skype but, within a few seconds, it was likely at her end she would cease receiving sound and image and get a message from Skype which said: "loading." This was telling her that Skype was doing its best to make available to her the video and audio signals I was sending. However the loading never completed. At the U.K. end I would get a message telling me the connection was poor or had been lost and Skype was doing its best to recover it. We both learned that the best thing to do was to end the call and then try again. Sometimes this would work but most times it didn't; often we would chat with written messages and do without the audio/video link. The time we had most success in having a live video chat was between five and seven in the morning Philippine time, which was mid to late evening in the U.K.

Some background information about the woman I have married will be useful as the story of our path to the altar and the present is told. RB worked full-time looking after a child with serious physical disabilities. Full-time in this context has a very different meaning to that which we understand in the developed world. It meant she was expected to look after the child all day and all night, every day and every night. She slept in the same area as him, fed him, bathed, toileted and cleaned him, and took him to the various places he needed to go. Transport was always provided through the family who employed her. Whilst the conditions in which she worked were pleasant and safe, in a private gated housing area with routine security patrols, there were no days off. She was well treated, respected her employer and, generally, enjoyed her work. She had, and still has, a big commitment to the child. He is now nine years old and she worked with him from just before his first birthday to a month before his fifth birthday. In effect she was treated as a member of the extended family much of the time. There were other members of staff around her with different responsibilities and, together, they supported a couple in their seventies and an elderly lady who was a parent to one of them. Their son, his wife and their three children, one of whom was the disabled child also lived there. RB lived on site and I had the impression this was the case with all the other staff members. The house is in a lovely area but, as soon as one leaves the gated community, you are back into the rough and tumble of the real Philippines.

Having effectively retired from work in mid-2014, a couple of months before Jo's arrival in the U.K., my diary was clear. These days it often is! I got a positive feeling about RB soon after we first met online. There were many similarities to May but without the negative family influences around her. The sort of comments she made were completely consistent and normal for a young woman in her position. She did not try to bamboozle me with any sort of waffle; never asked for any money, if she didn't know the answer to something, she said so and if she didn't understand something she asked. This was a two-way street. I also came across situations where I did not fully appreciate the local context and she was patient with me and explained, to the best of her ability, what was happening.

We chatted frequently online and, although I had a flight and accommodation for a Cebu trip reserved for mid-January to mid-February, I did not mention this to RB until after New Year, a couple of weeks in advance of the planned departure date. She acknowledged this without any great song and dance and I later discovered that was because, until we met, she did not go online or use social media or the dating website very often and, when she did, had been told all sorts of rubbish by the people she met. Her initial thoughts were that I was just someone else spinning her a yarn. When I asked if she would be able to meet me she replied she would need to check that out with her employer. A day or two later she said she would but her employer would expect to join us as she would not be meeting anyone without a chaperone. I agreed we would meet and then took things a step further. From the online chats we had had I knew she had not visited her family for the best part of four years so I asked if she would speak to her employer about getting a few days off so we could meet her family together. A couple of days later she came back to say we could do this and she gave me the name of a hotel, local to where her family was based, where we could stay; Lalimar in the Negrenses. I looked for the hotel online and it looked good but it was obviously well off the beaten track for the western tourist. That said it was a nice looking site, right on the shoreline, and with a decent sized swimming pool. However when I came to make a reservation I found there was only one organisation I could use. That was a holiday company based in Dubai but with an office in Manila. However I booked a cottage at the hotel for five nights, made flight reservations and then sent her a message through the dating website telling her what I had done. I got the impression she did not believe me so I asked her to open an e-mail account telling her that I would copy the reservations to her. This took several days because, to do this, she needed to borrow the mobile of one of her colleagues. When you have 24/7 care of a child with serious disabilities you cannot just drop into an internet café, particularly when you have little or no experience of using a computer. I sent the e-mail but I don't know if she ever received it. Even up to the day before I was due to depart she still seemed to have problems accepting that this man she had met on the dating website was actually coming to the city where she worked to see her.

I arrived on schedule at Mactan Airport, walked across to the Airport Hotel and checked in. As a thank you for my business they had ungraded me to an Executive Suite, a very pleasant surprise. Once settled I called her mobile. When I told her I had arrived and where I was staying she seemed to be in shock. She asked me to call her back about three hours later as she was busy with her work. It transpired that when I made the initial call she had been in a car with the disabled child being transported from a therapy session back to their home. Once there she knew he would need changing and to be fed, etc. So, in the mid evening, I called back. By this time she had regrouped. She told me that she hadn't really believed I would come to Cebu. I assured her I was in town and she gave me the address at which she worked. To ease her concern I also gave her the hotel telephone number and my room number so she could call me back to prove to herself that I really was in Cebu City. We agreed that we would meet at her employer's home at 5pm. the following afternoon and go for a meal together, with her employer acting as chaperone.

I arrived on time but it took the best part of quarter of an hour to get into the gated site. The Guard House had not been told that I was expected and it took a while for them to confirm with the house that I was a legitimate guest. When the taxi finally dropped me off I was greeted by a pleasant chap about ten years my senior who spoke very good English. We chatted for twenty minutes or so and it became apparent, in a positive way, that I was being vetted. He told me that RB was returning from the daily therapy session with their grandson and offered me a beer. I thanked him but turned down the offer. I was at the beginning of a period of quitting alcohol and, getting on for six years later, am still on the wagon. I accepted a glass of lemonade, sat on a small first floor balcony area looking out into the countryside to the north of Cebu City and was surrounded by religious icons. Obviously catholicism was a major element of life for this family, (as is the case with many Filipinos). After an hour or so RB arrived with her charge. The boy's Mum (our chaperone to be) was driving and also in the car were her other two sons and a second nanny. We went to the chaperone's favourite Chinese restaurant and the three boys and their nanny joined us. At the time they were seven, three and eighteen months old respectively so took a bit of looking after but were not big eaters. We had a couple of hours out in total and then the chaperone returned us all to their home before going on to her night shift. She worked in the health care business and was a shift supervisor; her husband ran what I have always assumed to be the family business. From the very limited discussions we have had I think this was some form of engineering consultancy and workshop. They were both good company and intelligent, articulate people. I asked RB if she would like to meet on the following day and she suggested I join her before the young boy's daily therapy session so that we could travel there together and maximise our time whilst she was working. It was during this trip that the chaperone, this time the father of the disabled child, asked for confirmation of our intended visit to RB's home. I showed him our tickets and confirmation of our accommodation reservation which showed a cottage hire. This was important because, as chaperones, he and his wife had a responsibility for the well-being of RB; they took their responsibilities seriously and considered that this also included her moral well-being. We had what was described by the hotel website as a cottage within their complex; that implied the availability of private sleeping arrangements. I do not know if RB's employers contacted her parents, however the trip was sanctioned.

There were still four or five days before the trip to meet RBs family and we met each day. The child was always with us and we were unable to spend any meaningful time alone. However we did demonstrate to each other, probably without realising it at the time, how we were with children. It was only when the child was sleeping whilst at the hotel that we could go further than chat together. I have to say that whilst RB was very inexperienced she displayed a great willingness to learn. We got no further than a kiss and a cuddle but we were both fully engaged. I got the impression that she enjoyed those moments as much as I did. They were brief and we did not go any further because we did not want to risk the child waking up and witnessing behaviour he would find confusing or that might worry him.

One oddity with RB was that she would not travel alone; she expected to be collected and returned home in person. All the other women I have met in the Philippines were happy to agree a venue at which we would meet. We would then do whatever we wished and, at the end of the date, if we were close to her home, I would take her there. If not I would hire a taxi and pay for it. RB wanted to be collected and returned. I think that she had lived in the gated community so long she was fearful of what lay outside, a lack of confidence which pushed her into needing to be accompanied. I certainly got that impression from the couple for whom she worked. They made regular reference to the dangers that lurked outside the gates of their community.

Maybe it is because of my size, maybe self-confidence or perhaps just plain stupidity on my part, but I have very rarely felt much at personal risk anywhere. As I am now a little age worn I am starting to revise those positions a little, but not much. I believe a lot of the fears we have are generated by false perceptions; by stories which hit the headlines about all the risks encountered if alone. I accept there are risks but do not think they are very great provided you do not put yourself in a situation where you become vulnerable. If you are in a busy place waving around a wallet or the latest mobile phone there is a much heightened likelihood of a theft occurring. So I suspect RB's concerns had been amplified through being looked after and kept in a cloistered community for almost four years. Linked to this if she did venture out unaccompanied she would probably feel uncomfortable; signs of this would be visible to others which, in turn, would heighten the likelihood of a ne'er do well choosing her as a victim. Keeping their staff under the thumb like this also suggests that her employers, whilst wanting to keep their staff safe and protect them from taking unnecessary risks, would also benefit as those staff members would be unlikely to develop the skills necessary to go out, participate fully in the world and thrive, effectively becoming institutionalised. If they did get out and about they might find another employer or a better deal. I don't think this occurred deliberately; it was just a consequence of living in an island of security within a sea of fairly serious deprivation. Whatever the reasons it was apparent from the outset that RB hated the idea of travelling alone. Dealing with this sort of issue is straightforward when at home; it's simply a case of getting in the car. However, when living in a hotel in a foreign country where dangers may lurk, this meant allowing much more time and a bit more expense. For example, if she was going to join me at the Waterfront Airport for a meal I needed to take a forty minute taxi journey from the hotel to the house where she lived and worked. Once she was ready; and, in fairness to her that was dictated by the situation with the boy she was looking after and the other domestic responsibilities she had picked up, we would make the return trip. So the actual date would begin around two hours after I set out. A similar situation would occur in reverse when the date ended. A two hour date could take six or seven hours for me. That presupposes we did not hit a difficulty with taxi drivers or travel during rush hour – which begins around 6 am in Metro Cebu and doesn't really finish until after 9 pm. Right through the day traffic is dense and slow moving across the city!

When we were ready to leave her employers home they would call the gate house to get a taxi for us. The distance from their residence to the gate house was about 600 metres down a steep hill. It was far enough to work out if we had a genuine taxi driver or one of the many who set their meter at an enhanced rate. Another trick they routinely tried was to not zero the meter from the previous fare. I also had a couple of drivers who, when I pointed out their meter was not set to the P40 standing charge, said that my fare began when they were called off the main road, not when I got in the cab at the house. We usually agreed on a zeroed meter, otherwise we would have called for a different cab; competition is fierce. Probably because this was an exclusive private housing estate and many users would be charging the taxi to their employer or a client, or maybe had an arrangement with a driver like a monthly account, over half of the drivers called to the house behaved in this way. Elsewhere it was probably somewhere between a quarter and a third. From the Airport Hotel it is a rare occurrence.

Now we have here a good example of 'amor propio' in action; and the clashing of Philippine and western cultures. Whilst the taxi driver would know full well he had set the meter to charge an enhanced rate he could never admit it; to do so would be tantamount to an admission of thieving and to admit such a thing, apart from anything else, would be to lose face. However, in me, he had a customer who had no intention of being ripped off. So, when this happened, as we approached the gate house, I would tell the driver to stop. I would then get out and ask RB and the child she was carrying to do likewise. I would pay the driver what was shown on the meter and tell him, in no uncertain terms, why we would not go any further with him and what I thought of him. From my perspective he was taking me for a fool and trying to take money from me by deception. He was treating me differently to locals because I was European; which seems to be a very common occurrence in the Philippines. The customer is often priced rather than the goods or service. From the perspective of the taxi-driver he had collected a fare in a wealthy area, with a westerner paying to boot, and believed it was his right to exploit the opportunity. But by doing this he was exploiting me and I was having none of it. This presented a problem because, not only was he losing his fare, he also needed to deal with a loud mouthed European telling him he was a thieving so-and-so. More importantly still this performance was taking place in the public arena, usually within earshot of several people including the security staff in the guard house. They had to get involved as the driver needed to have the barrier raised before he could leave the site. I was also presenting a challenge to the 'amor propio' of the guards. They were the ones who had chosen that particular taxi and sent it to the house. By giving the taxi driver the run down on why we would not use him, I was also implicitly taking a swipe at the guard house staff. Coupled with this I would then walk onto the street and find my own taxi; this did not go down well with the gate house staff at all.

So, whilst I saw myself as the victim of a cheating taxi driver, in terms of local culture everyone else around judged me to be the villain of the peace because of the affront I was creating to the driver's self-esteem whilst doing the gatehouse staff no favours. In the Philippines this is not the way to do business. The drivers hated it. The security staff understood what was happening and knew exactly what the driver had been up to; but the driver was a male Filipino, a working man with a poor wage, just like them, and was being abused by a wealthy westerner when, despite his actions, he deserved to be treated in accordance with local culture and with dignity. Any sympathy that was going went to the driver. It was also a problem for the same reason for RB. She knew I was right as far as the meter was concerned but was shocked that anyone would deal with such a matter so bluntly. As an aside she was also probably more aware than I that these practices routinely occurred and this was likely a major contributory factor to her feeling the need to be escorted everywhere. She would not have had the self-confidence or the nous to deal with a cheating taxi-drivers if travelling alone.

So, in general terms, after getting to the venue our date would begin. After we had eaten, chatted and relaxed and the evening was drawing to a natural conclusion, I would ask the hotel concierge, or waiter if we were at a restaurant, to call a taxi. If my date and I were going in a broadly similar direction then we would share the cab and she would be taken to the place where she chose to disembark; if not I would call a cab for her and ensure the cost of her journey was covered. I would then make my own way back to the hotel. However RB would have none of this. Her expectation was that I would join her in the taxi, get her to the front door, a quick good night kiss, and in she would go. I would then stay with the taxi and go back to the hotel. For her this was being properly looked after, or kept safe; for me it meant a lot of time in taxis which I did not need to be in. If it was a case of keeping her safe then it was time and money well spent but, I have to admit, I found it a bit frustrating. Although I am a romantic at heart, there is a thick streak of pragmatism running through me. At these times the two emotions clashed. If we were eating at the Airport Hotel it meant I had to allow a minimum of ninety minutes before the date and ninety minutes afterwards to deal with transportation and it would probably take longer. I was led by the heart which told me to take good care of such a precious cargo; but my head gave me a right royal rollicking each time I did it!

The day of the trip to RBs home arrived. We had to check-in at the domestic terminal of Mactan Airport no later than 8.30 am. This meant I had to get a taxi from the Airport Hotel for the forty minute ride to her house and make the return journey together for breakfast. In turn, this meant a very early start. An early morning call at 4.15 am. meant I was able to clear my room, check out then lodge the cases with the concierge before getting a taxi to collect RB around 5.00 am. She took a while to get ready whilst the taxi waited and the return trip began as traffic began to build up. We arrived back at the hotel and shared breakfast together around 7.15 am before walking across to domestic departures. It was RBs first break from work in around four years. She had never been to an airport before let alone flown. Nor had she stayed overnight at a hotel except whilst working, i.e. looking after her charge during a family holiday or trip. Whilst I wanted to spend this time together and to meet her family and friends, I also wanted to take the opportunity to allow RB to learn how to travel. It is very easy for a seasoned traveller to go through the airport systems; the first time may be a challenge. We agreed that, on the outward journey, I would lead her through the process. On the return trip she would lead but I would be alongside her perchance anything untoward occurred. One of the oddities I found with the internal flight was that, because the plane was small, a thirty seater or thereabouts, they did not just weigh the cases we checked in, they weighed each passenger whilst holding their hand luggage. This would be to ensure an even distribution of weight across the plane. However the weight shown on the scale was clearly visible to everyone in the airport. There was no hiding place; if you were a fatty it was announced to the whole world! Well, at least that part who were in the departure hall. I am a very tall guy with the build to match and probably would have been one of the heaviest people they had every encountered. Thankfully I am also fairly thick-skinned so I was not fazed by the gasps from the queue behind me. However RB is a slip of a girl. Our average weight came down to that of two regular European men. However, that is significantly heavier than a regular Filipino couple.

In terms of RB's circumstances a bit of background information may be useful. She has five siblings. There are two older sisters; the eldest is now thirty-three, and has three children, and, when RB and I met was working in the Gulf, Oman I think, sending money home to her partner who was also working whilst looking after their first child. Having completed her contract in the Gulf she returned home but, after a couple of months, went off to work in South Korea for a few weeks; since when she has back at the family home whilst her partner works away. During this time they have had their second and third children, the second being born the day after RB and I had our Philippine wedding ceremony. The eldest sister is the only member of the family who has tried to tap me up for money. At least that was my interpretation of what happened. She asked via Facebook if I knew of any organisation which might be prepared to sponsor the education of her eldest child. I referred her to a Luxembourg based charity I know of and heard nothing from her subsequently. The second eldest sister is now thirty years old and living with a de-frocked American priest in his 70's. When RB and I first met he was subject to U.S. extradition proceedings, allegedly for gun-running, but the court case in Manila has passed and I have heard no more talk of this since our first visit over five years back. He does visit the U.S. occasionally so any legal issues must have been resolved. When he visits the U.S. he closes down the apartment they live in and the sister and their son, return to the home of my in-laws until he returns. Also living my in-laws is the eldest child of this sister. The American won't entertain her at their apartment so she is being raised by her grand=parents. Her natural father died a few years back. RB also has three younger siblings; a sister aged twenty-one who had her first child last month. The father is a policeman well into his thirties who has a family with another woman. RB also has two brothers aged twenty three and eight. The elder one lives with his girlfriend and their child. Pre Coronavirus he lived and worked in Cebu; he returned to his own family home just before individual islands locked down and is currently flitting between his and his girlfriend's family homes. The younger brother attends junior school in the village where the family live.

The journey to the family home was a trip of eight to ten hours from where RB was working. The final section of the journey at the time of our visit took the best part of three hours although it is probably less than twenty miles. The terrain covered was difficult on roads which are mostly unsurfaced, often little more than rocky, boulder strewn dirt tracks. A four wheel drive vehicle might make it, dependent upon weather, mudslides, avalanches and the skilfulness of the driver, but it was usually only attempted by motor bikes. Even then some of the track was so steep and boulder strewn that it has to be walked. Since our first trip I understand there have been some improvements; a stream has been bridged and the last section of the climb now has a fairly narrow concrete surface.

The local town one sets out from, La Libertad, is the closest community with a handful of shops and cafes. The nearest supermarket is around thirty miles away in Guihulngan which is also where you need to be for anything bordering on a reliable internet connection. The area I am describing is also home to the N.P.A. (New People's Army) a communist group which is fighting a continual battle with local, regional and national government. Locally this group is occasionally referred to, incorrectly, as Abu Sayyaf. However Abu Sayyaf is an offshoot of the Moro People's Liberation Army. They are based exclusively in the west of Mindanao Island in the south of the country and the nearby islands in the part of the Sulu Sea which separates the Philippines from Indonesia and Malaysia. This is an area the British foreign office has advised tourists to avoid for many years. It is nowhere near Guihulngan. There are no links between the N.P.A. and Abu Sayyaf, the former is communist, the latter muslim fundamentalist. They operate in a similar manner with assassinations, kidnap, etc. but they are two completely independent militias. None of this matters much to the westerner or tourist visiting the area. What is important is that there have been the top side of a hundred killings in the last four years in and around Guihulngan. My wife monitors these fairly closely. Last week, whilst completing this document, the death count was as follows:

Sunday	0
Monday	0
Tuesday	1
Wednesday	2

Thursday	0
Friday	4
Saturday	1
Sunday	0

Most are only reported locally and one of them that week was a young man with whom my wife attended school. The deceased are mostly either NPA, law enforcement personnel or alleged drug users and dealers with innocent locals occasionally getting caught in the crossfire. Oddly, the Guihulngan area, currently one of the most dangerous in the Philippines, has yet to be listed by the U.K. government as a no go area!

Tourists visiting the Guihulngan area are likely to be fine but there is a much heightened risk of kidnap or an accidental assassination, so why bother! For any westerner visiting the area travel insurance is now difficult and, given the risks involved, unless there are seriously extenuating circumstances, visiting the area is reckless.

RB's parents are farmers who have a small shop as part of their property. Shortly after meeting RB we invested in four piglets, two of which died young, and these were fattened for market at the family home. Her siblings are also involved in the farm in their own ways. The family have a radio but there is no TV. The only telephony available is the mobile phone. Signal strength has improved slightly in recent years but is still highly variable. You need to know where to stand to make and receive a call. Because the village is so small and isolated no one has an address. There is only one Mrs. Bloggs or Mr. Smith, so there is no need for official road names or house numbers. We mentioned earlier that, politically, towns and cities in the Philippines break down in Barangays. The Barangay breaks down into what is called the Sitio or Purok. A Sitio can be further broken down with a number. So, whilst Jo was able to provide the name and number of her Sitio and the Barangay name, RB did not have such luxury. The village is so remote that, whilst it is a Barangay in its own right, it is much too small to break down in Puroks, and there is certainly no need to consider Purok numbers.

I quickly established that RB had no papers beyond her birth certificate and a letter from her employer to identify herself. I have no idea what RB's wages were; that was none of my business, but I do know she had no bank account and operated in a cash only environment where she had little cash and no control over it. She had left school as soon as she had been able to, around the age of fourteen. Continuing education would have meant costs which the family could not meet and work away from the family home would mean one less mouth to feed whilst that 'mouth', RB, might be able to repatriate a little income if she found work. The other children seem to have followed a similar pattern. Please don't think this could reflect neglect or idleness of her parents. They are hardworking the problem is that what they do does not produce much income.

We flew from Mactan Airport to the only airport in Negros Oriental Province, located close to the provincial capital, Dumaguete. This town has now been listed by the U.K. foreign office as an area which Britons should not visit; the insurance companies have followed their lead. The airport is little more than an air strip running from the sea into a field. Each day saw a return flight to Cebu and several return flights to and from Manila. When I made my first trip the earliest plane of the day was an arrival shortly after 8am and the last plane of the day a departure around five in the afternoon; outside these times the site was closed. Airport security is not comparable to the U.K.; in fact it is virtually non-existent. Check-in procedures are similar as are processes around baggage. However the town end of the runway ends in a busy urban area adjacent to the main road around the island. All that separates the two is a fence about three feet/one metre high which could be stepped over by a tall person. Having landed shortly before noon RB decided that, before we travelled to the hotel, we should meet her second eldest sister in town. So we got a habal-habal, (motor bike taxi) and had a meal with her, a very pleasant young woman. Whilst the two women were obviously happy to see each other there was nothing like the affection two European sisters who had been apart from each other for around four years would be likely to show. It was all very reserved; maybe this is the Philippine way, I thought.

We had booked accommodation at Hotel Lalimar, near La Libertad, the hotel which RB had recommended. I had taken a look at it online. It seemed to be okay if somewhat remote. None of the regular travel sites used it. However it not only looked good but turned out to be excellent value for money. That said it is not the type of establishment a western holidaymaker would expect. By nine most evenings everywhere is closed.

After having lunch with her sister we went to the local bus station where, for £1.50 each we had a ride of over three hours. This took us through the provincial capital, past the Airport and onwards through seven or eight towns of varying size. The island had suffered an earthquake around three months prior to our trip. Whilst this had not affected RB's family directly, it had created havoc for local communications. Whilst Negros is a big island, larger than Cebu Island, the only really substantial road acts as a ring road around the coast which is just over four hundred miles long. Off this there are four or five roads running very approximately east to west across the mountains connecting one side to the other. But most of the roads leading off the coast road are, ultimately, cul-de-sacs. The island is very mountainous, the highest peak being Mount Canlaon which tops 8,000 feet, (2,700 metres), and also happens to be a fairly active volcano. It is continuously monitored and has erupted twenty-eight times in the last century. The base cone has a circumference of around nineteen miles (thirty kilometres). At various points the coast road is bridged over rivers, creeks and estuaries. The earthquake had taken many of these out and most were still undergoing repair.

We eventually alighted from the bus in what looked to me to be an isolated spot. All I could see were a few cottages set back on the left side of the road and a couple of huts on the right and a small unsurfaced road leading past a purpose built guard house in the general direction of the sea with an insignificant signboard telling us we had reached our destination. We walked down this track for a couple of hundred metres going through a glade of trees before a sharp right turn gave us sight of some activity. We found a delightful small hotel with an infinity pool overlooking the Tañon Strait with the west side of Cebu Island in the distance. There is a rocky beach and seven cabins of varying sizes. These were nicely spread out to one side of a modest reception area. A large entertainment hall which was roofed but had very little by way of walls and a small bar and restaurant which was part of the pool complex are on the other side. There was a substantial parking area as the hotel works closely with the local authority and, most days, some group or other will use the facilities for work/education related activities. It is also a venue used by children and local families for party type events. The hotel had no problem with food being brought onto site although, in all honesty, the kitchen produces very acceptable food at the right price. It is a pleasant surprise in an area which tourists would rarely think of visiting. This was to be our base for five nights and a place where we spent ten nights on our second visit; twenty-three nights during our matrimonial trip and, more recently a nineteen night stay. Sad to say in April, 2019, Lalimar was now in need of a deep clean and some love and attention from its owner. I understand this has happened but, because of Coronavirus, we have not yet been back. Lalimar is geared up for use by local people and local tourists. To the westerner, at its best, it would be described as basic. It is functional, safe and operates in keeping with its surrounds and local cultural norms.

For RB our visit was an opportunity to meet old acquaintances and to arrange to see her parents and younger siblings again. It was a fairly quiet time for me but RB was on the go right through the day, every day. We did spend time with her family but, because of the remoteness of their home, much of it was spent travelling. RB seemed surprised that I was prepared to make the journey and, it was only after I had made the trip that, I understood why. The journey was difficult. We travelled on a 150 c.c. motor bike. Prior to this trip I had been on the back of a motor bike twice in my life. One of these occasions had been as a teenager with a seriously reckless former colleague who had taken me round part of the inner ring road of one of our larger cities, travelling the wrong way, against three lanes of traffic, in the early evening rush hour. How on earth we did not get ourselves seriously injured or killed I will never know. We exited by going the wrong way up a slip road onto a roundabout which we hit still going in the wrong direction before shooting up the first available side street. It had been a salutary lesson and I have subsequently avoided two wheels like the plague.

The dangers for this journey were of a different order but were still there. To begin with I had no idea at that outset of the type of journey we were about to embark upon. I was expecting a ride of a few miles on a normal road. I dressed accordingly. I was wearing a T shirt, lined swimming shorts a pair of sandals and no socks. Loading the bike was an interesting exercise. For a start, whilst Filipinos are small, I am large. The owner of the bike, a man in his late twenties, rode it; I was pressed up close behind him, clinging on for dear life, and RB was gaily sat third in the line, holding onto me and waving to all around us. RB wanted to take some supplies for her family and I had made it clear that, whilst I did not want to appear rude or bad mannered, the last thing I needed when visiting my future in-laws was to get a dose of the trots again. So I carried my own water which was all I intended to consume. To make matters worse, having set off on our journey, after a few hundred yards our 'guide' pulled into a market. There he collected another passenger, a middle aged woman who I now know to be my wife's godmother. She perched on the front mudguard clutching a variety of items and shopping bags which poked out in all directions. With a seriously obstructed view through the godmother's shopping the rider struggled to see the road. She was with us for the first half an hour or so before alighting outside a hut in the middle of nowhere. Overall the journey took three hours and, most of the way, we were climbing. For the first two hours the climb was gradual and the scenery sensational. We reached the village of Pacuan where RB had received her some of her education. It was little more than a strip of houses and huts alongside what was now a two-way dirt track. She met her younger sister and eldest brother here. They were in their mid-teens at the time and there was obvious affection and delight at seeing each other and catching up but, as with her older sister, their greetings were quite restrained compared to what I would have expected in the west. After a short break we rode out on the only road; a continuation of the one we came in on. We had about five miles to go.

After a few hundred yards we had to ford a shallow but fast flowing river. It was probably about twenty-five yards wide and we needed to keep to stepping stones. I was too busy getting myself across and helping RB to notice how the rider got his bike across, but he managed somehow. I guess someone must have helped him. I understand this river has subsequently been bridged.

From this point the road started to climb more sharply and, the further we went, the more serious the climbing became. After three or four miles we slowly passed through another much smaller village which had developed alongside the right hand side of the track. To our left was a sharp drop into a ravine that bottomed out far below us. The road itself was so steep at this point that some concrete slabs had been put in so a two wheeled vehicle could keep its momentum going whilst a four wheel drive would at least have something which two of the wheels could grip. We passed a small junior school and the children ran to the road edge to look at us. My guess is that they saw few vehicles; there was certainly no evidence of tyre marks, and we were now on roads which could only be accessed by motor bikes or four-wheel drive vehicles with plenty of clearance beneath them. We were travelling slowly because of the gradient. As we left this village the bike finally gave up. Even in first gear it could not maintain forward momentum. So we resorted to shank's pony. I was reassured by RB telling me "we are almost there". It took about half an hour of walking up steep, gouged and boulder strewn inclines whilst travelling, intermittently on the back of the bike, to reach her home village. During this time we passed thirty of forty other people walking one way or the other, but there were no signs of any other vehicles at all.

We arrived in the village on a track which broadened out considerably as we approached but became increasingly grassed over before disappearing altogether. I saw small houses and huts dotted around me and there were a few very rudimentary tracks, one of which we rode along. It was bordered by grass and undergrowth which began at the height of around a half a metre and rose to over three metres here and there. We passed a few small huts by the side of the track but barely visible because of the amount of undergrowth before arriving at the home of RBs family. We were met by her parents, her youngest brother and her niece. The reception we received was very friendly and encouraging. However I noted again that, given the time RB had been absent, it was not the celebration I had anticipated. But we were both made very welcome. A meal had been prepared which RB shared with her family; there was a significant seed and nut content. I had sent word in advance of the trouble I could expect if I partook of anything which had a hint of local water, so I stayed with my water bottle. Some food and drink was taken out to our rider. The impression I got was of a family who, compared to their immediate contemporaries, were doing quite well. The building was of several rooms; at one end it had been made into a small shop, and there was plenty of land around it which seemed to belong with the building. Whilst it was obvious there was not a lot of money about everything was very clean and tidy and I was made most welcome. I felt more comfortable here than in any other house I had been to; including the one where RB worked. After the meal was completed RBs mother took me for a walk around the house and the surrounding land. There were many fruit trees and bushes and evidence of small scale crop production which I now know is tobacco. She also took me to a place about thirty yards from her house where, at some point, the footings had been dug so a second property might be constructed, but they were beginning to grass over. At least that was my initial interpretation of what I saw. We shared smiles and gestures but had no shared language. Perhaps she was suggesting RB and I develop this plot as a home and live there; I was just guessing from my western, developed world perspective. I subsequently discovered that what I had thought were the footings for a proposed new build were actually where the earth had been torn open as a consequence of the earthquake which had occurred a few months earlier! We stayed for two or three hours before our motor bike rider/guide indicated we had to go as he wanted to get back onto good dirt roads before nightfall. I invited her family to join us at the hotel the day before our departure and they agreed to come. They would have been welcome every day, they knew that, but they had work to do and did not want to give the impression they were taking advantage.

The journey back was far worse than the trip out. Then we had been climbing; the descent was perilous. I had finished my water whilst with RB's parents. It was a good job. Whilst there were areas we had to walk because it was far too dangerous to attempt on the motor bike, there were also many occasions where our rider assumed his passengers shared the confidence he had in his ability to keep us upright, safe, and seated on the bike! We clung on for dear life! To be fair, whilst we had to stop several times, that was because I felt so scrunched up behind him and kept getting cramp in my legs, so I needed to be able to stretch a little and unwind myself. The journey back took half an hour less than the outward trip and I was very glad to be back at the hotel. I was dry, hungry, dirty and aching in places I had forgotten existed. After some well-earned and enjoyable relaxation we had an evening meal in the hotel restaurant. As mentioned earlier, the quality of the food was good. What was radically different to anything I have ever witnessed anywhere before were the cats. I suspect there were a lot of rodents about and the hotel had some feral cats around. They had bred and their kittens were at an age where they were learning to be predatory and to scavenge. The so and so's were everywhere in the public areas of the hotel. If any food was being served in the restaurant area of the hotel, there was a line-up of cats waiting to pounce on anything edible. It was impossible to leave a table; within seconds they would have leapt up and be golloping down everything in sight; no invitation was necessary. Even before you ate, given the opportunity, they would be walking around your legs and jumping onto tables. What I found even more surprising was that not only the staff but all the guests treated this as the normal state of affairs. Call me an old fashioned tourist but when I am dining with my woman I take the view that one pussy per table is sufficient!

On subsequent visits to Lalimar I have seen cats, dogs, hens, chickens, geese and turkeys wandering freely around the grounds, and a couple of cockroaches. I have only seen one rat, and that was right on the edge of the site.

During our stay at Lalimar we visited several friends and family of RB. She had worked briefly at the municipal offices so we called there. Also we took a ride of a couple of miles inland to the home of an aunt and uncle. There were several older children here, in fact some were young adults. Again my recollections are all positive. What I did notice on this trip was the remains of an avalanche. To me, with my very limited British experience, an avalanche might block a path or cause a similar minor inconvenience. This one was never reported in the western media so far as I can establish. It had occurred a couple of years prior to our visit and the debris ended about a mile away as the crow flies from the house we visited. About a third of the side of a hill had collapsed onto the farmland below. And this was not a small hill. It topped out at over 1,200 feet, (400 metres) and the base was not much above sea level. Avalanches are fairly common in the Philippines. Hills and mountains liable to slip and mudslides are identified locally and people encouraged to make their homes well away from the danger areas. However soil from landslides tends to be very fertile and is farmed intensively in poor communities. Some people will know the risk but choose to live in a dangerous spot; their choices and horizons are very limited by circumstance. That is what had happened here. We discussed this during the visit and it was still very much an open wound. People this family had grown up with had just disappeared. In areas such as this, once the avalanche falls there is no equipment or expertise to do a serious rescue dig. In any case, this particular avalanche had dropped thousands of tons of earth and rock on top of the homes beneath it. It was obvious that anyone caught up in the event would, more than likely, have been instantly crushed so there was little point in mounting anything other than a very perfunctory search of the area. The first reports of the earthquake which triggered this avalanche are timed at 5.42 am. It is scant consolation that those who died may still have been sleeping and would know nothing of the tragedy which took their lives. When I got back to the hotel I used its wifi hotspot to log on and discovered the final casualty list was 42 dead, 66 missing and 54 injured. Two years on it is assumed that those missing are dead.

How would a natural disaster which had claimed the lives of over a hundred people be reported in the west? You would not be able to keep the film crews and journalists away. Here, it is a part of everyday life. There is little information available about such events beyond what locals might post on social media and the occasional article in the local newspapers. The family we visited had a 24/7 reminder of the fate of their relatives and friends. They looked out of their home and saw a bald stretch of mountainside rising steeply above them with a massive pile of earth below which was slowly being returned to the wild. Beneath it were the remains of people they knew and loved, from babies to grandparents.

There had been no effort to clean up or to stabilise the remaining parts of the hill. There was nothing much left to fall on this particular community but, around the remainder of the hill, livestock was still being tendered to and crops grown, and people living on the edge.

During our five nights at Lalimar we moved from two beds to one; and a good time was enjoyed by all.

Whilst at Lalimar I had reinforced to me a huge cultural difference between the west and the Philippines. This concerned alcohol. Earlier I have made a variety of comments about my relationship with alcohol. I am fairly happy now to acknowledge that I am an alcoholic; to the discerning reader that has probably been fairly obvious. I had stopped drinking about seven weeks before travelling out to meet RB. Before embarking on this trip I had had serious worries that a mixture of being on holiday, alcohol costing much less, needing a liquid replacement for local water, being alone much of the time, particularly late evenings, and in an environment where many around me were on holiday or relaxing, would see me quickly tippling off the wagon and back onto the bottle. However that was not the case.

Having first consumed alcohol at the age of eleven or twelve when I sipped the drinks of everyone who would let me at my grandparent's Boxing Day bash; and having got giggly and inebriated; alcohol had

become a very normal part of life. I was first served in a pub when I was fourteen years old and, by the time I reached sixteen, was drinking regularly, not heavily as I could not afford to, although my Dad's supplies were often attacked. I recall my parents and younger brother going on holiday when I was in my late teens. I spotted that my Dad had placed a mark on the label of a bottle, presumably so he could tell if his son and heir had been helping himself whilst they were away. I used the same biro to place identical marks around the rest of the label. Neither of us said a word and the issue was only discussed about forty years later!
So alcohol had been a routine part of my life for the best part of fifty years. The previous trips I had made to the Philippines had all been whilst I was in full-time work. This was my first visit as a retiree. For around ten years I had been playing with the idea of stopping drinking alcohol altogether. There had been a couple of 2-3 month stretches when I stayed dry and there had been a period of a couple of years running up to retirement when I had only been drinking at weekends and whilst on holiday. This particular trip began in mid-January and I had given up drinking altogether a few weeks before Christmas. In retrospect I think the big difference which triggered what has, so far, been a successful quit attempt, is my retirement. I am sure the stresses of my work environment played a part in driving this but I think the biggest driver has been that I am now fully in charge of my own life, I do not have to chase employment and a wage, I do want to wake up with a clear head and enjoy each day as it comes, and I do want to spend my income on things that matter to me. I suppose I have at last learned that alcohol does not matter as much to me as I do.

On this particular visit to the Philippines, before taking the break with RB, I had spent the first seven nights alone. For five or six of those nights I had been with her during the evenings, but, usually by nine thirty or ten I was left to my own devices as she had her work to concentrate on. So I was back in the lobby of the Airport Hotel. This is a big area. As one entered from the taxi drop off point a long reception desk faced the visitor across a lobby area about thirty-fives paces wide. To the right you passed a small stage a couple of offices and conference rooms, one of which was good for a function for five hundred or more.

At the end of this area were steps down to the pool area and up to a Korean style bar. Straight ahead and to the left was the lobby lounge and, to its left, up a couple of steps, the bar and main restaurant area. At weekends entertainment was provided in the lobby lounge. This began around 7.00 pm and concluded about eleven. Sunday evening would be a pianist, Friday and Saturday, a singer and/or a band. I usually took a table with my back to the bar and restaurant but with a view across the lobby towards the main entrance, the stage, the meeting rooms. I would have a book with me and pass the time with some reading but I also undertook of a fair bit of people watching; or general nosiness if you prefer! On this trip I was drinking mineral water and other soft drinks. The staff made no comment but their expressions acknowledged that their stocks of vodka and gin were not being depleted at anything like the rates they had anticipated based on previous visits. Also, instead of meandering through the lobby to the lifts at one in the morning, I was disappearing to my room before midnight, and then sleeping rather than continuing to drink in private. I was appearing for breakfast before seven some mornings and was in the swimming pool by nine. This was a totally different routine to my previous trips. I had been arriving for breakfast at best half an hour before the ten o'clock cut-off point and might have reached the pool by midday, if at all.

Whilst sat relaxing in the lounge I would see other travellers coming and going. Most guests were from South Korea and Japan and their flights arrived at Mactan in the late evening, departing in the early hours of the morning, roughly between eleven and two. So there was a steady throughput of people. Now I was sat in the lounge of an airport hotel which was a walk of about three hundred yards from the check-in desks at an international airport. Had I been in a similar situation at a European Airport which attracted tourist travel, there would have been high spirits and a fair amount of alcohol around. Amongst the Orientals there was very little drinking; and certainly none on the part of those people returning home. That pattern was repeated night after night. The few people behind me sat at the bar were mostly of western extraction. Probably because I was so busy knocking it back myself I hadn't noticed this previously. It was the same in all the restaurants I visited. Drinking alcohol, when it happened, was definitely ancillary to the meal. This same experience was reinforced at Lalimar. I spent a lunch-time with my in-laws to be and several other relatives and friends. We arrived around eleven and stayed until around two thirty. We were a party of around twenty people. No alcohol was ordered. It was offered; but the preference was cans of pop and mineral water. Other guests and visitors were using the bar/restaurant, again there was no evidence of alcohol. It wasn't until shortly before we moved on that two western couples arrived for a meal and then the wine and beer began to flow. It would seem that alcohol is just not a significant element of Philippine culture. This was also the case in the evening. An occasional bottle of beer was served, and would be shared amongst a group of friends, but almost everything else was non-alcoholic. Perhaps, given my relationship with drink, my view was exaggerated. But, following this realisation, I kept an eye on this for the remainder of the trip and noticed that is was rare for Filipinos socialising together to consume much beer or wine. If a westerner was involved then the alcohol flowed but, left to their own devices, there was very little and usually none. The only exception I can make to this was on my third trip when visiting June for one of the parties to celebrate her Dad's return from Qatar. Lager was available but it was bought from a nearly sari-sari store when supplies began to run low. It was then decanted into small plastic cups, and consumed in moderation and exclusively the preserve of the male. There was no sign of any wine or spirits. Across all my visits I have only seen drunken Filipinos twice. The first time was a man alone. He was drinking bottled lager and sat well away from the bar and anyone else. That in itself was telling as most Filipinos in company will go out of their way to be sociable and inclusive. They were completely ignoring this guy which makes me think something beyond alcohol may also have been in play; perhaps drugs or, maybe, a mental health issue. He sat alone loudly cursing the foreigners who came to his country, tried to take over and took his work; themes not entirely alien to Brexit Britain!

The second occasion was on our most recent visit. A group of young men who had spent the day at a fiesta in Guihulngan called in on their way home. They had been drinking all day and were plastered. They eventually left with a police escort.

I have not visited many bars in the Philippines but, where I have, Filipinos seem to consume alcohol in serious moderation; that said the bars I have visited tend to be in hotels or touristy areas. If I couple this observation to the experiences Jo had with the Tia Maria we might conclude that a western man who has a Filipina in his life will not need to concern himself much with bar bills and other alcohol related issues. Nor is he likely to have a partner wanting to go to the pub on a regular basis. The downside will be if the man himself enjoys pub culture, a Filipina may be the wrong partner. All that said, my sample size is small. However it did make my trip much more manageable. I was not under any pressure from peer groups or fellow guests to have a drink and that was beneficial.

We completed our time at Lalimar and had a Sunday flight back to Cebu scheduled to depart Dumaguete Airport at 11 am. so we had to check-in by nine. Lalimar is set back a couple of hundred metres from the coastal road around the island and is on the main bus route between Dumaguete, San Carlos City and Bacolod. There is a bus stop immediately outside the hotel. It is a three hour bus ride so, to make the airport check-in, we checked out very early deciding to catch the bus scheduled to pass the hotel a few minutes after six in the morning. I had no idea of how punctual or otherwise the bus service would be. If there was a problem with this one a second was due twenty minutes later. However if neither appeared we would then have a wait of an hour and a half which would put us on the last minute for the flight. I need not have worried. Between six and five past the bus arrived. I had thought that as this was early on Sunday morning there would be few people on it but, again, I was wrong. It wasn't full but it wasn't far off and, during our trip, it filled up quickly. We arrived at the airport to find a problem with the flight. The plane on which we would be travelling had been delayed on its departure from Mactan Airport on its outward journey. Having been scheduled to depart Mactan at 9.30 am. it had now been put back to midday. So we could have had a couple of hours longer in bed and enjoyed breakfast before departing the Lalimar. C'est la vie! We eventually left Dumaguete Airport shortly after one in the afternoon.

Before finishing my trip with a week at the Airport Hotel I had six nights at a beach hotel in Maribago called White Sands. This was not the place I had stayed at during the first three trips; that was nearby. One of the big benefits of staying at the Airport Hotel had been getting to better understand the layout of the airport and facilities surrounding it. It used to be a pain to have to deal with all sorts of chancers trying to make a few cents from carrying luggage or calling a cab. However I had discovered that there was a properly regulated taxi rank at the airport. This was situated close to domestic flight departures; well out of sight of international flight arrivals. So we came out of the arrivals hall with our bags, crossed a busy eight lane road, climbed a set of steps and joined a short queue at the taxi rank. Within twenty minutes we were checking into White Sands. RB had told her employers she would be back on Sunday afternoon but, once we got notice of the delay at Dumaguete Airport, had advised them she would be back as soon as possible. In the event we had a few hours at White Sands together and a meal at the Maribago Grill before I took her back to work. From White Sands to her workplace was now an hour and ten minutes by taxi each way; but she was worth it. We had enjoyed a great time together and begun to feel that, despite our massive age gap, we might make a good couple. We had the beginnings of some shared interests. RB seemed to be very close to the sort of person I was looking for educationally. She had an enquiring mind and wanted to learn. Her actions demonstrated this as well as the things we discussed. She also had a bit of backbone coupled with a sense of humour and loved laughing. She had been born into a culture where religion had far greater importance than it does in my bit of the west which was borne out by some of the things she did. However she did not find my atheism to be an issue nor, so far as I know, did her family. My guess is that her employers could see this as a problem as the strength of their beliefs were clear for all to see with the icons with which they had surrounded themselves in their home and their vehicles. However that was an issue for them, not me. I respect their right to believe what they think is right for them.

As I began my recollections of this particular trip I mentioned arriving during Sinulog on the day after the pope had ended a visit to the Philippines. On a wet day in Manila six million people were reported to have attended a papal mass. The man left the country with a message for Filipinos to look after their families, look after their children and not to use contraception. As a recent and fairly regular visitor to the country I can confirm that Filipinos do have a strong tendency to look after their families as best as they can; they know that no one else will. They also look after their children as best they can; again because no one else will. There is a high birth rate amongst young Filipinas, strong evidence of underage sex, a burgeoning adult entertainment sector and increasing levels of H.i.V and other sexually transmitted infections. To discourage the use of contraception, particularly in these circumstances, is dangerous; in fact to anyone bar a bloody fool it is a ridiculous stance to take; it encourages disease, loss of life and loss of quality of life. All that said, given the acute poverty seen in many of the areas I have visited, a decent afterlife will be the best many can hope for.

The ostensible reason for the papal visit was to show solidarity with the people of Tacloban who had suffered the consequences of Typhoon Yolanda/Haiyan some fourteen months earlier. He did this, briefly, the visit being cut short because of the approach of a wet and windy weather system. It is good to know that solidarity in a practical papal sense translates to bailing out at the first sign of trouble thus abandoning those who suffered the most devastating wet and windy weather on record; the very people with whom you are supposedly expressing solidarity.

It is interesting that the pope did not visit the Sinulog festival in Cebu however this makes perfect sense from a security perspective as the streets are frequently gridlocked which would be a nightmare for the papal guard.

Sinulog began before Spanish colonisation was first attempted in 1521 therefore it preceded catholicism. At that time it represented the local people honouring the wooden artefacts which had become the totems of their pre-religious world. However the eventual arrival of the Spanish in 1565 saw this celebration being absorbed by the catholic church who replaced these icons with santa niño, literally saint son or saint jesus. Jesus is not god and his image was kept in the form of a child and borne through the streets for worship as the local saint. Worshippers shout out their requests for resolution to their problems as the procession winds its way through the city streets, two steps forward and one step back. The word Sinulog is derived from the Cebuano word sulog which means 'like the movement of a current of water'.

That is the basic idea. I know I am very short on detail and my lack of religious belief makes me view much of this as nonsense, but, from my perspective, that is religion for you. I can certainly see the virtues of Sinulog as a cultural event which can help bind communities together and bring a lot of pleasure to a lot of people. I think the celebrations are great for this; I just can't accept a link to a supernatural being. I also see it as a way of continuing to brainwash a gullible population, particularly children and young people. I am happy to accept that the brain is a very powerful tool and, if a celebration such as Sinulog can help that brain to deliver messages to the body which, in turn, allow it to make recovery from illness, then I am all for it. But my bottom line really is that by accepting and practising scientific knowledge we will have a much better chance of healing our ills. Certainly if I need an operation I am going to seek a qualified doctor rather than someone who will pray for me.

During the remainder of my visit, six nights at White Sands and a further week at the Airport Hotel, RB and I met daily whilst she was working and were able to create time almost every evening in which we would have a meal together and, when this occurred at the Hotel, spend some quality time together developing our friendship/relationship. However, once back from Lalimar, we were never alone. Her young charge might spend some time sleeping but was always there, and properly cared for.

We agreed that RB would give her employers three months' notice of her intention to leave and discussed our plans with them. From their perspective they said they would support her in this decision and find another nanny to look after their child. We helped with this. RB's younger sister agreed to take over the role.

The employers also agreed they would support us in making sure RB had the necessary documents to support a passport application and open a bank account. Whilst I was present they took her to their bank but discovered that, as the correct identification documents could not be provided, the bank would not allow her to open an account.

On reflection this should have had warning bells ringing for me. The next two years were a continual war of attrition with bureaucracy. Whilst the nature of bureaucracy has much to do with that we also have to consider the inputs, or lack of, from RB and myself.

The conversations and chats we had whilst together were not deep. Except for our time at Lalimar we had a small disabled child with us constantly. He was generally well behaved and a pleasure to be with, but it did mean that much of our time and effort was concentrated on dealing with his needs. The moments we had to ourselves were infrequent and little more than the opportunity for a quick kiss and cuddle, on a good day maybe some low scale intimacy. But deep and meaningful conversation did not feature.

When my return date arrived I left Mactan Airport in the hope that RB would join me in the U.K. a few months later. In the event it took in excess of two years and a further visit. There was a never ending catalogue of issues which had to be dealt with.

We saw earlier the level of documentary proof of identity required in the Philippines to open a bank account and to successfully apply for a passport. In mid-February, 2015, I left RB at her place of work/home in Cebu City, in a pleasant upmarket housing development. It took two months to get a bank account opened and from February to October to obtain the passport. The reason was that RB had few identity documents. With being in full time employment she should have had the full set of documents but I can only assume her employer had kept her invisible in the system as she was unable to produce any evidence of health insurance or pension scheme, and was not visible to the taxation authorities. She was not known to the Government Service Insurance System, the Social Security System or the Bureau of Internal Revenue. Her employers had promised us they would provide support to RB as she began this new part of life's journey; I have to say that at no point have they said or done anything negative. We were allowed to meet and she was supplied with a T.I.N. card (Taxpayer Identification Number) which could be used as a support document when applying for a passport. But the biggest problem for RB was having no free time in which to pursue her application. Having a disabled child with you 24/7 means that queuing for anything is difficult. He was unable to stand or walk and, at that time, had no trolley or chair; he needed to be carried everywhere. So, although she had had police and barangay clearance when working in her home province, these documents had expired long ago. Whilst we were at Lalimar she renewed them, however that identified her as being a resident of a Barangay in Negros Oriental Province, not Cebu City, so, having returned to Cebu for her work, she needed to find time to get police and barangay clearance for the address where she worked and lodged. This was sufficient for her to be able to open a bank account. However that was not the bank of her employer's choice; that one still refused to open an account. I found this odd, but I have found many of the systems in the Philippines odd. To Filipinos I am sure western systems will seem equally peculiar. The good news was that the bank at which she opened the account was listed as acceptable to the U.K. Border Control Agency. Once we got a bank account open I wanted to test how she behaved with money. It was the opportunity to see if I would be ripped off. The initial issue we needed to resolve was to improve communications between us. RB was routinely borrowing the mobile phone of a co-worker and this was beginning to cause problems between them. I checked Cebu City prices for mobile phones online looking for something fairly basic which would allow us to maintain contact with Facebook, Skype and the a communication system provided by the dating website. I dug around online and got a feel for prices in Cebu. I then told her I would put some money into her bank account so she could purchase her own mobile phone. I also wanted her to start to become familiar with using a bank account. This excited RB. I asked her to find out the price of a suitable phone and, perhaps predictably, much the same as a teenager is prone to do with a parent, she immediately came back to me with a price for the newest 'must have' top of the range iPhone then available. I asked her to be realistic and a couple of days later she came back with three or four options from different suppliers which were all comfortably within the price range I had found when checking online. So the money was sent across to her account and the new mobile purchased.

It lasted five or six weeks. She contacted me via Skype in tears one evening using the mobile of her co-worker. She had been in the Ayala Shopping Centre that afternoon with the child she cared for. Whilst playing a game on her phone which kept both of them amused a youth came past on a skateboard and snatched it. That was the last she saw of the mobile phone. She had little by way of description of the offender but had managed to cancel her phone account before any illicit use could be made of it. She was devastated. Her devastation seemed to me to be absolutely genuine. However a difficulty was presented as we were back to square one so far as communications were concerned. She tried to maintain contact with the co-operation of her colleague but that co-operation was, at best, irregular. I decided to send some money across to get a replacement. That one also only lasted for a few weeks before the younger brother of the child she cared for deposited it into a glass of cola. This time there were witnesses. Even so, when she asked her employers to replace it, they refused. They took the view that she should have had more sense than to leave a mobile phone in a place where a young child could get hold of it. A bit harsh I thought, but that may also have reflected that she only had two or three weeks left with them. Her colleague used her mobile to send me images of the damaged phone. It was obviously not working. Before she left their employ I replaced it again with a fairly cheap mobile so that once she left her employment we would be able to maintain contact.

After she left her work RB had, unfortunately, to lead something of a gypsy existence. Up until then accommodation and full board had been part of the payment for her work. By finishing her job she became simultaneously unemployed, incomeless and homeless. The impact of this was very pronounced initially. We had agreed that, provided we kept making progress towards her visiting the U.K. and marriage, I would place a set amount into her bank account around the middle of each month. The amount was modest by U.K. standards but well above the average earned by an unskilled person in their early twenties in the Philippines. It was more than she had expected and I now know more than three times what she had been earning; allowing for bed and board.

Having left her work she found herself a room in a boarding house with several other single women. This was done on the recommendation of a friend. It didn't work out. Within a few days her mobile was being used by other people who also accessed her Facebook account. Through this I became aware that people I am linked with in the U.K. began receiving odd messages and a couple I know were asked for money for the most ridiculous things. We came close to losing contact. There were a couple of occasions where we were exchanging messages on Facebook it became apparent to me that I was communicating with someone pretending to be RB. On one occasion I was contacted by a person telling me RB had been admitted to hospital and that funds were needed immediately to cover the costs. I had been there before and asked for the name of the hospital and doctor so I could establish the prognosis and costs. That produced the response that they were looking after RB as she had been discharged from the hospital but had no one else to look after her. So all payments would have to go through them. A few hours later RB contacted me through Facebook and was obviously completely oblivious to the earlier exchange of messages I had been involved in. I told her what had occurred and she told me this was the first she had heard of it; she knew nothing of the hospital issue but had been walking without footwear on the shoreline earlier that day and had some small cuts on the soles of her feet. The time she told me she had been walking coincided with the time I had been solicited for medical costs. She told me that, having experienced having her phone snatched, she had left it in her room for safety. She also told me she had left the room locked and it had been locked when she returned. We both now knew that, in her absence, someone was accessing her room and using the mobile or had cloned her Facebook account, or both. When I initially told RB what had happened she did not seem to understand the implications and potential dangers of this.

Over the next couple of weeks our communications reduced and I was worried about both our developing relationship and RBs ability to survive solo. Knowing that the birthday of the child she had looked after was coming up and that RB would be visiting, I contacted the family she had worked for and told them what was happening. I explained that both RB's phone and Facebook were compromised and that she had to sort this out. A new Facebook account was straightforward enough but she also needed to be talked through resetting her mobile and understanding she might have to change her memory card and number. They did this and, on the boy's birthday, we had a long chat on Skype. We agreed it would be a good idea for her to review her accommodation arrangements.

Her only immediate local alternative was to stay with an aunt in an area of Cebu City called Guadalupe, an aunt who I had met and knew could do without another body in her hut. However from late July to February RB migrated between the home of the aunt and returning to her home island where she lodged with other family members and friends. I found that she seemed much happier and her behaviour and life style was much improved when on her home island so encouraged this to become the place she stayed more regularly. That may also have been happening naturally as she made the psychological readjustment from being employed doing physically hard work 24/7, to a situation where she could relax more and take her time over things.

This nomadic existence became necessary as delays occurred first with her passport application and then with the visa application. Let's deal with the passport first.

RB insisted on using an agent to obtain a passport for her. She told me that this woman had recently obtained a passport for a cousin so she was confident her application would be successful as the agent had a proven track record. Two difficulties occurred which were not directly the fault of the agent, although she should have been aware of them and advised RB accordingly. Firstly the initial application was made from the address of her former employer. Given that RB had identity documents from her home island this was a daft thing to do. The application was refused because the address she claimed to be living at did not accord with the addresses on her identity documents. It was common sense that she should have used her home island address. However, in consequence of the initial application, she needed to get her support papers sorted out so they all related to the same address. So, under the guidance of the agent, she obtained the Barangay and police clearances and then got a Postal i/d for the Guadalupe address. A second application was submitted and refused because she had only lived at the Guadalupe address for a couple of weeks. The authorities demanded a further level of 'acceptable' id. The only one from the government list which RB believed she could obtain was what is referred to as Old College i/d. To obtain this she had to visit her home island and return to the last school she attended. The request was made at the school on a Monday afternoon; RB's mother made the trip with her. The document was prepared and ready for collection on the Friday of the following week. She then returned to Guadalupe and the agent. A third submission was made in the middle of August using her correct home address. Unsurprisingly this was accepted; at last. We expected to receive her passport in early September. It didn't arrive. I asked her to contact the agent and find out why. The reply I got indicated it was delayed because of industrial action. As soon as I checked online I discovered that the Philippine government was in the process of outsourcing its passport printing services. This had led to industrial action earlier in the year and a huge backlog in dealing with applications. Priority was being given to

Filipinos working overseas whose passports were coming up for renewal and to those applicants with a promise of work overseas. Otherwise delays were expected. Eventually her passport was handed over by the agent on 15th October, 2015. The date on which the passport was issued was 8th September. It expires on 7th September, 2020. We hoped, by then, to have made some progress!

We had agreed that we would try for a Visitor visa for RB. I knew that had failed with Jo but I also knew that we had not properly established that we knew each other. It was different with RB. We had photographs together in various places with different people, family, colleagues and friends. We had shared a flight together and had our tickets and boarding passes, we had shared a hotel room together and had a reservation receipt to that effect coupled with photographs of us together at the hotel. What could go wrong?

Plenty!

We had a major delay in making the application because of the postal service. To support RB's application she needed to prove she had a place to live in the U.K. and would not become a liability to the U.K. tax payer. Whilst she was able to print some of the documents in support of her application, I needed to prove ownership of my property, that all issues around mortgage were covered, that I had a decent income, that I was paying my bills, etc. Furthermore that we knew each other and that I was formally inviting her to stay with me whilst she visited the U.K.. To prove this I sent copies of bank statements, pay slips, tax records, utility bills, certified copies of my passports, (there had been a recent renewal), and birth certificate. By the time this package of information was complete it consisted of several hundred sheets of A4 paper all contained in a see through plastic box. If it fell into the wrong hands I could expect my identity to be stolen.

A transparent package is important when making a visa application. V.F.S. will remove and discard any other type of packaging. Using an envelope or folder is a waste of time. I used the Post Office to mail these out using a service called international track and trace. The Post Office website told me they expected delivery would be made within seven working days. I followed its progress. Initially it was in transit and then 'arrived Manila'. And that was where it stayed. Seven days came and went. After two weeks I advised the Post Office who confirmed it had reached Manila (they would, wouldn't they; we were using the same software!) They told me that I could not report it lost until 28 working days after the package had been posted and no investigation would take place into its whereabouts until I had made that report. They probably meant four weeks; 28 working days would be five weeks and three days, an odd cut off point! However after 28 working days the package was still recorded 'arrived Manila'. I reported the matter. No one contacted me. Around three weeks later I received a cheque through the post to recompense the cost of postage and the plastic container. They refused to pay any further compensation. The fact that they had lost materials from which my identity could be stolen did not matter a jot to them.

By now we were in late November. RB and I discussed how we should take this matter forward. There seemed to be no point in me posting papers out the same way again; they could just as easily be lost or stolen again. However, without the supporting documentation she was unable to make any progress with her visa application. As we entered December I remembered I knew someone who was travelling out to the Philippines to spend Christmas and New Year with their family. I contacted them and they agreed that, if RB met them at Manila Airport, they would be happy to hand over a set of documents to support her application. Whilst this would be a fairly expensive way of getting the papers delivered, as it would mean RB having a return flight and overnight stay in Manila, it was definitely a more secure method of delivery, and, given very recent experience, safer and more reliable than using our postal services. However it would also be a good opportunity for RB to manage a short return flight by herself. So this is what happened. But it was a few days before Christmas, 2015, before the documents were handed over. After the Christmas and New Year holidays in Cebu City it was the beginning of Sinulog so there were still days when the rest of the world was returning to normality following the Christmas break whilst a different type of normality prevailed in Cebu City. In consequence it was towards the end of January, 2016, before the visa application was finally fully submitted.

Again RB insisted on using the agent. She had proved she could get a passport, (eventually – third time lucky), so she had to be good! I had railed against this. However an application was submitted and U.K.V.I. again refused to issue the visa. What I did not know until that point was that, over a year earlier, our government had changed the rules and refused any right of appeal against their decisions on visitor/tourist visas. The only appeal which can now be made would be through the European Court of Human Rights; a route which is likely to be lost altogether during the negotiations the U.K. is having as it plans to leave the E.U.

The reasons given for refusal were as follows, (my italics):

The decision

I have refused your application for a visit visa because I am not satisfied that you meet the requirements of Paragraph 4.2 of Appendix V Immigration Rules for Visitors because:

The onus is on the applicant to demonstrate that they meet the requirements of the UK Immigration Rules. The UKVI Website provides information to visa applicants about the types of documents that they should produce so that they can demonstrate to an Entry Clearance Officer that they meet the rules. We advise applicants that the failure to submit such documentation may result in refusal of their application. This decision has been made on the basis of the information and evidence that you have provided with this application.

You are applying to visit the UK for 6 months as a General Visitor. I recognise that your sponsor proposes to bear the cost of your visit. However I must also take into account your own circumstances when considering the intentions behind your proposal to visit the UK.

You state that you are single, unemployed and receive £x per month from other sources including friends and family. In support of your application you have provided evidence that your sponsor sends monthly remittances to you in the Philippines. However you have produced no evidence of any assets, property or savings. Neither have you provided any evidence of who you live with in the Philippines. Therefore you have not shown any responsibilities or ties to your home country. Your sponsor intends to support your trip and it is apparent from the evidence provided that you will be reliant on your sponsor for all of your expenses during your stay, as you are already reliant on him for your only evidenced means of support in the Philippines. Given the above I am not satisfied that you are a genuine visitor and will leave the UK at the end of your visit.

In view of your current economic standing along with the fact that you have no evidenced income of your own, I am not satisfied that you have shown significant ties to the Philippines that would induce you to leave the UK. In view of the above, I am not satisfied that you are genuinely seeking entry to the UK as a visitor for the limited period stated by you or that you intend to leave the UK at the end of that period. Appendix V 4.2 (a) and (c).

I have therefore refused your application because I am not satisfied on the balance of probabilities that you meet all of the requirements of the relevant paragraph of the United Kingdom Immigration Rules.

Future Applications

Any future UK visa applications you make will be considered on their individual merits, however you are likely to be refused unless the circumstances of your application change.

Before commenting on this decision let us take a look at the section of the Immigration Rules this application allegedly fails to satisfy, (again, my italics):

Appendix V, section 4.2 The applicant must satisfy the decision maker that they are a genuine visitor. This means that the applicant:
(a) will leave the UK at the end of their visit; and
(b) will not live in the UK for extended periods through frequent or successive visits, or make the UK their main home; and
(c) is genuinely seeking entry for a purpose that is permitted by the visitor routes (these are listed in Appendices 3, 4 and 5); and
(d) will not undertake any prohibited activities set out in V 4.5 – V 4.10; and
(e) must have sufficient funds to cover all reasonable costs in relation to their visit without working or accessing public funds. This includes the cost of the return or onward journey, any costs relating to dependants, and the cost of planned activities such as private medical treatment.

U.K.V.I. is clear that the application was refused because it did not satisfy Appendix V 4.2 of the Immigration Rules. There are five elements to this section, (a) to (e).

Parts (b) and (d) are of no relevance to this application so we can ignore them. Part (b) is used to refuse a Visitor visa when U.K.V.I. suspect an applicant is making repeated use of it as a means of basing themselves in the U.K. This was RB's first application so (b) cannot be of any relevance. Part (d) refers us to parts 4-10 of the Appendix. In brief 4.5 – 4.7 covers work in the U.K. and payment for it. Part 4.8 covers study and 4.9 covers medical issues. Our application was very clear that RB would not engage in any of those activities. 4.10 bars anyone using a Visitor's visa to marry in the U.K. Our application was explicit on our intentions around that issue.

Part (e) relates to RB being able to fully fund her visit. Ass you will see the application we submitted fully covered this issue. This leaves us with parts (a) and (c) as being the only legitimate elements of the section which may be used to refuse issue of the visa.

V4.2(a) states - the applicant will leave the U.K. at the end of their visit, and,

V4.2(c) states - the applicant is genuinely seeking entry for a purpose that is permitted by the visitor routes (these are listed in Appendices 3, 4 and 5).

If you wish to check the e-link is:
https://www.gov.uk/guidance/immigration-rules

As far as V4.2(c) is concerned when we look at the Immigration Rules we are clearly told that Appendices 3, 4 and 5 have been deleted. By using these Appendices to deny the issue of the visitor visa the Entry Clearance Officer is using something which no longer exists, by their own Rules. This leaves the grounds for refusing the issue of a visa to be based on part (a) only, i.e. the applicant has not satisfied the decision-maker they will leave the U.K. at the end of their visit.

Within the finance section of RB's visa application she stated: (my italics):

> *5.18 My friend has agreed to cover all costs. This includes return air fare, accommodation, clothing and food. The reason for this goes to the purpose of the visit. My friend and I met online. We have also met in person in the Philippines; shared a room together and visited my family together. We*

want to understand if our friendship will grow into more. Online and for a four-week visit we think this may happen. But living together for up to six months will allow us both to understand if we might become a couple. My air ticket will be return. Should the short term visa be issued there are three potential outcomes, each of which means I will return to the Philippines within the terms of the visa. The potential outcomes are:

(a) We get on well. We agree to marry in the Philippines. I return to plan the wedding after which make application for the correct visa to re-enter the U.K.

(b) We get on well. We agree to marry in the U.K. I return to the Philippines to take the language and TB tests and then apply for the correct visa to re-enter the U.K. to marry within six months.

(c) If we do not get on well I will return and pick up my life in the Philippines within the terms of the visa.

5.19 The cost to me has been resigning from full-time work in June in order to make this trip. (I have then had a delay whilst waiting to receive the correct documents to apply for my passport and also experienced the delays currently being experienced in the Philippines in the issuing of passports.)

My letter inviting RB to visit read as follows (with some information adjusted solely to protect identities and locations):

I write to support RB, born (date provided) in (address provided) in her application for a six month Visit and Short Term Stay Visa to the United Kingdom. Documents referred to in this letter of support have been provided to RB in sequential order for her to hand in when she presents hard copies of her application. I hold almost all of them electronically. Please contact me at the above e-mail address should anything appear ambiguous or should any clarifications be required.

RB and I met online in October, 2014, using a dating website. We communicated using the website, Skype and Facebook until January, 2015, when I visited her in Cebu, the Philippines. I stayed for four weeks and, during that time, we met almost every day and took a trip to visit her family in (location stated) together. We are applying for this visa as we enjoy each other's company very much but also know there are huge differences between us, particularly with regard to age. During her visit she will stay with me for a period of up to six months having the opportunity to experience normal day to day life in the United Kingdom; a different climate and culture and to improve her knowledge of the English language through day to day use. I will be providing her with a return flight ticket from the Philippines to the United Kingdom. The length of visit will be the choice of RB. She may choose to stay for a few days or up to the full term of the visa should it be issued. The purpose of her proposed visit is for us to understand if the differences are too great or if we feel we have the basis of a long-term relationship. We do understand that were our chosen path to formalise our relationship by marriage then RB would return to the Philippines where we would either marry, or plan a marriage in the U.K. and then apply for the appropriate visa to facilitate her return to the U.K. In view of this I have provided a copy of the decree absolute from my marriage, which ended in 2003, to evidence that I am entitled to re-marry should we choose to follow this path.

Whilst she is in the United Kingdom I will assume full responsibility for her financially. She will live at my address as shown above. I am expecting her to arrive with no money, little luggage and inappropriate clothing for the British winter. We will deal with this. To support her application I have provided documents to prove my identity and to demonstrate I have ample funds to support her throughout the visit. Furthermore there is additional information to evidence that we have spent time together, that we have visited her family together in a remote part of the Philippines, that I have assumed a role of financial sponsor and that we have maintained contact over a significant period of time.

We had hoped to apply earlier however the supporting information I mailed to RB was either lost or stolen within the Philippine postal service area. Because of the risk of loss I had sent certified copies of original identity documents perchance this occurred and have done this again. However the supporting information on this occasion is being delivered by hand by (person and relationship details provided) who is a Philippine citizen. You will find colour photocopies of my birth certificate and passport; also pages within my passport to show I have visited the Philippines on six occasions. These copies have been certified as genuine and endorsed to that effect by my solicitor. I have included the passport stamps to demonstrate that I am not a one-off opportunist.

You need to be assured that I have the wherewithal to look after RB and that she will not require any assistance from public funds whilst in the U.K. To this end you will find documentary evidence of my ownership of the property we will live in (mortgage and rent free). (This) is a five bedroomed semi-detached property with two bathrooms and gardens to the front and rear. I currently live there alone; there is ample accommodation for RB.

I cannot provide payslips for several months as my income is made up of pension payments from previous employment with (former employer named) and (former employer named). These bodies only issue a pension payslip when the net pay differs by £10 on the previous month. I have included the most recent pension payslips, April for (organisation specified), May for (organisation specified). There is also proof of a substantial cash investment. Bank statements cover a six month period up to (date specified). These show, amongst other things, the pensions have been paid in each month. They also show monthly outgoings for Council Tax, TV Licence, Utilities and TV/Communications. You will note that there are no monthly payments for credit or a loan. That is because I have no debt to service. Also shown are payments made to RB via Western Union to support her; for completeness I have also included the e-mail receipts received from Western Union for these payments. A copy of my current Council Tax demand is enclosed as it shows a 25% reduction on full tariff to evidence my current single status. For completeness there are also copies of utility bills. These can also be triangulated with the bank statements. In short this information demonstrates that I live well within my means and have the financial wherewithal to fully support RB, which I have been doing, fully, from July, 2015, and partially from March to June, 2015 inclusive. In addition to the above, should a visa be issued and once RB arrives here, I will purchase a private health insurance package for her so that, in the event of unforeseeable illness or accident, she will not become a burden to the U.K. tax payer. I have been quoted £365 for this by B.U.P.A. Global.

There is documentary evidence of the trip we made to (RBs home identified) consisting of the reservation confirmation from the hotel we used; a copy of the return flight ticket and copies of our outward bound boarding passes. Also included are copies of photographs of us during that trip showing I have visited her family home and met her family. Whilst we stayed in (location specified) RB's family home in (location specified) is 20 miles from the hotel. Over 80% of the route is on dirt tracks. Our journey was mostly by motorcycle but partly on foot as some of the paths were unsuitable even for a motor cycle due to steepness and roughness of the terrain. Furthermore, as a check of the Philippine media will show this is a region in which the New People's Army, (N.P.A.), is active. Two people were murdered in the village of (location specified) close to (location specified) at the end of June. A further murder occurred in (location specified) itself in July. For me as a foreigner to visit that area had an element of risk, particularly kidnap. However I felt it was important to make the trip given the potential future of the relationship RB and I were considering. I advise you of this as I want to be clear that the visit to (location specified) was neither frivolous nor a simple soft option. It took some planning and effort and, from my perspective, was well worthwhile.

I returned to the U.K. on 17th February, 2015 and have subsequently maintained contact with RB. Unedited copies of transcripts of conversations can be provided by e-mail if required but they run to hundreds of sides of A4 paper. What I have printed is a copy of the index a folder containing e-mail and Facebook exchanges relevant to our friendship almost all of which have been automatically dated by Facebook, etc. This shows that we spend frequent time online together. Please note that not included here is use of Skype which has been fairly frequent and telephone calls which have been occasional.

I trust that the information provided will assure you that RB:

is making a genuine visa application; is fully aware that she must leave within the time span of the visa;

has a responsible sponsor who will ensure, if a visa is issued, she fully complies with it and will leave within the terms of the visa; and,

through me has the financial and other means in place to ensure no need to draw on public funds.

I can also confirm we are fully aware that she:

cannot and will not undertake any work, paid or voluntary; and,
will abide by the restrictions regarding educational activity.

Yours faithfully

xxxxx

I know that I am biased but think the reason given for refusing to issue this visa is thin to say the least; concern *that "the applicant will leave the UK at the end of their visit."* Perhaps that reflects the fact that the person making the decision knows full well that it cannot be appealed. So they are free to assume 'the applicant will not leave the U.K. at the end of the visit' based simply on their own opinion rather than on anything objective or that may be tested or queried. The only way this opinion can hold water is if both RB and I were lying. That was not the case. If it were then we could both be prosecuted as we would be conspiring to obtain a visa under false pretences.

If representatives of the U.K. government are making important decisions on people's lives on their personal opinions rather than objective evidence then anyone applying for a visitor visa can be refused anytime. In consequence I have no qualms in suggesting we have a government which is encouraging its immigration arm to use the visitor visa application process as a piggy bank. An application is made, £85 collected then, £95 now, application refused on the opinion/whim of the assessor only, no need to consider the evidence, no right of appeal. And we call ourselves a developed country! It is a system in which the most corrupt of banana republics could take pride. As a cynic I would suggest that applicants for visitor visas are actually evaluated on their ability to spend (money as well as time) for up to six months in the U.K.. Those with substantial funds will get the visas, those who are not well heeled will not. The reasons given for not issuing the visa clearly state that part of the reason was that RB had no income of her own. We did not try to hide this and did provide substantial evidence that, as her sponsor, I was well able to provide for her.

In this instance either the applicant and sponsor are conniving together and lying to the Entry Clearance Officer, in which case they should be properly investigated, or there are no checks and balances on the Entry Clearance Officer who is then free to refuse any application as no right of appeal means no come back on them. Given that U.K.V.I. keep all past applications on file there are further implications for future applications?

However we were where we were.

Perhaps Private Eye had it right in a cartoon in issue number 1415 which showed an Entry Clearance Office saying to a visitor to this country making a visa application: "You'll need to fill in this new form," and handing over a document with the reference PI55.OVV.

It is not just RB and I who have issues with small print in immigration matters, it is reflected across all aspects of society when access to the U.K. is sought. In sport, for example, Nigerian footballer Taiwo Awoniyi signed for Liverpool football club in 2015. Because he cannot yet get a work visa he has continually loaned out to other clubs. For the season which has just concluded, (2019-20), he is in Germany with FC Mainz 05. He is still ineligible for a work permit. It seems quite bizarre to me that a professional footballer, with a contract at one of the top clubs in the world, is not allowed into the country where the business which holds his contract is based. It smacks of both free trade being impeded, and racism.

I am sure other football clubs will have similar stories.

More seriously the family of an elderly man have had to appeal a decision to return him to Pakistan from his home in Oldham. This man was living with his family, suffering from dementia and dying. He was in a caring environment, was not reliant on public funds, and his disease had advanced to a place where he did not fully understand what was going on around him.

May Brown, a young Mum of Nigerian descent, living with her ex-British soldier husband and child, spent some time under a death sentence imposed by U.K.V.I.. I will let items from the web tell the ridiculous story of this case; it is also worth noting that our mainstream media only got involved once events had turned to favour the 'immigrant'; God forbid they might do something positive to support her cause!

> On 13 October 2016 a May Brown launched an appeal to the Home Office/UK Visa & Immigration to allow her sister to visit the UK from Nigeria for a lifesaving stem cell (bone marrow) transplant.

The ACLT, African Caribbean Leukaemia Trust, has been supporting May with help and advice, hospital visits and emotional support since her relapse earlier this year.

May was diagnosed with Acute Myeloid Leukaemia last year and lives in Dorset with her husband Mike, an ex-British soldier, and their two year old daughter Selina May.

After receiving four cycles of chemotherapy, May went into remission. However, sadly, nine months later she relapsed (the cancer returned), this time more aggressively.

Consultants have confirmed May's only chance of survival is to receive a stem cell transplant from a donor with a matching tissue type.

May who is scheduled to start a second round of chemotherapy at King's College Hospital, London, has been told that *"they are running out of time"* if they are to start chemotherapy treatment and carry out the transplant post getting her back into remission.

The medical tests show May's sister Martha, who resides in Nigeria with her two children, has been identified as a 10 out of 10 match for her sister and therefore has the ability to save her sister's life by donating her stem cells.

Despite letters from hospital consultants confirming Martha's status as the only available matching donor for the urgent stem cell transplant. Martha, who is a school teacher in Nigeria, has been refused a visa to enter the U.K. as she did not meet economic requirements. This is despite her sister May, agreeing to sponsor her trip to the U.K., covering her return flights, accommodation and any living expenses during her short stay.

(https://madnewsuk.com/2016/10/17/woman-left-distraught-after-sister-is-refused-uk-visa-to-donate-stem-cells-video/)

The letter from U.K. Visas & Immigration states:

> "I am not satisfied that you are a genuine visitor and will leave the UK at the end of your visit or that you have sufficient funds available to cover your costs whilst in the UK without working or accessing public funds."

May, who had been in hospital for the last three months said:

> "I was elated when I received the news Martha was a 10 out of 10 match. But when I received notification her visa was rejected I felt distraught and helpless. My two year old daughter Selina needs me. She needs me to be back home with her, looking after her. To know my life isn't important to those who have the power to help me is deeply upsetting."

She added:

> "My life can be saved if my sister is granted leave to enter the UK to donate her stem cells. This is a six hour journey which will help save my life. I am begging for the UK Home Office to review their decision and grant my sister admission to the UK."

The B.B.C. later chipped in with:

> A woman undergoing treatment for leukaemia said she was "overjoyed" that her sister has been granted permission to travel from Nigeria to donate bone marrow.
>
> May Brown from Weymouth, Dorset was told her sister Martha was a "10 out of 10" tissue match.
>
> Martha was initially refused a visa to the U.K. because her income was too low.
>
> The Home Office said it reversed its decision on her visa application due to "exceptional circumstances".

It comes after more than 61,000 people signed a petition against the refusal.

(http://www.bbc.co.uk/news/uk-england-dorset-37728275)

Had the B.B.C. shown concern earlier perhaps the 'exceptional circumstances' would have been recognised earlier! It might have prompted some members of the public to sign up which, in turn, would have generated more publicity. But the B.B.C. is funded from government and we have a government committed to reducing levels of immigration. A knock-on effect is that we have a U.K.V.I. under pressure to say 'no' unless there is no alternative or explicit evidence of a very healthy bank balance.

May Brown died a few months later. Whilst one cannot blame that on directly on U.K.V.I. or the Home Office it is quite legitimate to flag up that their actions were far from helpful. Compassion was sadly lacking in both these arms of government.

Compared to these examples our case is trivial. However, I took legal advice from a specialist immigration barrister. To summarise, his advice was that whether or not the decision to refuse the visitor visa was right, there was no right of appeal so it was pointless to even consider that option. He agreed that this effectively handed carte blanche to the Entry Clearance Officer to refuse the issue of a visa on a whim. He advised against making a second application for a visitor visa. His view was that, even if we found some way to assure U.K.V.I. that RB would return, if we submitted another application for that type of visa, they would find an alternative reason to refuse it. His view was that, from the U.K.V.I. perspective, a visitor is someone who comes into the country to do some shopping, attend a sporting event or visit stately homes, i.e. spend their money; nothing else. The opinion he gave was that we should never have considered applying for a visitor visa. His recommendation was that the only type of visa which the authorities would consider for our circumstances was a matrimonial visa, Family of a Settled Person (Fiancée). It was pointless to consider anything else.

He also asked me why I was looking to the Philippines to find a wife. His view was that there were many young women of Asian descent already legally in the U.K. who would see me as a good catch. He told me to find one, get her pregnant, and then return to him and he would guarantee a successful visa application. This may have been sound practical advice given the adventures and misadventures I have experienced, but it took love and RB right out of the equation. I wanted them both in the equation, and still wanted them here with me! In any case a woman of Asian descent already legally in the U.K. should either be on top of her visa situation or not need one.

So I was back in fiancée visa territory again. The upside of all this was that I had previous experience where I had been successful. So, here we go again.

Success, at Last.

And so we are approaching a conclusion of sorts to our story. RB took and passed her TB test in Makati City, Manila, in early April, 2016. This would support visa applications made within six months of the date of issue. As with Jo we did the TB test first because, if she had latent TB, she would need a six month course of medication to cure it. She then took her English language test. The format for that test had changed. There is now only one organisation in the Philippines which offers tests which U.K.V.I. and Entry Clearance Officers will accept. That is presented by the British Council. This is a British based organisation with charitable status but part funded by the Ministry of Foreign Affairs, i.e. financially under the ægis of the government. So, having made language testing compulsory for the applicants of many visas, our government has now centralised the assessment process and brought it under its own control. So much for encouraging free trade! All for a free market and competition but doing just the opposite when it comes to the issue of immigration; well, at least in the field of language skills testing. However finding politicians who are inconsistent and playing to the gallery is hardly a surprise!

The test has six levels – A1, A2, B1, B2, C1 and C2. For the visa which RB was applying she needed to pass at either level A1 or A2. We decided on A1 as the object was to pass and this was the most basic option on the scale. There was no need to make matters more difficult than necessary.

C2 indicates a person has the English language skills necessary to study at degree or higher degree level. Online I found a mock test and took it expecting to be classified C2. I was told my level was between B1 and B2. This made me wonder about how the now centralised testing system was being geared; at what level the bar was being set. By nature I abhor conspiracy theories but the thought has crossed my mind that the language testing system may be used as a backdoor way of refusing to issue a visa. If an applicant is unable to pass the language test then, in most cases, they will not be able to take their application for a visa any further. As no visa means no travel to the U.K. setting the barrier at which one would pass this test at a high level would prevent many a visa application. This would mean many would-be visa applicants would be prevented from submitting their application as they would be unable to satisfy the language requirement; a situation likely to play well with many politicians and the media.

It has to be accepted that RB's English language skills were modest at the point she took the test; she had no experience of the examination environment and not much self-confidence. In mid-June, 2016, she took her A1 Life Skills English language test and failed. Whilst it is not a difficult test, when you only learn a language for 2-3 years and are tested on it six years later, you are likely to be a bit rusty.

A couple of things need to be discussed here as they could also be contributory factors to RB's failure. Firstly, within the Philippines, the British Council offer the A1 Life Skills tests in two formats; one is accepted for the purposes of visa applications; the other isn't. Testing for both versions are available at the same centres on the same days in Manila and Cebu. However the test which is not valid for visa applications can also be taken at various other centres across the country. Any would-be visa applicant needs to be sure that, when booking and paying for this test, they choose the correct option. Inevitably when the outcome of the test is going to be used to support a visa application, the cost is higher. I reserved and paid for the correct test. Following the reservation of the test we were sent a confirmation e-mail which told us the start time would be 1 pm. However this was only for the speaking part of the test; we were advised that the listening element of the test would take place earlier and that we would be notified of that time by the examiner at a later date. Registration was no later than 8am. on the day as staff needed time to ensure all candidates were correctly registered and that listening testing were arranged. The testing was undertaken at a hotel close to the Ayala Centre in Cebu City. RB had to make the six hour journey, find accommodation, and then register no later 8 am.

She actually arrived at the test centre at 7am. In the U.K. it was 11 pm. when I received a message from RB telling me she had visited the hotel reception and been told there was no language testing taking place at the hotel that day. I went to the web site and discovered there was and passed this information back to RB. It was not until 9.15 am (1.15 am in the U.K.) that RB discovered what the problem was. The information she fed back to me was quite bizarre. The reception staff at the hotel were split across two functions; one to look after guests, the other to look after events. RB, nor anyone else attending the hotel, could hardly be expected to know this. Initially she had approached the guest receptionist who knew nothing about the language testing event. It was only a couple of hours later as RB persisted in her efforts to find out what was happening that she discovered what was going on; and then it was largely down to good fortune. She had been speaking with the guest receptionist and the events receptionist apparently overheard the conversation and intervened. It was explained that the tests were taking place but it would be later in the day. The hotel receptionist advised RB that the British Council examiner had not realised they were examining candidates in Cebu City and had reported to their centre in Manila. When the error was discovered they were immediately rushed to Manila Airport and flown into Cebu. At the time this conversation was taking place the examiner was in the air! Their arrival at the test centre was expected between noon and 1 pm.

The testing did take place but was seriously delayed. It was partly just good fortune that RB discovered what was happening. It would have been very easy for her to have left the hotel once she was told there was no testing that day. Her persistence was a good sign. She believed me rather than the reception staff and continued to try to establish what was happening. Eventually she was successful in her attempts. However the situation which had developed was hardly one conducive to taking an important test. She had arrived at the venue around 7 am. The test, both parts, were scheduled to last fifteen minutes in total; it was 3.20 pm. when she left the test centre.

The poor quality of service continued when the results were announced. RB was told, and the British Council in the U.K. reinforced this to me when I spoke with them, that the result would be known seven days after taking the test. RB would receive a certificate. This would be delivered by a courier service used by the British Council in Manila. The result would also be available in RB's account with the British Council. The problem with that, whilst an account had been created for her, she was never given the password to access it, despite several requests by both of us in our respective countries. The result, apparently, is available online for 28 days. It was over four weeks after the test that the courier service delivered the result. And then they did not deliver it to RB but left it at their own offices in a town which was 6-7 miles away. RB had to travel in and collect. It was not until she did this that we discovered she had failed the test.

In fairness to the British Council I must add that RB and I have had subsequent experience of the hotel they use for testing. When RB took her second test she stayed at the hotel with her sister the night before the test. They enjoyed their overnight stay so, on a recent trip, as a couple who are now married, we reserved a room for three nights. On arrival reception told us that the room with breakfast which we had reserved and paid for about four months in advance was not available so they had upgraded us. However our original reservation was for the same type of room my wife and sister-in-law had used on their previous visit. When we got to the room RB told me this was definitely not an upgrade; if anything just the opposite. We were at the rear of the hotel on the tenth floor overlooking a building site. The music on the building site began at 6.30 each morning and construction work commenced shortly afterwards with the noise making sleep almost impossible. During our stay staff entered our room without knocking whilst we were making love; thankfully the sight of a large western bottom heaving away provoked a hasty retreat. Maybe they did knock on the door; the noise from the building site below would have ensured we could not have heard them. On our final day I was refused entry to the breakfast room on the grounds that I was in breach of the hotel's dress code. The item which caused offence was a sleeveless top. This was not a running vest, only my arms were uncovered. However women with sleeveless blouses were allowed through. I briefly argued my case to no avail. Frankly I was glad to be out of the place. I mention this because, if the reception staff are consistent, then the truth of what they told RB with regard to her first language test might also be considered to be debateable.

But, let's not get ahead of ourselves. We had a failed English language test to deal with. I went online and found an English language tutor for RB. Such services for Negros Oriental Province were all based in Dumaguete City or its immediate surrounds. Not surprising as that is by far the largest population centre in the Province but is was a six-hour return bus trip for RB. We agreed with the tutor that she would have three lessons a week, Monday, Wednesday and Friday, and homework, a combined time of 10-15 hours study per week. Each lesson would be for two hours with 2-3 hours homework being given. The rate of pay for tuition was modest, P150 per hour (£2.40; €2.63; $3.04), so we assumed a nine week course and aimed for a retest in early September. Payment for tuition was agreed in two blocks. I would pay 75% upfront as a gesture of goodwill and also to keep the number of service payments to Western Union to a minimum. The remaining 25% would be paid in the final week of RB's tuition. In addition to payments for tuition I agreed with the tutor that she would purchase and supply RB with a couple of books to support her learning. There was also a need to increase RBs monthly allowance to cover off travel, etc.

Perhaps unsurprisingly, once the initial payment had arrived in the tutor's account, I received an e-mail from her advising a parent had died and hospital and funeral costs needed to be paid. A loan was sought; and refused. What I promised was a bonus to be paid when the British Council advised RB that she has passed the test.

Half way through RB's course the tutor and I discussed which test date to reserve for RB. From my perspective the objective was simple. I wanted RB to pass the test; I did not want a second failure and the fallout from that, and the tutor wanted her bonus. So I told the tutor we needed a date when she, the tutor, would be confident of a pass. We decided to extend the nine weeks to twelve weeks and a test date towards the end of September. The opinion of the tutor was that RB was good enough to pass the test with ease; the problem was her lack of self-confidence; not knowing how she would react to the examination room environment; and, given the abysmal performance of the British Council for the first test, worries about a repeat performance. When it came to the second test RB asked me if she could take her younger sister with her. She also said they would need somewhere to stay. Following the fiasco of the first test I wanted to do everything possible to support RB, which is why a room was reserved at the hotel in Cebu City in which the testing took place. The hotel had no single rooms so her sister travelling made no difference financially.

We have another example here of how costs differ between the Philippines and the west. The lessons RB took entailed a three hour journey each way using public transport. A return fare was not available; the single fare was P120 each way. The tuition at P150 per hour for two hours was P300. That is a total of P540 which works out at around £8.50 per session. Three sessions a week for twelve weeks is thirty-six sessions. At £8.50 per session that comes to £304, (€333; $385). What would that cost in the west? Two hours of private one-to-one tuition with attendance necessitating three hours on public transport each way. It is unlikely there would be much change from £100 per session. For thirty-six lessons you would probably be looking at a price of at least £3,000, (€3,291; $3,804). I should be thankful that I do not have to produce a certificate showing I have a beginner's level understanding of Bisaya/Cebuano or Tagalog whenever I visit the Philippines!

Between arranging lessons and the date of the second test there were many Facebook chats and definite signs of RB's standard of English improving. On one occasion I called RB's mobile. The ring tone was unfamiliar and then a seductive pre-recorded male voice said: "Hi there, you are through to the … Gay Chat Line. Please tell us which of our Hunks of the Day you wish to chat with by pressing buttons 1, 2 or 3 on your handset. Calls will be charged at our standard rate of £1.50 per minute." At that point I hung up. I had known RB for almost two years and still, for a split second, thought she had sold the mobile phone I provided her with on and was using a cheaper, locally obtained, version. But it was just that split second. I then thought: that voice was in English; the cost of the call was in British currency! Then the penny dropped: I realised that I had forgotten to add the international dialling code of 0063 for the Philippines. Mobile phone numbers across the Philippines all begin with the digits 090. Without the international dialling code I had got straight through to a premium rate number in the U.K.!

Towards the end of September RB re-took the language test and the British Council notified us in early October that she had passed. Delight! The bonus was paid to her tutor.

I was immediately good to my word and reserved accommodation and a flight to Cebu with Cathay Pacific. Our opening night would be at a budget city centre hotel close to South Bus Terminal. Our last night, as a treat, would be back at the Waterfront Airport. For the ten nights between the two we would return to the Lalimar. I could look forward to being with RB shortly after the second anniversary of meeting online. We have different recollections of the date but it was around that time. I also wanted to share her birthday with her. However the most important reason for the visit was to be sure that the fiancée visa application was correctly completed and submitted. Apart from anything else, at £1,195, (€1,311; $1,515), it was not something to be taking chances with. I wanted to be with RB throughout the application process and to be sure she did not seek the support of an agent. I took all the necessary supporting documents with me. What could go wrong? Well, for a start, RB had to return to Manila as her April TB clearance expired a couple of days after receiving the language test result. A new TB test was reserved for the day before I travelled out to meet her but, with there being a seven hour time difference, it was possible I would not discover the outcome of the test before leaving the U.K.. Also, it was now the middle of the typhoon season so that could present a problem.

The money situation had also radically altered since my last trip. Whilst I was getting 72 pesos for my pound four years back and noted that the rate peaked around P75. The last transaction I made gave me an exchange rate of P58; a Sterling devaluation of over 20% against the Philippine Peso. Following the Brexit referendum the British currency was quite volatile and devalued significantly. (As I write in mid-2020 it has bounced back a bit but is currently caught up amongst all things Covid. However, in October, 2016, I found I was being offered between P49 and P56 to the pound; which came as a bit of a shock when I was more familiar with P70 plus. I decided to carry Sterling with me and buy my Pesos locally from supermarket based money exchanges; previously their rates have never been lower than what I could get in the U.K. and they are usually a bit higher. That said on previous trips Sterling had probably been a more attractive investment currency than the Philippine Peso. There are many street trading currency exchanges in the Philippines; every taxi driver will find the best one for you. Beware; the best one will be the one who gives the driver the best cut, the cost of which reduces the exchange rate to you! I have never used them even though their rates are usually slightly higher. I worry about forged notes, which I would not recognise, and being set up for a subsequent mugging.

When we submitted the new visa application we would still be dealing with Entry Clearance Officers pursuing a government agenda to reduce the number of immigrants entering the country. Would they continue thinking they were dealing with two liars and cheats? I hoped not. We would make an application for a fiancée visa. That meant their decision could be appealed if necessary. It also implied that, were they to refuse to issue the visa, solid grounds would be needed.

I was due to fly out of my local airport on a Thursday; an overnight flight, which would land in Hong Kong the following morning, Friday. That afternoon I had a reservation on a connecting flight to Cebu. The day before I was due to leave the U.K. I received good news and bad news. The good news was that RB had passed her TB test. The bad news was that, whilst the Philippines had been hit by a typhoon on the Sunday before I travelled, a second typhoon was forecast for me day of departure. The second typhoon was forecast to directly hit Hong Kong Airport during my transfer times. So, whilst they did not affect me directly at this point, they became an issue. The morning I was due to travel I checked the Cathay Pacific website to find that my flight from Hong Kong to Cebu the following afternoon had already been cancelled. I tried several times to call Cathay Pacific. Unsurprisingly given the circumstances the lines were continually engaged. I decided that I had to go to my local airport. If I did not try to check in then the ticket would be lost. So, off I went, fully expecting to be back home within 2-3 hours. However Cathay Pacific excelled themselves. I presented myself at check-in and was immediately directed to a desk they had set up specifically for travellers caught up in events created by the typhoon. They were ready for me with a very positive solution. They had effectively sold my outward flight on to Emirates Airlines. So, although my departure from the local airport was ninety minutes or so later than anticipated, because Emirates had a significantly reduced transfer time in Dubai, I actually arrived in Cebu over three hours ahead of the original schedule.

It had been eighteen months since I had last passed through Mactan Airport during which time it seemed to have seriously cleaned up its act. I left the arrivals hall expecting to do battle with the hustlers after a few cents to carry my bags, etc., but the area outside was orderly and fairly quiet. I crossed the road and climbed the steps into the domestic departures area to get a taxi only to find the taxi rank had gone. Looking down onto international arrivals and departures I saw it was now at one end of that area; most convenient had I noticed it initially! I walked back and was able to get my own cab with almost no interference. I also saw posters telling me the airport was going to be having a second terminal built which would be completed in 2018. Is this a consequence of a Duterte Presidency? Maybe. Sadly my next trip proved the lack of hustlers was a freak event; they were back out in force.

So I made the Cebu City rush hour. We had a one night reservation at Hotel ABC in Cebu. This is close to the South Bus Terminal; but not too close. The bus terminal is in a seriously run down part of town; not a place to hang about in. We were about a mile away, opposite a hospital, in a downtown side street. It worked out very well. My plan had been to use that evening and the following morning to complete and electronically submit the visa application. We would then need to make an appointment to hand in the supporting paperwork and have biometric data collected. This would entail a return trip from RB's home island to Cebu City; six hours each way.

These ideas were thwarted by several things I had not fully considered. Although RB had agreed to meet me at the hotel she did not do this. The reason was a knock-on effect of the typhoon and my flight changes. The last thing I did before leaving home was to send her a message through Facebook telling her of the cancellation of my connecting flight at Hong Kong and that I did not know when I would arrive. At worst it could be 2-3 days later than we hoped. Having no mobile phone with me and no access to e-mail I had asked an Emirates rep to send RB an e-mail telling her of the current situation. This occurred at my local airport but I had no way of establishing if she had received this message or replied to it. When I called her from the hotel she was with the young boy she used to look after full-time. The e-mail from Emirates had been received and she knew that I was on my way, but so did he; and he was also expecting to see me. So I had little choice but to call a cab and pay them a visit. Before leaving I established that the hotel did have wifi but it could only be accessed from the lobby area. It was a small hotel with a small lobby, half a dozen seats at most and no tables.

(A way for locals to by-pass the need to pay at an internet café is to find a wifi hotspot they can tap into it. Local people, often teenagers, will take advantage of the hotspot; some hotels actively exploited this. So it was not really the sort of place to set up for a few hours to complete and submit a legal document when uninterrupted online access was necessary.)

When I met up with RB there was a lot of emotion about and we put our time to better use than applying for a visa; a case of getting one's priorities right. I put an engagement ring on her finger, a gold band set with a solitaire diamond, and gave her a birthday card and gift. We had not seen each other in the flesh for eighteen months – so we did.

Meeting again was great and we decided; well I suppose I decided really, that we would complete the application once we arrived back at Hotel Lalimar. We knew they had wifi as we had stayed previously and used it. So we enjoyed supper, a slightly late breakfast and each other.

We had established that to submit the visa application online we would need a guaranteed wifi link for at least a couple of hours. Whilst at home I had printed off a completed application form and intended simply copying the information across onto the electronic version. There were also two other mandatory forms supplied by the U.K. authorities which needed completion and submission. One was a breakdown of my finances to demonstrate I had the wherewithal to maintain RB; the other was a form which I had to complete and sign promising to financially underwrite RB's visit for up to five years from the date of her arrival.

Having changed some money at P57.1 to the pound, ten o'clock the following morning, Saturday, found us at the South Bus Terminal in Cebu. We needed to get to a wharf called Tangil; part of the small town of Dumanjug on Cebu Island's west coast. It was either bus or taxi. The bus trip cost around £1.20 each, and the trip took three hours; at those prices I did not consider getting a price for a taxi but now know it would be around £50. The ferry crossing took about one hour and twenty minutes. Our tickets, which cost £2.50 each including port taxes, told us we would land in Guihulngan, the nearest town of any size to the hotel. However, whilst Hotel Lalimar in 5-6 miles south of Guihulngan, the port we arrived at was 7-8 miles north. Technically it was within the administrative limits of Guihulngan but, to all intents and purposes, it was stuck in the middle of nowhere. That said it was on a bus route, but there was no timetable or sign of a bus stop. We ended up getting a moped taxi which got us to the hotel in around three-quarters of an hour for a price of around £5. We stopped en route to buy some bottles of pop and water; and were welcomed back to the Lalimar in the late afternoon.

We had a reservation for ten nights; RB had paid a small deposit, less than £10, to secure our booking. The remainder of the payment was made in cash on arrival.

It should be noted that there is nowhere close to the Lalimar where money can be changed or a cash card used. The nearest bank is in Guihulngan. It has a cash machine which makes a charge for its use; and offers abysmal rates on currency transactions. The six-hour return trip to Dumaguete by bus is necessary to find a market where there is some competition and a reasonable exchange rate. All transactions at Lalimar are in cash. The hotel worked out about £25 per night, (€27.50; $32), for two people; £12.50 each. So the price was modest and that reflected the accommodation. Lalimar is not a luxury hotel, but it is well located and the beds are fairly comfortable; excellent value for money. However, as a westerner, it is as well to understand a little about local culture before deciding to stay there. As we have discussed earlier Filipinos generally are not big drinkers and the day splits to almost twelve hours of daylight and twelve hours of darkness, with a brief dusk and dawn. The day for rural Filipinos tends to work with daylight and nightfall. Once dawn breaks there is activity; once it goes dark activity ceases. This does not work well with the mind-set of the western tourist anticipating a typically western resort nightlife. Daylight arrives at approximately 5.30 am. That is when noise from other guests begins. The 'other guests' are likely to be Filipinos, often young Filipinos. They live life to the full and do not consider that other guests may be sleeping as they assume 'other guests' will be fellow Filipinos. Darkness arrives around 5.30 pm. Last orders at the Lalimar restaurant are at 8.30 pm. and last orders at the bar follow half an hour later; with a little give at weekends if there is plenty of activity. Lalimar is about three miles north of Jimalalud and a bit further south of Guihulngan. The village of La Libertad is a mile or so north. It has schools, a municipal office, a market and a variety of shops, including a pharmacy. There is one small internet café, one small café open for a few hours during the day, no restaurants and no bars.

The advanced weather forecast for my visit had not been at all appetising. Rain was forecast every day and, on eight of the twelve nights I was staying, there was a high likelihood of thunderstorms. It had been raining when I landed at Mactan and it had obviously rained overnight, but, for our trip to Lalimar we saw no daytime rain. Once settled I hit the pool. It was lovely. I really enjoyed an hour or so just floating around and enjoying the late afternoon/early evening ambience. As it began to go dark I could see there was a thunderstorm rolling down the west coast of Cebu Island. The lightning flashes were well over twenty miles away. I was looking across the Tañon Strait and could see the storm slowly move down the coast from Alcantara to Moalboal and onwards across Badian Bay towards Alegria, whale watching country. It was strange to be able to watch a weather system. A mass of grey clouds then an area where the clouds were replaced by the rain storm. It was like an area which had hundreds of vertical lines drawn down the sky with the occasional horizontal flash within them. Then the grey clouds resumed. Watching from across the sea was fascinating. Also watching was a man around fifteen years my junior who seemed to be looking for an opportunity to chat. After my previous experiences of the ex-pat western male that was something to be avoided so I showered off and returned to our 'cottage'. That is the word used by Lalimar to describe our en suite room.

Our room had neither TV nor radio. There was a good lock on the door, a decent air conditioning system, a sea view from the patio area and proper bathroom facilities. It had two windows but the glass in them, whilst not darkened, was very opaque. There were no curtains. There was a wardrobe with a couple of drawers for storing clothes; a double bed and a single bed. That was it. One needs to note that the beds are constructed with Filipinos in mind. When my mass arrives they cease to be fit for purpose! When I lie down the centre of the double bed and arms and legs (rather than hands and feet) dangle off the corners. That's life, I guess. I found that the two of us in the double together was splendid for love but thoroughly uncomfortable for sleeping. Most nights, after initial negotiations, I took myself to the single bed. This did not exactly meet with approval but it did mean we could both sleep; I could also return to the double if/when I felt up to it!

During this trip a knock-on effect of the weather meant we experienced what was for me two very peculiar evenings. The long range weather forecast hadn't been particularly accurate and the weather was generally fairly good. However, one day there was quite a lot of rain around. We had taken a late lunch and, as we were planning to go to the Lalimar bar for something to eat in the evening the heavens opened. Looking out there was no sign of any clear sky. So around half past eight, we went to bed with the purpose of sleeping. I cannot remember when I was last going to sleep at that time. The effect was to wake up early. By five in the morning I was raring to go, but there was nowhere to go to. The pool and restaurant/bar did not open until seven. Wifi became available when the office staff arrived. Whilst they tended to arrive a few minutes early for work, the advertised time for wifi was also seven in the morning.

Two or three days later the rain arrived just after 6pm. It was accompanied by some fairly high winds; sufficient to blow a tree down between our cottage and the one next door. Many tropical trees stay upright through a mass of rhizomes running shallowly just beneath the surface of the soil; they have not evolved the deep root systems we are familiar with in the west. Trees and shrubs supported by rhizome systems blow over much more easily in the wind and that was what had occurred here. However, in terms of our activities, it meant we were in the cottage from around 6.15 pm. RB promptly went to sleep. Whilst it felt seriously unnatural, I followed her example around fifteen minutes later. When I first awoke it was just before midnight. I dropped off to sleep again and dozed for several hours before getting up with the daylight. It felt very strange but did provide an insight into the daily routine of the rural Filipino; it may also go some way to explaining big families. We were together in a cottage where there was no TV, no radio, no mobile phone signal, no wifi, and no video or music centre. The weather pre-empted any thoughts of going out. Even if we did everything in the hotel was closed after 9 pm. If we tried to get to the next town we knew there was nothing there that would be open. Nor were there any taxis. Given the weather it is very unlikely there would be any of the moped or bicycle taxis in our neck of the woods. There was absolutely nothing to do except use the bedroom – sleep, sex, shower and read! Well, life could be a lot worse!!

As soon as we arose on Sunday morning I went to the reception area of the hotel. That was where the wifi was located and it was generally good within around fifty yards. I experienced great difficulty until realising that, not only were reception staff busy on their mobiles, but so were several other guests. The bottom line was that the wifi connection was poor because of the volume of traffic. It remained that way throughout the day. I managed to do a quick check of e-mail during Sunday evening but that was my lot. No chance of doing anything visa related. During the day we also encountered a couple of weather related brief brownouts.

The usual security arrangement my bank has with its customers are that, if the client intends to make a payment upwards of £1,000 from a current account, the bank are notified and agree a time slot during which that transaction will be honoured. Our need to make a payment during the process of making the visa application was a non-standard situation. So, before travelling, I had agreed with the bank they would honour the payment anytime on either Saturday, Sunday or Monday, i.e. on one of the first three days of my visit. I had believed this would be sufficient time to do all the paperwork, etc. but was wrong. Monday was the only day on which we could make progress on the visa application but we hit a difficulty. We had to have guaranteed access to the U.K.V.I. website whilst making our application and had to do this at an internet café in Dumaguete which meant a three hour bus trip each way.

So, on the Monday morning, before 6 am. we caught the bus outside the hotel to Dumaguete City. We got seats but there were few left and, within fifteen minutes, it was standing room only, which included some standing on my feet. Buses made for Filipinos mean that the only seat where I have a chance of legroom is where the aisle meets the back seat. That one was occupied so I was sat on a seat designed for a local person and had one bum cheek and leg crammed in behind the seat in front of me and the other in, and hovering over, the aisle. Timewise it's a long trip. I was cramped and thoroughly uncomfortable, had had no breakfast and was in the frame of mind to whinge. I stopped myself just in time. How selfish was I being? I was a guest in the country and at least had a place to park my backside. Virtually everyone else on the bus was either working or travelling to work. This was a cramped and thoroughly uncomfortable environment for everyone and my fellow travellers had to put up with it twice a day every working day. Okay, my feet were a bit sore, but no one was treading on me with malice. I was a much bigger creature than they normally found on the bus – so I owed it to everyone to be bigger in every way and to keep my mouth shut!!

We arrived in Dumaguete and, after an acceptable bus station breakfast, found an internet café. Having logged on to RB's account I discovered U.K.V.I. were trialling a new method of online application which we had no choice but to use. This meant that, whilst the preparation I had done in filling out draft forms in the U.K. prior to departure was not totally wasted, it did not make life anything like as straightforward as anticipated.

To begin with we had to negotiate three drop down menus to choose the version of the application form we needed. This should not have been difficult. However it was. The fiancée visa had now become part of the visa application process covered by the term 'Family of a Settled Person'. I knew this from the work I had done before leaving home. However on the sub-menu of 'Family of a Settled Person', there was no mention of fiancée, but there was mention of 'marriage'. That created an issue. A visa to enter the U.K. can be issued to a person wanting to visit the country to marry. That was the position RB and I were in. We were engaged and, by this time, had the paperwork to prove we had set a time and date to marry at a U.K. registry office. However the Marriage visa is for people wanting to marry in the U.K. and then return and live in their own country. A similar situation to a British couple deciding to go to an exotic location to get married. That was not what we were looking for. RB was coming to the U.K. to marry me and live with me on a permanent basis; she was coming to the U.K. ultimately to settle and build our lives together. Marriage was a part of that process. The other major difference between these two types of visa is cost. The Marriage visa had a cost of £85, against the price tag of £1,195 for the Family of a Settled Person visa. This difference is significant.

We completed the Family of a Settled Person (Marriage) visa and nowhere in it was the word 'fiancée' mentioned. Towards the end of the form was a drop down menu which asked the applicant to specify their relationship with their sponsor, i.e. what was RB's relationship with me. The menu included grand-parents, civil partners, nephew, niece, parent, aunt, uncle, etc. The only relationship it failed to mention was fiancée!

At this point we were almost at the end of the form. I completed it and found a second problem. The final section of the form asked for 'any other information'. The version of the form I had printed off and completed in the U.K. had a similar section which clearly stated that, if there was insufficient space, add extra sheets. I had happily been typing away with our additional information when I discovered that the online version limited us to around fifteen lines of text. So we then had to very carefully craft our 'additional information' and leave out some information we believed was important altogether. The space provided should have allowed us to fully explain our circumstances and evidence the genuineness of the application. It was also an opportunity for us to guide the reader through the papers which we would hand in to support the application. For example rather than include transcripts of Facebook/Skype conversations, which would run to thousands of sides of A4 paper if printed, we had printed off the index of a folder which all our communications had been copied into. The pages printed covered messages we had exchanged between April of our first year and April of the second year. They had been automatically timed and dated by the e-mail provider. This proved we were in regular contact with each other and had been consistently for over a year. However there was no room to provide such an explanation.

I saved the incomplete application and sent an e-mail to the helpline provided. Replies were promised within 24 hours. The question was simple. It was written on behalf of RB and asked "I am making an application for a Family of a Settled Person visa as I wish to join my fiancé in the U.K. and to marry him there and settle with him in the U.K. On the drop down menu which asks me to specify my relationship to my sponsor the word 'fiancée' does not appear. I am worried that I may not be using the correct application form. Please can you confirm that the Family of a Settled Person (Marriage) form is the right form for my application?" We then had a late lunch with RB's former English language tutor and took the bus back to Lalimar. We had left the hotel at 5.45 am and got back at 5.30 pm.

The answer from U.K.V.I. arrived the following day. It went some way to answering a question we had not asked. The reply said: "When choosing an application form you have three drop down menus to choose from. Choose 'settlement' from the first and second and then choose the type of 'settlement' you are applying for." It was the 'type of settlement' where the options were ambiguous! We were also reminded that it was the responsibility of the applicant to choose the right type of visa, the appropriate application form and to submit the correct paperwork in support of that application. Later that day U.K.V.I. had the gall to send a second message asking us to comment on how well they had done. To answer that question truthfully may well have jeopardised this and any future applications!

We repeated Monday's journey to Dumaguete on Wednesday. I had again been in e-mail contact with my bankers, apologised for the messing about we were doing, and agreed they would allow a payment through on the Wednesday, allowing for the eight hour time difference. I knew we had chosen 'Settlement' on the first two drop down menus. I reviewed the third one and 'Marriage' was the only realistic option, so we stayed with it. The total cost was £1,250. This was made up of two elements; £1,195 for the visa application; £55 for making an appointment to hand in our papers at the U.K.V.I. office in Cebu City rather than Manila.

U.K.V.I./V.F.S. were still charging in U.S. dollars and the £1,250 settlement was automatically exchanged into $1,600, which was then taken from my account. To do this they applied a £/$ exchange rate of

£1=$1.28. The £/$ exchange rate my bank operated that day was £1=$1.2153. On the reputable money markets of the world no organisation offered a rate anywhere close to that. By using a seriously inflated exchange rate U.K.V.I. skimmed my account for an additional $80.88, (£66.55, €75.20); nice work if you can get it! I wonder how many similar scams were practiced worldwide that day by U.K.V.I.?! Maybe as many as there were in the internet chatrooms and dating websites of the Philippines! I am sure the authorities would explain this away as an exchange rate fluctuation or such like, however the exchange rate U.K.V.I. applied was way out of line with any other financial institution that day. The £/$ rate only reached that level again the following year a couple of days after a general election was called.

After making the payment we then had to choose a date and time to hand in the signed application form and supporting documents. We had two choices. Either two days hence before mid-day or the morning I began my journey back home. We chose the latter. Even if we could get from Hotel Lalimar to the U.K.V.I.'s Cebu office in six hours, which was debatable and would mean a 4.30 am. start, we would certainly not be able to make the last ferry back; it would entail another night in Cebu City. So we picked a 7am. appointment on 2nd November. To some extent this worked in our favour as we had time to meet and photograph visits with family and friends. On returning to Cebu Island we checked in at the Waterfront Airport Hotel and, to our delight, discovered we had been upgraded from a Superior Double to an Executive Suite. Much appreciated. When we entered the room there was a nice display from the hotel saying 'welcome back'. We photographed ourselves with it for the application. This was evidence that an independent organisation was acknowledging we had been there previously as a couple; good solid evidence that we were a genuine couple submitting a genuine application.

So the papers were submitted and the application was in the lap of the gods; the gods being some nameless, faceless bureaucrat appointed by U.K.V.I.. When we handed our papers in at the Cebu City office no comment was made on the veracity of our application. V.F.S. required a further payment to cover the return of papers to RB once a decision had been made on the issue of a visa. One would have thought that would have been included in the fee paid online but that was not the case. The U.K.V.I. website advised applicants that 95% of applications would be dealt with within three weeks. VSF, advised that applications were taking between three and four months. Apparently, following the Brexit referendum, they had been deluged with citizenship applications from European Union citizens who live and work in the U.K. I am not going to try to guess how that should impact on the bureaucratic process in the Philippines. However VSF were fairly accurate. It was two days short of thirteen weeks when we got the great news that the visa has been issued; three weeks later RB walked into my arms at our local airport; twelve weeks after that we married.

It was at this point that the original story concluded by posing two rhetorical questions. The first was that, given the issues I have had to deal with, how many foreign nationals wanting to come to the U.K. are likely to try the legal route? A British national trying to obtain a visa for his legitimate girlfriend/fiancée will be continually beaten back by the system at every opportunity unless able to pay a high price for a matrimonial visa which will, in effect, allow a short period of courtship followed by marriage or the applicant returning home. Secondly was a question I asked of myself at the outset of these recollections. Am I sane? What man in his right mind would embark upon an attempt to find a wife who is not a European (or, post-Brexit, of pure British) descent? Whilst the answer to the first question is that there is no answer, the answer to the second is simple. A man who is in love.

This story began as an exploration of the journey a westerner must make if they look for love in foreign climes and find it. As I reach the end of the story I realise I have probably done Tories and Brexiteers a great big favour; not to mention the U.K. Visa and Immigration Service. They may not care very much for the image painted of them but, given the risks, the commitment and time necessary, the hurdles that must be jumped and the costs involved, they can be sure that any reader of this story will think long and hard before even considering getting involved with a partner whose nationality is different from their own.

Together for ever.

This book was first published in the summer of 2017 and concluded at the bottom of the previous page with RB arriving in the U.K. and our marrying just under three months later. It was published under the title of 'Hello Daddy!' With a title like that it is perhaps unsurprising sales were almost non-existent.

However life has continued and we have navigated the top side of three and a half years together now with a good degree of success. By this time in my first marriage the seeds of destruction, from my perspective, were well rooted. This time around I am still enjoying life and full of optimism.

Once RB arrived in the U.K. we fully honoured the visa. One day short of twelve weeks after her arrival the knot was tied. The following day we began our honeymoon back on her home island. The civil marriage in the U.K. was completed by the local Registrar followed by a small get together of family and friends, the main celebration with a church service and reception was in La Libertad. It was very similar to a full church wedding however the legal part of the wedding was completed before leaving the U.K.; the Philippine side was purely ceremonial. And that worked well. The U.K. is good at officialdom and getting the paperwork right; the Philippines are good at ceremony, colour and celebration. If you follow this link it will take you to around eighty five minutes of YouTube video of our celebration in the Philippines.

https://www.youtube.com/watch?v=V99i8nJ0I2M

This video almost didn't happen. The leader of the video team was ill on the day of the ceremony and it was shot by three of his junior colleagues. They had much less experience and, unfortunately, it shows! That said, you will see the preparations at Hotel Lalimar, the trip to the church in nearby La Libertad and all that happened there, (the service is different to that we are familiar with in the U.K.), and then the return to Lalimar and the reception. What is not obvious from the video is that events began around 6.00 in the morning. Church was 9.00 to 11.15am and the reception began around 11.45 am finishing around 1.30 pm.; no afternoon or evening event, none that can be public and shareable anyway. Very odd timing from a western perspective. The reasons were largely two-fold. The main one was that guests came from several places. Many had set out the day before and needed to get a ferry back to their home island following the reception. The second reason was the clerical diary. The Minister's first service of the day began at 7.30 am in a remote part of his large rural parish. This over ran meaning our 9.00 am event began around 30 minutes late.

RB and I have had some great times together. From my perspective I would also say we have yet to experience any significant problems in our marriage/relationship; no major surprises, either way. There's the odd upset but nothing that has had to be slept on. Doubtless we will get our share of troubles as time progresses; that said, whilst we each have a fairly strong streak of stubborn in us, neither one of us much likes arguing and we both seem prepared to make compromises. So, to date, it has been fairly plain sailing. I am sure RB would agree with the caveats that her life in the U.K. is still well and truly going through a cultural adjustment process; and it is almost always cold here! Some of the days during the lovely summer of 2018 were okay but pretty typical of coolish days in Cebu City or on Negros Island. Rural life and living in a metropolitan gated community in the Philippines is a world apart from suburban England. We have both had some major personal issues to deal with. In my case the death of my father, expected but still traumatic. For RB this has been about being isolated from family and friends. However 21st century communications systems help massively. She is able to chat with many members of her family and with friends by using Facebook, Viber, Skype, etc. There are also a proliferation of providers competing to provide international telecoms services which force prices down. She is currently able to phone home for a few pence per minute. But there is no substitute for actually being there. Family is such a big thing in the Philippines and RB misses them. After three years this is beginning to improve but the gap in her life is there. To help with this we are hoping to bring her parents, young brother and niece across to the U.K. for a 3-4 week holiday next year.

Whilst we have had three trips back since her initial arrival our fourth visit had to be cancelled thanks to the coronavirus pandemic. A fifth is planned to coincide with the five hundredth anniversary of Sinulog in January, 2021.

There will be another trip planned in the not too distant future as our travel agent has refunded us for the cancelled trip with what they call a flexible ticket. This allows us to re-book and provides a voucher for an extra £20 as a goodwill gesture. We are told these can be accessed via their app but there is no sign of them yet. A couple of weeks later we were advised that the £20 goodwill gesture could only be used for a trip reserved after the one they refunded has been used. We will see how this pans out but it does seem they have a different understanding to us of what constitutes goodwill! We may use the flexible ticket to help fund a visit here for Lory's family but the agent may also have a different understanding of the word 'flexible'. Time will tell. We could always make an early reservation for the Christmas and New Year the year after next!

During RB's absence her eldest sister has become a mother for the second and third times, her second child being born the morning after our wedding event in the Philippines which she attended. Her younger brother has become a father for the first time and her youngest sister had her first baby in June, 2020. As for us, well there is no pitter patter of tiny feet here yet but we are working on it. RB may have had a very early miscarriage around fifteen months back but we are regularly counting days and engaging in frantic bouts of horizontal activity when prime time approaches. We have both been medically tested and found to be firing on all cylinders but have yet to hit the jackpot! We have discussed matters with our G.P. and been referred for assisted A.I. However, due to coronavirus and a back log of referrals, it is likely to be between one and two years before we hear from the clinic. I guess the egg and sperm we produce are as stubborn as their originators which does not bode well for a natural conception!

At the personal level the biggest event for me since marrying is receiving a diagnosis of Asperger's Syndrome. Given my age this is odd to say the least. However all the online tests place me well and truly on the spectrum; and there is GP agreement. Whilst this explains some of my foibles, it is not something I'm likely to be bothering the medical profession with much further. A diagnosis at pension age is likely to be a bit late for any significant inputs to be made. However it gives me some peace of mind in knowing I have an explanation for my dislike of flashing lights, bright light, unexpected touches, sounds, aromas and movements etc. On a daily basis it explains my passionate loathing of mobile phones and the like. It explains why flying at night is a problem because of light and sound associated with all the electronic devices which are in use. Also why I find xenon headlights on vehicles such a blinding experience. It may also explain why I rarely feel as though I fit in anywhere; which, in turn, suggests that when I am in places where I don't understand the language, (such as the Philippines), being able to switch off and relax is far easier. All my school reports mentioned a 'lack of concentration'. The reality was an unrecognised information and sensory overload and difficulties in dealing with it.

RB is aware of the diagnosis. It is something we talk about and she is beginning to understand the implications; one of which is that there is around a 25% chance of it becoming an inherited condition. It could become a bigger issue should we eventually have a family.

RB continues to discover the differences between life here and back in the Philippines. She has work. Not full time but very close. A 33 hour contracted week with fairly regular additional hours at present. The difficulty for her is that, whilst she really loves her work, to get to it is a fourteen mile (22 kilometre) return trip. She works overnight at a residential home for the elderly and there is no public transport available to get her there and back so I take her. Provided the car and driver are in good condition this works well, but we both know that RB passing her driving test would be a great benefit. However this presents a major problem. RB has had driving lessons and she and her instructor are both confident she will be able to pass the practical test. The big problem links directly with language and culture; and this is the theory test. For a person whose first language is English the theory test can be challenging. To pass you need to correctly answer 43 out of 50 multiple-choice questions in 57 minutes. RB's English language skills have improved dramatically since her arrival here, but to answer a multiple choice question you not only have to understand the driving skill which is being tested, but also local context, and the way in which the English language is being used in both the question and possible answers. This is do-able but quite a challenge. She is enrolled on an online course which she works at and her scores are gradually improving which is encouraging.

A few months back she discovered her driving test will include hazard perception. Whilst driving her home from work one morning, pre-lockdown, she told me she had done an online hazard perception test and her score had been zero! Three years ago I would have been horrified; not so now. I am learning a little about the Philippine psyche. Her zero score was a cultural issue. Remember we earlier discussed the Philippine 'yes' which can mean anything from 'yes' to 'no'? If you add this into being a product of what Filipinos themselves acknowledge is a very judgemental society, this is the type of outcome one will get. RB discovered she had to pass a test called 'Hazard Perception', so she found one online, took it and failed magnificently. When she told me this I asked her what 'hazard perception' meant. At best her idea was unclear. So she had embarked on a test without properly understanding what she was being tested on. No surprise she failed to score.

As we drove along quiet country lanes on the way home I explained as best I could what the phrase meant. We still had 5-6 miles to go so I told her I would make that drive a learning experience for her. Decades back I had undertaken advanced driver training with the police. An examined part of that training was to do a commentary drive. It is something I have continued to do occasionally just to keep my hand in, (although I must be pretty rusty by now). But for the remainder of that trip home, fifteen minutes or so, I commentated on everything that was happening related to the drive and related this back to the concept of hazard perception. Whilst this included talking about road signs, vehicle and pedestrian movement around us, junctions, etc. I also mentioned things like: "We are near a school and here is a line of parked cars so we have to take our time and keep our wits about us as there is always the possibility a child might run out in front of us. Or "We have just passed a bus stop. There was no one stood at it. Does that mean a bus has recently departed and we will come up behind it?"

RB must have listened because a few days later she presented me with a hazard perception test she had found online and completed very successfully. The only error she had made was not seeing approaching the brow of a hill as a hazard. We have no plans for the driving test just yet but I'm hopeful we will get there in the next 2-3 years. And we both know that, whilst a new addition to our family would be loved and cherished, should that happen then a full driving licence would be very beneficial.

She is a bright woman, a good learner and I am proud of her. Does that sound a little paternalistic?! Maybe a bit of that has had to enter our relationship; with the difference in our ages. I have recently celebrated my 66th birthday; she is still 26. There is also a huge difference in life experience and, to the best of my ability, I want to provide RB with the best opportunities in life that I can. A big issue there is that the Philippine education system has trained her in low expectations and to be an effective part of her extended family. The U.K. education system is about helping young people make their own decisions, becoming independent and developing their own 'family' in whatever form that might take. Shifting from one set of outcomes to the other may be impossible; it will certainly take many years. Had I been moving to the Philippines I would also be very reluctant to change much!

The little boy RB looked after Cebu City has now moved with his family to the eastern seaboard of the U.S.A. He happily lives with his family and now attends a school through which he is better supported. To help with his cerebral palsy and quadriplegia he now has a purpose made wheelchair and computer which he is learning to operate using his eyes. Communication links are much improved and a trip to see him is do-able.

RB can access her favourite soap opera within a couple of hours of its local transmission in the Philippines and a couple of clicks on the laptop thanks to services provided by the Philippines government to their O.F.W.s, (overseas foreign workers) and will spend a couple of hours most days catching up with all things Philippine.

Her initial visa allowed her to stay in the U.K. for up to six months on condition we marry within that time. Prior to marriage she had no right to work and very limited educational opportunities. Following marriage we had to renew her visa. The initial visa expired a month or so after we returned from our honeymoon and applications needed to be submitted up to three months before the expiry date of her fiancée visa. This was supposedly a routine application however it took just over six months and the intervention of our M.P. to get the visa issued. During this time we knew RB had the right to work. However U.K. law puts an obligation on all employers to ensure a job applicant has the right to work before offering them a job. For RB, and those in a similar position, this is generally done by producing their passport and visa. The visa in RBs case is in the form of a Residence Permit. It is a plastic card similar in size to a credit card and shows her photograph, the dates between which she is entitled to be in the U.K., and that she has the right to work but has no access to public funds. It has been issued in her maiden name, not her married name. We are told this is because her passport at that time was in her maiden name.

After we married but prior to receiving the Residence Permit RB took classes at a local adult education centre in English, Maths and I.T. Once we received it she began to look for work. Within a week of getting the permit she began unpaid voluntary work in a charity shop. A few dozen job applications were submitted online and we hit the same issue with every potential employer. Her married name is not the name on her Residence Permit so additional information had to be submitted as proof of right to work. This confused several of the online application systems. On one occasion we went to see the employer, a well-known national supermarket chain. The manager advised that RB should do what every other woman would do and get her name changed in her passport. She made it clear that she would not open her employer up to employing anyone who might not have the right to work when there were plenty of local people who would satisfy the requirement simply by producing their British passport. This opinion may be legally questionable but demonstrates the difficulties faced by legitimate foreigners when looking for work in the U.K. A Residence Permit issued in the married name, the name she chooses to use, would have made life much simpler. However RB continued with her studies and voluntary work several days a week before finding paid work which she commenced around six months after receipt of the permit.

There are differences in our life styles and the way we do things. Most reflect culture, lifestyle and experience.

Food provides a very simple starter. Unless dining out it is rare for us to eat together. We eat at different times of the day and enjoy different foods. When RB is not working she only recognises one seven or eight o'clock, and that is not in the morning, (a situation she knows will have to change when we have a family). On the odd occasion she takes breakfast this will be rice based; boiled rice, not rice in cereal form. In fact rice forms the basis of almost all of her meals. It replaces bread and potato in the traditional British diet and is often accompanied with noodles and sardines. I love sandwiches, and enjoy plenty of salad and fresh fruit. I'll eat a bit of meat occasionally but most of my protein intake is fish based. Much of RB's food she prepares herself. This is not really out of choice. The various prepared foods offered in western supermarkets do not take her fancy. She likes strong flavours but not hot spices. She likes to cook in vinegar and soy sauce with oodles of salt and garlic. Apart from rice all food will be prepared in the frying pan. This reflects her life prior to coming to the U.K.. Many Filipino foods will be sun dried and preserved in salt, (corned), and RB loves them. Whilst she will have salmon or cod when we eat out her preference is for fish she knows prepared in a familiar way. This means shopping at specialist south Asian grocery stores from time to time and her stocking up on frozen and dried foods. These trips do not present any problem but it does seriously restrict her options on the food front. Where we do have a difference of opinion is around food preparation. To the average westerner the smells created by traditional Filipino cooking can be challenging. Perhaps for the next birthday or Christmas I should consider an electric frying pan and a lengthy extension cable or plug point in the back garden! Now that might just bring on a bout of 'tampo'.

Bringing a Filipina to the west brings a variety of unexpected issues. For example I had not given any consideration to either bras or sanitary protection. The U.K. offers a wider range of each product, some new ones and greater choice. There were some which RB had not previously encountered; so be prepared for discussions in this area. You should also expect knowledge of contraception to be nil and prepare yourself for a few old wives tales.

As I mentioned in the opening chapters of this book I have spent plenty of time living alone. Whilst that may have its downside one of the things I quickly learned was that if anything went wrong, accidently or otherwise, it was down to me. I have also learned how to run a house. I may not have the best routines; I may not be the most squeaky clean of individuals, but I do know that a house has to be managed and that jobs need doing. When I first got a house it took a few months but I fairly quickly realised that if I didn't do these things, no one else was going to. So, when someone new comes into the house, whoever it might be, I will notice pretty well immediately. I don't have a problem with this but I do have an expectation that if I am living with someone they will work with me to deal with the routine running of our domestic affairs. Where I do find a bit of a clash of cultures, or maybe generations, is in how this is dealt with.

RB's domestic skill level was very low. This was simply because the work was done by her mother and elder siblings whilst she was at school. At home she looked after her two younger siblings. On being taken out of school early she went straight into work outside the home. In her work environments cooking, cleaning, washing, in fact everything domestic, was the role of other people. Defining her work roles in the Philippines is fairly straightforward. Serve in a small shop and fill the shelves. Look after a severely disabled young child. So far as I am aware she fulfilled these roles well. However she never had to plan anything; and was familiar with being told to do this, do that. Any kind of autonomous act would be discouraged. Firstly, in a highly judgemental society, one does not risk being judged by initiating an action. Secondly there is always the risk that, only knowing a small part of the overall picture, mistakes can be made. In consequence she has never had to plan, think of a bigger picture or think beyond herself and immediate surrounds. She has certainly never had to learn how to shop for a week or a few days nor how to plan meals for a few days, or how to run a house. In consequence she has never learned how to use most domestic appliances. Having had to leave school and work in her mid-teens the art of learning does not come easily; particularly when it is something one doesn't really want to do. During my working life I would often take the view that, if someone else was prepared to do a job, I was prepared to let them! Seeing RB adopt that mode is making me aware of the frustrations I must have caused others. However I have to say that, whilst she can be a slow learner, she has made a remarkable adjustment so far. Her efforts around the house are much appreciated and we are fairly close to sharing the workload evenly; even though it is a workload neither one of us particularly enjoys! Also one of my major faults is that I am a terrible completer/finisher. My mind is always racing ahead to the next job. So RB also being a terrible completer/finisher is a major frustration; probably for both of us.

And I have learned too; particularly around humility. I had the benefit of an upbringing in a solvent household with hard working parents. Many things that are taken for granted here are not available to many Filipinos. An earlier chapter dealt with the availability and quality of water. We have mentioned the idea of a toilet being any place where there are large leaves and I have also had a bit of a whinge about not having legroom when travelling on local buses. But that is just a beginning. What I have not mentioned are things such as having a brother-in-law who, despite being a father and 23 years old, had never been in a road vehicle until we gave him a lift home one day. Similarly with my in-laws. Their first time in a vehicle with four wheels was when they joined us for a couple of days at our hotel near the Airport on one of our trips. Even more of a surprise was when my wife told me that her mother had asked her not to buy a fridge for the family. That was because they couldn't guarantee the electricity supply and that would become a major problem. Instead would she think of buying a foam mattress?! Until that point I had not realised all her family at their home sleep on the floor. I had not known that, when we invited them to join us at a hotel for a couple of days, that was their first experience of sleeping on anything close to what we would call a bed. When RB took her second language test, the night before she stayed in the hotel which was used as the test centre. Her sister shared the room with her. This was a city centre three star hotel. It had two single beds and a bathroom which included bath and shower. The girls understood how the shower worked but we had been married for a couple of years before I discovered RB never used the bath because she did not know how to. She told me that she and her sister had pondered this the evening before the language test. But rather than experiment they kept away from it. Recently I have had a birthday; RB's mother's birthday is a week before mine. I got a pair of trousers as a gift; we sent her Mum a 50 kilo bag of rice so the family could eat. The differences are that stark. The cost of the rice was about two thirds that of the trousers. I have begun to think of my family in the Philippines along the lines of the original Beverly Hillbillies; a TV series which ran from 1962-1971. They may be simple people but their hearts are very much is the right place. They work hard and their lives are generally uncomplicated. From a western perspective everything they do is reduced to basics. However that pokes fun at the rest of us as we tend to create complications where there aren't any. My in-laws ask for little, they have little and, what they have, they share.

Finally I would like to briefly return to the reason this book has been written and thank you the reader for making this purchase. I hope the read has been of interest.

The situation faced by some Philippine children due to acute poverty and the increasing availability of technology is still being exploited by paedophiles almost exclusively based in the west. We hope the sales of this book will provide sufficient income for us to employ a local person to work alongside the police and teachers in RBs home area to support all youngsters in having a solid understanding of how to stay safe online and what to do if they feel uncomfortable or at risk. We anticipate this being done in collaboration with other local agencies and organised through schools. There are twenty seven Elementary Schools in the region and three Secondary Schools, one of which is operated privately.

On 2nd September, 2020, RB will be making a 15,000 feet tandem parachute jump for which we are also seeking sponsorship in the hope that between us we can raise the £7,500 necessary to do this. The jump cannot be shown live but a video of the event will be made and posted. We have a fundraising site with GoFundMe and the project title is SOS-keep children safe online.

AUTHOR'S NOTE (2):

Zig and RB first met online in September, 2014. Their first meeting in person was in January, 2015. They got engaged in October, 2016 and were married in May, 2017. He is now 66 years old; she is 26 years old; they are working hard at living happily ever after and thank you for sharing their story.

Zig is a pseudonym, a contraction of the name under which the original script 'Hello Daddy!' was published. The author is an Englishman who has spent many happy times in the small German market town of Merzig; a love he is now able to share with his Philippine wife.

APPENDIX 1.

Various forms used by U.K. Visa and Immigration at the time Jo visited the U.K..

VAF1A (Application for a short stay visa)
https://www.gov.uk/government/uploads/system/uploads/attachment_data/file/589170/VAF1-visitandshorttermstay.pdf

VAF4A (Application for a family of a settled person visa)
https://www.gov.uk/government/uploads/system/uploads/attachment_data/file/274029/VAF4A.pdf

VAF4A (Application for a family of a settled person visa – financial requirement)
https://www.gov.uk/government/uploads/system/uploads/attachment_data/file/270484/VAF4A-Appendix2.pdf

APPENDIX 2.

Here is the index to the Immigration Rules as it stood in mid-2016:

Immigration Rules: Index
The rules are divided into different documents. The index page will help you find the part you need.

Introduction (Paragraphs 1 to 6C)

Implementation and transitional provisions
Application
Interpretation
Public funds clarification

Part 1: General provisions regarding leave to enter or remain in the United Kingdom (Paragraphs 7 to 39E)
Leave to enter the United Kingdom
Exercise of the power to refuse leave to enter the United Kingdom
Suspension of leave to enter or remain in the United Kingdom
Cancellation of leave to enter or remain in the United Kingdom
Requirement for persons arriving in the United Kingdom or seeking entry through the Channel Tunnel to produce evidence of identity and nationality
Requirement for a person not requiring leave to enter the United Kingdom to prove that he has the right of abode
Common Travel Area
Admission for certain British passport holders
Persons outside the United Kingdom
Returning residents
Non-lapsing leave
Holders of restricted travel documents and passports
Leave to enter granted on arrival in the United Kingdom

Entry clearance
Variation of leave to enter or remain in the United Kingdom
How to make a valid application for leave to remain in the UK
Withdrawn applications or claims for leave to remain in the United Kingdom
Specified forms and procedures in connection with applications for administrative review
Undertakings
Medical
Students
Specified documents
Indefinite leave to enter or remain
Power to interview a person with limited leave to enter or remain
Exceptions for overstayers

Part 2: Persons seeking to enter or remain in the United Kingdom for visits (Paragraphs 1 to 4)
Transitional provisions Part 2 and Appendix V: Immigration Rules for Visitors

Part 3: Persons seeking to enter or remain in the United Kingdom for studies (Paragraphs A57A to 81)
Persons seeking to enter the UK for short-term study
Spouses or civil partners of students granted leave under paragraphs 57 to 75 (but not A57A to A57H)
Children of students granted leave under paragraphs 57 to 75 (but not A57A to A57H)

Part 4: Persons seeking to enter or remain in the United Kingdom in an "au pair" placement, as a working holidaymaker or for training or work experience (Paragraphs 122 to 127)
Spouses of persons with limited leave to enter or remain under paragraphs 110 to 121

Children of persons with limited leave to enter or remain under paragraphs 110 to 121

Part 5: Persons seeking to enter or remain in the United Kingdom for employment (Paragraphs 128A to 199B)
Work permit employment
Requirements for indefinite leave to remain as a highly skilled migrant
Representatives of overseas newspapers, news agencies and broadcasting organisations
Representatives of Overseas Business
Private servants in diplomatic households
Domestic workers in private households
Overseas government employees
Ministers of religion, missionaries and members of religious orders
Airport based operational ground staff of overseas-owned airlines
Persons with United Kingdom ancestry
Partners of persons who have or have had leave to enter or remain under paragraphs 128 to 193 (but not Paragraphs 135I to 135K)
Children of persons with limited leave to enter or remain under paragraphs 128 to 193 (but not paragraphs 135I to 135K)

Part 6: Persons seeking to enter or remain in the United Kingdom as a businessman, self-employed person, investor, writer, composer or artist (Paragraphs 200A to 245)
Part 6A: Points-Based System (paragraphs 245AAA to 245ZZE)
General requirements for indefinite leave to remain
Documents not submitted with applications
Specified documents for students previously sponsored by an overseas government or international scholarship agency
Tier 1 (Exceptional Talent) Migrants

Tier 1 (General) Migrants Tier 1 (Entrepreneur) Migrants
Tier 1 (Investor) Migrants Tier 1 (Graduate Entrepreneur) Migrants
Tier 2 (Intra Company Transfer) Migrants
Tier 2 (General) Migrants, Tier 2 (Minister of Religion) Migrants and Tier 2 (Sportsperson) Migrants Tier 5 (Youth Mobility Scheme) Temporary Migrants
Tier 5 (Temporary Worker) Migrants
Tier 4 (General) Student
Tier 4 (Child) Student

Part 7: Other Categories (paragraphs A246 to 276BVI)
Persons exercising rights of access to a child resident in the United Kingdom
EEA nationals and their families
Retired persons of independent means
Partners of persons who have or have had limited leave to enter or remain in the United Kingdom as retired persons of independent means
Children of persons with limited leave to enter or remain in the United Kingdom as retired persons of independent means
Long residence
Private life
HM Forces
Spouses, civil partners, unmarried or same-sex partners of persons settled or seeking settlement in the United Kingdom in accordance with paragraphs 276E to 276Q (HM Forces rules) or of members of HM Forces who are exempt from immigration control under section 8(4)(a) of the Immigration Act 1971 and have at least 5 years' continuous service
Children of a parent, parents or a relative settled or seeking settlement in the United Kingdom under paragraphs 276E to 276Q (HM Forces rules) or of members of HM Forces who are exempt from immigration control under section 8(4)(a) of the Immigration Act 1971 and have at least 5 years' continuous service

Spouses, civil partners, unmarried or same-sex partners of armed forces members who are exempt from immigration control under section 8(4) of the Immigration Act 1971
Children of armed forces members who are exempt from immigration control under Section 8(4) of the Immigration Act 1971
Limited leave to enter for relevant Afghan citizens
Parent of a Tier 4 (child) student

Part 8: Family members (paragraphs A277 to 319Y)
Transitional provisions and interaction between Part 8 and Appendix FM (paragraphs A277 to 319Y)
Spouses and civil partners
Victims of domestic violence
Fiance(e)s and proposed civil partners
Unmarried and same-sex partners
Children
Parents, grandparents and other dependent relatives
Family members of relevant points-based system migrants
Other family members of persons with limited leave to enter or remain in the United Kingdom as a refugee or Beneficiary of humanitarian protection
Parents, grandparents and other dependent relatives of persons with limited leave to enter or remain in the United Kingdom as a refugee or beneficiary of humanitarian protection

Part 9 - General grounds for the refusal of entry clearance, leave to enter, leave to remain, variation of leave to enter or remain and curtailment of leave in the United
Kingdom (paragraphs A320 to 324)
Refusal of entry clearance or leave to enter the United Kingdom
Refusal of leave to enter in relation to a person in possession of an entry clearance

Refusal of variation of leave to enter or remain or curtailment of leave
Crew members

Part 10: Registration with the police (paragraphs 325 to 326)

Part 11: Asylum (paragraphs 326A to 352H)

Part 11A: Temporary Protection (Paragraphs 354 to 356B)

Part 11B: Asylum (Paragraphs 357 to 361)

Part 12: Procedure and Rights of appeal (Paragraphs 353 to 353B)

Part 13: Deportation (paragraphs A362 to 400)

Part 14: Stateless persons (Paragraphs 401 to 416)

Part 15: Condition to hold an Academic Technology Approval Scheme (ATAS) clearance certificate

Appendix 1: DELETED
Appendix 2: Countries or territories whose nationals or citizens are relevant foreign nationals for the purposes of Part 10 of these Rules app 2
Appendix 3: DELETED
Appendix 4: DELETED
Appendix 5: DELETED
Appendix 6: Disciplines for which an Academic Technology Approval Scheme certificate from the
Counter-Proliferation Department of the Foreign and Commonwealth Office is required for the purposes of Tier 4 of the Points Based System

Appendix 7 - Statement of Written Terms and Conditions of employment required in paragraphs 159A (v), 159D (iv) and 159EA (iii)
Appendix A: Attributes
Appendix AR
Appendix Armed Forces
Appendix B: English language - English language
Appendix C: Maintenance (funds)
Appendix D: Immigration rules for leave to remain as a Highly Skilled Migrant as at 28 February 2008
Appendix E: Maintenance (funds) for the family of Relevant Points Based Systems Migrants
Appendix ECAA: ECAA Nationals and settlement
Appendix F: Archived Immigration Rules
Appendix FM: Family members
Appendix FM-SE: Family members - specified evidence
Appendix G: Countries and territories participating in the Tier 5 Youth mobility scheme and annual allocations of places for 2014
Appendix H: Applicants who are subject to different documentary requirements under Tier 4 of the Points Based System
Appendix I: DELETED
Appendix J: Codes of practice for Tier 2 sponsors, Tier 5 sponsors and employers of work permit holders
Appendix K: Shortage occupation list
Appendix KoLL: Knowledge of language and life
Appendix L: Designated competent body criteria for Tier 1 (Exceptional talent) applications
Appendix M: Sports governing bodies for Tier 2 (Sportsperson) and Tier 5 (Temporary worker - creative and sporting) applications
Appendix N: Approved Tier 5 Government authorised exchange schemes
Appendix O: List of English Language tests that have been assessed as meeting the UK Border Agency's requirements

Appendix P: Lists of financial institutions that do not satisfactorily verify financial statements, or whose financial statements are accepted
Appendix Q: DELETED
Appendix R: DELETED
Appendix S: DELETED
Appendix SN: Service of notices
Appendix T: Tuberculosis screening
Appendix V: Immigration Rules for Visitors

This link will take you to the index to the Rules as they exist at the end of June, 2020.

https://www.gov.uk/guidance/immigration-rules/immigration-rules-index

APPENDIX 3.

Fiancé(e)s and proposed civil partners

289AA. Nothing in these Rules shall be construed as permitting a person to be granted entry clearance, leave to enter or variation of leave as a fiancé(e) or proposed civil partner if either the applicant or the sponsor will be aged under 18 on the date of arrival of the applicant in the United Kingdom or (as the case may be) on the date on which the leave to enter or variation of leave would be granted.

Requirements for leave to enter the United Kingdom as a fiance(e) or proposed civil partner (i.e. with a view to marriage or civil partnership and permanent settlement in the United Kingdom)

290. The requirements to be met by a person seeking leave to enter the United Kingdom as a fiancé(e) or proposed civil partner are that:
(i) the applicant is seeking leave to enter the United Kingdom for marriage or civil partnership to a person present and settled in the United Kingdom or who is on the same occasion being admitted for settlement; and
(ii) the parties to the proposed marriage or civil partnership have met; and
(iii) each of the parties intends to live permanently with the other as his or her spouse or civil partner after the marriage or civil partnership ; and
(iv) adequate maintenance and accommodation without recourse to public funds will be available for the applicant until the date of the marriage or civil partnership; and
(v) there will, after the marriage or civil partnership, be adequate accommodation for the parties and any dependants without recourse to public funds in accommodation which they own or occupy exclusively; and

(vi) the parties will be able after the marriage or civil partnership to maintain themselves and any dependants adequately without recourse to public funds; and

(vii)(a) the applicant provides an original English language test certificate in speaking and listening from an English language test provider approved by the Secretary of State for these purposes, which clearly shows the applicant's name and the qualification obtained (which must meet or exceed level A1 of the Common European Framework of Reference) unless:

(i) the applicant is aged 65 or over at the time he makes his application; or

(ii) the applicant has a physical or mental condition that would prevent him from meeting the requirement; or;

(iii) there are exceptional compassionate circumstances that would prevent the applicant from meeting the requirement; or

(vii)(b) the applicant is a national of one of the following countries: Antigua and Barbuda; Australia; the Bahamas; Barbados; Belize; Canada; Dominica; Grenada; Guyana; Jamaica; New Zealand; St Kitts and Nevis; St Lucia; St Vincent and the Grenadines; Trinidad and Tobago; United States of America; or

(vii)(c) the applicant has obtained an academic qualification (not a professional or vocational qualification), which is deemed by UK NARIC [National Academic Recognition Information Centre] to meet the recognised standard of a Bachelor's or Master's degree or PhD in the UK, from an educational establishment in one of the following countries: Antigua and Barbuda; Australia; The Bahamas; Barbados; Belize; Dominica; Grenada; Guyana; Ireland; Jamaica; New Zealand; St Kitts and Nevis; St Lucia; St Vincent and The Grenadines; Trinidad and Tobago; the UK; the USA; and provides the specified documents; or

(vii)(d) the applicant has obtained an academic qualification (not a professional or vocational qualification) which is

deemed by UK NARIC to meet the recognised standard of a Bachelor's or Master's degree or PhD in the UK, and
(1) provides the specified evidence to show he has the qualification, and
(2) UK NARIC has confirmed that the qualification was taught or researched in English, or
(vii)(e) has obtained an academic qualification (not a professional or vocational qualification) which is deemed by UK NARIC to meet the recognised standard of a Bachelor's or Master's degree or PhD in the UK, and provides the specified evidence to show:
(1) he has the qualification, and
(2) that the qualification was taught or researched in English. and
(viii) the applicant holds a valid United Kingdom entry clearance for entry in this capacity.

Leave to enter as a fiancé(e) or proposed civil partner

291. A person seeking leave to enter the United Kingdom as a fiancé(e) or proposed civil partner may be admitted, with a prohibition on employment, for a period not exceeding 6 months to enable the marriage or civil partnership to take place provided a valid United Kingdom entry clearance for entry in this capacity is produced to the Immigration Officer on arrival.

Refusal of leave to enter as a fiancé(e) or proposed civil partner

292. Leave to enter the United Kingdom as a fiancé(e) or proposed civil partner is to be refused if a valid United Kingdom entry clearance for entry in this capacity is not produced to the Immigration Officer on arrival.

Printed in Poland
by Amazon Fulfillment
Poland Sp. z o.o., Wrocław